Reading Gender and Space: Essays for Patricia Coughlan

© Piaras Mac Éinrí

Reading Gender and Space
Essays for Patricia Coughlan

ANNE FOGARTY AND TINA O'TOOLE
EDITORS

CORK UNIVERSITY PRESS

First published in 2023 by
Cork University Press
Boole Library
University College Cork
CORK
T12 ND89
Ireland

Library of Congress Control Number: 2023932121
Distribution in the USA: Longleaf Services, Chapel Hill, NC, USA

British Library Cataloguing in Publication Data
A CIP record for this book is available from the British Library.

ISBN: 978-1-78205-564-8

Printed by BZ Graf in Poland
Print origination & design by Carrigboy Typesetting Services
www.carrigboy.co.uk

COVER IMAGE – Margaret Clarke, *The Dressmaker*, 1924, collection Crawford Art Gallery, Cork © the artist's estate

www.corkuniversitypress.com

Contents

ACKNOWLEDGEMENTS ix

NOTES ON CONTRIBUTORS xi

PREFACE *Margaret Kelleher* xviii

INTRODUCTION *Anne Fogarty* and *Tina O'Toole* 1

While Bleeding 13
Doireann Ní Ghríofa

Cuimhne an Uisce 15
Nuala Ní Dhomhnaill

PART 1. THE POLITICS OF GENRE

Stabat Mater 19
Eiléan Ní Chuilleanáin

1 '*Gente Blanca*' in the Green Atlantic: Selfhood, victimhood, whiteness, and early modern Ireland 21
Patricia Palmer

2 Transformational Transactions: Eochaidh Ó hEodhasa's poem (1603) to James I 37
Sarah McKibben

3 The Ghost Comes to Town: Le Fanu and the urban Gothic 51
Nicholas Daly

4 'Very little to have been so long about': Pastoralism and William Morris in Yeats' *Poems, 1899–1905* and related writings 65
Alex Davis

5 *Fianaise Lom* / Bare Witness: Surrealism and life writing in the work of Celia de Fréine 80
Máirín Nic Eoin

PART 2. THE FAMILY ROMANCE AND SIBLING RELATIONS

Home Sickness 109
Bernard O'Donoghue

6 Siblings: Juliet Mitchell and Malory's *Morte Darthur* 111
Catherine La Farge

7 Fathers and Sons, Mothers and Daughters: The family romance in Katherine Cecil Thurston's *The Fly on the Wheel* 128
Clíona Ó Gallchoir

8 'Now in the city there are two worlds': Maeve Brennan's Dublin sequences 144
Eamonn Hughes

9 The Law of the Mother and the Sibling World: Leeanne Quinn's queer ecologies 158
Moynagh Sullivan

PART 3. RETHINKING FEMININITY/MASCULINITY

The Lionhearted 181
Paula Meehan

City Without God 183
Thomas McCarthy

10 Female Personal Names in Old English 185
Elisabeth Okasha

11 Writing Irish Women in South America 192
Laura Izarra

12 'All I am is feeling': Samuel Beckett, aesthetics, and the matter of mother 207
Seán Kennedy

13 'Mind Our Men': Fragile masculinity in post-crash Irish men's writing 221
Anne Mulhall

14 'a permeable membrane gives at the slightest touch': The ecopoetics of houses in the poetry of Vona Groarke and Sinéad Morrissey 242
Margaret Mills Harper

15 Alienated Subjects: Post-feminist control and contemporary Irish femininity 259
Claire Bracken

NOTES 275

PATRICIA COUGHLAN PUBLICATIONS 311

BIBLIOGRAPHY 315

INDEX 341

Acknowledgements

In the long process of compiling this book, many people have assisted us. We are grateful to colleagues at University College Dublin and the University of Limerick for their support and advice. Anne Fogarty would like to thank Ulf Messner for technical help and vital emotional support. Tina O'Toole would like to thank Joan Murphy for keeping the circuits connected and Siobhán O'Dowd for everything else.

Our heartfelt gratitude to Margaret Kelleher for her astute preface, to our contributors for their enthusiasm, scholarly insights, and unstinting patience, and to Doireann Ní Ghríofa, Nuala Ní Dhomhnaill, Eiléan Ní Chuilleanáin, Bernard O'Donoghue, Paula Meehan, and Thomas McCarthy for enriching the collection with their poems. Thanks are also due to Michael Waldron for facilitating the reproduction on the cover of Margaret Clarke, *The Dressmaker*, 1924, Collection Crawford Art Gallery, Cork © the artist's estate.

We would also like to thank the anonymous readers for their generous and keen-eyed observations and Maria O'Donovan and Mike Collins for their stewardship and professional oversight in bringing this volume to fruition.

'While Bleeding' by Doireann Ní Ghríofa from *To Star the Dark* (2021) is reproduced by kind permission of the author and Dedalus Press, www.dedaluspress.com

'Home Sickness' by Bernard O'Donoghue from *Clutag Five Poems Series. No. 13: Bernard O'Donoghue* (2016) is reproduced by kind permission of the author and Andrew McNeillie of Clutag Press, www.clutagpress.com

'Stabat Mater' by Eiléan Ní Chuilleanáin from *The Boys of Bluehill* (2015) is reproduced by kind permission of the author and The Gallery Press, www.gallerypress.com

'Cuimhne an Uisce' / 'A Recovered Memory of Water' by Nuala Ní Dhomhnaill translated by Paul Muldoon from *The Fifty Minute Mermaid* (2007) is reproduced by kind permission of the author, the translator, and The Gallery Press, www.gallerypress.com

'The Ghost Comes to Town: Le Fanu and the urban Gothic' by Nicholas Daly from *The Demographic Imagination and the Nineteenth-Century City: Paris, London, New York* is reproduced in edited form by permission of Cambridge University Press, www.cambridge.org

Notes on Contributors

CLAIRE BRACKEN is an Associate Professor in the English Department at Union College, New York. She is co-editor with Susan Cahill of *Anne Enright* (2011) and with Emma Radley of *Viewpoints: Theoretical perspectives on Irish visual texts* (2013). Her book *Irish Feminist Futures* was published by Routledge in 2016. In 2017, she co-edited with Tara Harney-Mahajan a double special issue of the journal *LIT* entitled *Recessionary Imaginings: Post-Celtic Tiger Ireland and contemporary women's writing*. She has co-edited a special issue with Cara Delay on Reproductive Justice and Women's Health for *Éire-Ireland*, published in autumn 2021.

NICHOLAS DALY is Professor of Modern English and American Literature at University College Dublin, and a member of the Royal Irish Academy. His publications include the monographs *Modernism, Romance, and the Fin de Siècle* (1999), *Literature, Technology, and Modernity* (2004), *Sensation and Modernity in the 1860s* (2009), *The Demographic Imagination and the Nineteenth-Century City: Paris, London, New York* (2015), and *Ruritania: A cultural history from The Prisoner of Zenda to the Princess Diaries* (2020). For Oxford World's Classics he has edited Baroness Orczy's *The Scarlet Pimpernel*, Anthony Hope's *The Prisoner of Zenda*, and Arthur Conan Doyle's *A Study in Scarlet*.

ALEX DAVIS is Professor of English at University College Cork. He is the author of *A Broken Line: Denis Devlin and Irish poetic modernism* (2000), and many essays on anglophone poetry from the 1880s to the present day. He is co-editor, with Lee M. Jenkins, of *Locations of Literary Modernism: Region and nation in British and American modernist poetry* (2000), *The Cambridge Companion to Modernist Poetry* (2007), and *A History of Modernist Poetry* (2015); and, with Patricia Coughlan, of *Modernism and Ireland: The poetry of the 1930s* (1995).

ANNE FOGARTY is Professor of James Joyce Studies at University College Dublin and founder and co-editor with Luca Crispi of the *Dublin James Joyce Journal*. She was Associate Director of the Yeats International Summer

School 1995–7 and has been Academic Director of the Dublin James Joyce Summer School since 1997. She was editor of the *Irish University Review*, 2002–9. She has written widely on aspects of twentieth-century and contemporary Irish writing. A collection of essays on the novelist Deirdre Madden, co-edited with Marisol Morales-Ladrón, was published by Manchester University Press in 2022. She is completing an edition of *Dubliners* for Penguin.

MARGARET MILLS HARPER is Glucksman Professor of Contemporary Writing in English at the University of Limerick. She researches and teaches twentieth- and twenty-first-century Irish and American (US) literature in English, especially poetry. She is the author of *The Aristocracy of Art: Joyce and Wolfe* (1990) and *Wisdom of Two: The spiritual and literary collaboration of George and W.B. Yeats* (2006). Scholarly editions include two of the four volumes of *Yeats' 'Vision' Papers* (1992 and 2001, with Anthony Martinich and George Mills Harper), and both the 1925 and 1937 versions of Yeats' *A Vision* for *The Collected Works of W.B. Yeats* (2008 and 2015, with Catherine Paul). Recent work includes the edited volume *Dance and Modernism in Irish and German Literature and Culture: Connections in motion* (2019, with Sabine Egger and Catherine Foley) and a special issue of *International Yeats Studies* on *Wheels and Butterflies* (with Alexandra Poulain, 2021).

EAMONN HUGHES was a Senior Lecturer in the School of English at Queen's University Belfast for many years. He specialises in Irish literary and cultural studies. Recently he has worked with Van Morrison on two volumes of lyrics: *Lit Up Inside* (2014) and *Keep 'Er Lit* (2020). He is currently Chair of the board of governors and President of the Linen Hall Library.

LAURA IZARRA is Full Professor of Literatures in English at the University of São Paulo, Coordinator of the W.B. Yeats Chair of Irish Studies/USP, and former President of the Brazilian Association of Irish Studies – ABEI (2009–18) and of the Society for Irish Latin American Studies (SILAS). She is author of *Mirrors and Holographic Labyrinths: The process of a 'new' aesthetic synthesis in the novels of John Banville* (1999), *Narrativas de la diáspora irlandesa bajo la Cruz del Sur* (2010), and *Cultural Trauma and Literary Irish Resonances* (2020); editor of *Da Irlanda para o Brasil: Textos críticos* (since 2009) and *Roger Casement in Brazil* (2010) with two exhibitions (2010, 2016); co-editor of *ABEI Journal* (since 1999), *Lectures* (since 2010), and the Portuguese translation of *The Amazon Journal of*

Roger Casement (2016). She has published widely on Irish contemporary literature; at present, her main research interests are literature of the diaspora, cultural trauma, and memory studies.

MARGARET KELLEHER is Professor and Chair of Anglo-Irish Literature and Drama at University College Dublin. She received a BA in English and History from University College Cork (1984) and a PhD in English from Boston College (1992). Her book *The Maamtrasna Murders: Language, life and death in nineteenth-century Ireland* was published by UCD Press in 2018 and awarded the Michael J. Durkan Prize for Books on Language and Culture by the American Conference of Irish Studies in 2019. Other publications include *The Feminization of Famine* (1997), *The Cambridge History of Irish Literature*, 2 vols, edited with Philip O'Leary (2006), and a special issue of the journal *Éire-Ireland* on the topic of 'Ireland and the Contemporary', edited with Nicholas Wolf (2017). She is Chair of the Irish Film Institute and was UCD academic lead for the Museum of Literature Ireland (MoLI), a collaboration between UCD and the National Library of Ireland.

SEÁN KENNEDY is Professor of English and Coordinator of Irish Studies at Saint Mary's University, Halifax, Nova Scotia. Recent publications include, as editor, *Beckett Beyond the Normal* (2020), *Samuel Beckett and Biopolitics* (2019), and a special issue of *Estudios Irlandeses*.

CATHERINE LA FARGE lectured at the University of Galway. She is interested in medieval texts and psychoanalysis and has written on a range of subjects including early travel writing, gender in Chaucer, and blood, conversation, and genre in Malory.

THOMAS MCCARTHY was born in County Waterford and educated at University College Cork. His many collections of poetry include *The First Convention*, *The Sorrow Garden*, *Merchant Prince*, *The Last Geraldine Officer*, *Pandemonium*, and *Prophecy*. He has also published two novels, *Without Power* and *Asya and Christine*, as well as three works of non-fiction, *Gardens of Remembrance*, *Out of the Ashes*, and *Poetry, Memory and the Party: Journals 1974–2014*. He is a member of Aosdána. He has won the Patrick Kavanagh Award, the Alice Hunt Bartlett and O'Shaughnessy Prize for Poetry as well as the Ireland Funds *Annual Literary Award*. He was editor of *Poetry Ireland Review* and *The Cork Review*. He worked for many years at Cork City Libraries, resigning in 2014 to write full-time.

SARAH MCKIBBEN is Associate Professor of Irish Language and Literature at the University of Notre Dame. She is author of *Endangered Masculinities in Irish Poetry, 1540–1780* (2010) and essays in *North American Journal of Celtic Studies*, *Éire-Ireland*, *Irish University Review*, and various collections, including *Early Modern Ireland: New sources, methods, and directions* (2018), *Modernist Afterlives in Irish Literature and Culture* (2016), *The Edinburgh Companion to Irish Modernism* (2021), and (with Danielle Clarke) *A History of Irish Women's Poetry* (2021). She is working on a new book provisionally entitled *Tradition Transformed: Bardic poetry and patronage in early modern Ireland, c.1560–1660*.

PAULA MEEHAN was born in Dublin where she still lives. She studied at Trinity College Dublin and at Eastern Washington University in the US. She has published seven collections of poetry which have received both popular and critical acclaim. She has moderated workshops in the community, in prisons, and in recovery programmes, and has worked extensively with emerging poets inside and outside the universities. She has written plays for children and adults and some of her work for radio is published in *Music for Dogs* (2008). She has received the Butler Literary Award for Poetry presented by the Irish American Cultural Institute, the Marten Toonder Award for Literature, the Denis Devlin Award for *Dharmakaya*, 2000, The Lawrence O'Shaughnessy Award for Poetry, 2015, a Cholmondely Award for *Geomantic*, 2017, and the PPI Award for Radio Drama. She was honoured with election to Aosdána in 1996. She was Ireland Professor of Poetry, 2013–16, and her public lectures from these years, *Imaginary Bonnets with Real Bees in Them*, was published by UCD Press in 2016. Her selected poems, *As If By Magic*, was published by Dedalus Press, Dublin, in 2020 and by Wake Forest University Press, Winston-Salem, in 2021.

ANNE MULHALL is a Lecturer in the School of English, Film, Drama and Creative Writing at University College Dublin, where she is Co-director of the Centre for Gender, Feminism and Sexualities. Her writing and teaching are in the areas of queer, feminist, and critical migration studies, and contemporary Irish writing and culture.

MÁIRÍN NIC EOIN is Emerita Professor of Irish, Dublin City University, and author of *An Litríocht Réigiúnach* (1982), *Eoghan Ó Tuairisc: Beatha agus saothar* (1988), *B'Ait Leo Bean: Gnéithe den idé-eolaíocht inscne i dtraidisiún liteartha na Gaeilge* (1998), and *Trén bhFearann Breac: An díláithriú cultúir agus nualitríocht na Gaeilge* (2005). She has published many articles and book chapters on modern and contemporary writing in Irish and her current research focuses on the international contexts of that writing. She has edited or co-edited literary anthologies and collections of critical essays, including the two-volume *Litríocht na Gaeilge ar fud an Domhain* (2015). The book *Cumadóireacht Uí Chadhain*, an edition of a number of unpublished works by Máirtín Ó Cadhain, co-edited with Mícheál Briody, was published in 2020. She is a member of the Royal Irish Academy.

EILÉAN NÍ CHUILLEANÁIN is a Fellow and Professor of English (Emerita) at Trinity College Dublin and a member of Aosdána. She served as Ireland Professor of Poetry from 2016 to 2019. She was a founder member of *Cyphers*, a literary journal. She won the Patrick Kavanagh Award in 1973, the O'Shaughnessy Award of the Irish-American Cultural Institute in 1992, the 2010 International Griffin Poetry Prize, and the 2020 *Irish Times* Poetry Now Award. Her collections include *Acts and Monuments* (1972), *Site of Ambush* (1975), *The Second Voyage* (1977, 1986), *The Rose Geranium* (1981), *The Magdalene Sermon* (1989), *The Brazen Serpent* (1994), *The Girl Who Married the Reindeer* (2001), *Selected Poems* (2008), *The Sun-fish* (2009), *Legend of the Walled-up Wife* (2011, translations from the Romanian of Ileana Malancioiu), *The Boys of Bluehill* (2015), and *The Mother House* (2019). Her *Collected Poems* was published in October 2020.

NUALA NÍ DHOMHNAILL is one of the most prominent poets in Ireland today. Her poetry has been translated into English by a number of well-known Irish writers, including Seamus Heaney, Medbh McGuckian, and Paul Muldoon. Irish themes, including language, are central to her poetry and range from ancient myths to small details of contemporary life. As a student at University College Cork she studied Irish and English and became part of a group of Irish-language poets who were published in the literary magazine *Innti*. Her first collection was published in 1981, and the translation *Selected Poems: Rogha dánta* appeared in 1986. In addition to poetry, she has written plays in Irish, and her work has been translated into French, German, Polish, Italian, Norwegian, Estonian, Japanese, and English. Ní Dhomhnaill has held the Burns Chair of Irish Studies at Boston College, the Humboldt Chair of Irish Studies at Villanova University, and the Naughton Fellowship of Irish Studies at Notre Dame University. She held the Ireland Chair of Poetry from 2001 to 2004. She is the recipient of several awards including the Lawrence O'Shaughnessy Award for Poetry, the American Ireland Fund Literary Award, and the Seán Ó Ríordáin Award, which she won for all four of her Irish poetry collections.

DOIREANN NÍ GHRÍOFA is a poet and essayist. Her prose début *A Ghost in the Throat* was awarded Irish Book of the Year 2020, and described as 'glowing' (Anne Enright), 'sumptuous' (*The Sunday Times*), and 'captivatingly original' (*The Guardian*). She is also author of six critically acclaimed books of poetry, each a deepening exploration of birth, death, desire, and domesticity. Ní Ghríofa's artistic practice encompasses cross-disciplinary collaborations, fusing poetry with film, dance, music, and visual art, and her work has been commissioned by institutions such as The Poetry Society (Britain), Poetry Ireland, The Embassy of Ireland in Britain, and the Department of Foreign Affairs. Awards for her writing include a Lannan Literary Fellowship (USA), the Ostana Prize (Italy), and the Rooney Prize for Irish Literature. Her most recent book of poems is *To Star the Dark*.

BERNARD O'DONOGHUE was born in Cullen in north-west Cork in 1945 and he still spends part of the year there. Since 1965 he has lived in Oxford where he taught medieval English and modern Irish literature at Wadham College. He has published seven books of poetry of which the most recent was *The Seasons of Cullen Church* (2016).

CLÍONA Ó GALLCHOIR is a Lecturer in English at University College Cork. Her research focuses on the literature and culture of the long eighteenth century, focusing particularly on Irish writing, women's writing and constructions of gender, sexuality, and childhood. Her publications include *A History of Modern Irish Women's Literature* (2018), co-edited with Heather Ingman, *Maria Edgeworth: Women, enlightenment and nation* (2005), *Maria Edgeworth* (2021), and essays and articles in *European Romantic Review*, *Irish University Review*, and *Irish Literature in Transition, 1700–1780* (2020).

ELISABETH OKASHA worked as Professor of Anglo-Saxon Literature in the School of English, University College Cork for forty-two years, and was Director of the UCC Language Centre, before retiring in 2019.

TINA O'TOOLE is Senior Lecturer in English at the School of English, Irish, and Communication, University of Limerick. Her scholarship focuses on the literary representation of genders and sexualities, concentrating on late-nineteenth- and twentieth-century Irish writing; publications include *The Irish New Woman* (2013), and essays for *Modernism/Modernity*

(2014), *A History of Irish Women's Writing* (2018), and *Irish Literature in Transition 1880–1940* (2020). As editor, she has produced special issues of *Irish University Review* on Elizabeth Bowen (2021; co-edited with Anna Teekell), *Éire-Ireland* on 'New Approaches to Irish Migration' (2012; with Piaras Mac Éinrí), *Women Writing War* (2016; with Gillian McIntosh and Muireann O'Cinnéide), and *Irish Literature: Feminist perspectives* (2008; with Patricia Coughlan).

PATRICIA PALMER is the author of *Language and Conquest in Early Modern Ireland: English Renaissance literature and Elizabethan imperial expansion* (2001), and *The Severed Head and the Grafted Tongue: Translating violence in early modern Ireland* (2014). She has published articles with *English Literary Renaissance*, *Translation Studies*, *Renaissance Quarterly*, *Irish Historical Studies*, and *Literature Compass* and has contributed book chapters on subjects as diverse as the body in pain, the Flight of the Earls, travel writing, and colonial rhetoric. After graduating with an MA from University College Cork, she worked in Athens and Brussels before taking a D.Phil. in English Literature at the University of Oxford. She was Senior Lecturer in the University of York (2000–8) and Reader in King's College London (2008–16), and took up the Chair of Renaissance Literature in Maynooth University in 2017. She is Principal Investigator on the MACMORRIS project which seeks to map the full range of cultural activity, across languages and ethnic groups, in early modern Ireland. *Early Modern Criticism in a Time of Crisis* which she co-edited with David J. Baker was published by the University of Santa Barbara in 2022.

MOYNAGH SULLIVAN is Associate Professor in English and Associate Dean for Equality, Diversity, and Inclusion at Maynooth University. Her research focuses on motherhood, gender, and sexuality in Irish culture from a variety of psychoanalytical perspectives. She has published widely in these fields, with a particular attention to the mechanics of hetero-patriarchal interpretation and neglected women poets, exemplified by her recent essay 'Rematriating Mid-Century Modernism: Carla Lanyon Lanyon', in *A History of Irish Women's Poetry* (2021). She is currently writing a monograph on motherhood in Irish culture. Awarded the Department of Foreign Affairs Fulbright Fellowship in Irish Studies at the University of California, Berkeley in 2009, she was recently Principal Investigator on the Irish Research Council funded project, Mamecology (2020–1).

Preface

MARGARET KELLEHER

In 1973, Patricia Coughlan began her teaching career as junior lecturer at St Patrick's College, Maynooth, following doctoral studies at Queen Mary College, University of London funded by the prestigious National University of Ireland Travelling Studentship which she won in 1970. Her doctoral thesis was entitled 'Classical Themes in the Non-Satiric Poetry of Andrew Marvell'. In 1977, she became lecturer in the Department of English, University College Cork, where she was later appointed professor; she retired from this academic post in May 2014. The publication of this volume of essays provides a welcome occasion to celebrate her highly influential teaching career and to underline the significance, scope, and impact of her scholarship and research.

To reflect on the range of Pat Coughlan's scholarship is genuinely humbling and not a little daunting. Chronologically, her chosen subjects extend from Edmund Spenser and Sheridan Le Fanu to Sinéad Morrissey, Máire Mhac an tSaoi, and Paula Meehan; generically, her research covers poetry, fiction, historical writing, theory, criticism, bio-bibliography, and memoir; thematically, her interests span gender representations by female and male writers, feminist theory and cultural history, diaspora literature, modernism, life writing and social history, colonial discourse in and about Ireland, Irish Gothic, psychoanalytic theory, subjectivity and gender in Irish postmodernity, and literature written in Irish. Yet even such a list does poor service to the intellectual brilliance, suppleness, and vivacity of her work as literary critic – qualities cherished by her readers and students and to which the following brief survey can only begin to pay tribute.

In 1990, *Spenser and Ireland: An interdisciplinary perspective*, edited by Patricia Coughlan, was published by Cork University Press. The volume was a ground-breaking collection, not only for its topic, but also in disciplinary terms, demonstrating the converging interests of literary scholars and historians working on the early modern period, along with a constructive wariness as to overly simplistic identifications. Coughlan's own contribution to the volume provides an especially nuanced engagement with a controversial subject, namely the 'radical alterity' of Ireland in Spenser's writings. These she treats 'as the site of a single complex of thought ... riven by contradictions, but richly repaying a comparative approach seeking to comprehend the continuity of symbolic representation with social behaviour'.[1] Such a formulation is noteworthy not only as an early statement of a fundamental theoretical stance but also as a fine example of her distinctive critical practice whereby methodology is made explicit and self-reflective, and the conceptual implications of one critical essay extend far beyond its stated subject.

A highly influential cluster of articles (on dramatist Henry Burkhead, 'the English anatomy of Ireland in the seventeenth century', the political thought of Vincent and Daniel Gookin, and the Hartlibian project for a natural history of Ireland) published over the next decade examines the developing discourse about English colonisation of Ireland in the mid-seventeenth century, and the opposing views expressed at the time. These essays by Coughlan are similarly characterised by the integration of historicist and literary-textual approaches or, to employ her own more elegant formulation, by a commitment to 'investigate the various writings of the period in themselves as symbolic representations (as distinct from seeing them as relatively inert and transparently readable pieces of evidence for the views or political positions of various factions)'.[2] Viewed together, these essays also offer especially rich insights into the precise textual dynamics of colonial discourse – more usually generalised by literary critics than specifically examined – and vividly illuminate the 'close and nervous relation' of colonial discourse in and about Ireland 'to the ideology actually seen to govern political actions'.[3] Her introductory essay to the 2009 edition of Henry Burkhead's *A Tragedy of Cola's Furies or Lirenda's Miserie* consolidates and extends her investigation of early modern writing.[4]

Coughlan's work on nineteenth-century Irish writing, which was first published in the late 1980s, has paved the way for many later critical practitioners. Her 1988 essay on James Clarence Mangan was one of the first to recognise the richness of his intertextuality, 'the complex fabric of his writing and doubleness of tone': 'always bifocal'.[5] The succeeding essays on Joseph Sheridan Le Fanu and Charles Maturin are key texts in defining the 'Irish Gothic' and its domestic preoccupations; rereading them now, what distinguishes them even more sharply is their determined insertion of Irish authors into a tradition of European writing (Mangan's use of Byron; the influence of Maturin on Balzac; the significance of German Romanticism for Le Fanu). Fittingly, these essays were first delivered and published in international fora – in Birgit Bramsback's Uppsala series and in Heinz Kosok and Wolfgang Zach's *Literary Interrelations* volumes – a significant reminder of Coughlan's long-standing support for Irish literary studies in Europe over many decades.

Samuel Beckett's fiction and poetry have been enduring subjects, from her first published essay '"A noise of wet kisses and washing in a tub": Samuel Beckett and the idea of fiction', published in the *Maynooth Review* in 1980. Her 1996 essay '*Entre le galet et la mer*: Reading a Beckett poem between two languages' is a beautiful example of her own impressive linguistic sensitivity (more brio than panache), exploring 'the interpretative possibilities, or chinks, offered by the fact of the poem's two versions and their small disparities'.[6] Once again the occasion of publication is itself notable: part of a literary conference organised by seven departments from the then School of Languages and Literature, UCD, whose objective was to 'highlight the influence and impact which different literary traditions have had and continue to have on each other'.[7]

A year before, *Modernism and Ireland: The poetry of the 1930s* appeared, edited by Coughlan and colleague Alex Davis. The deep and rapid impact of the volume – in bringing back to attention the writings of the 1930s poets and with them the 'fate of modernism in Irish literature after the first modernist generation' – may itself obscure the full pioneering nature of their project, since what was then a very real critical neglect is now difficult to imagine. Yet the scholarly agenda so precisely delineated by Coughlan and Davis (and inaugurated in their own essays on Beckett and Coffey respectively) continues to be fresh and vibrant: 'to investigate what relations may be posed between the master narratives of international modernism, with all their internal variations and contested issues, and the nature of Irishness and how it was framed in terms of institutions, on the one hand, and selfhoods, on the other'.[8]

'Tá sé in am dúinn na téacsanna a athléamh ar shlíte eile: mar fhriotal mná, i gcomhthéacs litríocht na mban.' This manifesto for renewed critical attention to the symbolic and contextual dimensions of women's writings appeared in Coughlan's 1999 Irish-language essay on Peig: 'An Léiriú ar Shaol na mBan i dTéacsanna Dírbheathaisnéise Pheig Sayers' ('The Representation of Women's Lives in the Autobiographical Texts of Peig Sayers').[9] Originating in a lecture at the 1998 *Ceiliúradh an Bhlascaoid* seminar, her talk sparked a 'sraith litreacha', with a stream of letters to *The Irish Times* as well as many discussions in radio and local newspapers.

What resulted was, as Coughlan notes in the 2007 English-language version of her article, 'an unlikely, sometimes hilarious, controversy, about who owned Peig, who might think and write about her, and in what ways', though the manner of those ideological demarcations also had a more ugly form.[10] Regrettably less visible within the controversy, and poorly served by headlines such as 'A Feminist Peig Sayers Chafed at Being a Chattel', was the delicate sympathy of Coughlan's textual reading, most especially her treatment of the themes of faith and religious feeling in Peig's work and of Peig's legacy as creative writer rather than ideological foil ('léargas domhain agus corraitheach ar dhearcadh na mban a bhí mar chuid den phobal san agus ar an tuiscint a bhí acu ar an saol, ó bhreith go bás …').[11]

In 1991, Coughlan's famous 'Bog Queens' essay was published, a study of representations of femininity in the poetry of Seamus Heaney and John Montague. The essay has been republished three times to date, and its critical genealogy includes responses by Heaney in an interview published in 2002 and Coughlan's revisiting of the subject in her *Irish Review* article of 2007. It has generated a host of engagements by other critics, many of which credit the essay's enabling force and others which take a more oppositional stance, often in combative footnotes – their placing a telling indication of the unease that Coughlan's starkly fundamental questions about aesthetics and gender can still provoke.[12] The opening question in the 1991 essay has lost none of its charge: 'can poetry's implicit claim to universality of utterance and to utopian insight be upheld in the face of a reader's awareness of its gendered and therefore (perhaps unconsciously) partial perspective?'[13] Similarly, her later rebuttal of the complaint that 'ideology drives out aesthetics' continues to inspire: 'Yet to enquire into the meanings of poems is not necessarily to strip them of their formal qualities. It is perfectly possible, and is the ideal of all responsible criticism, feminist or not, to arrive at an interpretation which takes account both of form and of meaning, in their inextricable interweaving.'[14]

A compelling engagement with the pleasures of textual 'interweaving' is a hallmark of Coughlan's criticism, evident in her sensitive and non-idealising reading of Kate O'Brien's fiction, her nuanced treatment of '[Elizabeth] Bowen's delicate, skeptical anatomy of the permissible modes of being feminine', and her unflinching scrutiny of 'abjection' and agency in the work of Edna O'Brien, to name just some examples. Her 2006 essay on Edna O'Brien is a wonderful instance of the multi-faceted quality of a single Coughlan essay: it begins with compelling commentary on O'Brien's deployment of Joycean tropes, proceeds with an intricate detailing of the 'building-blocks and small-scale constituents' which account for 'the texture of her prose', constructs a deeply suggestive analogy between O'Brien and Kristeva, and concludes with a subtle and persuasive evaluation of the complex ideological force of O'Brien's fiction.[15] The following short quotation provides a fine example of the continuing richness of psychoanalytic theory for her work and of the delicate critical interplay of theory and literary text: 'I see Kristeva, therefore, not as the *advocate* of abjection, but as its searching and eloquent *analyst*; it is pointless to shoot the messenger. And likewise in O'Brien's case, she does not *celebrate* the abjection of the maternal and of Ireland in her work; she rather chronicles, agonizes and mourns over it.'[16] Psychoanalytical criticism and specifically object-relations theories continue to be an especially important theoretical resource for Coughlan: in her recent work she strongly argues that psychoanalysis and social feminism are 'continuous' with one 'illuminating the other and leading to a broader view which is ethical and ideological, as well as emotional'.[17]

In 2005, Coughlan and colleagues Tina O'Toole and Eibhear Walshe produced the *Munster Women Writers* project, a dictionary and a database, which constituted one of the first digital humanities explorations in Irish literary studies. The project, part of an interdisciplinary, three-strand research initiative on Women in Irish Society, was supported by the Programme for Research in Third-Level Institutions, Cycle 1, and the provision of such resources in 1999 was a landmark in humanities funding. Placed alongside the 2008 collection *Irish Literature: Feminist perspectives*, edited by Coughlan and O'Toole, a key distinguishing characteristic of Coughlan's feminist scholarship comes to light, namely the ability to integrate historicist and textual approaches with fresh and diverse theoretical perspectives. A further striking quality is the collection's inclusion of both younger and established critics, with subjects ranging within and beyond the canonical.

Since 2003, Coughlan has published key critical studies of poets including Eiléan Ní Chuilleanáin, Thomas Kinsella, Moya Cannon, Vona Groarke, and Máire Mhac an tSaoi; and of novelists Ronan Bennett, Anne Enright, John Banville, Edna O'Brien, Eilís Ní Dhuibhne, Anne Haverty, Mary Morrissy, Alice McDermott, and Elizabeth Bowen. Many of these influential articles provided remarkably assured and substantial engagements with very recently published works, such as her 2005 reading of Enright's *The Pleasure of Eliza Lynch* (2002) or her 2006 article on Banville's fiction including *The Sea* (2005).[18] To choose just one year, in 2009 she published an eloquent meditation on a single lyric – Kinsella's 'High Tide: Amagansett' and its intertexts – and a powerful critical championing of Cannon and Groarke, which included a piercing indictment of current critical trends in poetry reviewing and their 'fiercely regulatory' approaches. Here she exposes how conventions of poetry criticism, especially in reviewing, 'have been, or have become, decidedly unwelcoming even to much thematic, let alone social or ideological, discussion (and especially when that explicitly critiques social-structural gender arrangements)'.[19] Her diagnosis of the consequences of this condition is worth reproducing as an especially valuable insight into what matters for Coughlan as a critic: 'I see this distaste for the visibility even of ideas themselves, let alone a politics, in poetry, as a kind of self-denying ordinance which risks impoverishing the realm of poetry and has the effect of further isolating it from audiences and from recovering its traditionally powerful role in society at all.'[20]

Her 2012 essay on Alice McDermott, published in the *Éire-Ireland* special issue on 'New Approaches to Irish Migration' (edited by Piaras Mac Éinrí and Tina O'Toole) attests to Coughlan's commitment to the still-neglected domain of diaspora literature. This essay also illustrates her lasting critical interest in postmodern narratives of subjectivity and gender, which Coughlan reads as part of a continuing and coherent project of decolonisation 'but with a difference'.[21] The conclusion of her 2007 *Irish Review* essay on Seamus Heaney provided a tantalising foretaste of the scholarship to come: 'For sceptics, as I am, of post-nationalist positions, can the old nation-narratives be recuperated? In Irish postmodernity, it is not yet clear whether the baby (the sense of what, however loosely, unifies our various Irelands and makes the country its changing, developing self) must be thrown out with the bathwater of old-nationalist and patriarchal appropriations, subordination and containment of the feminine. But that is another day's work.'[22]

Such work has continued apace following her 'retirement' from UCC, and to Irish studies' benefit. In 2015, two essays on Irish-language poet Máire Mhac an tSaoi appeared, one published in a festschrift for Coughlan's close friend and colleague Máire Herbert, and the second as part of a bilingual collection edited by Louis de Paor. Her fine close reading of Mhac an tSaoi's 'Love has pitched his mansion', as a 'dark fantasy of failed mothering', elucidates not only the Irish-language poet's rewriting of the Yeatsian 'Crazy Jane' figure but also her wider repudiation of the lyric form as consolatory mode.[23] Conversely, in '"An t-éitheach; is an fíor? …": A note on two late poems by Máire Mhac an tSaoi', she analyses two lyrics where the poetic impulses move towards 'connection, attachment, mutual recognition between self and other, and the sense of achieved insight, transcending emotional pain'.[24] Her most recent work on Mhac an tSaoi, for the Cambridge University Press *History of Irish Women's Poetry* (2021), traces what Coughlan terms the 'core ideal of human kinship' and the ultimate 'indivisibility of love' across the four-and-a-half decades of the poet's career.[25]

Coughlan's enduring power to combine close textual inspection with a commanding breadth of reference and suggestion is evident throughout her recent publications. To name just a few instances, her essay on sibling and family relations in contemporary Irish literature, for a collection edited by Luz Mar González-Arias, ranges from the poetry of Ní Chuilleanáin, Bernard O'Donoghue, and Nuala Ní Dhomhnaill to the fiction of Enright and Maeve Brennan, culminating in a masterful comparison of funeral scenes in Enright's *The Gathering* and Joyce's *A Portrait*.[26] In her chapter for the 2018 Cambridge University Press *History of Modern Irish Women's Literature*, she returns to the work of Elizabeth Bowen with an in-depth assessment of the author's career presented in three phases, along with thought-provoking comments on theme and style. All this in an essay of twenty-two pages which manages also, with characteristic incisiveness, to set the critical agenda for generations to come: 'Within Irish criticism, contrasting reductionist pitfalls have risked distorting Bowen's reception. On the one hand, she is found wanting on political grounds for not having disavowed gentry privilege and hegemony. On the other, Ascendancy dispossession is problematically equated with other, far more oppressive, forced displacements, encouraging nostalgia. While a more informed understanding of the nature of her Irishness has emerged, she is still in the process of admission to the Irish canon.'[27] Her ensuing contribution to the *Irish University Review* special issue on Bowen (2021), entitled '"We get all sealed up": An essay in five deaths',[28] features a series of deeply moving reflections on the affective life; this is at once a constant of her work as critic and newly explicit. One eagerly awaits what will follow.

The adjective most frequently associated with Pat Coughlan as supervisor and mentor is 'generous' ('rigorous' and 'supportive' also make high appearances, but second always to 'generous'). Her contribution can be seen in the many master's theses and doctoral dissertations which she has supervised or externally examined, the postdoctoral and visiting fellows whom she has mentored, and the countless others influenced through her scholarship rather than personal contact. Her work with the Irish Research

Council's committees since 1998 has supported and guided many scholars and research projects in the humanities in Ireland, to cite just one of her many time-intensive public service contributions whose value can too often go unnoticed. The importance of her service to UCC's governing authority in the term 2001–4, and of her courage and integrity as staff representative, are on public record. Nationally, she has been an active contributor to arts programmes in English and in Irish, for Raidió na Gaeltachta, RTÉ, and BBC Radio 4, and a cherished participant in and director at the Merriman Schools. Internationally, the influence of her ambassadorial work for Irish literature and Irish studies is immense, as demonstrated by her Fulbright Scholar award in 2014, and as colleagues from many centres for Irish studies warmly attest: extending from Concordia and New York to Leuven and Sweden, and further in the years ahead.

Teaching and research have always been deeply intertwined in Pat's work; studying her career, it is clear that many of her most innovative and influential research subjects have begun life in the seminar room and lecture theatre and return there. Those of us fortunate enough to have sat in those classes can still remember their intellectual charge many years later. Students from the late 1970s onwards recall, for example, her 'brilliant' Beckett lectures and her sparkling lectures on Renaissance poetry, her lectures on *Lolita* for their 'sheer cleverness and ingenuity', and her introduction to the mysteries of *Bleak House* among other 'stand-out' lectures on nineteenth-century fiction. More recent graduates have been treated to courses on contemporary Irish poetry and fiction, along with seventeenth-century poetry, an enduring passion. Many contributors to this volume can date the beginning of our own graduate careers to a course by Pat Coughlan, whether the course on literary theory which she introduced to students of English in the early 1980s – and which was audited by many others – or the course on feminist literary theory co-taught with Anne Fogarty in the mid 1980s, one of the first in the country; or the ground-breaking interdisciplinary English and history programme developed with Tom Dunne. Her contributions to IASIL conferences are spellbinding; one personal highlight was in July 2013, at Queen's University Belfast, when we were treated to a sparkling tour de force plenary lecture entitled 'Desolation, Haunting, Power: Changing the city imaginary', in which Pat ranged from writings by Edna O'Brien, Neil Jordan, and John Banville to recent works by Sinéad Morrissey, Keith Ridgway, and Tana French.

And lest her mischievous sense of humour and keen sense of fun fail to receive its place before ending, I'm grateful to Nick Daly for reminding me of his favourite of Pat's jokes, part of her lecture on Russian formalism and defamiliarisation:

> 'What is green, has three legs, and waves in the wind?'
> 'I don't know.'
> 'Grass.'
> 'But grass doesn't have legs.'
> 'Yes, but otherwise the question is too easy.'

Introduction

ANNE FOGARTY AND TINA O'TOOLE

The essays in this collection were composed, not only in tribute to Patricia Coughlan, but also in active dialogue with her work. References to her multi-faceted publications thread their way through them and bear testament to the diverse and consequential debates they have instigated and their long-lasting and ongoing impact. These essays participate in lively and continuing conversations, not alone with Coughlan's influential scholarly output, but also with her inspiring and enduringly involving teaching, public lectures, and conference presentations. Her intellectual passions, in sum, undergird the work gathered together here. Above all, these essays mirror the variety of her interests, detailed in Margaret Kelleher's preface, and the span of her academic curiosity, historically, socially, politically, emotionally, and thematically. Their premises, as a consequence, are various. However, two central themes, gender and space, dominate and cross-connect these essays, as our title indicates. Methodologically, moreover, a unifying approach is the attentiveness that all of the authors devote to variously conceived texts and artefacts, created in a wide span of historical eras. The possibilities and findings of close reading are married with insights gleaned from historical and theoretical investigation in all of these pieces.

The overview of this volume outlined here will first consider how it intersects with feminist debates in the current moment and then touch on the varying notions of space and the environment that inform several of the essays and cross-connect the findings that they put forward. The importance of engaged and responsive reading exemplified by Patricia Coughlan in her influential essays and talks is a mainstay of the interventions here. The differing ways in which these pieces signal how an engagement in attentive and detailed interpretation is crucial to literary, historical, and political understanding will be pinpointed in the course of profiling their variegated but mutually illuminating and overlapping arguments.

In Ireland, as elsewhere, feminism has been going through a period of consolidation, revival, and change in the past decade or more. Many pressing social events have borne out the necessity for maintaining feminism as an activist platform and a mode of social and cultural inquiry. They have also made evident that social justice and parity between the genders can be attained only if intersectional interests are pursued and advocated for. The campaigns for marriage equality legalising same-sex marriage in the 2015 referendum and the removal of the ban on abortion in the 2018 referendum were enabled by cross-sectoral engagement and a widespread public debate on issues of human rights for members of the queer community and for all people of reproductive age. Yet, these landmark advances have been overshadowed by the halting recovery of the occluded history of the incarceration and silencing of women and children in institutions, most prominently the mother and baby homes. The report commissioned by the government from a tribunal set up in 2015, following Catherine Corless' exposure in 2014 of the undocumented burial of hundreds of anonymous infants in the grounds of the former Bon Secours home in Tuam, issued in January 2021 has been vitiated by omissions and a reluctance to take survivor testimonies adequately into account.[1] A failure to recognise the voices of those who have been damaged and maltreated and to grant access to vital records about the circumstances surrounding individual adoption have marred attempts at piecing together a shamefully erased history and efforts to achieve a modicum of redress. Moreover, current controversies reveal that institutional abuse is not confined to the past, nor can it easily be held at a distance. It is compounded and continued in the present. As a consequence, the unfolding debates about the pernicious and enduring maltreatment of women and children by state and religious bodies have refocused attention on the endemic nature of patriarchal discrimination in Irish society and the imbalance of power that it ruthlessly foments and pursues.

In the cultural sphere, this gender imbalance became particularly evident on two recent occasions: the omission of works by female artists, with the exception of Ali White's *Me, Mollser*, from the Abbey Theatre's commemorative 2016 'Waking the Nation' programme and the neglect of female writers in *The Cambridge Companion to Irish Poets*, edited by Gerald Dawe in 2018. A prevailing and deep-seated male bias in relation to poetry, playwriting, and all the creative aspects of theatre practice, including direction, costumes, set lighting, and sound design, was thus uncovered. The fallacy of assuming that advance in some areas with regards to women's rights extends to every aspect of society was exposed. The invisibility and marginalisation of female contributions to the arts led to a prolonged outcry. Conspicuously, the response marshalled the resources of third-wave feminism, with its emphasis on intersectionality, the multi-perspectival, the use of social media, and the politics of coalition, in setting out to undo the damage of these omissions in the first instance and to extend and champion awareness of women's roles in the cultural sphere.[2]

The year-long #WakingTheFeminists campaign spearheaded by Lian Bell and encompassing a wide array of artists in the theatre sector devised a carefully worked out set of objectives.[3] Its central goal was to negotiate the adoption of a new code of conduct by key Irish theatre companies whereby they undertook to ensure gender equality and to protect employees from harassment and sexual exploitation. Similarly, the sidelining of poetry by women has given rise to measures that aim lastingly to change social values and practices. While Twitter streams such as #FiredIrishPoets and #WakeUpIrishPoetry channelled indignation at the neglect of women poets, the recognition of a deficit in our knowledge of this general field also prompted the publication of several key volumes, including *A History of Irish Women's Poetry*, edited by Ailbhe Darcy and David Wheatley, and *Irish Women Poets Rediscovered: Readings in poetry from the eighteenth to the twentieth century*, edited by Conor Linnie and Maria Johnston, which will, it is fervently hoped, materially advance investigation of this subject area into the future and, simultaneously, make wilful ignorance less feasible.[4]

Concurrently, many of the key precepts and adages of feminist thinking about the operations of patriarchy and deep-seated prejudices against women, formulated with especial plangency during second-wave feminism in the 1970s and 1980s, have been re-articulated for the contemporary era.[5] Indeed, Linda Connolly in her pivotal study of the Irish women's movement persuasively argues for the continuities between the discourse and activism of second-wave feminism and the women's rights sector in previous decades of the twentieth century.[6] Connolly thus pertinently queries the breakage model that conceives of feminism as proceeding in waves that are discrete and disconnected.

In this spirit, Ailbhe Smyth, who worked prominently in the Repeal campaign, reiterated the relevance of a well-established feminist precept for the present moment. Reflecting on why LGBT+ sexualities are demonised and ostracised and why female sexuality and all aspects of reproduction are so policed, she concluded that it is because, digging down through many layers of power, 'patriarchal society is founded on the control of women'.[7] In a similar vein, but concentrating on the literary public sphere, Anne Enright isolated troubling exclusionary practices: greater attention is accorded to works by men in regular reviewing outlets, such as the literary pages of *The Irish Times*, lower numbers of female authors are published by Irish presses, and men are rarely called on to review books by women, although women regularly evaluate male texts.[8] This non-reciprocity in reviewing culture and in general readership, which has been widely attested to, means that publications by women are ignored by men and dismissed as niche and having a less universal purchase. Enright, sizing up the damage caused by this imbalance, adduced that, while an automatic granting of esteem to male culture may sometimes seem merely heedless, it is vital to recognise that it amounts to a devaluation of works authored by women and often to their entire exclusion from the literary scene. She declared, moreover, that the further problem with such silence is that 'it is also a silencing'.[9] Obliteration rather than marginalisation is the upshot of a skewed and inequitable system.

The intertwined workings of power and space, whether conceived of as a dwelling, a habitat, a geographical zone, pastoral romance, a country, an ecosystem, the environment, the printed page, or a literary genre or mode, provide a focus for several essays in this collection. Henri Lefebvre has persuasively argued that space should be conceived of as dynamic and a product, not as something static or fixed.[10] In his eyes, societies are underwritten by spatial practices. In thus arguing, he refuted a dominant and seemingly immovable western view of space as abstract and an entity divorced from matter. Space in Lefebvre's re-conceptualisation is malleable and infiltrated by ideologies that fashion and determine it; in the modern era these encompass capitalism, neoliberalism, and essentialist and discriminatory understandings of race, ethnicity, sexuality, and gender. In step with Lefebvre's contentions, an interrogation of the spaces broached by the writers under investigation is carried out in these interventions. In particular, the manner in which ideological concepts of abstract space function to underpin gender, ethnic, and racist prejudices is drawn out. Also, the countering of seemingly fixed social and political presumptions by representations of more inclusive, relational worldviews is identified and examined. Above all, the authors examined, from Thomas Malory to Leeanne Quinn, are shown variously to uphold or quarrel with the bifurcation of space and nature and of self and Other, entrenched and invariably destructive principles in western culture, and often hardwired, as several contributors demonstrate, into the psychodynamics of the subjects and families depicted.

The fluidity and ambiguity of literary genres are central concerns of the essays in the first section of this collection. Taking her bearings from Latin American magical realism, Patricia Palmer sifts through the elusive and scattered traces left behind across a widespread archive of multilingual sources by Irish Jesuit missionary Thomas O'Fihily, and the adventurer Bernardo del Carpio, who journeyed to Brazil and Paraguay in the sixteenth century. The emphasis in letters and commentaries about travels in these two countries on the exotic, miraculous survival, heroic feats, and providential intervention, as she notes, uncannily prefigures aspects of later fiction writing from these regions and also gives their stories of conversion and privateering a novelistic allure. The multiculturalism and shape-shifting identity of the two figures that she documents, however, are at odds with more sinister aspects of their exploits. They are involved in colonial exploitation and enslavement and rarely exhibit any sympathy for the indigenous peoples with whom they come in contact. Above all, as Palmer persuasively argues, despite coming from a country that is a colony, they use the mantle of their whiteness to assume an automatic and unquestioned right to prey on and dispossess others.

Both Sarah McKibben and Nicholas Daly treat authors who deploy genres in unusual ways, subtly but purposefully reorienting them. Eochaidh Ó hEodhasa's poem marking the accession of James I in 1603, though partly constrained by the conventions of the panegyric in the Gaelic tradition, nonetheless repurposes the mode to endow his text with monitory aspects. Even as he praises James and pre-emptively celebrates his fairness and the transformative nature of his reign overall, he also implicitly advises the monarch on how to handle Irish affairs and to listen to his Irish subjects. As McKibben indicates, the poem demands to be read slowly as only an attuned dissection of its key tropes and rhetorical strategies can reveal their doubleness and persuasive intent. Ó hEodhasa writes a metamorphic poem that uses its Ovidian frame of reference to bring together jarring political objectives and to smuggle the subaltern viewpoint of the colonial Other into a display of royalist fealty. Nicholas Daly revisits Sheridan Le Fanu's permutations on the ghost story, which have frequently been assumed to be an offshoot of his antiquarianism and penchant for oddity. He makes the case that these Gothic stories are shot through with anxieties about the quotidian, not the past, and prompted by modern transport's unsettling invasion of people's privacy. Specifically, the jostling intimacy experienced on omnibuses sparked unease among passengers. Likewise, the remodelling of urban streetscapes for the construction of railway lines led not only to controversy but also prompted worries about the encroachment of this new transport mode on middle-class dwellings as people feared being subjected to the gazes of those on passing trains. Consequently, as Daly contends, public spaces are as haunted and perturbing in Le Fanu's tales as domestic interiors. In essence, the baleful spectres in his stories are distinctive in being urban emanations that breach personal and civic spaces and betoken the alienated and repressed affects of modernity.

Alex Davis argues in his examination of Yeats' *Poems, 1899–1905*, published in 1906, that a calculated moulding and finessing of pastoral symbolism drive Yeats' reworking of his earlier lyrics. In particular, his intertextual refashioning and interrogation of images gleaned from William Morris' fantasy fiction endow this volume with a new cast and political direction. Taking issue with views that dismiss the poet's middle period as flaccid and negligible, Davis shows that delving into the minutiae of Yeats' intense reading of Morris in this period enables us to discern how he revises his earlier work for the 1906 collected volume, adumbrating future political directions he will take. Contrary to Morris, he gives the symbolism of his love lyrics links with the workaday world as well as continuing to utilise the exotic charge of images derived from *fin-de-siècle* romance and esoteric teachings. Máirín Nic Eoin sets out similarly to circumscribe an aesthetic, that of the Irish-language poet Celia de Fréine, and also to consider how her outstanding work *Fiacha Fola / Blood Debts* fits in with her overall artistic trajectory. Reading across de Fréine's many collections, Nic Eoin notes her use of indirection, fragmentation, the serendipitous, the surreal, and the theatrical to structure individual poems. Although the unfinished, the unspoken, and the uncertain are hallmarks of de Fréine's verse, her epochal collection *Fiacha Fola*, published in Irish in 2004 and in translation as *Blood Debts* in 2014, differs from her other works because of its overt social concerns and its political engagement. These volumes are a series of meditations on and reckonings with a scandalous and prolonged case of medical malfeasance in which pregnant women and haemophiliacs in the late 1970s and early 1980s contracted Hepatitis C and HIV from contaminated blood products administered to them. The poems particularly arraign the failure of male doctors to grant credence to women's felt, bodily experience and their blanketing over as a result of the medical problems from which they were suffering. The prejudice of the medical system is, however, countered by the exactitude with which de Fréine captures the embodied reality of illness and of the subaltern position of the female patient. As Nic Eoin contends, she lends a startling and heart-rending immediacy to the poetic sequence as mode and augments its political and affective impact in deploying Gothic images of contamination and vampirism that underline the horror of the scandal. Yet, at the same time, the sequence through its interweaving of poetic and everyday language endows the woman speaker with a witty and incisive voice that permits her not only to take the system to task but also to re-establish agency.

Differing psychoanalytic perspectives are applied in the second section of this collection to dissect literary representations of siblings and the family. Although Arthurian knighthood is purportedly built on ideals of brotherhood and fealty, Catherine La Farge in her compendious analysis of siblinghood in Thomas Malory's *Le Morte Darthur* demonstrates that it is linked rather with violent conflict, misrecognition, and obsessive cathexes that remain stubbornly unresolved. Consonant with Juliet Mitchell's provocative theories, she notes how in Malory sibling relations are founded on deep-seated psychosocial traumas and primal fears of death. For Mitchell, the initial murderous responses to the sibling as a rival can be overcome through the recognition of Otherness, thus allowing the self to mature. Yet, as La Farge shows, dysfunction, violence, and failure are the invariable hallmarks of sibling strife in *Le Morte Darthur*. But, by the same token, repeated narratives of sibling discord are central to the narrative dynamics of this text and explain in part the power it wields over its readers.

Clíona Ó Gallchoir's investigation of Katherine Cecil Thurston's 1908 novel *The Fly on the Wheel* probes aspects of this New Woman fiction, particularly its subversion of realist conventions through its querying of aspects of the family romance. Bearing out the radicalism and multivalency identified as hallmarks of New Woman writing by Tina O'Toole, Ó Gallchoir considers how Thurston's scrutiny of the social undercurrents in middle-class Waterford goes beyond the remit of realism in laying bare the psychosexual formation of the two central subjects, Stephen Carey and Isabel Costello, who conduct a brief affair.[11] Thurston's testing of bourgeois values, Ó Gallchoir proposes, is arrived at through her depiction of the contradictory underpinnings of masculinity founded on identification with the father, and the authority he embodies, and on the policing of desire, fault-lines that are visible in the central male protagonist. Chiming with Marianne Hirsch's suggestive hypothesis that the banishment and the silencing of the mother are preconditions for the female narrative, Isabel

Costello, unlike Carey, identifies with her maternal origins and subversively pursues sexual freedom and self-expression. Yet, nonetheless, she is trapped within a phallic economy; her suicide at the close of the novel suggests that the patriarchal prerogatives constituting bourgeois normality can be challenged but not ousted.

Horizontal and vertical family relations are of moment in Moynagh Sullivan's essay. She contends that sibling relations in Leeanne Quinn's *Before You* are generative and have utopian dimensions because they are linked with sisterly connection, queer identity, and an apprehension of the fluid continuities between human embodiment and the material dimensions of the natural world. Quinn's volume of poems, which sets out to mourn the premature death of her sister Caroline, does not shirk the realities of sibling rivalry. But it renders them differently to Malory because of its recognition of the mother as a mediating and creative presence and its ability to oscillate between sameness and difference. The rifts between the two sisters hence result not in a reinforcement of originary trauma and a retreat to narcissistic selfhood as in *Le Morte Darthur*, but in the overturning of human and non-human dichotomies and the cross-relating of all life on a cellular level. *Before You*, Sullivan winningly advances, not only rethinks gendered and sexual identities, but also space. Instead of depicting the home as a place for female entrapment, it queers it and situates it as part of the dynamic of ecosystems to which it belongs. A preoccupation with the home, in her fictional re-workings of her family's house at 48 Cherryfield Avenue, Ranelagh, works to contrary ends in Maeve Brennan's Dublin stories, as Eamonn Hughes explains in his essay. Space in these narratives is implosive and claustrophobic. In following the fates of three different overlapping families who occupy this address in her tales, the Brennans, the Derdons, and the Bagots, she dissects the stifling effects of domestic space and a middle-class ideology of conformism for all family members, but especially women. In particular, the stories forensically examine the subjugation of women in their function as wives and housekeepers, their loss of agency, and their negated role in the public sphere. But, as Hughes establishes, Brennan's stories also variously calibrate different aspects of the married woman's fate; Delia Bagot, especially through her intimacy with the spectre of her dead mother and her projections of her children's futures, seems a more hopeful representation than Rose Derdon, who is cowed by her marriage. Nonetheless, home, even though represented as a place that triggers overwhelming affects, remains an ambiguous site in Brennan's work, linked primarily with psychic deadlock and emotional stultification.

The essays in the third section of this book approach the topics of gender and space from a wide number of angles. They all touch on issues of burning concern within feminism, including racism, misogyny, masculinity, the environment, and post-feminism. Elisabeth Okasha in her intervention contends that the axiom that grammatical and biological gender coincide in Anglo-Saxon names has been too readily applied and has led to data bias. In particular, the principle has been invoked to mask the presence of women, as in the instance of a ring found in Sussex which bears a male name but whose size points to a female owner, or name-stones from a monastic graveyard in Cross Close, Hartlepool, which, despite including male names, likely point to the burial of nuns in the same space. In sum, Okasha concludes that the time-honoured precept that the grammar of Anglo-Saxon names is a reliable indicator of gender is a modern convenience and needs now to be cast aside. Laura Izarra tackles gender imbalance in a different area, histories of the nineteenth-century diaspora in South America which invariably concentrate on men. Her examination focuses on memoirs, letters, and fiction written by Irish women who settled in Argentina. She contends that perusal of these works uncovers female desires and points of view while also revealing their imbrication in a white, racist stance on the indigenous peoples they encounter. Yet, she also recognises that much remains occluded, as they usually circumvent emotion. Because emigrant women tend to be involved in families whose members were scattered around the globe, ultimately their letters, as Izarra proposes, are translocational and conceive of home as a network of cross-connections between different places. Diasporic identity hence is hybrid and fluid in part, even if contradictorily caught up also in racist thinking about skin colour and ethnicity.

Seán Kennedy squares up to a discomfiting aspect of Beckett's writing: the overt misogyny of his early work. He adduces this to be a deep-seated philosophical as well as aesthetic problem, since the quest to achieve freedom from necessity and dependence is seen as crucial in the theories of art and reason proposed by Kant and Hegel. Even if Beckett dates a key epiphany that spurred him to rethink his art to a moment in his mother's room in Dublin in 1945, the maternal and the feminine represent counter-ideals for the male figures of his early work to be decried, feared, and evaded. Yet, as Kennedy argues, the vituperation of women and the maternal is so overdetermined and pronounced in his writing that it warrants further scrutiny. Women are denounced, he avers, because they reveal the chimerical nature of the male goal of self-sufficiency, while acting as an unwelcome reminder of men's dependency on the sensual, the material, and the affective, all of which are associated with the feminine. 'First Love', read in this light, can be deemed to problematise rather than simply uphold the male pursuit of rational detachment, disembodiment, and devotion to the father and to lay bare the protagonist's dependence on the prostitute, Lulu, sexually, economically, and psychically. His nonchalant final declaration, 'either you love or you don't', belies the impasse in which he finds himself, determined to be free of matter and the maternal but forever yearning for them and confounded and infantilised as a consequence by these repressed feelings.[12]

Different facets of misogyny and gender bias are unearthed in Anne Mulhall's analysis of the celebrated post-crash fiction by Donal Ryan, Colin Barrett, and Kevin Barry. She uncovers how unexamined hypotheses about the recession caused by the banking crisis conceived it to be a consequence of feminism and women's greater participation in the employment market. Concurrently, men were assumed to have borne the brunt of the economic downturn and to have suffered more calamitous psychic damage. The portrayal of masculinity in Barry's *The City of Bohane*, Ryan's *The Spinning Heart*, and Barrett's *Young Skins* is underpinned by these unexamined assumptions, as Mulhall's detailed examination demonstrates. Even if the dereliction of fathers is sometimes castigated, traditional masculinity is vaunted as a social balm in these texts while female independence and economic success are seen as emasculating. To boot, violent misogyny is problematically depicted as the outcome of male disempowerment and not the result of a pernicious patriarchy. These narratives that concentrate on masculinity in crisis while overtly attuned to the contemporary *Zeitgeist*, Mulhall claims, have many blindspots: they do not challenge the subordination of women, nor do they unpick the assumption that violence is either an innate tool for male expression or a legitimate outlet for male frustration.

If masculinity as a driver of genealogies of power is of moment for Anne Mulhall, Margaret Mills Harper is preoccupied by the differences between second- and third-wave feminisms and the way in which they implicitly shape the work of Irish women poets. To this end, she pits Vona Groarke and Sinéad Morrissey against Eiléan Ní Chuilleanáin and Medbh McGuckian. The latter writers push against the boundaries of the lyric poem and the forms of authority and gendered identity it usually enshrines. The persistent focus on the ligatures between built and human environments in the poetry of Groarke and Morrissey likewise evidences distinctive concerns not only with gendered inflections of the lyric 'I', but also with the nature of space, the contours of the human, and the subject's emplacement in the world. Hierarchies are broken down in their poetry, Harper asserts, and binary oppositions between self and Other, subject and world, are undone. Ultimately, their work evinces a self-conscious aesthetic which reaches beyond itself to articulate what cannot be expressed or articulated, thereby continuing but also pushing forward the writing of their immediate forebears. In a similar fashion, Claire Bracken inspects the dynamics of post-feminism and tests the ways in which it colours the subjects of Anne Enright's 'Natalie' and Leanne Sullivan's *Waiting for My Clothes*. The girls in these texts are portrayed as alienated, vulnerable, and fractured, hallmarks, as Bracken advances, of the splitting of the self and the severing of links between women promoted by neoliberalism and post-feminism. In particular, the equation of female liberation with empowered consumerism is shown to be debilitating for these subjects who anxiously police themselves and also cleave to images of physical perfectibility. Yet, countering the insidious hold of such ideologies of femininity hinging on the commodification and the surveillance of the self are images of female relationality and wayward desire. Thus, Bracken argues that the writing of Enright and Sullivan, while uncovering the negative effects of neo-liberalism on the subjects they represent, also point to the modes of resistance that are possible within post-feminism and the diverse forms of female identity that proliferate in the face of the conformism imposed by global capitalism.

In her recent study *Hooked*, Rita Felski has expanded on what she sees as a fresh groundswell in literary studies, variously titled the new formalism, the affective turn, the environmental humanities, and surface reading, that places a stress on attachment rather than disinterested investigation. This emphasis, as Felski explains, is about 'how people connect to art and how art connects them to other things'.[13] She further argues for the salience of first-person attachment and for a more enabling way of conceiving of relations 'as sustaining both aesthetic experiences and the work of criticism'.[14] In conversation with and taking inspiration from the critical writings of Patricia Coughlan, the diverse essays in this volume reflect variously on gender and space and in so doing put such a philosophy of reading into practice; they attest to the many ways in which literary texts can hook us and the differing means by which they in turn are sewn into the historical and political contexts which they mirror and with which they interact.

While Bleeding

DOIREANN NÍ GHRÍOFA

In a vintage boutique on Sullivan's Quay
I lift a winter coat
with narrow bodice, neat lapels,
tight waist, a fallen hem.

It's far too expensive for me,
but the handwritten label [1915]
brings it to my chest in armfuls of red.

In that year, someone drew a blade
through a bolt of fabric and stitched this coat
into being. I carry it

to the dressing room, slip
my arms in; silk lining spills
against my skin. To clasp
the belt is to draw a slow breath
as a cramp curls again
where blood stirs and melts.

In glass, I am wrapped in old red –
        red pinched into girl cheeks
        and smeared from torn knees,
        lipstick blotted in tissue, scarlet
        concealed in pale sheets, all the red
        that fell into pads and rags –
        the weight of red, the wait for red
        that we share.
In the mirror, the coat blushes.

This pocket may once have sheltered
something precious: a necklace, a love letter,
or a fresh egg, feather-warm, held gently
so it couldn't crack, couldn't leak through seams,
so it couldn't stain the dress within.

Cuimhne an Uisce

NUALA NÍ DHOMHNAILL

Uaireanta nuair a bhíonn a hiníon
sa seomra folctha
ag glanadh a fiacla le slaod tiubh
is le sód bácála,
tuigtear di go líonann an seomra suas
le huisce.

Tosnaíonn sé ag a cosa is a rúitíní
is bíonn sé ag slibeáráil suas is suas arís
thar a másaí is a cromáin is a básta.
Ní fada
go mbíonn sé suas go dtí na hioscaidí uirthi.
Cromann sí síos ann go minic ag piocadh suas
rudaí mar thuáillí láimhe nó ceirteacha
atá ar maos ann.
Tá cuma na feamnaí orthu –
na scothóga fada ceilpe úd a dtugaidís
'gruaig mhaighdean mhara' nó 'eireabaill mhadraí rua' orthu.
Ansan go hobann téann an t-uisce i ndísc
is ní fada
go mbíonn an seomra iomlán tirim arís.

Tá strus uafásach
ag roinnt leis na mothúcháin seo go léir.
Tar éis an tsaoil, níl rud ar bith aici
chun comparáid a dhéanamh leis.
Is níl na focail chearta ar eolas aici ar chor ar bith.
Ag a seisiún síciteiripeach seachtainiúil
bíonn a dótháin dua aici
ag iarriadh an scéal aisteach seo a mhíniú

is é a chur in iúl i gceart
don mheabhairdochtúir.

Níl aon téarmaíocht aici,
ná téarmaí tagartha
ná focal ar bith a thabharfadh an tuairim is lú
do cad é 'uisce'.
'Lacht trédhearcach,' a deir sí, ag déanamh a cruinndíchill.
'Sea,' a deireann an teiripí, 'coinnibh ort!'
Bíonn sé á moladh is á gríosadh chun gnímh teangan.
Deineann sí iarracht eile.
'Slaod tanaí,' a thugann sí air,
í ag tóraíocht go cúramach i measc na bhfocal.
'Brat gléineach, ábhar silteach, rud fliuch.'

PART I

The Politics of Genre

Stabat Mater

EILÉAN NÍ CHUILLEANÁIN

At last the page is peeled away,
the last page, like a covering from a wound,
and the transparent sheet beneath is another page
on which is written, '*You have no enemy*'.
– Just look. It is damage itself, and what lights up
the scarred flesh to the view
of the flinching eye, of the one
who saw it all and let us know, in words
we can't read rightly, until touch teaches –

as you can only find out by pushing
forward in the crowd
until your body is pressed
flat against the glass.
Behind the glass is the shadow of suffering,
and it shivers because it feels your touch,
it's alive. But others are pressing
behind, and you must move along,
and when you look back
to the house of mourning
the shutters inside shutters have closed
down, folded, each one with a day's date.

When the calendar was in its force
they all fitted together
as the leaves fit the tree
of atrocities, and even now
you can still hear the elation
of the strings, their long hopping
as the alto fills her lungs
to lead off *Stabat Mater*.

CHAPTER 1

'*Gente Blanca*' in the Green Atlantic: Selfhood, victimhood, whiteness, and early modern Ireland

PATRICIA PALMER

In 748, Pope Zachary wrote to Boniface accusing the Irish cleric of 'perverse and abominable teaching ... that there [is] another world and other men beneath the earth'. To believe that the Antipodes existed defied Catholic orthodoxy. Early Irish literature, however, imagined worlds beneath the sea. *Saltair na Rann* dared to wonder in the late tenth century:

> Cialín nasluag, srethaib drong,
> dosceil tonn muad mara mind,
> ceti arbair trebait ann
> dondleith tall dontalmain tinn?
>
> What is the number of the hosts, with ranks of companies,
> which the noble wave of the clear sea conceals?
> What are the multitudes which dwell there,
> on the other side of the solid earth?[1]

By the sixteenth century, of course, voyages to 'the other side of the solid earth' had passed from the realm of fiction into fact. (Three Galway cabin-boys rounded the Horn with Magellan aboard the *Trinidad* and *Conceptión.*)[2] This essay follows two other voyagers to South America, to a place where, narratively, fact shears off towards the fictional and events become unsteadied in the telling. But it brings us, also, to lives ignored by our texts but whose presence at their margins disturbs everything. Narratives framed as *rites* of passage have as their undersong a presumption that only certain groups of migrants enjoy the *right* to pass from abjection to mastery, from being colonised to colonising others.

In an important essay on *The Pleasure of Eliza Lynch*, Pat Coughlan shows how the book's Paraguayan setting is central to Anne Enright's success in inserting a feminist postmodernism into the canon of contemporary Irish fiction. Paraguay provides the imaginative space for Enright 'to show the melting away of apparently solid European systems of order and belief in the utter difference of South America'; it provides, Coughlan argues, an analogue for 'a world in disintegration, of European values, knowledge, and order being tested to destruction'.[3] By way of a prequel to Coughlan's essayist excursion to Paraguay, '*Gente Blanca*' tells the story of two earlier Irish migrants to South America.[4] It suggests that while their identities were being 'tested' and rewritten in the contact zone, 'destruction' was reserved for those at the sharp end of the system of 'values, knowledge, and order' in which our two travellers found a berth. That unequal encounter forces us to rethink R.F. Foster's jibe that 'the old victim-culture ... was also, in its way, a culture of superiority', by setting it alongside Sara Ahmed's assertion that whiteness is 'a category of experience that disappears as a category through experience'. We need to keep Ahmed's suggestion that 'this disappearance makes whiteness "worldly"' in mind as we follow our two victims of colonisation in Ireland to the other side of the world.[5]

Undertaking to write a biography of Richard Creagh, archbishop of Armagh, the historian Colm Lennon remarks, 'Biographies of sixteenth-century Irish figures, lay or ecclesiastical, are rare.'[6] Autobiographies are even rarer. Neither of the Irish exiles on whom this essay focuses – one rendered spectral by hagiography, the other made fantastical by his own picaresque travelogue – participates in the discourses of interiority which writers like Montaigne were contemporaneously making available.[7] Tracing the emergence of a recognisably modern, Cartesian subjectivity in *The Tremulous Private Body*, Francis Baker distinguishes between the narrated self of *Le Discours de la Méthode* and earlier biographical and autobiographical writings. Whereas for Descartes, 'the narrated self becomes for the first time not only the exemplum but the ground of truth', earlier kinds of life-writing were mainly hagiographical. In hagiography, the self is not individual but exemplary, pointing to a truth beyond itself.[8] This is certainly the case with Thomas O'Fihily, a Limerickman and a pioneer of the Jesuit mission to Paraguay. The difficulty with sketching even a brief life for him starts with naming. In his only autograph letter, he signs himself Thomás Philidius. Ruiz de Montoya SJ, whose labours in the Paraguayan *misiones* overlapped with those of O'Fihily, speaks of him, in a work written fourteen years after his death, as 'Father Toma Pildi, an Irishman by birth, a man of great age and rare virtue'.[9] His father, William Fihily, a doctor, was admitted to the 'English Liberty' of Limerick in 1555, in exchange for anglicising his surname to Field.[10] His mother was Janet Creagh, possibly a sister of Archbishop Creagh.[11] He was educated in David Woulfe SJ's grammar school in Limerick and went to the continent in 1568, 'to avoid', as one Jesuit historian put it, 'the dangers of heresy'.[12] He studied in Paris and Douai, and took his master's in Louvain before entering the Jesuit novitiate in Rome in 1585.[13] Shortly afterwards, he and the English Jesuit John Yates were selected for the Brazilian missions. Funding his journey with alms begged along the way, O'Fihily walked from Rome to Lisbon, detouring to Santiago de Compostela to kiss the relics of the apostle.[14] After a year's study in Coimbra, he sailed for São Salvador de Bahia and served for eight years in Jose de Anchieta's Misión San Vincente.[15] He is sighted only once in those years. John Yates reported condescendingly to Fr Good, one of O'Fihily's grammar-school masters, 'News of Father Thomas Felie … he was very unapt to learn this Brazil speech, but he did always edify us with his virtuous life.' He assures his correspondent that he has sent 'Felie' 'his portion of the blessed grains and images that came unto my hands'.[16] Then, in 1587, the Jesuits received an invitation from the province of Tucumán, in northern Argentina, to found a mission there. O'Fihily, along with four other Jesuits, sailed from Bahia for Buenos Aires.

We have four primary accounts of the voyage: Nicolás del Techo's *Historia de la Provincia del Paraguay de la Compañía de Jesús* (1673), condemned by its nineteenth-century editor for its 'inverosímiles y absurdas narraciones'; Pedro Lozano's *Historia de la Compañía de Jesús en la Provincia del Paraguay* (1754) which filters the Jesuit 'Cartas Anuas' through a haze of awe and adulation; an anonymous Jesuit chronicle of 1600 which alludes to the episode; and a first-hand account by the bishop of Tucumán's agent.[17] Lives get blurred in these tellings; in del Techo and Lozano, *historia* shades into fable. For both, the story comes alive as the ship transporting the Jesuits to Buenos Aires enters Rio de la Plata. Suddenly, English 'pirates' attack. Lozano introduces them as Queen Elizabeth's 'thieving vassals', robbing their way around the globe:

> mientras su infame Reyna Isabela divertia en amores, y en derramar, qual Harpya cruelissima, sangre de Catholicos en su Reyno, theatro abominable de la Heregìa.

> while their infamous queen … amused herself in amours and, cruel Harpy that she was, in spilling the blood of Catholics in the abominable theatre of heresy that was her realm.[18]

Once aboard the Jesuits' boat, the pirates pillage a cache of communion hosts blessed by the pope; one stomps on the *agnus dei*. Fr Ortega grabs the blasphemer by the leg who, unsteady with drink, slips and bangs his foot. His shipmates throw Ortega overboard and, outraged to find one of the queen's 'subjects' in the vestments of her *capitales enemigos*, they threaten to do the same with O'Fihily. But just then the 'malignant postule' that had formed on the drunken blasphemer's foot starts to spread through his entire body. In panic, his shipmates amputate the foot. But within twenty-four hours he is dead. This self-evidently miraculous intervention chastens the heretics and they tow the Jesuits south towards the Straits of Magellan. In those icy latitudes, they strip the evangelists' boat of tiller, riggings and sails and, in what could be a topos from an early Irish voyage tale, they set it adrift. In the manner of an *immram*, too, fate takes command and the little boat sails serenely into the harbour of Buenos Aires.[19] In all this time we hear only one word from O'Fihily. The anonymous chronicler recounts that the pirates nearly hanged him from a yard-arm when they heard him speaking a word of English, *como el Padre era de Escosia* [since the priest was Scottish].[20] The bishop of Tucumán's agent never mentions him. He flickers into existence only as an essentially anonymous *exemplum* of Jesuit heroism.

After a crossing so saturated with the marvellous, re-entering the ordinary was never assured and accounts of the Jesuits' progress overland continued to participate in a discourse of wonder. Having arrived 'almost naked' in Buenos Aires, they walk 120 leagues to Córdoba, seat of the bishop of Tucumán. They traverse not so much a physical landscape as a world poised on the edges of extinction. They are given an escort because

> à la sazon todo estaba poblado de Infieles, que consumieron despues la codicia, y malos tratamientos de los Españoles, y no han quedado de aquellas poblaciones, ni vestigios, ni aun los nombres.[21]
>
> in that time, the whole place was occupied by the Infidels, whom greed and the ill-treatment of the Spanish would afterwards consume [lit. the Infidels who consumed afterwards greed ...], so that nothing has survived of those people, no trace, not even their names.

This is a world not just at the boundaries of the known but at one of its vanishing points. Lozano's syntactical sleight-of-hand sets the reader's coordinates spinning. The original Spanish, reversing the conventional subject-verb-object word order, trips us into assuming that the *Infieles* will do the eating – that cannibals ply the road to Córdoba – only to up-end such expectations: here, it is Europeans who eat Indians. This is a world upside-down, where '*Antipodes* in Shoes, / Have shod their *Heads* in their *Canoos*'.[22]

The onward peregrinations of the Jesuits continued to press against the boundaries of the known. From Córdoba they walked to Santiago del Estero, to study the language of their new mission, Tonacote. But their instructor fell ill and O'Fihily and his companions sought permission to travel to Paraguay because the indigenous language, Guarani, was cognate with Tupi which they already knew *muito bem* from Brazil where they previously evangelised.[23] As O'Fihily and Ortega struck out north-east from Asunción, becoming the first Jesuits to enter the province of Paraguay, the sense of going beyond the known world intensified. They traversed the jungle on foot and paddled upstream in canoes; they went from village to Indian village, 'to the ultimate bounds of the Crown of Castile's dominions'.[24] After seven years on their own, O'Fihily and Ortega received a visitation from the mother-house in Peru: it took the visitants two months to travel the 200 leagues from Asunción to the two Jesuits' *misión*, crossing swollen rivers, 'an interminable lake, or an immense sea, from which nothing could be seen but water and sky ... marshes ... swamps in which the mules sank up to their ears'; they arrived on the feast of the Epiphany, to witness O'Fihily and Ortega's *obras maravillosas*.[25]

What the Jesuit accounts present – and from Córdoba on, we rely exclusively on them – is not just a geography of extremity but the performance of marvels commensurate with such physical exorbitance. O'Fihily and Ortega are merely ciphers in an eye-watering arithmetic of conversion: in forty days (Christological echoes abound) in 1590 alone, they perform 1,000 baptisms, hear 1,500 confessions, and celebrate 140 marriages.[26] The adulatory imprecision of hagiography privileges the after-sheen of achievement over the actual texture of what must have been profoundly complex processes; its recourse to metaphor abstracts not only the mechanics of catechesis but also the humanity and agency of all the actors. The two missionaries, Lozano tells us, converted 'innumerable Infidels, polishing minds that hadn't been broken in, and domesticating the untamed natives'.[27] Apart from one cacique's daughter rich enough to earn a fleeting mention for endowing the Jesuits' first church, the Guarani are utterly undifferentiated. Only rarely do they achieve even the visibility of the exotic, as when the two Jesuits encounter a 'barbarous' tribe who 'sing to the sound of instruments little pleasing to the ear'. They are 'demented by the Devil with mad persuasion'; their cacique is 'naked, made grotesque by the various dyes and colours with which he painted his body and face'; his hair grows down to his knees and he wears a head-dress of feathers. But O'Fihily and Ortega

> dieron à enterder la astucia, con que Satanàs los tenia reducidos à aquella vida de brutos, para tenerlos mas lexos de su mayor bien, y arrastrarlos al abysmo de penas sempiternas.
>
> gave him to understand the trickery with which Satan had reduced them to that brutish life, to keep them away from their best interests and to drag them into an abyss of sempiternal pain.[28]

This encounter, between Counter-Reformation militants and Guarani hunter-gatherers, brings us to a limit-point between two irreconcilable understandings of the world. In keeping with the adulatory narrative of inexorable conversion, Lozano says nothing about how, precisely, the cacophonous tribesmen were 'given to understand' the tenets of Tridentine Catholicism. All we know is that 350 Guarani shuffled off to take their place in a new *reducción* and the two priests 'made a short catechism which contained only what was strictly necessary for saving one's soul'.[29] The bare-bones instrumentality of the catechism is telling. Melià and Nagel show how the '*Reducción*' of the Guaranis was, above all, a huge linguistic enterprise which entailed the profound 'reduction' of the Guarani language itself, shrinking it down grammatically, syntactically, discursively and culturally to the evangelising needs of the missionaries.[30] The new converts appear, in their reduced state, like 'living portraits of death, or lively skeletons'.[31] In her analysis of *Eliza Lynch*, Pat Coughlan shows how the novel's emphasis on food, eating and 'the irreducibility of the body', on moments of 'dissociated and discrete' sensation, power Enright's construction of a fractured, postmodern subjectivity.[32] The construction of premodern, hagiographical subject-hood works in precisely the opposite direction. The wonder-tale quality of the Jesuit accounts means that there are no 'living portraits' of O'Fihily, no flesh-and-blood counterpoint behind the performance of the miraculous feat. He functions in these 'Historias de la Compañía' like one of the emblematic characters in the didactic pageants which he himself used as a tool of evangelisation.[33] If, in the postmodern construction of identity, 'metonymy is always poised to become metaphor', in hagiography the subject is always already metaphorised.[34] O'Fihily's identity migrates onto a pasteboard stereotype of Ignacian Christian militancy. He and Ortega are '*Soldados de Christo*', two 'unbeaten champions to fight the battles of the Lord'; 'like valiant soldiers, they return triumphant, rich in the spoils of so many heathens captured for the Gospel'.[35] Interchangeable ciphers in a godly conquest, they exist only by analogy: they are 'like two drops of water in dry land' or 'two Angels come from the sky ... flying from place to place like speedy seraphim'.[36]

The O'Fihily who left Limerick in 1568 passed through successive *liminae*: through the Pórtico da Gloria of the great cathedral of Santiago de Compostela, through rites of spiritual passage in the South Atlantic, across the linguistic boundaries of Irish, English, Latin, Spanish, Tonocote and Tupi-Guarani, before being finally apotheosised through hagiography. He is like a figure deliquescing in the shimmers of a heat-haze. But just once, in 1601, in his fifty-second year, we hear from him directly. The occasion is a long, impassioned letter which he wrote to the superior general asking that the Brazilian province take over the Paraguayan mission from the Peruvian authorities who no longer have the manpower to administer it. O'Fihily writes from Asunción, in a time of dissolution and disillusionment. All the other Jesuits have been recalled from Paraguay. Only he, 'suffering from a painful illness', has been left behind by Divine Providence – left, Lozano complacently intones, to 'minister to innumerable souls and numerous tribes'.[37] But O'Fihily's voice, when it comes, is neither the voice of an angel nor of a champion in the lists. It is a voice of despair:

> Así quedamos sin favor, remedio, sin ayuda, sin compañeros, desconsolados, tristes, que Dios sabe qué será de nos.[38]
>
> Here we are without favour or remedy, without help, without comrades, sad and disconsolate, so that God alone knows what will become of us.

His text continues to screen off the Guarani behind metaphors: they are 'ripe corn' ('*mies*') or 'fruit' harvested by priestly labourers (p. 72). But in petitioning on their behalf, O'Fihily gives us the different perspective of one well advanced on what he calls 'this pilgrimage' ('*esta peregrinación*'). Left 'stripped of all human solace in this land' ('*desamparados de todo consuelo humano en esta tierra*'), he has come up against the limits of language. What he has to say cannot be conveyed:

> hay tanto que escribir a V.P. de estas cosas, que había menester mucho papel y un buen escribano, y no se puede escribir todo: "quoniam dies mali sunt" y suceden naufragios a las veces, a las cartas. Y escribimos

> unos y otros a los provincials de Perú y no hay remedio, más que consolarnos con palabras.
>
> there is so much to write about these things ... that it would need much paper and a good scrivener, and one cannot write everything: *quoniam dies mali sunt* and sometimes letters are shipwrecked. And we write to the provincials in Peru and [they offer] no solution, except to console us with words. (p. 71)

He is so far away, unable to say 'face to face' ('*cara a cara*') what needs to be said. He has written often, never knowing whether his letters arrive. A sense of failure stalks his words: the enterprise to which he has given so many years 'is being lost' ('*se va perdiendo*', p. 71). His plea is bounded by an awareness of death: '*morir*' and '*muertos*' echo through his text. Even if reinforcements were to come from Peru, a five-month walk away, they would arrive 'already half-dead' ('*ya medio muertos*', p. 70); he himself may die ('*yo muriera*') before the hoped-for answer comes (p. 72).

In 1620, Thomas Shelton, a Dublin recusant who had fled, first, to Hugh O'Neill's protection in Ulster and thence into exile in Antwerp, published *The History of the Valorous & Witty Knight-Errant Don Quixote of the Mancha*, the first English translation of *Don Quixote* (Part 1). Shelton's translation is wry, lively, and fast-paced, as we see from his telling of the deleterious consequences of Señor Quijada's addiction to chivalric romances:

> In resolution, he plunged himselfe so deepely in his reading of these bookes, as he spent many times in the Lecture of them whole dayes and nights; and in the end, through his little sleepe and much reading, he dryed vp his braines in such sort as he lost wholly his iudgment. His fantasie was filled with those things that he read, of enchantments, quarrels, battels, challenges, wounds, woings, loues, tempests, and other impossible follies. And these toyes did so firmly possesse his imagination with an infallible opinion, that all that Machina of dreamed inuentions which he read was true, as he accounted no History in the world to be so certaine and sincere as they were.[39]

One of the Don's favourites – and, therefore, one of the principal villains of the piece – was Bernardo del Carpio who 'slew the enchanted Roland in Roncesvalles'. By a curious coincidence, one of Shelton's fellow exiles came to be known as 'Bernardo del Carpio' by the Portuguese whom he met on the Amazon: this Bernardo del Carpio from County Clare returns us to South America as the site where 'apparently solid European systems of order' melt away; but, this time, it produces not a dissolution of the self but its reinvention. In the mid-1630s, one 'Don Bernardo Obrien del Carpio of the noble house of Thomond' petitioned the king of Spain.[40] O'Brien was a fabulist of the contact zone, a self-penned *picaro* who invented an identity for himself much more robust than the hagiographical commonplaces foisted on O'Fihily. In his *petición*, O'Brien recalls finding himself, aged seventeen, in London when he received news that his father's three castles had been attainted and granted to English settlers. Reminding us that the push of exile and the pull of wanderlust can be hard to disentangle, O'Brien jumped at the chance which dispossession offered to travel and see 'new things' ('*novedades*'), sailing to the Amazon with Sir Henry Roe.[41] O'Brien, eleven other Irishmen, and four English-Catholic servants disembarked 60 leagues up the Amazon to establish a trading post. Joyce Lorimer, in *English and Irish Settlement on the River Amazon*, argues that 'it is hard to escape the conclusion that the Irish were, on the whole, more efficient in their approach to exploiting Amazonia than the English': whereas the English were intent on creating a monopoly, the Irish wove in and out between the many communities jockeying for position on its shifting frontier. They gained that mobility, she argues, by knowing the local languages and by being better attuned to the changing political realities of the region.[42]

Pat Coughlan argues that Eliza Lynch's experimental performances of identity are possible precisely because she is linguistically 'unfixed [and] floating':

> She knows several languages, which gives her potential leverage in terms of her own identity and perceptions, making her an interpreter between forms of difference themselves irreconcilable and an expert at passing between systems.[43]

O'Brien is a kindred linguistic chameleon. His *petición*, written in Castilian, testifies to the plasticity of reality for one inhabiting the borderland where fact met fantasy; as he crossed the borders between languages, solidities dissolved. Though he sailed to the Americas under an English flag, he returned, three years later, with 16,000-escudos worth of cotton and tobacco, on the Dutch fleet; he went back to the Amazon in 1629 as captain general, pilot, and interpreter of a Dutch expedition. He then switched sides again, by signing over the fort and followers which he held for the Dutch and English 'heretics' to the Spanish, drawing up the documents conveying ownership in Portuguese and Irish (p. 96). He hoodwinked the English by communicating in Irish with a compatriot in their ranks; and he acted as '*intérprete*' between the Spanish and Portuguese (p. 99). But it was O'Brien's command of Amazonian languages that secured his passage to a world stranger still. Sir Henry Roe's ship had first made landfall at Sipinipoca on the mouth of the Amazon and O'Brien and his companions made friends ('*amistad*') with the villagers, using sign language until they mastered Arrua, and, subsequently, Arawak (p. 98). Encountering a canoe-load of fishermen off Surinam, he greeted them in '*differentes lenguas de Indios*' before conversing with them in Arawak (p. 98). Later, when an alliance of convenience with the Portuguese broke down, they sent him into exile ('*destierro*') among the Cururi cannibals (p. 97). He does no more than mention that they eat human flesh ('*comen carne humana*') and quickly settles in to learning their language and finding out all he can of their '*medicinas y secretos*' (p. 97). (When, subsequently, he found himself in Caracas during an outbreak of the plague, he cured more than forty people with native herbs and drugs.)

After his first year in the Amazon, he and 'four Irish scholars and Latinists' and fifty Indian guides, helpers, and interpreters ('*lenguas*') paddled 700 leagues up-river. They came to a region inhabited only by women. These were the *Cuña Atenare*, he told the king, the 'manly women' ('*mugeres varoniles*') whom the Christians called 'Amazons' (p. 92). A magic realist *avant la lettre*, O'Brien crosses between myth and truth-claims. The *Cuña Atenare* may be characters out of romance – they have very small white breasts like men, treated '*con artificios*' so as not to grow – but they are real in his narrative. More importantly, these are not the Amazons of misogynistic European tradition.[44] South America, Coughlan argues, provided Enright with a perspective from which she can mount a 'powerful interrogation ... of the gender-system of the West'. In one way, the 'counterweighting' of colonially inflected prejudice provided by Eliza Lynch's 'quickness of feeling' is interestingly anticipated in O'Brien's encounter with the Amazons.[45] Their right breasts may be doctored 'in order to shoot arrows' – he can confirm that 'the left breasts are as large as other women's' – but these are not the belligerent harridans of legend. Instead, O'Brien recounts an irenic exchange marked by reciprocal courtesy and mutual self-interest. Hearing that their queen, Cuña Muchu, is 'at that time on an island in the river', he sends

> in his canoe an Indian woman as an ambassadress (*embaxadora*), and she carried with her a mirror and a Dutch linen shirt as a gift and a sample of the merchandise he was carrying, and orders that she should say that he had not gone to harm her; rather if it would please her that she should look at what he was sending to her, and if she was pleased, that he might go and speak with her; and that she should send him hostages.

With the courteous circumlocution of O'Brien's diplomatic language out of the way, they can get down to brass tacks. Cuña Muchu

> sent him three of the most distinguished of her women and asked him to go and speak with her. He did so. She asked him if it was he who had sent a gift. He said yes. She asked him what he wanted. He replied peace and permission to pass through her kingdom and to trade in it. She replied that it was granted to him and gave three of her slaves in exchange for trade goods (*mercaderías*, p. 92).[46] He had her dressed in the Dutch linen shirt, of which she was very proud, and at the end of the week, when he took his leave promising to return, she and her subjects signified that they were grieved by his departure. (p. 266)

While O'Brien gives us no sense that the 'grief' was reciprocal, there is a striking mutuality about their self-interest. Three slaves the richer, he moves on to spend a further three years exploring the Amazon and attracting 4,000 Indian warriors '*a su devoción*' ('under his control') (p. 93). When he sailed back to Europe with the Dutch flotilla, he used some of the profit from selling his cotton and tobacco to secure his father's release from prison and to buy back a sixth of his land.

In the end, the identity of the chameleon-exile, dispersed through so much role-playing, so many tall tales, hangs in doubt. His genius at navigating shifting alliances in the contact zone becomes a liability when petitioning Philip IV: a life of trimming had to be reinvented as a story of unwavering loyalty to Spain and the Catholic Church; his *petición* recasts his recent negotiations with the Amsterdam Company and, subsequently, the London Guiana Company as, in fact, manoeuvres designed to wriggle *out* of acting for heretics. So, he tells the king, he had been on the Spanish *flota* bound for Seville when he was captured by the Dutch. Examined by the authorities back in Holland, he escapes their further attention by pretending to be a Londoner. He walks around the streets of Amsterdam, conversing '*en Indio*' with, variously, a '*renegado*' and the Indian '*muchacho*' ('boy') – the son of an Amazonian chief – who is his constant companion (p. 101).[47] He makes his way to London and is poised to lead another expedition to Guiana – until the English require him to swear allegiance to the crown. Unwilling to make a 'conquest for heretics', he is kitted out in the habit of Santiago by the Spanish ambassador and prepares to sail for Spain. He sends a Basque boy ahead with books and papers which include his '*descripción y cosmographía*' of the Amazon, written in Irish (p. 105). But the boy evanesces and, with him, the cosmography of a realm situated half-way between exploitation and the imagination. If O'Fihily's letter uncovers a redoubt of selfhood that resists inscription, hagiographic or otherwise, O'Brien's lost '*cosmographía*' perfectly emblematises the space that its writer himself occupied: a space of self-invention where identity is suspended between the colonial victimhood of a dispossessed Clareman and the voracious imaginings of a journeyman colonist on the make. Ultimately, the liminality that attaches to both O'Fihily and O'Brien is narratival as much as geographical: the spaces of expression available to – or about – both, whether hagiographic or picaresque, rendered the truth of their peregrinations inaccessible and accounts of two very real lives strangely fictional. But behind form lies politics and, so far, this essay has taken the form of a biographical quest. But, as we will shortly see, the biographical impulse – *Finding Fr Field*; the picaresque adventures of a mercantile freebooter with a *chanson-de-geste* name – privileges the life of the one over the lives of the many.

In the words of Fr Lozano, O'Fihily and his two companions struck out for the Paraguayan mission 'like the greedy merchant who, weighing up the profit by sight, put more back into the business' ('*como el Mercader codicioso, que al ver al ojo la ganancia, se empeña mas en el negocio*').[48] To think about the Jesuits, in line with their own metaphor, as covetous merchants investing in '*el negocio de … conversion*', 'the business of conversion', allows us to move away from thinking, biographically, about the good – or bad – that they did and to consider instead the *goods* that they carried with them.[49] One of the things they carried was the miraculous severed head of one of St Ursula's martyred virgins. Fr Lozano takes up the story in his account of the pirates' attack:

> Fue el caso, que entre las demàs cosas dignas de veneràcion, conducian estos Missioneros una Cabeza de las once mil Virgines, para colocarla con la mayor decencia en el primer Templo, que erigiessen en el Tucumàn. Al reconocer, que las Naves de los Pyratas apressarian la

> Nao Portuguesa, escondieron tan preciosa Joya en parte donde no la pudiessen encontrar los pèrfidos Hereges, y no quedasse expuesta à álgun desacato, si cayesse en sus manos, ò la lanzassen al Mar, donde fuesse pasto de sus monstrous, tan estimable tesoro. No diò con el la diligencia codiciosa de los Pyratas: ya à la verdad ni podia dàr, porque invisiblemente se desapareciò la Reliquia ... sin duda no quiso el Cielo fuesse el despojo Sagrado de aquella Virgin testigo de los horrorosos sacrilegious, que cometieron sus Compatriotas: con que al passo que les llegò al alma à los Missioneros pèrdida tan considerable, tuvieron materia de consuelo, venerando los profundos Jucios del Altissimo, que obrò tal maravilla.[50]
>
> It so happened that, among other venerable objects, the Missionaries carried the Head of one of the 11,000 virgins, planning to place it, with all due solemnity, in the first church which they would erect in Tucumán. When they saw the Pirates' carrack bearing down on their Portuguese *Nao*, they hid the precious Jewel where the perfidious Heretics couldn't find it and where it wouldn't be exposed to contumely of the kind that would happen if that inestimable treasure were to fall into their hands, or be thrown into the Sea as grist to their monstrous mill. For all their greedy diligence, the Pirates couldn't find it: nor, to tell the truth, had they any hope of doing so because, invisibly, the Relic had disappeared ... No doubt, Heaven didn't want the Sacred booty of that Virgin to witness whatever horrific sacrilege her Compatriots might commit: so that, despite the soul-destroying blow which such a loss entailed for the Missionaries, they had cause for consolation, seeing the deep judgement of the Most High who worked such a miracle.

With Lozano fixated on the miraculous, we have to go to the bishop of Tucumán's agent, our one contemporary source for the voyage, for a more materialist telling. He had sailed north from Buenos Aires to São Salvador de Bahia to collect the Jesuits. But he had other passengers and a substantial cargo to load onto the *San Antonio* and the smaller, thirty-five-ton *nao* which had been built to the bishop's specifications in Bahia. His inventory of the lading makes no mention of a virgin martyr's miracle-working death's-head; instead, he records only 'saints' relics, among them 'big bones'.[51] Nor is that all he sees. Del Techo and Lozano focused exclusively on the Jesuits and their holy goods; the anonymous Jesuit chronicler mentions that, eventually, the pirates cut the five Jesuits adrift 'with the rest', '*con los demás*', but gives no hint as to the identity of those others.[52] The bishop's agent, however, keeps his eye firmly on the lading:

> el padre armiñio ... diose á cada uno de los padres á costa del Reverendisimo de Tucuman, trenta mill maravediz para el vestuario y caliz, y trayan muchos libros y muchos rreliquias de santos, entrellos huesos y muchos anusdeies, muchos ymagenes, y diego de palma carillo y el padre francisco salzedo trayan de las cosas de la tierra, las que heran menester para esta, como son campanas, yerro, acero, calderas de cobre vaçias, peroles para hazer azucar, y negros para el servicio del Reverendisimo Obispo; y finalmente venian en los navios cantidad de Hacienda, de mas de cinquenta mill pesos, asi de su Señoria, como de particulares, y de diego de palma como muy solene presente de esclavos y otras cosas que el governador general [Manuel Telles Barreto] enviaba al Reverendisimo de Tucumán.
>
> Father Armiñio ... gave 30,000 maravedis from His Reverence the Bishop of Tucumán's account to each of the priests, for clothing and chalices, and they brought on lots of books and lots of saints' relics, bones among them, and lots of rosary beads, lots of holy images, and Diego de Palma Carillo and Father Francisco Salzedo brought on farm produce which is necessary for where they're going, as are bells, iron, steel, empty copper cauldrons, pots for making sugar, and blacks for the service of the Reverend Bishop. And finally, a quantity of revenue was brought on board, more than 50,000 pesos, both from His Lordship and other individuals and from Diego de Palma, as well as a very formal gift of slaves and other things which the governor general was sending to the very Reverend Bishop of Tucumán.

In this very different economy where miraculous relics become merely 'bones', a whole other '*negocio*' takes shape in the hold – the terrible '*ganancia*' of slavery. Bahia was not just a quayside where six expectant Jesuits waited for passage to their new mission; it was, along with Pernambuco and Rio de Janeiro, the centre of the Brazilian–Angolan slave trade.[53] In the hull of the *San Antonio*, the Green Atlantic suddenly comes face-to-face with the Black Atlantic; saving souls and enslaving bodies set sail in the same boat.[54] For Paul Gilroy, the ship is the 'first of the novel chronotopes' which enables us to 'rethink modernity via the history of the Black Atlantic'; 'concentrated within [the] timbers' of the *San Antonio*, we find, to paraphrase Peter Linebaugh, 'all the contradictions' of the intersecting *negocios* of mercantile capitalism and colonial conversion.[55] They are concentrated, too, in the person of the first bishop of Tucumán (from 1582–90), Francisco de Victoria, who, having failed as a silver merchant in Potosí, became a Dominican friar.[56] In one voyage, Bishop de Victoria brought together Jesuit evangelisation and the trade in south-west African bodies. If the bishop's manoeuvring brought the institutions of *reduciones* and slavery to Argentina in the same boat, we have to ask how coincidental that simultaneous introduction was. Though the English pirates made off with pots, bells, and dark iron, the agent tells us, they had, reluctantly, to leave the enslaved behind with the Jesuits because they did not have food or water for them.[57] And while he later informs us that the bishop of Paraguay gave blankets to the Jesuits to cover their nakedness once they landed in Buenos Aires and that he donated sackcloth to two or three 'decent' men, we hear no more of the '*piezas de esclavos*', 'units of slaves', as they make their unclothed way to Córdoba and the slave auction of Potosí and, ultimately, servitude in the bishop of Tucumán's vast *encomienda*.[58]

Later on, during an outbreak of the plague, O'Fihily and Fr Solano, his Catalan colleague, became 'everyone's slaves in order to save everyone', '*esclavos de todos, para salvarlos à todos*'.[59] But they were metaphorical slaves in a world of real – and really occluded – slavery. O'Fihily himself would argue that the Jesuit mission in Paraguay provided the 'only refuge and protection' ('*refugio y amparo*') for the 'helpless souls of the pagans'.[60] But while the *reduciones* unquestionably saved countless Guarani from the excesses of Spanish colonisation, '*la Espiritual Conquista de las almas*', 'the spiritual conquest of souls' which they advanced was inextricably bound up with the secular *conquista*.[61] Meanwhile, further north, there was nothing in the least metaphorical about the three slaves which Cuña Muchu bestowed on Bernardo O'Brien in an island on the Amazon; and an acceptance of – and willingness to profit from – slavery is taken for granted in his text. When, for example, he negotiated the surrender of Tauregue Fort with Pedro Texeira, he requested that 'the Irish and other foreigners with them should have the freedom of their lives, slaves (of whatever nation), free Indian servants and goods'.[62] Moreover, when he 'obliged' ('*obligó*') the Indians '*a su devoción*' (which can be translated as 'under his thumb') 'to cultivate tobacco and cotton for him, and to give him the food and drink of that country'; or when he offered Texeira 'lands and Indians to cultivate tobacco', we are left to wonder just how 'free' those '*Indios libres de su servicio y devoción*' actually were.[63]

When, years before, in the mouth of the Rio de la Plata, the English pirates found a cask of tin *ex votos* which the Jesuits intended for the '*yndios*', they smelted them down and turned the holy images into shot for their arquebuses.[64] The distinction between the sacred and the profane melted very easily. The distinction between doing good works and turning people into goods, between fleeing oppression at home and imposing it overseas, was equally plastic. The 'innocent' ethnocentrism[65] behind Irish studies' fascination with the Irish abroad is usefully challenged by an alertness to the unnarrated lives that intersected with theirs – lives that complicate and sometimes reverse the narratives (and the vector of victimhood) with which we are more comfortable. Bernardo O'Brien was very clear about why he first set out with the Amazon Company:

> dela qual terra se tenía noticia, y mucha fama de ser buena y de muchos provechos, y no estava poblada antes por gente blanca.
>
> that land had, by report, the reputation of being rich and very profitable and it had not been settled before by white people.[66]

In the 'Green Atlantic', the Irish did not have to 'become white'.[67] As Bernardo O'Brien knew from the outset, and Thomas O'Fihily was forcibly reminded on a hot quayside in São Salvador de Bahia, they were always, already, *gente blanca*.

CHAPTER 2

Transformational Transactions: Eochaidh Ó hEodhasa's poem (1603) to James I

SARAH McKIBBEN

Pat Coughlan's foundational work on the 'radical alterity' of early modern Ireland in the English imagination addresses texts not 'as relatively inert and transparently readable pieces of evidence', but 'as symbolic representations' of the local context and traditions in which they are 'totally imbricated'.[1] This critique applies equally well to early modern Gaelophone writing: attention has been devoted to its occluded historical referents but criticism has failed to examine its complex symbolic functioning. Only recently have bardic poems, the most substantial body of Irish-language writing from early modern Ireland, begun to receive close reading and semiotic analysis highlighting their deft artistic and political craft, seen in relation to their charged historical moment. This essay takes up Coughlan's charge, revisiting an early modern poem in Irish whose 'symbolic representations' are far more complex than has typically been understood.

Critical tardiness in attending to bardic poetry stems in part from its technical difficulty. Single works may consist of twenty, fifty or even ninety quatrains of highly allusive, densely ornamented, syntactically complex, sometimes obscure Classical Modern Irish in syllabic metre, posing an interpretive challenge. The poems' epideictic nature has also given pause: most bardic poetry does not typically offer private sentiments, opinions or perceptions free of politics or financial concerns. Instead, bardic poetry overwhelmingly addresses patronly concerns and 'reflects the ideological priorities and aspirations' of its Gaelic and gaelicised elite recipients, authors and audiences.[2] Bardic poetry overwhelmingly sought to legitimate the authority and prestige of elite patrons, to elicit generous remuneration. Poets celebrated patrons' ancestry, deeds, character, physical appearance, and conformity to dominant codes of conduct, whether or not actual circumstances fully supported this politically necessary fiction. Poems also proffered diplomatic counsel: cosmopolitan, hereditary, professional poets were reservoirs of 'shrewd and healthy political advice', which they 'deftly expressed in terms of formal panegyric'.[3] Such poetry thus offers a window onto a world misrepresented by surviving historical documents, even if it discomfits those who imagine literature above partisanship, self-interest or politics.

As a deeply rooted, elite genre, bardic poetry is conservative in its values: literally in seeking to conserve the culture that produced it, as well as to police gender, societal, behavioural, and artistic norms over time. This does not mean that native culture was, as some critics would have it, static or inflexible. As Mícheál Mac Craith explains, the struggle 'between the Crown and Ireland's dynastic lords has traditionally been presented as a conflict between a progressive modern civilization and a stagnant archaic one, the latter being inevitably destroyed, a victim not of colonial aggression, but of the march of progress'.[4] In fact, bardic poets' sense of conservatorship – and tradition, understood as an enabling rather than stultifying force – empowered them to react strongly to threats to their society, culture, and profession. As Louis de Paor remarks of our poet '*Ní scarann sé leis an traidisiún ach oibríonn sé ar fad laistigh de*'.[5] More broadly, Brendan Bradshaw, Breandán Ó Buachalla, Mícheál Mac Craith, Marc Caball, Peter McQuillan, Clare Carroll and others have demonstrated that the indigenous Irish literary tradition responded dynamically and resourcefully to the challenges of English colonial attention from the 1540s to the consolidation of state control after 1603. Though constraints of professional occasion limited individual poets' ability to speak out directly, we nonetheless can discern the emergence of a national political consciousness: an ethnically inclusive, Catholic imagined community, and the marshalling of religious, societal, and gender norms in defence of Gaelic cultural heritage. The crafting of an oppositional native historiography that redeployed traditional tropes and mechanisms exemplifies this 'change within continuity' characteristic of native Irish cultural tradition, which lives on rather than ending with the loss of political power.[6]

Yet, even as poets defend their native culture, counter colonial misrepresentation and promote an Irish Catholic identity to unite those of Anglo-Norman and Gaelic ancestry in resistance to Tudor–Stuart incursions, they also apply for pardons, serve as translators to the new regime, and even compose poetry for newcomers and loyalists.[7] In the poem that is the subject of this essay, Eochaidh Ó hEodhasa's thirty-four-quatrain *Mór theasda dh'obair Óivid* ('Much is wanting from Ovid's work'), the Fermanagh master-poet and *ollamh* to the Maguires even formally acclaims James VI and I following his accession to the triple crown of England, Scotland, and Ireland in 1603, elegantly claiming that the resulting unprecedented metamorphosis has rendered Ovid's work lacking.[8]

James Stuart's Gaelic ancestry and his Catholic connections (as the son of self-styled martyr Mary Queen of Scots, and husband of convert Anna of Denmark) initially prompted joy and hope for tolerance among Catholics across the king's new realm.[9] James' acceptance by the Irish learned class was, however, 'a conscious decision based on a realistic assessment of recent politico-religious developments in Europe ...', insists Breandán Ó Buachalla.[10] Simply put, James 'was Ireland's first "High-King" and the ultimate source of power, favour, preferment and patronage'; while the Irish continued to seek military aid from Spain to reverse their degradation, 'in the meantime reconciliation with the ultimate source of power was the only practical course available'.[11] Validation of the king through a praise-poem 'did constitute an acceptance of the *de facto* power of the King, as King of Ireland', but 'it did not entail an acceptance of the socio-cultural changes' that followed.[12] As the first poet in Irish to anoint a Stuart (or any foreign king) as, in stanza 16, '*ár rí*' ('our king'; 63), Ó hEodhasa may exemplify a sea-change in the attitudes of the Irish literati, but does not abandon hope for an end to ongoing Catholic Irish subordination.

Praise is only part of what the poem proffers. Like Fearghal Óg Mac an Bhaird's better-known but far less interesting twenty-nine-quatrain *Trí coróna i gcairt Shéamuis* ('Three crowns in James' charter'), *Mór theasda dh'obair Óivid* has usually been taken as a straightforward affirmation of James Stuart, as if the mere fact of praise exhausts what can be said about it.[13] With the exception of acute readings by Marc Caball and Clare Carroll (cited below), this poem has been dismissed as proof of bardic insincerity, narrow self-interest, or myopia. Yet, close critical attention illustrates how it brilliantly instantiates political and intellectual transformation. Reworking familiar materials, the poet pragmatically welcomes James, assesses the new status quo in light of past suffering, discerns reasons for hope, counsels caution before English authority, appeals to the monarch for clemency, moderation and tolerance, and thereby models a nuanced response to the novel historical moment. It both speaks to and shapes the poetic transaction with patron and communal audience alike, decisively demonstrating the bardic poet's insight and relevance in early Stuart Ireland.

Indeed, the poem is striking for its novelty. Metaphors of transformation are an obvious recourse for the poet of inauguration, and classical allusions are familiar enough in bardic verse, but the framing conceit is unusual.[14] The same poet employs transformation in an inaugural poem to Hugh Maguire of point: *c.*1589, using the classical story to legitimate his leadership by the usual sovereignty motif.[15] By contrast, the first two stanzas of *Mór theasda dh'obair Óivid* centre a distinctly European humanism – rhetoric employed to legitimate conquest in Ireland and elsewhere – to launch its exorbitant praise. James' accession demands a supplement to the work of 'the most imitated and influential classical authors' of the era[16] because Ovid's pioneering work has been retroactively rendered 'wanting' by an epic transformation unforeseen in the *Metamorphoses*, despite its exhaustive compendium of tales of '*fréamha cruthaidh is claochláidh*' ('the roots of creation and transformation'; l. 4). Ovid, '*dá maradh*' ('if he lived'; l. 7), would have added to the comprehensiveness of his masterwork (with surpassing praise for James).

The implications of the opening conceit are many. Ó hEodhasa's simple, unadorned language is supposedly unvarnished truth – a precocious Irish example of Jacobean plain style? – implying that James is a self-evidently superlative ruler.[17] James is a new, better Augustus – whose arrival on the throne overturns settled poetic and political precedent. Unlike contemporaneous English inaugural poems that address the new monarch only awkwardly, this poem deftly compliments the king's erudition.[18] Ó hEodhasa decorously references not traditional Irish mythography, but the great Latin poet and his august royal patron to address a notably learned king tutored in youth by the foremost Latinist of the day.[19] Moreover, by invoking the inadequate Ovid only to (respectfully) supply the missing praise, Ó hEodhasa boldly claims his own calibre as a successor to the Latin master and thus as a worthy poet for a king.

The conceit seems especially apropos, in both praising the king and promoting mutual regard – as we would expect from a master bardic poet who was professionally obligated to fit his praise expertly to the subject he sets out to celebrate. Yet, ironically, this was a time when Irish, and more broadly Gaelic, civility were derided – even by James himself.[20] Representations of the Irish, Patricia Coughlan notes, were 'based on the more general Renaissance typology of the wildness outside civil society', as in other early modern colonial encounters.[21] Claims of Irish barbarousness hark back to twelfth-century Gerald of Wales, who inaugurated centuries of attacks on the Celtic regions as requiring the civilising attentions of their neighbours, including the sixteenth-century violence of martial law, garrison government, and the scorched earth policies of the Nine Years War.[22] Ó hEodhasa asserts his civility, and, by extension, that of the community for which he speaks, by adroitly praising the king in complex epideictic verse – an act and genre that signal sophistication. His knowing lack of preamble name-checks a foundational author of the elite educational curriculum of the day, while signalling his insider's assumption of a shared intellectual inheritance.[23]

By invoking and then displacing Ovid, masterful author of *the* signal work of metamorphosis, Ó hEodhasa also trumpets the magnitude of the change he paints – thereby loudly sounding a note of shared perception despite radical differences in Irish outlooks and history.[24] James' assumption of the triple crown constituted a genuine transformation: not merely an accession, but that of a foreign king, *not* born of the late ruler's body, who faced private opposition and public disquiet, which contemporaneous and subsequent mythographers tried busily to erase. At once referencing and contributing to such mythography – like Ovid in *his* time – Ó hEodhasa appears keenly attuned to the larger historical moment.[25] For many Irish Catholics, James was a figure of radical promise, possibly more sympathetic and certainly more genealogically suitable than his predecessor, demanding thoroughgoing renovation of poetic and political ideology.

Recall that Ovid's *Metamorphoses* proffers multiple stories about metamorphosis, famously 'casts the knowledge of all disciplines in innovative form', and 'repeatedly meditates on the relationship between continuity and change in the universe, in individual lives, and within a poetic *oeuvre*'.[26] This is precisely what Irish poets had now to do, wrenching familiar practices and expectations into new alignment even while lamenting the loss of the old, all the while employing the resources of tradition to do so.[27] Ó hEodhasa's conceit provides a startlingly apposite frame for reflection by a bardic poet upon the ongoing transformation in his profession, community, patrons and function, and the larger sociopolitical moment, at the beginning of a new century during which 'the notion of change pervades ... Irish literature'.[28] Such resonance is no accident: in choosing his motif Ó hEodhasa demonstrates both the bardic poet's exquisitely trained judgement *and* his nuanced historical consciousness. Setting aside the passion but not the technical sophistication of his verse for his beloved patron Hugh Maguire, Ó hEodhasa makes the case for the importance of poetic '*obair*' ('work'; l. 36) in identifying, explaining, analysing, interpreting, and responding to this new world.[29] Just as Ovid sang to make the world, so too does Ó hEodhasa remake a dramatically defamiliarised one. This is manifest in his characteristically apt framing conceit, and throughout the poem, where generalisation (epitomised by some seventeen uses of '*gach/cách*' ('every')), profligate tropes of unity and collectivity, reiteration of at least sixteen synonyms for 'change' as well as multiple images for it, abstract rather than concrete terms, and self-conscious acts of interpretation and reflection, foreground bardic function as a public intellectual and voice of the collectivity, performing crucial *ideological*, *cognitive*, and *poetic* work at once.

Reversing Ovid's portrait of changes for the worse, in stanzas 3 to 10 Ó hEodhasa's sweeping, optimistic generalisations offer hope. '*Rob iomdha ní ... / ar dtús a n-olc do iompó*' ('Many a thing ... changed to evil at first'), acknowledges stanza 3, referring to a political as well as a literary past, but '*fearr an cinneadh*' ('superior the fate') that makes '*gach ní d'fhilleadh ar fheabhas*' ('everything turn for the better'; ll. 9–12). Stanza 4 is more optimistic still: '*Tillidh deallradh gach doircheacht, / díbridh eagna anfhoirfeacht / an ghlóir a n-oighreacht re headh*' ('Brightness repulses all darkness, wisdom banishes imperfection for a time glory is their heritage'; ll. 13–14). The poet praises James' brilliance and wisdom emphatically enough to evoke, in the words of one critic, a '*ré órga*' ('golden age'), but Ó hEodhasa hardly forgets Irish preoccupations.[30] As Clare Carroll puts it, the poet 'both hopes for change and is all too aware of how dramatically everything has changed.'[31] Indeed, for the metamorphosis of the Stuart reign to be so epochal, the Tudor past – culminating in the brutality of the Nine Years War and the defeat of the confederated Irish forces headed by Hugh O'Neill – must have been terrible. Accordingly, stanza 4 sees darkness repulsed, imperfection 'banished' or 'exiled', and '*foirneart gach bróin*' ('violence/tyranny of all sorrow'; l. 16), 'vanquished' or 'drowned'. This violent lexicon of nouns and verbs as well as the sense of stunned transformation are deliberate, memorialising recent Irish suffering (as opposed to rebellion) in the Nine Years War to urge its permanent banishment to the past.

The peculiarly heightened language of these early stanzas and their insistent references to '(re)turns' from recent 'evil' to prior good and 'brightness' that banishes 'darkness' and 'imperfection' employ the phrasing and tropes of religious disputation, more specifically those of a Counter-Reformation truth resurgent in the face of destructive, yet ultimately temporary error.[32] This religious message might have been intended for a more proximate, Irish audience. (Sadly, the performance history of the poem or who saw it after its completion are both unknown.) The poet arguably signals the oft-expressed hope that James and his realms would (in the prototypical Counter-Reformation verb) 'return' to the true faith of Catholicism, defeat the 'darkness' of heresy, and embrace the 'glory' of his (maternal/ancestral) 'heritage' in order to 'vanquish' sorrow. The underlying message that the Catholic Irish were on the side of justice, destined to see the wheel of fate turn back in their favour once they repented – a message that would become the overwhelming burden of seventeenth-century Irish poetry – offered powerful consolation.

Further happy transformations are in store in stanza 5, as individual expression is set free:

Atá libeirte a labhra
'gun anbhfainne agallmha;
a bruth as éadána ar fhear,
guth na héagcára as íseal.

('The [man who is] very timid of utterance has freedom of speech; the voice of injustice is subdued, its fury is gentle towards one'; ll. 17–20). James' accession (if not his religion) frees those who were once afraid, like the poet, to speak, while 'injustice' is intimidated. The classic topos of good kingship as countering injustice contrasts sharply with *prior* violations of justice and freedom of expression and religion experienced under Elizabethan 'pacification', culminating in such 'furious' curtailments of speech as beheadings, the cutting out of tongues, and persecution of literati, clerics and dissidents.[33] Ó hEodhasa depicts James as a different sort of ruler. Moreover, by using the 'very sparsely attested' loanword '*libeirte*' ('liberty'), instead of the seemingly equivalent, 'well-established, native [word] *saoirse* ["freedom, liberty"]', the poet may advert to much-debated early modern political concepts.[34] But he may also reference the Chichester proclamation of 1605 affirming the Irish as free subjects of the king, thus opening the courts to Irish litigants to counter rampant weaponisation of the legal system against them.[35] In contemporaneous English discourse, freedom of speech was a yardstick of a ruler's affability and openness, a corresponding guarantor of his state's longevity and health, a much-parsed civic virtue, and an individual liberty in a properly free society.[36] Ó hEodhasa praises James as a proper ruler due to his openness to counsel, urges the maintenance of such freedom of speech, and celebrates it as indicative of a just reign. Given the degree to which Irish speakers were silenced not alone by English violence but by English courts, texts, and governing bodies – as indeed they continue to be in contemporary criticism on the early modern colonial encounter – he may have wished to underline this point in his own act of poetic voicing, as our close attention to his words enables.[37]

Coming on the heels of the prior stanzas' religious resonance, freedom of speech evokes its philosophical companion, freedom of conscience, a concept repeatedly invoked by Irish lords and clerics to justify insurgency in the last decades of the sixteenth century. That freedom is posed as a positive good that James should respect, as the Irish Catholic majority and the still-substantial English Catholic minority devoutly hoped he would. The term 'liberty' was for Counter-Reformation Catholics strongly associated with notions of personal freedom and popular will, alongside freedom of conscience, as articulated in early modern republicanism. The Jesuit philosopher-theologians Francisco Suárez and Robert Bellarmine (Roberto Bellarmino) disseminated those ideas, which were transmitted into Irish by the Salamanca-trained, Connacht theologian Flaithrí Ó Maolchonaire (Florence Conry) at around this time.[38] Without directly referencing resistance theory or indeed any sort of resistance at all, Ó hEodhasa subtly promotes toleration, hints at the need for reciprocal regard, and even references the need for dissent in a healthy body politic.

Ó hEodhasa next heralds the coming of peace (as opposed to pacification) after war. Stanza 6 portrays a happily inverted world in which brilliance replaces darkness and peace replaces violence once more, as war itself is unexpectedly transformed (ll. 21–2), exchanging '*a sgéimh dhothaobhtha dhuibh / a néimh chrothaobhdha chúthuil*' ('its black repellent appearance / for pleasant modest splendour'; ll. 23–4). Thus it is in stanzas 7–8 that the Furies (not, *pace* Breatnach, the Gorgons) of vengeance are subdued, no longer generating 'anguish' or 'combat' (l. 25). In a striking image that forms a centrepiece of the early part of the poem, their snaky tresses are said to be tied together (ll. 29–30) so that '*giodh beó bhead / aingcis ná gleó ní gheinead*' ('even if they be alive / they do not generate either distress or combat'; ll. 31–2), remaining in a kind of stasis.[39] These changes permit Ceres, in stanza 9, to be '*ag treabhadh thulach ndíoghuinn, / ag buain fhala d'arm Marsa*' ('ploughing hills of plenty, / wiping blood from the sword of Mars'; ll. 34–5). The goddess of agriculture happily transforms destructive war (and particularly the deliberate razing of crops and settlements during its course) into the fruitful peace, traditionally created by a rightful monarch by the terms of the Irish sovereignty motif, by cleansing the blood from Mars' sword, turning that sword into a ploughshare.[40]

This might seem a self-evident and anodyne good, but the apparently neutral ploughing metaphor raises another fraught issue: colonial transformation of land from pasture to tillage as territory passed from native to settler control. Witness Lochlainn Ó Dálaigh's *c.*1610 *Cáit ar ghabhadar Gaoidhil?* ('Where have the Gaels gone?'), which protests colonists' dividing '*ar bhfearoinn-ne*' ('*our* land'; emphasis in original, l. 39) and turning Ireland's '*lachtmhair*' ('milky'; l. 35) (that is, pastoral) plains into '*acraibh*' ('acres'; l. 36) (that is, tillage).[41] As if to anticipate Ó Dálaigh's contested image, Ó hEodhasa instead insists, '*marbh an fhala ón obar-sa*' ('enmity is dead due to this work'; l. 36), claiming that all is peaceful while covertly prodding the Irish to bury the hatchet in that ploughed earth. Employing the noun '*fala*' (meaning, resentment, grievance, grudge, feud), Ó hEodhasa advocates the end of retributive violence (as of vengeance in stanzas 7–8) in the interest of peace.[42] Here and throughout the poem, both implicit and explicit advice – a central function of the bardic poet – reflects the needs of the community for and to whom he speaks in welcoming James. The '*obar*' ('work') visible here is both the fostering of peace reflected in the metaphor and the production of that metaphor itself: that is, the poet's own imaginative and ideological work in promoting reconciliation by envisioning a way forward.

To be secure, Ireland must be peaceful, which in turn requires unity and accommodation, which the poet figures in terms of '*éincheann ar iomad colann*' ('one head on many bodies'; l. 38) or, alternatively, '*cuirp a n-aonchorp ré hannsacht*' ('[many] bodies united in one body by affection'; l. 40), two standard metaphors of royal supremacy and concord – many bodies with one head or many bodies fused into one.[43] This dual reference foregrounds the poet's interpretive role, the difficulty of performing it and of aligning and reconciling all the actual bodies in play, as Ó hEodhasa instructs his audience to imagine both their new status and the new Stuart state in which they live. His exquisitely condensed, decorous couplet links the twinned loss and joy of succession experienced by 'the men of London': '*lá a rathuirse bás a mbróin, / dob fhás athshoilse um iarnóin*' ('on their day of great grief their sorrow died; in the evening there arose a new brightness'; ll. 47–8). The king is dead; long live the king. Imaginatively projecting an English subjectivity, Ó hEodhasa suggests that the Irish understand, if they do not quite share, that state.

Stanza 13 recurs to the glittering vision of Stuart accession by discerning how '*An ghrian loinneardha do las*' ('The brilliant sun lit up'; l. 49) with the arrival of the luminous '*Cing Séamas*' ('King James'; l. 50). James has not just scattered mist (as properly discerning rulers do in Irish tradition); he *is* '*sgaoileadh gach ceo*' ('the dispersal of all mist'; l. 50) that transforms confusion and suffering into clarity and transcendence. Thus '*comhorchra cháigh*' ('the collective mourning of all') is transformed '*'na glóir*' ('into glory'; l. 51). All in all, '*móir na comhortha claochláidh*' ('great the signs of change'; l. 52), a line once more foregrounding the poet's own crucial interpretive function and pragmatic vision, phrased as unstinting acclaim.

Having characterised the hopeful, transformed world uniting the Irish with James' other subjects, in stanza 14 the poet at last distinguishes his community, thus far strategically subsumed. He terms them '*sionn, / popal imshníomhach Éirionn*' ('we, the troubled people of Ireland' ll. 53–4), framing them as a particularly suffering, distinctive '*popal*' (modern 'pobal', 'people'). Far from dwelling upon that distinctiveness, however, he terms it '*ionganta*' ('wondrous'; l. 53) that they have left that worry (reiterated with a cognate noun) behind, '*gur dhearmaid gach duine dhíon / treabhlaid na n-uile imshníomh*' ('that each one of us forgot / the tribulation of all anxieties'; ll. 55–6). That is, the Irish have been wonderfully transformed into such joyful new subjects of the king that they have abandoned the memory of their suffering – that is, history itself. The choice of verb here is instructive. Elsewhere in late bardic poetry, 'forgetting' delicately averts to a lord's failure to behave properly so as to restore him to proper comportment – see, for example, the reference to '*díoth cuimhne*' ('lack of memory', that is, 'forgetfulness'; l. 3,757) as the cause of Gaelic lords' inexplicable failure to defend their hereditary rights in Aonghus Ó Dálaigh's incendiary *c.* 1580 *Dia libh, a laochruidh Gaoidhiol* ('God be with you, O heroes of the Gaels').[44] Also, 'forgetting' often refers to faith cast aside for heresy. Here, by contrast, 'forgetting' signals that the violence of failed insurgency, which Ó hEodhasa had previously celebrated (for example, in *Fuar liom an adhaighsi dh'Aodh*), euphemistically evoked with the adjective '*imníomhach*' ('troubled'), must be transformed. Insurgency, already occluded as trouble inflicted upon the Irish people as a whole, should be replaced by peace and unity. The Irish have forgotten old wars, but equally their actions should be forgotten, through the legal instrument (perhaps evoked here) of 'forgetting': amnesty for former rebels, in return for their promise to 'forget' their grievances along with their former loyalties.[45] On Mountjoy's advice, an Act of Oblivion was in fact proclaimed in the spring of 1603, and reiterated in March 1605, for 'those rebels who swore due allegiance to the crown', much to the disgust of most of Dublin officialdom.[46]

Ó hEodhasa's reiterated reference to the *anxiety/troubledness* that distinguishes the Irish people evokes the insight that nationalism in fact arises out of collective threat (or anxiety), while his reference to *forgetting* anticipates Ernest Renan's 1882 insight that 'Forgetting ... is a crucial factor in the creation of a nation'.[47] Members of the nation must forget the violence with which it is brought into being, as '[u]nity is always effected by means of brutality'.[48] Ó hEodhasa's acute, contemporaneous perception of this crucial mechanism of state-formation strategically subordinates the emergent Irish national consciousness inherent in the stanza's subject, '*popal imshníomhach Éirionn*' ('the troubled *people* of Ireland', emphasis added), while advocating for the sort of mutual forgetting that might (but ultimately did not) safeguard their interests. Yet in insisting that the Irish forget, Ó hEodhasa incribes their distinctiveness as a *people*, thereby paradoxically acknowledging or even ensuring that they cannot.[49]

Beyond his own community's recalcitrant representations and memories, the poet hyperbolically declares it to be still *more* astonishing ('*roidhiongna*'; l. 57) in stanza 15 that the Irish are not blinded by James' brilliance '*do ghnáth na n-én n-oidhchidhe / ar tteacht fan ngrianshoilse ngloin*' ('like the nocturnal birds on coming into the clear sunlight'; ll. 58–9). He likens the troubled Irish to night birds unaccustomed to dazzling justice and right, although grateful and eager for it. Indeed, he continues self-consciously, '*Oirchios dúin, gé a deirim-sin, / ceiliobhradh dár ccuing imnidh*' ('It is fitting for us, if I say that, to bid farewell to our yoke of anxiety'; ll. 61–2). The Irish can abandon long-familiar negative emotions now that the paternal '*súil chobhartha ar ríogh*' ('helping eye of our king'; l. 63) overcomes '*bríogh ndomharbhtha ar ndobróin*' ('the lasting force of our sorrow'; l. 64). Similarly, '*Atá aigneadh gach fhir dín / do réir nádúire an nóinín*' ('The nature of each one of us accords with that of a daisy'; ll. 65–6), opening its petals to the sun. Inured to misery, the Irish can now gratefully turn towards the light.

Instead of the innately depraved, uncivilised, and prideful rebels of Protestant (and earlier Giraldian) imagining, the Irish are shown – probably quite accurately – as longing for peace and tolerance under the king's 'helping eye'. They are said to share '*aonbháidh isan am-sa*' ('one accord at this time'; l. 69) – united at last in affirmation of the new monarch – and to be moved '*le hursboradh ionmhoine*' ('by the urging of affection'; l. 72) like all of James' new subjects. Carefully chosen images, like the reiterated tropes of unity, portray Ireland's people sympathetically to a foreign audience and king, to urge clemency, rather than the dehumanising harshness characteristic of Tudor rule. Ireland is typically cast, as Ó hEodhasa knew well, and as Patricia Coughlan remarks in relation to Edmund Spenser's work, as 'a challenging otherness', 'a prime site of difficulty and complexity, both in its stubborn recalcitrant self, and in the dilemmas to which it gives rise in those who must have to do with it'.[50] Indeed, Ireland's deforming effect was a central theme for Spenser and his colonial contemporaries. Using the derided language of the 'other', Irish, normally seen as a source of rebellion and degeneration, and stressing the notion of positive change, Ó hEodhasa crafts a master-trope portraying a transformed world of happy liberation, recovery, and unification.[51]

The poet's representation of the Irish people is as canny as his portrayal of the king's 'helping eye'. Like other Catholic writers responding to James at this time, he uses the occasion of praise to urge outcomes Irish Catholics urgently desired: clemency, justice, moderation, and tolerance. Like fellow bardic poet Mac an Bhaird, Ó hEodhasa emphasises aspects of royal comportment much desired by the Irish. 'The emphasis, in both poems', Ó Buachalla argues, is 'on James dispersing enmity and strife', in keeping with 'traditional notions of legitimate and righteous kingship'.[52]

Earlier, Ó hEodhasa praised James for banishing injustice, intimating the need for freedom of speech and hinting at the cognate need for freedom of conscience. Stanza 19 urges equal treatment of the different nations under James' rule, declaring that '*luibh fhóirthe chiach gach cridhe, / ní fhóirfe ar iath dh'áiridhe*' ('the herb that relieves the grief of every heart will not succour any one land in particular'; ll. 75–6). That is, James must be the proper healing medicine for all, attending to all fairly. In the words of James' own *Basilikon Doron*, or royal gift of advice, written for his son, he should govern as 'a worthy king' who guides his 'people great and small'.[53] Accordingly, Ó hEodhasa, like his compatriot Mac an Bhaird, implies that despite past history, Ireland should be given the same care as other kingdoms by a king who brings accord '*d'oibriogbadh is d'eisiomláir*' ('by deed and example'; l. 78). Again erasing heretofore problematic Irish difference, Ó hEodhasa portrays '*lucht gach aoinchríche*' ('people of every single territory'; l. 81) as now ruled '*gan iomthnúth gan ainigin, / gan neimh thnúith*' ('without jealousy, without violence, without envious bitterness'; ll. 82–3) due to James' astonishing exemplarity.

The acclaim offered to James as a rightful king naturally comes encumbered with expectation, as did James' own conception of good kingship.[54] So, too, traditional Irish notions of kingship powerfully linked 'qualifications and obligations', implying 'mutual responsibilities between king and people'.[55] This medieval bedrock is implicit throughout this poem. Ó hEodhasa does include a more novel acclaim, however. In stanzas 22, 24, 31, 32, and 34 he unites older kingship motifs with distinctly Machiavellian praise in the personification of Fortune, figured as fighting with Nature over who has been more generous to the king. James has subdued Fortune into a 'female slave' or 'handmaiden' in stanza 32; as Carroll remarks, the 'skill with which Nature has gifted the king to transform Fortune is like the *virtù* with which the Prince must control *fortuna*', so that the poem describes a further metamorphosis in kingship, encompassing 'a newer Machiavellian analysis of the achievement of power as the interplay between contingency and skill'.[56] This extended allegory frames James as a modern king who nonetheless has two personified goddesses fighting over the right to claim him, occasioning further compliments about his superlative qualities.

The conceit of a marvellous transformation for the better enables Ó hEodhasa to repeatedly invoke justice and moderation, just as James did in his own writing on the nature of kingship.[57] In stanza 27, he describes the heat of pride, while stanza 28 depicts an eagle's nest in an image borrowed from Lucan, whose *Pharsalia* was popular among Irish literati (and was referenced in another poem by Ó hEodhasa). The obscure figure refers to the eagle-stone, which cools the over-heated nest, keeping its eggs safe.[58] Thus having conjured up imperial pride – through the Roman symbol of the eagle, particularly an inflamed, aggressive one – Ó hEodhasa in stanza 29 praises Nature's acts such '*go measraigh a meanmain*' ('that she moderates her feelings'; l. 115) and, in stanza 31, supplies '*múnadh mheasortha*' ('moderating teaching'; l. 122). Moderation was a well-known touchstone of royal ideology in Irish tradition, and, as recent work by Peter McQuillan illustrates, a key early modern moral-ethical precept of elite civility.[59] In emphasising this regal trait the poet both reiterates a given and emphasises a quality of pressing relevance to the suffering Irish.

The Irish (of whatever political persuasion) had little power to urge anything on the absolute ruler of a land that would remain persistently militarised after the resounding defeat of the confederated Gaelic forces in the Nine Years War. But Ó hEodhasa promotes Irish interests in the face of unpredictable and dramatic change. He acknowledges the tenuous Irish desire for stability: '*ar n-athchruthadh go hullamh; / gach athrughadh uaramar*' ('may no second change come for us soon again; we have experienced every transformation'; ll. 137–8). Tellingly, the poem's *dúnadh* (or recursive formal closing) does not repeat the opening word or phrase as in most bardic texts, suggesting the impossibility of returning to the past. In place of a circular return, the poet repeats just one syllable, the unstressed schwa of *-mar*, the final, first-person-plural suffix ('we') of the closing, past-tense verb, which forms a diminished consonantal near-rhyme between the initial stressed, long 'O' of '*Mór*' ('great') of the opening line. It is a sombre end to a poem of praise: instead of reiterating the patron's greatness, the conclusion returns to the anxious collective interest of the subject community. Notwithstanding the poem's ostensible burden, that last, ruminant, knowing communal syllable confirms where the poet's heart and hopes lie. If Ó hEodhasa has reminded his countrymen that James is a fearsome Augustan eagle who could burst into flames, revoking his promised mercy, banishing a poet or anyone he chose, as the relentlessly arbitrary, absolute powers in Ovid's *Metamorphoses* testified, in urging this modern Augustus to be merciful, then he has surely negotiated this complicated transaction with remarkable dexterity.

CHAPTER 3

The Ghost Comes to Town: Le Fanu and the urban Gothic

NICHOLAS DALY

While ghosts are often free of the temporal restraints that bind the living, the ghost story is far from being timeless: we can trace a longer history of oral tales of the supernatural, but the modern literary ghost story manifests itself in the nineteenth century, distilled from the more diffuse Gothic fictions of the eighteenth. In this essay I want to discuss the role played by the Irish writer Joseph Sheridan Le Fanu (1814–73) in this history. Le Fanu, I will suggest, brings the ghost story to town. In a number of his stories the otherworldly ordeals of the protagonists take place not against the residual Gothic backdrops of crumbling castles or remote country houses, but on city pavements and public transport. To this extent the intense private nightmares of his characters seem linked to transformations of public urban space in the early and mid-nineteenth century, which were driven in turn by developments in public transport. Here is horror for the age of the commuter.

Major Irish contributors to Victorian supernatural fiction include Mrs J.H. Riddell, Fitzjames O'Brien, B.M. Croker and Bram Stoker.[1] But as Patricia Coughlan has shown, J.S. Le Fanu stands head and shoulders above the others in shaping the modern ghost story.[2] Le Fanu is now read for his atmospheric sensation novel *Uncle Silas* (1864), and late erotic vampire story 'Carmilla' (1872), but he was a prolific producer of supernatural tales from the late 1830s onwards.[3] His first ghost stories, presented as the reminiscences of a Catholic priest, the Reverend Francis Purcell of Drumcoolagh, appeared regularly in the *Dublin University Magazine* from 1838 to 1840. Further stories appeared in the *Dublin University Magazine* in the 1840s and '50s, and he published in a range of English magazines in the 1860s and '70s (including *Temple Bar*, Sampson Low's *The Dark Blue*, *Belgravia*, and *All the Year Round*). After some early attempts at historical fiction, in the 1860s he began to write mystery novels of varying quality, which came from his pen with 'Braddonian rapidity', as his obituary in the *Freeman's Journal* phrased it. *Uncle Silas* was the most successful of these: to quote the *Freeman's Journal* again, 'there is a nerve, a fierce intensity in it, which keeps the reader spell-bound', and with it 'he took then a place which he never lost with library readers'.[4]

Like *Uncle Silas*, some of the other later novels create a curious sense of dislocation, the result, perhaps, of Le Fanu's use of fictional English settings in an attempt to court a larger reading public. Despite, or perhaps because of, their peculiar atmosphere, he enjoyed a measure of popular success in his lifetime. After his death in 1873, he was remembered by *Lloyd's Weekly Newspaper* in their round-up of 'The Great Dead of 1873' as a 'clever teller of thrilling stories that harrowed up many a nervous soul'; the *Times* also listed him among the illustrious dead of the year, alongside such figures as William Macready and Edwin Landseer.[5] A mythology has grown around Le Fanu's later life, and the idea that he was a reclusive 'Invisible Prince' still has a certain currency, despite evidence to the contrary. A cursory trawl through the social columns – 'Fashion and Varieties' in the *Freeman's Journal*, and 'Court and Fashion' in the *Belfast News-Letter* – suggests that Le Fanu continued to frequent society gatherings in these years, generally with one of his daughters.[6] He also kept up with some of his literary and legal acquaintance.[7] Nonetheless, as Victor Sage notes, 'the critical picture of Le Fanu's career as a writer is often shaped by the (biographical) notion of retreat'.[8] On such a reading, Le Fanu comes to stand as the representative of an isolated Protestant minority, haunted by the past, and increasingly besieged in the present by the growing sway of the Catholic middle classes, part of a specifically Irish Protestant Gothic tradition. In a study of the Irish short story, Heather Ingman, for example, presents 'Carmilla' as in part 'a political fable expressing Le Fanu's fear that the Anglo-Irish class to which he belonged was on the brink of dissolution'.[9] Here, I want to consider a different aspect of his supernatural tales, their immersion in the social and material realities of Dublin, notwithstanding their explicit antiquarianism and idiosyncrasy. In the examples I have chosen, it is the psychic disturbances of the quotidian present rather than the nightmares of history that are registered.

As Patricia Coughlan demonstrates, space is particularly important in Le Fanu's fiction, supernatural and non-supernatural alike. Thus, one of the recurring scenarios in his stories, early and late, is the locked room, often a locked room that turns into a death-trap. Where Edgar Allan Poe's 'The Murders in the Rue Morgue' (1841) takes a tale of horror, and famously turns it into one of the first detective stories, Le Fanu dwells on the murderous aspect of domestic space.[10] Where Poe offers a fantasy figure, the detective, who can unpick the tangled knots of urban mystery, Le Fanu offers a bleaker view – domestic space has mutated into something deadly. His domestic interiors thus recall Walter Benjamin's famous description in 'Paris, Capital of the Nineteenth Century' of the bourgeois home as a place of reverie, self-indulgence and phantasmagoria, but also of emotional cathexis, on which the pressures of the nuclear family and of heteronormative courtship bear. In his most pioneering work, Le Fanu explores some rather different aspects of the transformation of modern space. It is not just haunted private interiors that feature in these urban stories, but also public transport and the streets themselves. I want to argue that while Le Fanu's work everywhere registers the mutation in space effected by economic forces and changes in family structure, at times it also bears the impress of some technological factors, specifically the transport revolution of these years.

In the interests of concision, I will consider just three stories. Two of these appear in the late collection *In a Glass Darkly* (1872): 'The Familiar', which is almost word for word taken from an earlier story, 'The Watcher' (*Dublin University Magazine*, 1847); and 'Green Tea' which had first appeared in Dickens' *All the Year Round* in October–November 1869. The third was published in the *Dublin University Magazine* as an account of an actual haunting, 'An Authentic Narrative of a Haunted House' (1862).[11]

RAILWAY EXCAVATIONS

In 'The Watcher' / 'The Familiar', the unfinished streets of Dublin provide the striking setting for a series of events that are meant to have taken place 'somewhere about the year 1794' (p. 42).[12] The story's central character, Captain Barton, a retired naval officer, is menaced by a shrunken figure resembling one of his former crew, Sylvester Yelland, who is supposed to have died in Naples. He had been harshly treated by Barton in revenge for his ill-treatment of his daughter, with whom Barton had had some kind of relationship.

Barton has returned to Dublin and, though living quietly in lodgings 'in one of the *then* fashionable streets' (p. 43) and largely eschewing 'society', becomes engaged to a 'reigning toast' (p. 43), a Miss Montague, niece and protegée of Lady Rochdale. Walking home from a visit to his fiancée at the northside home of her aunt, he takes a route through an unfinished street 'which had as yet merely been laid out [with] little more than the foundations of the houses constructed' (p. 44):

> He had proceeded thus some way, when he, on a sudden, heard other footfalls, pattering at a measured pace, and, as it seemed, about two score steps behind him ... but though there was quite sufficient moonlight to disclose any object upon the road he had traversed, no form of any kind was visible there. (p. 45)

This aural persecution is followed by threatening notes from 'The Watcher', not unlike the Rockite letters that in the Ireland of Le Fanu's youth provided a sinister double to the ordinary post. Eventually the Watcher actually appears before Barton, fixing him with 'a look of maniacal menace and fury' (p. 51) as he is entering the House of Commons on College Green with our narrator. A diminutive figure in a fur cap (a travelling cap in the earlier version), he resembles the dead Yelland, and mutters angrily to himself as he approaches. The violence grows more explicit: Barton takes another nocturnal walk through the unfinished streets ('the road on either side was ... embarrassed by the foundations of a street, beyond which extended waste fields, full of rubbish and neglected lime and brick kilns' (p. 57)), and this time a musket is fired at him. He becomes convinced that he is the object of a 'system malignant, and inexorable' (p. 60) of persecution. The persecution takes on a peculiarly aural character, as he believes that he is 'pursued with blasphemies, cries of despair, and appalling hatred ... dreadful sounds called after me as I turn the corner of streets' (p. 62). At the urging of friends, he quits Ireland for a time, but the Watcher is there on the quay in Calais when he arrives in France. Back in Dublin, Barton stays at a secluded house in Clontarf, but the Watcher appears there too. Ultimately, the captain is found dead in his room, apparently frightened to death by the final visit of his nemesis.

In his introduction to *In a Glass Darkly*, Robert Tracy contends that the half-built streets that create such a strong impression in this story evoke Dublin during a phase of development in the 1790s, before the Act of Union made it a political backwater.[13] But I would suggest that this is a story whose historicism is a thin veneer, and that it is the pressure of the present rather than the past that is registered. Readers of the story in 1847 would have been well used to walking past excavated streets, lime-kilns, and the detritus of building. In the 1840s the fabric of Dublin (like that of other cities) was indeed being reshaped, not by the Georgian planners who had swept away the medieval city, but by the railway engineers who were cutting swathes through the urban fabric, and turning Dublin into a steam-age city.[14] The first Dublin railway terminus had opened at Westland Row in 1834, providing easy access to the busy harbour at Kingstown, as well as a service for commuters; by 1844 another terminus had been built at Amiens Street for the Dublin–Drogheda line; and by 1846 Kingsbridge (now Heuston) provided access to the south and west via the Great Southern and Western Railway. Ireland boasted its own railway newspaper, the *Irish Railway Gazette*, and from 1844 a telegraph system that grew alongside the network of rail. In 1847, the year of 'The Watcher', work began on a line between Harcourt Street and Bray, which railway entrepreneur and engineer William Dargan planned to turn into a seaside resort, complete with its own esplanade and Turkish baths. The same 'railway mania' that was abroad in England was sweeping Ireland too, and the public were invited to pour their money into new schemes, some of them of dubious merit. There was a wave of imaginative investment in the railways as a transforming utopian force in these years, as with John Grey C. Porter's 'A Few Observations Upon Our Present Railway System in Ireland' (1847), which envisaged a rail link from Westland Row to Valentia, County Kerry, providing a deep-water harbour for ships to America. Nor were such developments confined to the decade of railway mania. 'The Watcher' seems to anticipate a period in which ever more radical recreations of the city were contemplated. By the time Le Fanu had rewritten the story as 'The Familiar', Dubliners had been treated to an extended debate over plans to join all of Dublin's railway termini, which would mean extensive reshaping of the streets in between. There was stern opposition from the corporation, who resented what they saw as English capital carving up the city for its own ends, and more generally from those nationalists who saw a military agenda at work. Unfavourable comparisons were made with Baron Haussmann's modernisation of Paris.[15] In 1863 Frederick Barry controversially proposed a line that would run 20 feet above street level, and would feature a viaduct at Westmoreland Street. Dublin Corporation built a full-sized model of this projected bridge in order to show people exactly how intrusive it would be; a woman was seriously injured when some of the scaffolding fell. *The Irish Times* was hostile to Barry's Metropolitan Railway project, which it saw as taking passengers 'through gloomy tunnels and down steep declines' – they favoured the rival Dublin Railway planned by John Hawkshaw and James Barton.[16]

Le Fanu was not alone in turning the reshaping of Dublin into the stuff of horror. In 1862 'William Scribble' penned a Gothic comic drama, *Dublin*

Destroyed!, or, The Witches Cauldron of Railway Horror: A Mysterious Shakespeareana, in One Act, a sort of sequel to his *Old Carlisle Bridge*, a burlesque on Dublin traffic, which had been performed at the Queen's Theatre the previous year. Even this brief excerpt gives a sense of its comic flavour:

> Scene: The Railway Engine house of destruction ... distant rumbling noise, like thunder of railway train; bells, Railway whistles, etc. [two parliamentary agents and a solicitor discovered as three witches]
>
> 2nd Witch:
> Through each house, and through each shop,
> Nothing shall our progress stop.
>
> 3rd Witch:
> Let us e'en persuade the cits,
> 'Gainst their senses and their wits,
> That each bridge across the street
> Would be an architectural treat
> ...
>
> All:
> Dublin, Dublin, all great trouble in;
> We must lay our rails through Dublin.
>
> Railway Sprite [alias Barie]:
> Westmoreland-street, we've most, I think, to fear,
> And next to that the battle of D'Olier
> ...
> No, I'll engage the City well to shake,
> In imitation of some great earthquake;
> ...
> And all the architecture old and new,
> (When we have cut the city into slices)
> We'll hide by cunningly concealed devices.

Happily, the lord mayor prevails in scene 2, and Dublin is not destroyed.[17]

If Le Fanu was attuned to such developments, it was in part because he lived through them – by 1872 he lived about ten minutes' walk from Westland Row railway station. But the Le Fanu family were far from being simply observers of these seismic transformations of the fabric of the city, and indeed of the country more generally. Joseph's brother William was a railway engineer for more than twenty years, until in 1863 he was appointed commissioner of the Board of Public Works. Indeed, William's career followed the railways: he was aboard the very first train that ran in Ireland, from Dublin to Kingstown; between 1840 and 1846 he worked on the Dublin–Drogheda line, the second one in the country; he subsequently worked on the first lines to Cashel and Carlow; between 1846 and 1863 he oversaw, *inter alia*, the construction of the Great Southern and Western line from Dublin to Cork, the Dublin, Wicklow and Wexford line, and the Waterford–Limerick line, and designed the Cahir Viaduct over the river Suir.[18] Nor was Joseph completely insulated from this world: when William was asked in 1851 by the Great Southern and Western Railway Company to evaluate alternative Irish ports for transatlantic traffic to the US, his brother was roped in to promote his views using his contacts in journalism.[19] William was closely involved in the 'Dublin Destroyed' debate. In June 1863, the *Freeman's Journal* provided a detailed comparison of Barry's metropolitan railway and that proposed by William Le Fanu. By this time the grand plans to link all of Dublin's railway termini had been cut down to a scheme to link Westland Row to Kingsbridge. Like rival schemes, Le Fanu's envisaged a central station at Aston Quay, but relied less on viaducts and more on tunnels:

> Mr Le Fanu's line will leave Westland Row and the important part of Brunswick Street (sc. Pearse Street) uninjured, and will pass under D'Olier Street, Fleet Street, and Westmoreland Street, leaving these important portions of the city just as they stand at present ... Mr Barry proposes a viaduct right through the city, passing every street from Aston's Quay, Parliament Street, Winetavern Street, all of them, say 12 or more in number, by bridges. Mr Le Fanu proposes to reach the same destination by again causing his line to dip and to cross Parliament Hill, Cork Hill and Christchurch Place by a tunnel. This tunnel at Cork Hill he, however, intends to construct in such a way as to open a new line of street in continuation of Dame Street behind Castle Street, with a gentle ascent to Christchurch Place ... It is plain that while one [scheme] would disfigure many of our best streets, the other would be almost invisible to the street traveller at the points of most interest; and ... would be the means of opening up a new lung for the city, and ... would also have an important influence on the sewerage of the city, and the purification of the Liffey.[20]

If Le Fanu had been inspired by the earthworks of the 1840s, the decade of railway mania, to write 'The Watcher', his own brother's active involvement in the restructuring of the city might suggest one reason why he dusted off the story for re-publication in 1872 as 'The Familiar'.

The same sense of being under a hostile and even murderous gaze informs other stories too, ones that at first glance seem more typical of the magazine fiction of the period, as they deal with haunted houses. Unsettling figures that come to gaze at the living include the ghost of the debauched Judge Horrocks in 'An Account of Some Strange Disturbances in Aungier Street', later extensively reworked for *In a Glass Darkly* as 'Mr Justice Harbottle', and the series of poltergeists in 'An Authentic Narrative of a Haunted House'. In 'An Account', the student inhabitants of an old house in Aungier Street, Dublin are terrified by various manifestations of a long-dead hanging judge. When the narrator tries to sleep in his new bedchamber he finds himself held by the gaze of a face full of 'malignant omen': 'the gaze of this hellish visage was fixed upon me, and mine returned it with the inexplicable fascination of nightmare' (p. 364).[21] In 'An Authentic Narrative', the narrator and his family rent a house 'at a moderate distance from the city … and connected to it by a railway' (p. 420). The house is 'quite a modern one', recently painted and decorated, and is 'one in a cheerful row … facing the sea' (p. 420). This could be a number of commuter towns on the Dublin–Kingstown line, though given the narrator's desire for rest, it is tempting to speculate that the house is in Bray, which expanded as a resort town after the 1854 opening of the railway line from Harcourt Street, through Milltown, Foxrock, and Dundrum to the coast. But in this sunny setting the relocated family are soon subjected to inexplicable knocking in the night, and various members of the household see shadowy figures: a ragged one-eyed woman, a small man with a red face, and a young woman with a scar on her neck. The servants believe that 'thieves had established a secret mode of access to the lower part of the house' (p. 421). But it becomes clear that their visitors are not of this world, and our narrator speculates that the trio are reliving their parts in a murderous drama – human teeth and a jawbone are found in the back garden. It turns out that the house is not so modern after all, but once formed part of a remote government store. Sharon Marcus has suggested that in an age in which the middle classes rented their homes, stories of haunted interiors encode anxieties about the divisions of public and private urban space, as well as concerns that the middle-class home could never be distinct enough from the crowded lodging houses of the poor.[22] But Le Fanu's stories, as we have seen, made public space just as haunted as the domestic interior. What we have here, I would suggest, is another series of ghosts that have been scared up by the spread of the new transport system, and its attendant reshaping of the built environment.

I want to turn briefly to some of the recurring images of the early railway the better to explore how exactly we might couple up ghosts and the transport revolution of the nineteenth century. In Dickens' *Dombey and Son* (1846–8), the railways are famously treated with some ambivalence: they appear at times monstrous, and are associated, at least in the mind of Mr Dombey, with death; but they also bring order, light and industry to the frowsy neighbourhood of Staggs's Gardens, and prosperity to the Toodles, and it is a train that Dickens uses finally to annihilate Mr Carker, the villain of the piece. At another imaginative level Dickens also presents the railway as a good spirit, an 'Asmodeus', who will lift the rooftops, and reveal the mysteries and miseries of urban life. The figure of Asmodeus is borrowed from Alain René Lesage's satirical novel *Le Diable boiteux* (1707), in which he is the demon who, released from a bottle, flies with his liberator, Don Cleophas, through the Madrid night to the top of the tower of San Salvador, and makes the rooftops disappear to show the people within. He then describes these citizens to Don Cleophas, including 'the hidden motives of their deeds ... [and] their unbidden thoughts', in order to unlock 'the secret chambers of the human heart'.[23] Lesage's book enjoyed great popularity, and his demon became a very portable resource for satirical writers in such publications as Charles Sedley's *Asmodeus; or, The Devil in London* (1808); Edward Bulwer Lytton's series 'Asmodeus at Large' in the *New Monthly Magazine* (1832); and the Liverpool *Mercury*'s 'The Magic Globe; or, the Bottle Imp' (1829).[24]

Dickens was not the first to equate the railway with the magical Asmodeus. Here is the *Dublin Penny Journal* on the opening of the Dublin and Kingstown Railway in December 1834:

> Hurried forward by the agency of steam, the astonished passenger glides, like Asmodeus, over the summits of the houses and trees of our city – presently is transported through green fields and tufts of trees, then skims along the surface of the sea, and taking shelter under the cliffs, coasts among the marine villas, and through rocky excavations until he finds himself in the centre of a vast port.[25]

In a considerably darker piece in the *Morning Chronicle*, the journey into London over the roof-tops of Bermondsey and Rotherhithe is described as a 'bird's-eye view ... of a mass of human struggle' in the closely packed tenements: 'Asmodeus himself, with all his burglarious tactics and invisible entries ... never collected domestic episodes half so full of emotion, so dramatic, so varied ... as here are mapped out in prodigal suggestiveness before the railway traveller.'[26] Dickens, then, is writing within a recognisable railway discourse as much as drawing on Lesage for his vision of social transformation (the flying spirit of Christmas Present, who in *A Christmas Carol* takes Scrooge on a tour of Christmas Eve festivities all over Britain in order to warm the locked chambers of his frozen heart, can be seen to be an earlier version of this same figure). A magic surveillance is opened up by the railway, one that conquers the opacity of the unknowable metropolis. A similar point-of-view fantasy is evident in some of Gustave Doré and Blanchard Jerrold's *London: A pilgrimage* (1872).

There are no flying demons in Le Fanu's stories, but at least some of his ghosts may derive from a similar source, the transformation of urban space by the cutting of straight lines right through the older bricks and mortar, the opening up of new vistas, and the destruction of some of the city's poorest quarters. The new lines allowed the traveller to 'glide over the summits of houses and trees' as the *Penny Journal* puts it, but they also at times threatened to destroy a stable environment, and to replace it with something new, and potentially frightening. What Dickens represents in terms of a magical panoramic and penetrative vision becomes something different in Le Fanu, in which that penetrative vision is reversed. Explicit or implicit allegory is transmuted into a more enigmatic supernatural: no allegorical reading of the stories adequately accounts for the affect they describe and evoke. But in particular the benign spirit of Asmodeus has been replaced by less well-disposed spirits. What we see is not the secret drama of metropolitan homes, but things that should perhaps remain unseen: a shrunken Watcher, an evil presence in 'An Account', the participants in a crime in 'An Authentic Narrative'. And these suddenly revealed entities look at us with a glance that is far from friendly.

PASSENGERS

While 'The Watcher' deals with a form of spectral surveillance that seems to be the opposite of the benignly progressive gaze associated with the railway, in 'Green Tea' Le Fanu deals with a different aspect of the transport revolution: other passengers.[27] The unfortunate victim of haunting in this case, the Reverend Jennings, has his first brush with his supernatural persecutor not in the *étui* of his comfortable bachelor home in London, where the story is set, but on an omnibus. While the story was written in the 1860s, it is set in the early 1800s, when such vehicles as omnibuses did not in fact exist, suggesting once again that for all their antiquarianism, it is the streets of his own time whose life informs Le Fanu's fiction.

It is worth considering the specific nature of the omnibus as setting, since by 1869 it was already a vehicle heavily freighted with social meaning. Omnibuses were large horse-drawn vehicles that from 1829 onwards contributed to the development of a commuter culture in London and other British and Irish cities, including Dublin (they are usually thought to have originated in Nantes in 1826).[28] The *Morning Chronicle* described the first London omnibus, which ran from Paddington to the City from 4 July 1829, as 'a handsome machine, in the shape of a van, with windows on each side, and one at the end', and capable of accommodating sixteen to eighteen passengers.[29] Edinburgh, Glasgow, Liverpool and Belfast followed suit. By the mid-1840s there were a number of 'bus' routes in Dublin, including services to Dundrum, Dollymount, Sandymount and Bray, despite opposition from operators of 'cars'.[30] (Enthusiasm for the system seems to have survived the check it received on 6 April 1861 when the 'Favourite' omnibus from Rathgar fell into the canal at Portobello, and six passengers were drowned.) From being a novelty enclosed in quotation marks, the omnibus journey soon became a familiar part of urban life, and likewise became available as a chronotope and symbol in popular and high culture alike. A comic play called *The Omnibus* was on the Sadler's Wells stage by the end of 1829 (this or a similar farce was a favourite afterpiece in 1844–5 at the Queen's Theatre, Dublin), and George Cruikshank borrowed the name for his comic illustrated magazine *Omnibus* (1841–2), and used the chronotope of the omnibus journey to structure the 'Omnibus Chat' sections. Music-hall songs described romantic omnibus encounters:

> I jumped into an omnibus
> That soon came passing by
> And sat opposite to a pretty girl
> Who giggled at me so sly.[31]

Novelists also realised the crowded omnibus' potential as a place in which random but fateful urban encounters could be staged. In Wilkie Collins' *Basil* (1852), the protagonist first sees the alluring Margaret Sherwin, source of his subsequent misfortunes, on a London omnibus; her momentary touch as he helps her in immediately stirs him deeply: 'I felt it thrilling through me – thrilling in every nerve, in every pulsation of my fast-throbbing heart.'[32] A random urban meeting on an omnibus journey produces a visceral response, that in turn starts the protagonist on his narrative journey.

Painters used the crowded omnibus to show the way in which the city quite literally throws people together, and in which we see and are seen at close quarters by strangers – William Maw Egley's *Omnibus Life in London* (1859) is a well-known early example; the Irish painter George William Joy's *Bayswater Omnibus* (1895) a late instance. Thomas Musgrave Joy's *The Charing Cross to Bank Omnibus* (*c.* 1861) shows a young woman carrying a terrier onto an already crowded omnibus, indicating that it was not just other humans who shared the cramped space.[33] An article in *Punch* ironically welcoming the new regulations of the London General Omnibus Company, which, *inter alia*, banned dogs, 'except small dogs carried in the hand, and then only with the consent of all passengers', suggests that the bringing aboard of pets had become a familiar nuisance – *Punch* mentions babies, band-boxes, crinolines and wet umbrellas as other sources of passenger misery.[34] Of course coach journeys had created such shared moving interiors too, but there was a quality of brevity, hurry and randomness to the omnibus journey that was quite different.

The world of commuting was scarcely unfamiliar to Le Fanu. As McCormack notes, between 1843 and 1850, when they settled in Merrion Square (in the house vacated by Le Fanu's father-in-law), Joseph, his wife Susanna and their growing family lived in the coastal towns of Bray, Malahide and Kingstown, from all of which he would presumably have taken a train or omnibus to the city to conduct his affairs as a newspaper editor and writer.[35] In 'Green Tea', he takes up the popular image of the omnibus as a site of difficult close encounters, but in his fictional treatment a fellow passenger turns out to be not only of another species, but not of this world at all. The scholarly Reverend Jennings, returning one evening from the house of a fellow bibliophile in the City of London to his house in Richmond, takes 'the omnibus which used to drive past this house' (p. 22) when he cannot find a cab. He initially believes himself to be the only passenger, but in the gloomy interior he makes out two reddish lights that he realises are the glowing eyes of a small black monkey. But this is no ordinary monkey:

> I fancied that one of the passengers had forgot this ugly pet, and wishing to ascertain something of its temper, though not caring

> to trust my fingers to it, I poked my umbrella softly towards it. It remained immovable – up to it – through it. For through it, and back and forward it passed, without the slightest resistance. (pp. 23–4)

Even a flesh-and-blood monkey might resent such treatment, but the spectral animal takes it very ill indeed, and subsequently becomes the clergyman's relentless persecutor, haunting him wherever he goes, growing increasingly malign, and squatting on Jennings' bible when he tries to read to his parishioners. Dr Martin Hesselius, the student of the paranormal upon whose papers the stories in *In a Glass Darkly* are supposed to be based, promises to help the afflicted clergyman, whose spectral persecution seems to be somehow linked to his interest in the paganism of the ancient world, which he terms a 'degrading fascination' (p. 21). Hesselius considers that too much study, and perhaps too much green tea, have opened Jennings' inner eye to allow him to see evil spirits.[36] However, the good doctor then absents himself when Jennings desperately wants him, and the distraught victim cuts his own throat.

Here again, then, we have the phantasmagoria not of the home, but of public space, in this case a specifically new kind of public space, the bus interior. As with Dickens' 'The Signalman', the supernatural takes up residence in the new circuits of transport, rather than in the temporally and geographically remote. Jennings does not so much appear here as a delusional, overworked scholar but rather as a nervous commuter for whom the silent gaze of others becomes a living hell. In *The Railway Journey*, Wolfgang Schivelbusch argued that railway travel trained people into a new way of being in the company of strangers, in which the conviviality of the coach journey turns into the polite silence of the railway carriage.[37] But at roughly the same time the commuters of the crowded omnibus also learned such skills, and were forced into the same silent intimacy as their steam-driven peers. 'Green Tea' suggests that such a retraining in being under the gaze of others came at a considerable psychic cost, and that this was a fraught period in the history of affect. We might see Jennings' story as the flip side of those fantasies of random intimate omnibus and railway encounters evident in popular songs of this period, and more rarely in painting, as in Abraham Solomon's *First Class – The Meeting ... 'And at first meeting loved'* (1854): where these suggest the potential pleasures of enforced random intimacy, Le Fanu renders that intimacy as nightmare.[38]

TERMINUS

Are the ghosts that haunt Le Fanu's work the half-glimpsed lives of others, fitfully visible from the railway carriage? Are they shadows of the past as it flares up before disappearing forever beneath the railway tracks? Or are the hostile revenants that populate the stories visitors from the hell that is other people in the modern city? The stories generate their sense of dislocation and unease without allowing us to answer such questions in any definitive way. It is worth noting that elsewhere Le Fanu seems equally pessimistic about transport. In *Uncle Silas*, Maud leaves Bartram Haugh for France. She arrives in London 'fatigued with the peculiar fatigue of railway travelling'; but after further journeys by train and by coach, she finds herself not in France, but once again at her uncle's house.[39] The protagonist of 'The Room in the Dragon Volant' travels by coach with a new friend, only to find himself paralysed, able to watch his fellow passenger, but powerless to move, 'a spirit in prison ... [in] dumb and unmoving agony', presaging the subsequent attempt to bury him alive.[40] In *Wylder's Hand*, Mark Wylder is about to marry his cousin, Dorcas Brandon of Brandon Hall, when he vanishes. Letters arrive from him from Boulogne, Marseilles, Frankfurt, Geneva and Venice to indicate his whereabouts, but he has been dead all along, and his body is ultimately found not far from Brandon Hall; the forged letters were sent by his killer.[41] There is a recurring sense that, however dangerous domestic space may be, the world of travel is just as deadly.

The 'Invisible Prince' of the doomed Ascendancy is, of course, a far more dramatic figure than Le Fanu the middle-class Irish Victorian commuter, uncomfortable with the railway mania that made his brother prosperous, and with the intimacy of his fellow passengers, perhaps more than a little sceptical of the vision of Victorian progress through technology. But the latter more prosaic figure is just as plausible, and, to me at least, just as interesting.

CHAPTER 4

'Very little to have been so long about': Pastoralism and William Morris in Yeats' *Poems, 1899–1905* and related writings

ALEX DAVIS

Like so many of Yeats' publishing ventures – up to and including the projected *Edition de Luxe* in the 1930s – the making of his *Poems, 1899–1905* was subject to the caprices of the book market; and the volume, as published in October 1906 by A.H. Bullen, was a product of compromise.[1] Although the title's span of years might suggest otherwise, the collection excludes poems from *The Wind Among the Reeds* (1899), as, despite Yeats' best efforts, that volume's publisher, Elkin Mathews, was understandably reluctant to relinquish rights on a book that, by 1903, had already gone into four English editions. Writing to Bullen on 22 June 1905, Yeats states that Mathews' 'assent' to 'the inclusion at once of "the Wind among the Reeds" in a book containing everything I have written in verse from 1895 to the present moment' is 'essential to my reputation just now'.[2] But, regardless of the dubious legality of his position, Mathews held firm. Thus, while Yeats managed successfully to negotiate the publication, in New York, of the revised contents of *Wind* – in volume 1 of *The Poetical Works of William B. Yeats* – by the Macmillan Company in November 1906, in Britain Yeats would have to wait until 1908 to see their appearance alongside his other work in *Poems Lyrical and Narrative*, the first volume of the sumptuous (and expensive) *The Collected Works in Verse and Prose of William Butler Yeats*.[3] Indeed, Yeats' (and Bullen's) original conception of *Poems, 1899–1905* – 'the first big mass of verse that I have published for years', as he hopefully described it to Lady Gregory on 30 May 1905 – might be said to have only been realised with the publication of *Poems: Second series* in March 1910, a comparably priced trade edition, in which *Wind* precedes the narrative and lyric poems originally collected in the Dun Emer Press' 1903 limited edition of *In the Seven Woods* (American edition: Macmillan Co., 1903).[4]

There is also something a trifle ad hoc about the cover to *Poems, 1899–1905*. On the volume's spine, Bullen and Yeats reused Althea Gyles' design – an enigmatic 'spear' – for the spine of *The Secret Rose* (1897), a cost-cutting measure which also has the marketable side-effect, as David Holdeman observes, of strongly connecting Yeats' new work to that which had established his reputation in the previous century.[5] (The same design is to be found on the spine of *Poems: Second series*.) The symbolism of this design has been variously interpreted; but in the context of *Poems, 1899–1905* (and *Poems: Second series*), it completely lacks the almost symbiotic relationship with the book's contents that exists between the bibliographical code of Gyles' entire cover design for *The Secret Rose* and the semantic code of passages to be found in the compositional history of that collection's final story 'Rosa Alchemica'.[6]

In the paratextual elements to *Poems, 1899–1905*, its preface and notes, Yeats chooses to emphasise a sense of his recent poems' falling short of the ideal that, as we have seen, marked the construction and production of the book itself. In the preface, Yeats laments that the volume's contents seem to him 'very little to have been so long about'; and employs an alchemical image to convey his sense of dissatisfaction: 'I am a little disappointed with the upshot of so many years, but I know that I have been busy with the Great Work, no lesser thing than that, although it may be that the Athanor has burned too fiercely, or too faintly and fitfully, or that the *prima materia* has been ill-chosen.'[7] Of the new, 1906 version of that most intractable text of his, *The Shadowy Waters*, he says that it is the work of which he is 'least confident'; while of the masterly revisions made to the play *On Baile's Strand* he flatly remarks, in a note, that 'It is now as right as I can make it'.[8]

Harold Bloom concurs with Yeats' expressions of dejection. The bulk of what he dubs 'Middle Yeats' is, in Bloom's opinion, 'indifferent work', written 'against the grain' of the poet's earlier visionary Romanticism, to which the poet would triumphantly return in *The Wild Swans at Coole* (1917 and 1919). Revealingly, Bloom considers the 1906 version of *The Shadowy Waters*, with which *Poems, 1899–1905* begins, inferior to its unfinished mid-1890s and first-published 1900 versions, tracing the alleged diminution in the dramatic poem's representation of Dectora to Yeats' changed relations with Maud Gonne in the wake of her marriage in 1903 – 'when the *epipsyche* suddenly became Madame MacBride', as Bloom memorably comments –

and her separation as Yeats revised the work in 1905.[9] The editors of the early manuscripts of *The Shadowy Waters*, who share Bloom's view of the superiority of the 1900 volume, summarise the 1906 text as 'concerned with the negative aspects of love, and the idealism of the earlier version is routed out to be replaced with a vein of cynicism'.[10] This is not wholly untrue; but it might be more accurate to see the 'cynicism' of the new version as gently ironising the work's *fin-de-siècle*, symbolist preoccupation – embodied in Forgael – with a supposedly self-transcending eros.[11]

In this respect, the aestheticism of *The Shadowy Waters* fills the gap in *Poems, 1899–1905*, left by the omission of *The Wind Among the Reeds*, the capstone to Yeats' late nineteenth-century symbolism. The dramatic poem balances the rewritten version of the play *On Baile's Strand* (which follows it), an earlier and weaker text of which had concluded the 1903 Dun Emer Press edition of *In the Seven Woods*. In its new form, Cuchulain's bruising engagement with the *realpolitik* of Conchubar contrasts sharply with Forgael's 'idealism', and provides a pertinent prelude to the poems from *In the Seven Woods* and the play *The King's Threshold* that succeed it.

The opening and title poem of *In the Seven Woods* shares its idyllic setting with the introductory rhymes to *The Shadowy Waters* ('*I walked among the seven woods of Coole*'). Preceded in the context of *Poems, 1899–1905* by the revised *On Baile's Strand*, however, the topicality of references at the very centre of 'In the Seven Woods' is enhanced by the play's new-found political astringency:

> I have heard the pigeons of the Seven Woods
> Make their faint thunder, and the garden bees
> Hum in their lime tree flowers; and put away
> The unavailing outcries and the old bitterness
> That empty the heart. I have forgot awhile
> Tara uprooted, and new commonness
> Upon the throne and crying about the streets
> And hanging its paper flowers from post to post,
> Because it is alone of all things happy.
> I am contented for I know that Quiet
> Wanders laughing and eating her wild heart
> Among pigeons and bees ...[12]

The poem's reference to 'Tara uprooted' alludes to controversial excavations at the Hill of Tara, originally instigated in 1899 by 'British-Israelites' Charles

Groom and Walton Adams, who believed that the Ark of the Covenant was buried at the site. Work had recommenced the year of Yeats' writing the poem: according to an angry editorial in the *United Irishman* (5 July 1902), 'the retired English pork butcher Groome', and others 'associated with the vandalism', now intending to present the Ark to the recently crowned Edward VII.[13]

Yeats introduces these topical issues by means of a masterly paralepsis (his claim, 'I have forgot …', is succeeded immediately by the mentioning of what is supposedly forgotten), the oratorical power of which is indicative of the new 'note of dramatic intensity' Terence Brown hears in *In the Seven Woods*: 'the poems of a man who has been listening to the voices of actors and performers on stage'.[14] But the rhetorical figure is part of a larger movement in the poem's opening twelve lines, well described by Helen Vendler as 'an evolving parabola from pigeons and bees to pigeons and bees … interrupted in the middle by a bitter contrasting glance … enclosed … within the two pastoral hums'.[15] To which I would simply add that the disenchanted 'glance' towards the desecration at Tara, and the 'commonness' associated with the coronation, might be read as central to its pastoralism, rather than an interruption of it. After all, the poem's 'pastoral hum' of 'pigeons and bees' recalls that heard in Virgil's first *Eclogue*, in the description of Tityrus' homestead by fellow-herdsman Meliboeus. Davidson's much-reprinted prose translation, which Yeats possessed in a late nineteenth-century revision, renders the relevant lines thus:

> On this side, a hedge planted at the adjoining boundary, whose willow blossoms are ever fed on by Hyblaean bees, shall often court you by its gentle hummings to indulge repose. On the other side, the pruner beneath a lofty rock shall sing to the breezes: nor meanwhile shall either the hoarse wood-pigeons, thy delight, or the turtle from his lofty elm, cease to coo.[16]

The 'Virgilian hinterland' (in Warwick Gould's phrase) of 'In the Seven Woods' is more explicitly evident in Yeats' introduction to his selection *Poems of Spenser* (1906), on which he was working throughout 1902 ('In the Seven Woods' is date-lined 'August, 1902').[17] There, Yeats says of Spenser's north Cork environs: 'All about him were shepherds and shepherdesses still living the life that made Theocritus and Virgil think of shepherd and poet as one thing.'[18] However, Yeats adds, 'though he dreamed of Virgil's shepherds', the English poet 'saw nothing but disorder': the native Irish disorder anatomised in *A View of the Present State of*

Ireland. From within the pastoral enclave of Coole Park, Yeats sees disorder in the present state of Ireland too, but of British origin – the English or 'Anglo-Israelite' vandalism at Tara and the tawdry celebrations in Dublin of Edward VII's coronation. Yet, the paralepsis that introduces these discordant elements into the poem is not a departure from pastoralism but one of its complementary poles. The Dublin of 'In the Seven Woods' is the 'ungrateful city' (*Eclogue* 1.34) of Virgilian pastoral. In Virgil's first *Eclogue* the herdsmen's Arcadia has been thrown into disorder owing to urban political machinations, the land confiscations reflecting those made to further the settlement of veterans in the aftermath of the battle of Philippi. By means of the self-cancelling rhetorical gambit of 'I have forgot awhile ...', 'In the Seven Woods' follows Virgilian precedent in juxtaposing the city and its urban mores with an Arcadian ease or *otium* threatened, like Tara, with being 'uprooted' by the 'bitterness' prompted by contemporary historical (and personal) events.

'In the Seven Woods' concludes with, in Vendler's words, 'a disturbing sonnet-close, in which an apocalyptic personage supervenes upon pastoral allegory':[19]

> I am contented for I know that Quiet
> Wanders laughing and eating her wild heart
> Among pigeons and bees, while that Great Archer,
> Who but awaits His hour to shoot, still hangs
> A cloudy quiver over Parc-na-lee.

Yeats' 'Great Archer' remains a shadowy figure. 'Sometimes glossed as a vision of Sagittarius', as Jonathan Allison summarises, 'and a portent of change or justice', he 'is a transcendent image of justice and a terrible spirit of the place'.[20] For David Holdeman, the 'Great Archer' 'symbolize[s] an indefinite apocalyptic hope', but he also has 'occult significance', drawing on the vision of a centaur and female archer Yeats experienced while staying at Tillyra Castle on 14–15 August 1896, an invocation to which the poet would return repeatedly over the next quarter of a century.[21] Other archers suggest themselves too.

One such is the figure who uneasily enters the pastoral world in the tenth, concluding poem to the *Eclogues*: the elegiac love poet Gallus, for whom the attractions of Arcadia finally cannot quell his unhappy longing for his mistress: 'Now over rocks and resounding groves methinks I roam: pleased I am to shoot Cydonian shafts from the Parthian bow: [Fool that I am!] as if these were a cure for the rage of love.'[22] Yet Virgil's Gallus seems an all-too-humanised figure to stand in the hinterland of Yeats' symbolic 'Archer'. Furthermore, the Roman elegist's hopeless desire for the unfaithful Lycoris is a despair rejected by the persona of Yeats' poem, in his claim to have 'put away / The unavailing outcries ... / That empty the heart', even if one feels that, in its strenuous denial, such emotiveness remains very much in the penumbra of his words. (Several months later Yeats would play the full Gallus to Gonne's Lycoris – metaphorically 'following another through snows and horrid camps' – when her intention of marrying John MacBride cruelly dawned on him in early February 1903.)[23] But another 'Great Archer' had been in Yeats' mind in the latter part of 1901, during the composition of his essay on William Morris, 'The Happiest of the Poets': the enigmatic warrior Steelhead, a central character in the English author's final prose romance, *The Sundering Flood* (published posthumously in 1897).[24] This is one of the texts in which Morris influentially reconfigures traditional pastoral as modern fantasy fiction, paving the way for the work of, among others, C.S. Lewis and J.R.R. Tolkien.

Steelhead's superhuman archery is adduced in the course of Yeats' answer to the question as to why exactly Morris is the happiest of the poets. Yeats' essay distinguishes Morris' 'genius' from that of Dante Gabriel Rossetti, which, he argues, 'like [P.B.] Shelley's can hardly stir but to the rejection of nature, whose delight is profusion, but never intensity. ... Men like him cannot be happy as we understand happiness, for to be happy one must delight like nature in mere profusion, in mere abundance'.[25] Yeats' essay identifies Morris' 'delight' in gratuity in a number of symbols scattered across his oeuvre, including Steelhead's 'miraculous' bow and arrows:

> I do not think it was accident, so subtle are the threads that lead the soul, that made William Morris, who seems to me the one perfectly happy and fortunate poet of modern times, celebrate the Green Tree and the goddess Habundia [in Morris' *The Water of the Wondrous Isles*], and wells and enchanted waters in so many books. ... To him indeed as to older writers Well and Tree are all but images of the one thing, of an 'energy' that is not the less 'eternal delight' because it is half of the body. He never wrote, and could not have written, of a man or woman who was not of the kin of Well or Tree. Long before he had named either he had made his 'Wanderers' [in *The Earthly Paradise*] follow a dream indeed, but a dream of natural happiness, and all the people of all his poems and stories from the confused beginning of

> his art in *The Hollow Land* to its end in *The Sundering Flood*, are full of the heavy sweetness of this dream. ... We know so little of man and of the world that we cannot be certain that the same invisible hands, that gave him an imagination preoccupied with good fortune, gave him also health and wealth, and the power to create beautiful things without labour, that he might honour the Green Tree. It pleases me to imagine the copper mine which brought, as Mr Mackail has told, so much unforeseen wealth and in so astonishing a way, as no less miraculous than the three arrows in *The Sundering Flood*.[26]

In *The Sundering Flood* the two central protagonists, the lovers Osberne of Wethermel and Elfhild, are geographically and emotionally separated by a mighty river, the Sundering Flood of the title. Early in the sprawling and unrevised narrative, the thirteen-year-old Osberne encounters, while shepherding, Steelhead, who gives him an extraordinary bow and three arrows:

> Then the man betook him the bow which he had in his hand and said: 'Here is one that shall make thee deft; for whoso hath this [i.e. the bow] as a gift from me shall hit what he shooteth at if he use my shafts withal, and here be three which I will give thee; and if thou take heed, thou shalt not find them easy to lose, since ever they shall go home. But if ever thou lose two of them, then take the third and go into some waste place where there is neither meadow nor acre, and turn to the north-east and shoot upward toward the heavens, and say this rhyme:
>
> A shaft to the north,
> Come ye three, come ye forth;
> A shaft to the east,
> Come three at the least;
> A shaft to the sky,
> Come swift, come anigh!
> Come one, one and one,
> And the tale is all done.
>
> And then shalt thou find the arrows lying at thy feet.[27]

Steelhead's rhyme encapsulates the providential nature of Morris' romance. Like Steelhead's arrows, Osberne and Elfhild are sent hither and thither by the vagaries of circumstance; yet, by the time 'the tale is done', the sundering flood dividing the lovers has been surmounted, albeit through a process of arduous maturation. Steelhead's arrows, and the overcoming of an amatory gulf their flight symbolises, are very different to Yeats' 'The Arrow', from *In the Seven Woods*:

> I thought of your beauty, and this arrow,
> Made out of a wild thought, is in my marrow.
> There's no man may look upon her, no man;
> As when newly grown to be a woman,
> Blossom pale, she pulled down the pale blossom
> At the moth hour and hid it in her bosom.
> This beauty's kinder, yet for a reason
> I could weep that the old is out of season.[28]

The 'Great Archer' of 'In the Seven Woods' keeps his shot in abeyance. He '*awaits* His hour to shoot': a state of readiness reinforced, firstly, by the pun in '*still* hangs'; and, secondly, in a poem dominated by enjambment, by the momentary uncertainty as to whether to read the verb at the very end of the penultimate line, 'hangs', as intransitive (the archer *hangs still*) or transitive – an ambiguity resolved in the latter's favour by the run-over line: 'still hangs / A cloudy quiver'.

In 'The Arrow' the bolt has been loosed and lodged in the speaker's innermost being. In *The Poetical Works of William B. Yeats* and *Poems Lyrical and Narrative* (volume 1 of the 1908 *The Collected Works in Verse and Prose of William Butler Yeats*) Yeats makes clearer the relationship between 'In the Seven Woods' and 'The Arrow' by moving the two narrative poems, 'The Old Age of Queen Maeve' and 'Baile and Aillinn' – which in the Dun Emer edition and *Poems, 1899–1905* intervene between the two lyrics – to a position after and before the *In the Seven Woods* grouping, respectively. The rearrangement not only foregrounds the related archery imagery between the two lyric poems but also draws attention to their different verse-forms: the heavily enjambed, blank verse of 'In the Seven Woods' cheek-by-jowl with the largely end-stopped rhyming couplets of 'The Arrow'.[29] As a consequence, one is made conscious of the close relationship between the two poems and their sunderingly sharp and painful difference: the vague apocalyptic hope of 'In the Seven Woods' has yielded nothing but dissatisfaction. Maturation in 'The Arrow' is not Morris' optimistic teleology (a constant in his late prose romances), but a loss – of 'the old' beauty, the disappearance of which finds meagre compensation in the 'kinder' beauty found in its stead.

The re-ordering of the poems in *The Poetical Works* and *Poems Lyrical and Narrative* also creates a poetic triptych of sorts: the blank-verse sonnet 'In the Seven Woods' is now balanced by another sonnet, in rhyming couplets, 'The Folly of Being Comforted' (which succeeds 'The Arrow' in the Dun Emer *In the Seven Woods* and thereafter), the sonnets framing the octastich 'The Arrow':

> One that is ever kind said yesterday:
> 'Your well beloved's hair has threads of grey,
> And little shadows come about her eyes;
> Time can but make it easier to be wise,
> Though now it's hard, till trouble is at an end;
> And so be patient, be wise and patient, friend.'
> But heart, there is no comfort, not a grain;
> Time can but make her beauty over again,
> Because of that great nobleness of hers;
> The fire that stirs about her, when she stirs
> Burns but more clearly. O she had not these ways,
> When all the wild summer was in her gaze.
> O heart! O heart! if she'd but turn her head,
> You'd know the folly of being comforted.[30]

The formal interrelationship between the three poems is intriguing. While the sonnets comprise an obvious pairing, the couplets of 'The Folly of Being Comforted' replicate those of 'The Arrow' – but not wholly, their admixture of heavily end-stopped and run-over lines connects the poem's movement to that of *both* of the preceding poems.

The resulting heightened prosodic interplay of 'The Folly of Being Comforted' with its immediate precursors, in collections subsequent to the arrangement of *Poems, 1899–1905*, reinforces its interlacing of certain thematics present in the previous two poems. Like 'The Arrow', 'The Folly of Being Comforted' is a poem fully cognisant of the beloved woman's having aged; yet, the assertion that 'Time *can but* make her beauty over again' is a forecast the confidence of which matches that of the speaker's prophetic words at the close of 'In the Seven Woods': 'that Great Archer, / Who *but* awaits His hour to shoot'. However, whereas such foreknowledge brings some form of unspecified 'content[ment]' to the speaker of 'In the Seven Woods', to the persona of 'The Folly of Being Comforted' it brings 'no comfort, not a grain'. With Gonne's marriage to MacBride, such discomfort would change to distress: a transformation first registered in *Poems, 1899–1905* by the inclusion after 'The Folly of Being Comforted' of 'Old Memory' and 'Never Give all the Heart', the second of which announces that the 'heart' apostrophised in the earlier lyric is now seemingly irretrievably lost.

To what extent Morris' 'miraculous' arrows (or, for that matter, Virgil's *Eclogues*) are part of the inspiration for 'In the Seven Woods' and 'The Arrow' – in their 'quiver', so to speak – is impossible to determine, although one cannot stress too much the extent to which Yeats' admiration for Morris' late romances is attested to by not only 'The Happiest of the Poets' but also his autobiographical writings, and the numerous mentions of Morris in his critical output at the turn of the century.[31] Certainly, Morris' example as a *bookmaker* was very much in Yeats' mind during the composition of *In the Seven Woods*. The first edition of the collection was the first publication of Dun Emer Press, founded in 1902 by Yeats' sister, Elizabeth Corbet ('Lolly') Yeats, with her brother's help, which drew upon the expertise of Emery Walker, 'who had been William Morris' close friend, [and] had aided in both the design and production of books printed at [Morris'] Kelmscott Press (founded in 1891)'.[32] David Holdeman goes so far as to argue that Morris' influence extends from material correspondences between the production of *In the Seven Woods* and the book-making at Kelmscott Press to thematic parallels between Yeats' collection and Morris' work: 'The narrative and lyric section of the volume concludes … with a populist apocalypse that celebrates a "happy townland" in terms recalling "The Happiest of the Poets"'.[33]

There's many a strong farmer
Who's [*sic*] heart would break in two
If he could see the townland
That we are riding to;
Boughs have their fruit and blossom,
At all times of the year,
Rivers are running over
With red beer and brown beer.

* * *

Michael will unhook his trumpet
From a bough overhead,
And blow a little noise

When the supper has been spread.
Gabriel will come from the water
With a fishtail, and talk
Of wonders that have happened
On wet roads where men walk,
And lift up an old horn
Of hammered silver, and drink
Till he has fallen asleep
Upon the starry brink.[34]

Following Holdeman's lead, the 'new commonness' – that 'is alone of all things happy' – in the opening title poem to *In the Seven Woods* secedes, over the course of the 1903 collection, to the happy prospect of a Morrisian democratic utopia. This interpretation approximately aligns the politics of *In the Seven Woods* with those of *The Sundering Flood*, the double-plot of which is not wholly dissimilar to that of Nora Ephron's heart-warming 1998 romcom *You've Got Mail*: Osberne not only wins his beloved but also successfully fights on behalf of a revolution of the 'Small Crafts' or artisanal workers (like those at Dun Emer industries) against a despotic king and the exploitative merchants of the 'tyrannous Porte',[35] Morris' merchants driven by precisely the kind of 'money interests' Yeats berates in a letter to the *Freeman's Journal* of 9 April 1903 in the course of protesting a royal visit to Ireland by Edward VII.[36]

If Morris' heroic-age romances, including *The Sundering Flood*, provide – in the words of 'Adam's Curse' from *In the Seven Woods* – 'Precedents out of beautiful [albeit *faux*] old books', then the same might be said of the two narrative poems first collected in the beautifully produced Dun Emer edition of *In the Seven Woods: Being poems chiefly of the Irish heroic age*: 'The Old Age of Queen Maeve' and 'Baile and Aillinn'.[37] The structure and music of 'Baile and Aillinn' asks to be read as, in part, a response to Yeats' muted praise for Morris' long narrative poem *The Earthly Paradise* (1868–70). In his introduction to *The Poems of Spenser* (written after Yeats had begun 'Baile and Aillinn'), Yeats writes apropos of Morris' poem: 'One finds a music smooth and unexacting like that of the old story-tellers, but not their energetic pleasure, their rhythmical wills. One too often misses in his *Earthly Paradise* the minute ecstasy of modern song without finding that old happy-go-lucky tune that kept the story marching.'[38] Yeats here might be said to be unjust to Morris: *The Earthly Paradise* is very carefully refracted through 'modern song'. In the words of Florence S. Boos:

> *The Earthly Paradise*'s narrative personae are a lyric 'outer' poet ('singer') and two sets of 'inner' storytellers, twelve 'Wanderers' and twelve 'Elders'. The poem is first introduced by the ironically self-identified 'idle singer', who recites the 'Apology', 'Epilogue', and lyrics of the outer frame. The twelve Wanderers then appear in the 'Prologue', and try to describe the gradually emerging insights of their flight from the Black Death. The larger chorus of twenty-four assembled Elders and Wanderers, finally, attempt to evaluate their lives and prepare for death as they respond to each others' tales.[39]

On a far less ambitious scale, Yeats' tale of the Irish heroic age is, like Morris' medieval narrative, filtered through a modern lyric sensibility:

> *We hold because our memory is*
> *So full of that thing and of this*
> *That out of sight is out of mind.*
> *But the grey rush under the wind*
> *And the grey bird with the crooked bill*
> *Have such long memories, that they still*
> *Remember Deirdre and her man;*
> *And when we walk with Kate or Nan*
> *About the windy water side,*
> *Our heart can hear the voices chide.*[40]

'The Old Age of Queen Maeve' also deploys this Morrisian blend of heroic past and contemporary relevance. Positioned in *Poems, 1899–1905* (as in the Dun Emer edition) immediately following 'In the Seven Woods', the narrative poem obliquely refers back to 'Tara uprooted' in the title poem, to those Anglo-Israelite workings to which Yeats and others had so strongly objected, in its description of the destruction of another sacred Irish hill-site, but here it is an excavation with strangely beneficial results. The god Aengus bids Maeve to awaken 'The children of the Maines … / And set them digging into Anbual's hill': 'while they uproot his earthly house', Aengus intends to take possession of 'Caer, his blue eyed daughter':

> And all that night, and all through the next day
> To middle night, they dug into the hill.
> At middle night great cats with silver claws,
> Bodies of shadow and blind eyes like pearls,

Came up out of the hole, and red-eared hounds
With long white bodies came out of the air
Suddenly, and ran at them and harried them.

The Maines' children dropped their spades, and stood
With quaking joints and terror-strucken [*sic*] faces,
Till Maeve called out: 'These are but common men.
The Maines' children have not dropped their spades
Because Earth, crazy for its broken power,
Casts up a show and the winds answer it
With holy shadows.' Her high heart was glad,
And when the uproar ran along the grass
She followed with light footfall in the midst,
Till it died out where an old thorn tree stood.[41]

Maeve's triumphalism encodes Maud Gonne's involvement in the *United Irishman*'s outraged response to events at Tara, having inspected, with Arthur Griffith, the site of the excavations on Christmas Day 1900.[42] Gonne's engagement in these events is implied in 'The Old Age of Queen Maeve' by the comparison the poem draws between her and Queen Maeve's disparaging reaction to the 'common men' (the adjective recalling loyalist Dublin's 'new commonness' in 'In the Seven Woods'):

Friend of these many years, you too had stood
With equal courage in that whirling rout;
For you, although you've not her wandering heart
Have all that greatness, and not hers alone.[43]

By the time Yeats had completed these two mid-length heroic poems, and during the composition of 'The Rider from the North' / 'The Happy Townland', he was coming under the spell of Nietzsche (from the autumn of 1902).[44] The 'strong enchanter' was not incompatible with Morris, as Yeats points out in a letter to John Quinn of 6 February 1903.[45] (Yeats was not alone in admiring both writers: Morrisite domestications of Nietzsche can be found, for instance, in the pages of A.R. Orage's *The New Age* – much to its editor's chagrin.)[46] Still, it is revealing that the Morrisian 'populist apocalypse' of 'The Happy Townland' has a somewhat unreal air. As the pragmatic 'little fox', the rider's companion, asks – and he is given the last words in the poem – '"O what of the world's bane?"':

> The sun was laughing sweetly,
> The moon plucked at my rein;
> But the little red fox murmured,
> 'O do not pluck at his rein,
> He is riding to the townland,
> That is the world's bane.'[47]

The little fox's scepticism is not unrelated to Yeats' tartly hard-headed comment, in 'The Happiest of the Poets', that what is singularly lacking in Morris' moral and poetic vision is the 'bane' of labour, a lacuna seen as the inevitable corollary of the Victorian socialist's considerable private income:

> We know so little of man and of the world that we cannot be certain that the same invisible hands, that gave him an imagination preoccupied with good fortune, gave him also health and wealth, and the power to create beautiful things *without labour*, that he might honour the Green Tree. It pleases me to imagine the copper mine which brought, as Mr Mackail has told, so much unforeseen wealth and in so astonishing a way, as no less miraculous than the three arrows in *The Sundering Flood*.[48]

Morris, of course, in a work like *News from Nowhere*, argues strongly for the recognition of the *dignity* of labour. In Yeats' essay, however, this fact is occluded by means of the comparison between Steelhead's gift of the three 'miraculous' arrows and Morris' dividends from the 'copper mine', the Devon Great Consuls, to which J.W. Mackail refers in his *Life of William Morris* (1899).[49] 'Adam's Curse' may constitute a riposte to this dimension of Morris, as construed by Yeats, in its contemplation of the requisite laboriousness of beauty, poetic and otherwise: 'a line will take us hours maybe; / Yet if it does not seem a moment's thought, / Our stitching and unstitching has been naught'.[50] By way of contrast, Yeats' essay on Morris charges the English writer, however unfairly, with prelapsarian idleness, albeit of a highly productive kind: 'His poetry often wearies us as the unbroken green of July wearies us, for there is something in us, some bitterness because of the Fall it may be, that takes a little from the sweetness of Eve's apple after the first mouthful; but he who did all things gladly and easily, who never knew the curse of labour, found it always as sweet as it was in Eve's mouth.'[51] Yeats' qualified yet intense response to Morris in the first decade of the twentieth century is arguably signalled in *Poems, 1899–1905* by the placing as the volume's concluding work a revised version of his play *The King's Threshold*. This revision still has the happy ending of the original 1904 version, in which Seanchan, the hunger-striking poet, triumphs over the obdurate king. (In *Seven Poems and a Fragment* (1922) and *Plays in Prose and Verse* (1922), Seanchan dies, the new ending influenced – it would seem – by the death of Terence MacSwiney in 1920.)[52] Seanchan's heroic near self-sacrifice dramatises, through his abjuration of bodily sustenance, a poetic asceticism quite opposed to the engorged sensibility of Morris as depicted in 'The Happiest of the Poets'. His fasting, likewise, is linked directly to the aesthetic labour extolled in 'Adam's Curse', that which, in Yeats' eyes, is absent from those romances of Morris he so enjoyed: 'I am labouring', says Seanchan, 'that they may have voices, / Even in anger, like the strings of harps'.[53] This is the voice of Yeats in the new century, the creation of which he had been 'so long about'.

CHAPTER 5

Fianaise Lom / Bare Witness: Surrealism and life writing in the work of Celia de Fréine

MÁIRÍN NIC EOIN

> A person who has truly decided to take the uncertain path of art, who has sailed on the translucent, airy currents of language or followed Orpheus into the underworld, does not deliberate about large and small languages, they just take hold of a subject, a story or a poem, and work with the matter in the language and life that they have at hand, in their head and in their heart.[1]

Celia de Fréine's first collection of Irish-language poems bears the title *Faoi Chabáistí is Ríonacha* [Of Cabbages and Queens] (2001),[2] thus drawing on and feminising the surreal imagery of Lewis Carroll's 'The Walrus and the Carpenter' from *Through the Looking-Glass* (1871), where 'cabbages and kings' are among the many things that attract the interest of the curious Walrus:

> 'The time has come,' the Walrus said,
> 'To talk of many things:
> Of shoes – and ships – and sealing-wax –
> Of cabbages – and kings –
> And why the sea is boiling hot –
> And whether pigs have wings.'[3]

In paying homage thus to the author of *Alice in Wonderland* and *Through the Looking-Glass*, de Fréine is setting the tone for a collection where the subject matter is as diverse and unpredictable as that envisaged by Carroll's Walrus. Twenty-three of the poems in this collection were published in English translation, along with forty-two English-language poems, in the collection *Scarecrows at Newtownards* (2005), a book similar in style and subject matter to *Faoi Chabáistí is Ríonacha*.[4] In these collections fragmented narratives are related and partial truths revealed in a voice that is assured and self-consciously that of a woman. De Fréine's second collection, *Fiacha Fola* (2004), published in English translation ten years later as *Blood Debts* (2014), is her most overtly political collection, in that it gives expression to the pain and outrage experienced by Irish women as a result of the Hepatitis C scandal, as it unfolded in the 1990s and early 2000s.[5] She resumes a more meditative style in the dual-language collections *imram / odyssey* (2010) and *Aibítir Aoise / Alphabet of an Age* (2011).[6] This essay will examine the manner in which de Fréine's poetry moves between the personal and political, from the stark dramatisations in the 2001 and 2005 collections to the journeys and in-between states explored in the later dual-language collections. Instead of adopting a straightforward chronological approach, the essay will commence with a discussion of *Faoi Chabáistí is Ríonacha* and *Scarecrows at Newtownards*, followed by a consideration of *imram / odyssey* and *Aibítir Aoise / Alphabet of an Age*, and then return to the narrative poem sequence *Fiacha Fola / Blood Debts*. Following this order will facilitate a discussion of de Fréine's surrealism, and especially her ability to communicate powerful physical and emotional experiences, and their associated ethical and political concerns, through an arresting central image or cluster of images. The focus of the essay, however, will be the manner in which de Fréine harnessed this surrealist aesthetic to produce a narrative poem sequence that is one of the most remarkable examples of life writing to be published in Ireland in the last twenty years. I offer this exploration of the work of one bilingual contemporary Irish woman writer as a token of gratitude to Patricia Coughlan as a critic who has made ground-breaking contributions to feminist criticism in Irish, ranging from a radical re-reading of the autobiographical writings associated with Peig Sayers to exemplary close readings of poems by Máire Mhac an tSaoi.[7] Patricia Coughlan's ability to 'take hold of a subject, a story or a poem' and to combine incisive textual analysis with rigorous political and sociocultural critique have been an inspiration to me and to many others working in the field of Irish literary studies. I cannot hope to emulate her approach or style in this essay, but I do aim to draw attention to a body of work deserving of the kind of critical attention Patricia Coughlan has given to modern and contemporary Irish women's writing.

SURREALISM AND LIFE'S EXIGENCIES

Most of the poems in the collections *Faoi Chabáistí is Ríonacha* and *Scarecrows at Newtownards* take the form of short dramatic sequences with strong pictorial elements. Powerful images are employed and events, both ordinary and extraordinary, are recounted in language that is as clear as the language of children's stories. It is the contrast between the well-crafted lines and the violence of the message that they portray that creates a sense of mystery and urgency in many of the poems, however. Violence is presented as a natural human impulse in the poem '*Ocras*' / 'Hunger' (*Faoi Chabáistí is Ríonacha*, p. 13; *Scarecrows at Newtownards*, p. 55), for example, where sexual exploitation in wartime is presented as an ordinary domestic occurrence. Many of the poems deal with the contingency and uncertainty of human life, particularly during periods of conflict. If a choice has to be made, whose life is deemed more valuable, that of a poet or that of a mother ('*Bhí Cogadh ar Siúl*' / 'There Was a War On', *Faoi Chabáistí is Ríonacha*, p. 43; *Scarecrows at Newtownards*, p. 68)? War is a persistent theme, and the soldier a recurring image, though, as Luz Mar González-Arias explains, de Fréine's texts dealing with war 'are deprived of any clearly identifiable context. Instead, her soldiers belong to a perception of warfare as timeless, and contribute to international debates on the trials of militarised masculinity beyond the national frontiers of Irish history.'[8] Thus, when the poem '*Fear sa Teach*' / 'A Man about the House' (*Faoi Chabáistí is Ríonacha*, p. 45; *Scarecrows at Newtownards*, p. 69) poses the question of whether the man who returns from the war is the same man who set out in the first instance, the question remains open-ended and the dilemma it poses unresolved. Through sparse imagery and dramatic suggestion, poems such as 'There Was a Soldier' dramatise the encounter of a uniformed soldier with his lover who imagines herself looking:

> … over his shoulder
> to where his uniform wavered on the wardrobe
> door and watched, as the man he was, struggled
> against the shape of the man he would become,
> just as the limbs of the condemned
> convulse when the hangman tightens the noose.
>
> (*Scarecrows at Newtownards*, p. 33)

A sense of the Gothic pervades poems like '*Cóisir Bhainise*' ['Wedding Feast'] (*Faoi Chabáistí is Ríonacha*, pp. 32–3), where a wedding feast is seen as an occasion of unease and uncertainty, and '*Theastaigh Griangbraf Bainise Uaithi*' / 'She Wanted a Wedding Photograph' (*Faoi Chabáistí is Ríonacha*, p. 79; *Scarecrows at Newtownards*, p. 76), where a woman prepares a lifeless uniformed man for the camera. In 'Tenders of His Affection', Shakespeare's Ophelia ponders on the behaviour of her distraught lover Hamlet, imagining in the process the scene of her own death (*Scarecrows at Newtownards*, p. 34). Human conduct is viewed as a performance, as in the poem '*Ag Gluaiseacht leis an gCeol*' ['Moving to the Music'] where a couple are seen stretched out on stage props '*ag bualadh craicinn le Beethoven a Naoi*' ['having sex to Beethoven's Ninth'] (*Faoi Chabáistí is Ríonacha*, p. 34), or a game, as in the poem '*Cluiche, Cor agus Comórtas*' ['Game, Set and Match'] (*Faoi Chabáistí is Ríonacha*, p. 59), where a personal relationship is likened to a tennis match.

In a manner reminiscent of folk tales, or certain kinds of science fiction, descriptions of events tend to be concrete and objective, eschewing the autobiographical or confessional. Despite the emphasis on action and performance, human beings are represented as having limited power and agency. Dreams of flight and suicidal imaginings are conflated in '*Stórtha Arda*' / 'Tall Storeys' (*Faoi Chabáistí is Ríonacha*, p. 15; *Scarecrows at Newtownards*, p. 57) and '*Ar Mhuin an Albatrais*' ['On the Back of the Albatross'] (*Faoi Chabáistí is Ríonacha*, p. 26), where images of dramatic escape reflect an underlying sense of despair and lack of autonomy. Similarly, the poem '*Cúraimí*' ['Responsibilities'] captures an image of an individual suspended between the desire and the ability to transcend the circumstances of her existence. Typical of de Fréine's conflation of the ideal with the actual in her depiction of women's social roles, the ethic of care expounded in the poem associates motherly love with institutional cleaning duties:

> Ba bhreá liom fanacht ar foluain anseo
> cac an domhain thíos fúm
>
> ach bheadh na gasúir ag éirí uaigneach,
> agus cé a ghlanfadh na téada damháin alla
> de shíleáil an tséipéil?
>
> (*Faoi Chabáistí is Ríonacha*, p. 39)
>
> [I would love to stay suspended here
> the world's shit below me

but the children would be lonesome
and who would wipe the spider webs
from the church ceiling?]

One of the most striking aspects of Celia de Fréine's poetry is the compact nature of so many of the texts, making it difficult to extract excerpts that might give a sense of the work in its entirety. Many of them rely on a subtle irony with each well-crafted line and word having a distinct role to play. Though references to particular social or political contexts are avoided, thus allowing readers to interpret them in different ways, certain poems do bear overt political messages. '*Nuacht*' ['News'] is an example of a political poem which is unequivocal in its exposition of the role of news media in reporting the horrors of war, yet the subtle irony of the final stanza is typical of de Fréine's approach to questions of social responsibility:

Ní scannán é seo.
Ní éifeachtaí speisialta iad
na lasracha,
ná tinte ealaíne ach oiread.

Gasúir a itheann blúirín suipéir anois –
níos deireanaí beidh orthu
dul faoi obráid
gan ainéistéiseach.

Beidh cuid acu siúd atá ciontach
básaithe – a mná á gcaoineadh
i ngrianghraif
a ghnóthóidh gradaim.

(*Faoi Chabáistí is Ríonacha*, p. 75)

[This is not a film.
The flames are
neither special effects,
nor fireworks.

Children eating a meagre supper now
will later have to be
operated on
without anaesthetic.

Some of those responsible will be
dead – their wives lamenting them
in photographs
that will win awards.]

It is the combination of emotional realism and pictorial surrealism that makes certain poems particularly powerful. The poem '*Picnic i Reilig sa Bhílearúis*' / 'Picnic in a Cemetery in Belarus', for example, presents the relationship between food and death through simple juxtapositions, both in the title and in the evocative image of a mother keening the cows that cannot be milked:

Is í mo mháthair an bhean sa ghúna dearg
atá ag bualadh a cloiginn i gcoinne an chlaí,
ag caoineadh na mbó nach féidir léi a chrú.
(*Faoi Chabáistí is Ríonacha*, p. 67)

That woman in red, beating her head
against a fence, is my mother.
She weeps for the cows she cannot milk.
(*Scarecrows at Newtownards*, p. 71)

If there is one central thematic thread running through the collections *Faoi Chabáistí is Ríonacha* and *Scarecrows at Newtownards*, it is the precarity of human life. Anything is possible in these poems, and the human will is depicted as fickle, non-stable, and limited by circumstances over which the individual has no control. De Fréine is particularly attracted to the liminal viewpoints of artists, musicians and circus people, as can be seen in the poem '*Trap an tSorcais*' ['Circus Trap'] where life is seen through the eyes of a trapeze artist:

Éist leis an ngáir mholta.
Conas a thuigfidís
go luíonn púic faoi scáth
do mhiongháire, go mbuaileann
croí cranraithe taobh thiar
des na matáin theanna uchtacha sin?
Tá cleachtadh acu
ar gach cleas sioncrónaithe:
nuair a sheasann tú, seasaim id scáth;

rothlaím nuair a smeachann tú do mhéara.
Ach an chéad uair eile
a luascann tú chugam, seans nach léimfead.
(*Faoi Chabáistí is Ríonacha*, p. 69)

[Listen to the cry of praise.
How could they understand
that behind your smile
lies a frown, that a
hard heart beats
behind those taut pectoral muscles?
They are accustomed
to every synchronised trick:
when you stand still, I stand in your shadow;
I rotate when you click your fingers.
But the next time you
swing in my direction, I may not jump.]

In the poem 'Escaping the Circus' (*Scarecrows at Newtownards*, p. 29), the dismantling of a circus suggests the disruption of mores and expectations in time of war. Events are presented in other poems as a form of ritual enactment in which everyone plays the role predestined for them. In 'Samhain in the City', for example, life is described as a 'Theatre of Chance' where the speaker's assigned role is to 'perform your greatest feat for a small / select audience too busy to watch' (*Scarecrows at Newtownards*, p. 26).

Many of the poems in these collections could be read as parables or fables, but the didactic tone of the classical fable is absent and the surreal images in most of the texts leave the reader with a sense of unease rather than moral assurance. The title poems of the collection *Scarecrows at Newtownards*, 'Scarecrows at Newtownards' (I) and (II), alluding as they do to a painting by Belfast painter Daniel O'Neill (1920–72) of ominous scarecrows in women's clothing, exemplify a poetic imagination populated by haunting images, be they natural or fabricated, communal or private. The poems' speaker inhabits the field of reference conjured up by the ghostly figures, as childhood memories and the narrative element in the painting combine to elicit a dramatic personal response. 'Scarecrows at Newtownards (II)' concludes with a call to the reader to observe the detail of the scene as depicted by the artist, thus illuminating the process whereby archetypal images are internalised:

... – look closely: at the back a young girl

beckons, her voice smoother than her elders',
her clothes sleeker, one foot poised, the other
grounded in the compass of your being.
(*Scarecrows at Newtownards*, p. 50)

The poems in the dual-language collections *imram / odyssey* and *Aibítir Aoise / Alphabet of an Age* are meditations on particular places or events, real or imaginary. With the same starkness and surrealism of her first collection, de Fréine again uses dramatic images to capture sensations, evoke memories, and pose questions about responsibility and agency. *imram / odyssey* opens with the poem '*Dóchas*' / 'Hope' and the image of a boat, which, like the Moses basket in Nuala Ní Dhomhnaill's '*Ceist na Teangan*' (translated by Paul Muldoon as 'The Language Issue'),[9] serves as a vessel for life's hopes and dreams.[10] As metaphor for the creative path of a poet, the boat is also a scene of challenge, of destruction, of emptying out and starting anew:

Agus muid ár dtuargaint ag na tonnta, breathnaím
sómas an fhómhair, a d'fhéadfainn a bhrath,
ag téaltú leis taobh thiar d'íor na spéire. Déantar
liobar is leadhb de bhileog chuile phlean, smístear
ina smidiríní gach iarracht ar iomramh is caitear an bád
lena phaisinéir aonarach i dtreo screabáin, áit
a dtagaimid i dtír, batráilte, briste, gan lasta ar bith.

Pounded by waves, I watch the autumn
ease I could have enjoyed, slink off beyond
the horizon. The leaf of every plan is torn
to shreds, all attempts at rowing pummelled
to smithereens, as the boat with its single passenger
is flung onto stony soil where we come
to rest, battered, broken, without any cargo.
('*Dóchas*' / 'Hope', *imram / odyssey*, pp. 14–15)

The image of the boat is still there at the end of the journey, a vessel emerging from a dreamworld of mansions, strangers and mermaids to bring the speaker home. This collection – associated with a residency in Koper in Slovenia – draws on the themes and imagery of travel literature, such as the smells and tastes of food ('*Giosta*' / 'Yeast', *imram / odyssey*, pp. 16–17), the difficulty in sleeping ('*Gadaí*' / 'Thief', *imram / odyssey*, pp. 18–19), the drama and mystery of borderlands ('*Talamh Eadrána*' / 'No Man's Land', *imram / odyssey*, pp. 22–3), the sense of history being inscribed on a landscape ('*Bíobla Lae*' / 'Daily Bible', *imram / odyssey*, pp. 24–5), the traveller's bag into which objects inadvertently fall ('*Mála*' / 'Bag', *imram / odyssey*, pp. 42–3), the local vegetation ('*Crainn*' / 'Trees', *imram / odyssey*, pp. 50–1), and the self-awareness of the traveller ('*Scáth*' / 'Shade', *imram / odyssey*, pp. 26–7).

The perspective of the displaced visitor allows a consideration of the possibility of disengagement from the relentless demands of contemporary life. The poem '*Gráinneog*' / 'Hedgehog', for example, adopts the perspective of dumb road carnage and imagines what would happen if a flattened hedgehog rose in revenge, or if a magnetic rainbow dumped the roaring cars in a quarry:

> ... dá n-aiséireodh an ghráinneog úd leis na boinn
> a pholladh, dá n-ardódh tuar ceatha maighnéadach
> na carranna úd lena ndumpáil sa chairéal –
>
> seans go líonfaí na lánaí le rothair ansin, plab
> a mbonn is cling-cling a gcloigíní i dtiúin
> le sioscadh an uisce is monabhar na gcrann,
> ceolbhuíon a chuirfeadh chun suain mé.
>
> ... were that hedgehog to arise and puncture
> the tyres, a magnetic rainbow to lift
> those cars and dump them in the quarry –
>
> perhaps the lanes would then fill with bicycles,
> the whoosh of their tyres and ting-a-ling of their bells
> in tune with the water's whisper, the rustling of trees
> an orchestra that would lull me to sleep.
>
> ('*Gráinneog*' / 'Hedgehog', *imram / odyssey*, pp. 32–3)

De Fréine's propensity to treat landscape as stage set and to present people as actors in a drama can be seen again in this collection. While the other world of the collection is often Slovenia or Croatia, the perspective is that of a personal journey of discovery rather than a straightforward political documentary. The political is never too far away, however, as the poem '*Cuireadh*' / 'Invitation' (*imram / odyssey*, pp. 48–9) conflates the image of writers and refugees, and the poem '*Teanga*' / 'Tongue' finds the speaker struggling to understand the complexities of another country's conflicts:

> *LJUDI FUCK OFF; G8 FUCK OFF* a mholann
> an graifítí san áit ina labhraíonn an scríbhneoir faoi:
> *perished partisans* a bhí *fussilated by the fascists*.
>
> Éistím le dreasa nua cainte ag bocáil
> thar líon na tuisceana, gach ceann acu ag baint
> pioc úr líonolla, slaod úr míthuisceana leis.
>
> Umhlaíonn muintir na háite dom, ag fiafraí díom anois
> is arís, cén chaoi a ndeirtear focal áirithe mar gur mise
> an t-aon chainteoir dúchais Béarla ar an láthair.
>
> *LJUDI FUCK OFF; G8 FUCK OFF* the graffiti
> urge here where the writer talks of:
> *perished partisans* who were *fussilated by the fascists*.
>
> I listen as new expressions ping back and forth
> across the net of understanding, each bringing
> with it an extra jot of lint, a new layer of confusion.
>
> The locals defer to me, asking now and then
> how to pronounce a certain word as I am
> the only native speaker of English here present.
>
> ('*Teanga*' / 'Tongue', *imram / odyssey*, pp. 52–3)

War is still an abiding theme, and the woman's perspective is always to the fore, as in the poem '*De Cheal an Chogaidh*' / 'In the Absence of War' (*imram / odyssey*, pp. 54–5), which reflects on the effect of war on children. Typically, de Fréine approaches this subject obliquely by focusing on the children raised between wars, whose childhood and youth are circumscribed nevertheless by conflict-induced tensions and partial freedoms.

The overall impression created by *imram / odyssey* is of an uneasy journeying, an acceptance that life is never as planned or expected. The poem 'Hotel Koper' refers to the unwritten poems, the escapees who flew away before this 'half-way house' (p. 77) (a hotel to which de Fréine was relocated in the final week of the residency) was made available:

Móra dhaoibh, a dhánta a d'fhéadfainn a scríobh
dá dtiocfainn anseo níos túisce. Eitlígí chuig
an gcufróg, más mian libh, is lorgaígí
tearmann inti go gcuire mé fios oraibh.

Poems I would have written had I come
here sooner, I salute you. Fly,
if you must, to the cypress tree and seek
refuge there until I send for you.
(*imram / odyssey* pp. 76–7)

The title of *Aibítir Aoise / Alphabet of an Age* would suggest that the poems therein will be an attempt to capture significant moments in a life, and yet the opening poem questions the relationship between the concept of 'an age' and the lifespan of a particular individual:

Céard is aois ann –
an tréimhse ina bhfuil cónaí orm,
dátaí a thrasnaíonn dhá mhílaois,

póca ina bhfuil rúin i bhfolach
nó ceann chomh folamh sin
go mbuaileann sé le gaoth?

What is age –
the time during which I live,
dates that span two millennia,

a pocket where secrets hide
or one so empty
it flaps in the wind?
('*Aibítir Aoise*' / 'Alphabet of an Age', *Aibítir Aoise / Alphabet of an Age*, pp. 14–15)

This uncertainty is what fuels de Fréine's poetry, so that both particular places and particular events can be evoked in a manner that increases their mystery, the beauty of a graveyard ('*Áit Álainn*' / 'Beauty Spot', *Aibítir Aoise / Alphabet of an Age*, pp. 16–19), for example, or the significance of a photograph or a scent ('*Boladh an Mhismín Fhiáin*' / 'The Scent of Wild Mint', *Aibítir Aoise / Alphabet of an Age*, pp. 20–1).

The longest poem in the collection is '*Féileacán ar Foluain*' / 'A Butterfly Aflutter' (*Aibítir Aoise / Alphabet of an Age*, pp. 40–7), which combines a realistic depiction of the final journey to a dying mother's bedside with childhood memories of love and conflict. With characteristic obliqueness, de Fréine focuses here on the significance of the concept of lateness as the daughter reflects on the moments just before and after her mother's death, using the folk image of the soul immediately after death (the butterfly hovering) as she observes the flutters and movements of the dead body. This poem illustrates de Fréine's power to deal with death and dying without descending into the macabre or into undue sentimentalism. Though the poem does acknowledge tension between the two women, it is also a compelling declaration of filial love and an acknowledgement of the importance of mother love.

For a writer who regularly addresses ethical issues, the poem '*Fianaise*' / 'Witness' is an acknowledgement of the limits of human communication and a refusal to simplify the complex:

> Cé sinne le scríobh faoina bhfuil le teacht
> nuair a theastaíonn uainn a bhfuil thart a dhearmad?
>
> Cé sinne le scríobh faoin am i láthair
> nuair nach féidir linn a bhfuil thart a dhearmad?
>
> Seans gur chóir dúinn scríobh faoina bhfuil thart
> ach cén chaoi a bhfuil a fhios againn céard a tharla
>
> nuair is gá cruthú ón duibheagán?
> Cruthú.
>
> Cé sinne a chaithfidh fianaise a thabhairt –
> sinne nach féidir a dhéanamh ach a n-iarrtar orainn?

> Who are we to write about the future
> since we want to forget the past?
>
> Who are we to write about the present
> when we cannot forget the past?
>
> Perhaps we should write about the past
> but how do we know what happened
>
> when we must create from the abyss?
> Create.

Who are we to bear witness
when we can do only what is asked of us?
(‘*Fianaise*’ / ‘Witness’, *Aibítir Aoise / Alphabet of an Age*, pp. 48–9)

Despite the limitations on the poet implied in these lines, Celia de Fréine has never shied away from the role of bearing witness to injustice, atrocity or inequality. Indeed, the poem ‘*Huth ná Hath*’ / ‘Here nor There’ (*Aibítir Aoise / Alphabet of an Age*, pp. 58–9) is an open condemnation of the cowardice and hypocrisy of self-serving politicians, while ‘*I gCoibhneas a Chéile*’ / ‘In Relation to Each Other’ (dedicated to Mileva Marić, Einstein’s first wife, *Aibítir Aoise / Alphabet of an Age*, pp. 60–1) addresses the gendered politics of recognition and forgetfulness. I will now turn to the collections *Fiacha Fola* and *Blood Debts*, in which de Fréine’s narrative power and surreal style become perfect vehicles to expose the details of one of the most horrific chapters in recent Irish women’s history.

GOTHIC HORROR OR POETRY AS LIFE WRITING

Unlike de Fréine’s other collections, *Fiacha Fola* and *Blood Debts* are direct and explicit in focus, as they document the physical and emotional journey of a victim of the Hepatitis C scandal, which came to public attention in 1994 and was subsequently recognised as one of the most serious examples of medical malpractice ever to occur in Ireland. The story dates from the years 1977–9 and 1991–4 during which periods over a thousand Irish women were infected with the Hepatitis C virus from contaminated Anti-D, a blood product given to them during childbirth. In the same periods, hundreds of haemophiliacs were also infected with both Hepatitis C and HIV from contaminated blood products. The symptoms of the illness included chronic fatigue and serious liver damage. It took a political controversy, including a battle for state compensation by infected Donegal woman Brigid McCole, who died in 1996, before two tribunals of inquiry established the scale of the scandal and the Irish Blood Transfusion Board admitted responsibility. Celia de Fréine’s collections chronicle the experience of one unnamed woman, including the debilitating physical symptoms exacerbated by the psychological pain of being ignored or not believed when she attempted to communicate her condition to medical professionals.

The opening poems in the sequence are meditations on the past and on what might have been. Religious imagery of blood sacrifice is employed in the first poem '*Cailís Mo Chuid Fola*' / 'Chalice of My Blood' (*Fiacha Fola*, p. 13 / *Blood Debts*, pp. 18–19) where the speaker expresses a desire to undo the cruel fate meted out to her, while at the same time acknowledging the desire to be a mother which is even greater than her need of physical relief. The poem closes with a bold declaration of the choice she would have made, even if she had been forewarned of the danger:

> Ach fiú dá mbeadh a fhios agam é
> táim dearfa go ndéarfainn
>
> tabhair dom mo ghasúir
> tabhair dom mo ghasúir ar ais nó ar éigean.
> (*Fiacha Fola*, p. 13)

> But even had I known
> I'm sure I would have said
>
> give me my children
> give me my children whatever the cost.
> (*Blood Debts*, p. 19)

As well as chronicling what happened, there is a pondering over what might have been, with '*Dráma Míorúilteach*' / 'Miracle Play' (*Fiacha Fola*, pp. 14–15 / *Blood Debts*, pp. 20–1) recording one of the first outings during the early stages of a relationship. The attention turns very soon to the site of the trauma, however, as the description of the blood transfusion in '*Meán Fómhair – Mí na mBreithlaethanta*' / 'September – Month of Birthdays' (*Fiacha Fola*, pp. 16–17 / *Blood Debts*, pp. 22–3) is followed by the symptoms of contamination in '*Lionn Buí na gCaolán*' / 'Yellow Humour' (*Fiacha Fola*, pp. 18–19 / *Blood Debts*, pp. 24–5). Here we see de Fréine at her very best, where the reality of physical pain and the anger of a woman whose experience and words were ignored are communicated with a combination of surreal imagery and tragic irony:

> fógraí na teilifíse dom ionsaí
> babhlaí bia á radadh chugam
> m'éasafagas ag tarraingt
>
> a bhfuil im phutóga aníos
> dath aisteach buí ag leathadh
> thar m'aghaidh is thar mo ghéaga

sa chlinic mo chosa ag lúbadh fúm
m'airíonna á gcur in iúl don dochtúir
eisean ag rá go bhfuilim rite síos

mo shála á gcur i dtaca agam
ag iarraidh a chur ina luí air
go bhfuilim buí

eisean dom thionlacan chuig a ghrianán
le breathnú orm i nglésholas an lae
ag dearbhú nach bhfuil a dhath

mícheart le dath mo chraicinn
gur dath nádúrtha atá air.
Is Indiach é an dochtúir.

(*Fiacha Fola*, pp. 18–19)

television ads revolving
bowls of food flying at me
my oesophagus dragging up

all that's in my intestines
a strange yellow spreading
across my face and limbs

in the clinic my legs go from under me
as I describe my symptoms to the doctor.
He says I'm run down.

I dig my heels in
insisting
that I'm yellow

He brings me into his conservatory
to look at me in the clear light of day
insisting

there's nothing wrong with my skin
that its colour is normal.
My doctor is Indian.

(*Blood Debts*, pp. 24–5)

A central theme of this collection is the manner in which the suffering woman's words are not believed, how doubt is cast on her ability to describe the functioning of her own body. The woman is forced to endure the diagnosis of an obstetrician ('*Coinnigh Ort*' / 'Pray Continue', *Fiacha Fola*, p. 21 / *Blood Debts*, p. 27) and the judgements of politicians, media people and medics ('*Tréadaí*' / 'Pastor', *Fiacha Fola*, pp. 22–3 / *Blood Debts*, pp. 28–9; '*Achainí*' / 'Petition', *Fiacha Fola*, p. 25 / *Blood Debts*, p. 31; 'I Wanna Sleep Forever', *Fiacha Fola*, pp. 26–7 / *Blood Debts*, pp. 32–3). The notion of life as a dangerous dramatic performance the outcome of which is never clear is explored in the poem '*Ar a Téad Rite Arís*' / 'On Her High Wire Again' (*Fiacha Fola*, pp. 28–9 / *Blood Debts*, pp. 34–5), where the image of the tight-rope walker is employed to describe the relationship between the ill woman and those who scrutinise her:

> Thíos fúithi plódaíonn
> an lucht leighis
> a ngnúiseanna ag glinniúint
> as adhastair a gcuid steiteascóp.
>
> Casann ar a hioscaidí
> ag machnamh di ar na gairmeacha eile
> a d'fhéadfadh sí a roghnú
> chun dráma mór an tsaoil a léiriú
>
> ionaid eile – fáinneán mar shampla –
> áit a ligfeadh an lucht féachana
> gáir mholta, is a mbeadh a fhios aici
> go raibh líon thíos fúithi.
>
> (*Fiacha Fola*, p. 28)

> Below her the medics
> congregate
> each face askance
> in the noose of the stethoscope
>
> She turns on her heel
> mindful of other professions
> she might have chosen
> to play out life's drama
>
> other venues – a big top – for example
> where the audience would cheer
> and she'd know
> there was a net beneath her.
>
> (*Blood Debts*, pp. 34–5)

De Fréine's sense of the Gothic has ample scope in collections where blood and blood relations are central. The poem '*Ailp na Seirce*' / 'Love Bite' refers to the woman's injured neck as the result of a liaison with a vampire ('*fear fada caol ón Rómáin*' / 'a tall thin man from Romania' (*Fiacha Fola*, p. 31 / *Blood Debts*, p. 37). This poem exposes the prejudices directed against a sexually active woman, thus linking blood-related disease to sexual promiscuity in a manner that conjures up debates about AIDS and sexually transmitted diseases in general.[11]

The political context of the collections' theme emerges gradually, de Fréine typically approaching the question of responsibility indirectly. In the poem '*Cluichí Oilimpeacha Los Angeles*' / 'Los Angeles Olympics', for example, we are told that the television can no longer relay the joy of Irish successes to the suffering woman. Caught up in her own distress, she finds no relief in her country's triumphs on the athletics track:

> Ná bac a rá liom má éiríonn le John Treacy
> an staidiam a bhaint amach.
>
> Nílim ag iarraidh bratach na hÉireann
> a fheiceáil ag guairfeach os a chionn
>
> ná cogarnach de chaoincí
> *Ambrán na bhFiann* a chloisteáil.
>
> (*Fiacha Fola*, pp. 32–3)

> Don't tell me if John Treacy
> makes it to the stadium
>
> I don't want to see
> the tricolour hoisted
>
> or hear the strains
> of *Ambrán na bhFiann*.
>
> (*Blood Debts*, pp. 38–9)

The woman's lack of agency in matters concerning her own body is explored in poems dealing with medicalised birth ('Not of Woman Born', *Fiacha Fola*, p. 34 / *Blood Debts*, pp. 40–1), and undiagnosed symptoms ('Comfort', *Fiacha Fola*, p. 35 / *Blood Debts*, p. 42; '*In Uisce Té*' / 'In Hot Water', *Fiacha Fola*, pp. 38–9 / *Blood Debts*, pp. 46–7). De Fréine's ability to represent physical conditions is remarkable, as she addresses the challenges of expressibility outlined by Elaine Scarry in her ground-breaking book *The Body in Pain*.[12] The fact that the speaking voice in the collection can be read as a representation of the experience of a group rather than an individual makes the poetry itself one of those rare avenues of communication mentioned by Scarry:

> Because the person in pain is ordinarily so bereft of the resources of speech, it is not surprising that the language for pain should sometimes be brought into being by those who are not themselves in pain but who speak *on behalf of* those who are. Though there are very great impediments to expressing another's sentient distress, so are there also very great reasons why one might want to do so, and thus there come to be avenues by which this most radically private of experiences begins to enter the realm of public discourse.[13]

Fiacha Fola and *Blood Debts* carry the dedication '*Do na Mná*' / 'For the Women'. One senses that this dedication is less a claim to speak *on behalf of* a suffering commonality than the expression of a gift-offering, the gift being de Fréine's own personal 'resources of speech', her ability as a writer to bring private experience into 'the realm of public discourse'. The most frightening aspect of the Hepatitis C scandal was the manner in which women's words were not trusted by the physicians, illustrating what Scarry acknowledges as the experience of many people 'that physicians do not trust (hence, hear) the human voice, that they in effect perceive the voice of the patient as an "unreliable narrator" of bodily events ...'.[14] De Fréine approaches this subject head-on by illustrating that the problem was less a question of expressibility or representability than an example of an inability or refusal to hear women's voices or to take their words seriously.

The woman's experience at the hands of doctors is presented in terms of trial remedies and wild hypotheses, as in the poem '*Faigh Réidh Leo*' / 'Nip It in the Bud' (*Fiacha Fola*, pp. 40–1; *Blood Debts*, pp. 48–9) where de Fréine's sense of the bizarre in the ordinary is communicated through the depiction of an actual encounter with a doctor who suggests that the primroses outgrowing their beds and thus causing the woman to roll up her sleeves and get to work to keep them under control is the underlying cause of the infection.

The voice becomes angrier as the woman disagrees with the judgements of the specialists, declaring the truth of her own bodily experience ('*Mochthráth an Mhic Tíre*' / 'The Hour of the Wolf', *Fiacha Fola*, p. 43 / *Blood Debts*, p. 50):

Fiafraíonn an speisialtóir díom
an bhfuil aon eolas agam faoi lúpas.

Freagraím gur bhásaigh
cara liom dá bharr. Dar leis

nach mbásaíonn éinne
dá bharr sa lá atá inniu ann.

Bhí mé ar a sochraid
agus is cuimhin liom a deirfiúr ag rá

gur dhúirt a liasa nach mbaineann
daoine a bhfuil lúpas orthu

meán an tsaoil amach.
Molann mo dhuine cortasón –

stéaróideach a atann an corp
go bhfios dom. Samhlaím mé féin

i riocht mná Michelin ar foluain
os a chionn ag breathnú anuas

ar mhaoil a chloiginn
fad a bhíonn sé dom fhuineadh.

(*Fiacha Fola*, p. 43)

The specialist asks
if I've heard of lupus.

I tell him a friend
died from it. *No one*

dies from lupus
nowadays, he says.

I was at her funeral
where her sister mentioned

that their specialist had said
people with lupus

don't reach middle age.
He prescribes cortisone –

a steroid I've heard tell that
bloats the body. I see myself

in the guise of a *Michelin*
woman float up overhead

stare down on his pate
as he pummels my stomach.

(*Blood Debts*, p. 50)

The woman's body is the focus of the collection until halfway through, when the story of the contaminated blood is made public on a radio show. The poems 'Morning Ireland' (*Fiacha Fola*, p. 49 / *Blood Debts*, p. 56), '*Scéal Scéil*' / 'Hearsay' (*Fiacha Fola*, p. 50 / *Blood Debts*, p. 57), '*Mac Tíre i gCraiceann Caorach*' / 'A Wolf in Sheep's Clothing' (*Fiacha Fola*, p. 51 / *Blood Debts*, p. 58), '*An Tromluí is Troime*' / 'The Worst Nightmare' (*Fiacha Fola*, p. 52 / *Blood Debts*, p. 59), '*Áit a mBíonn Toit*' / 'Where There's Smoke' (*Fiacha Fola*, p. 53 / *Blood Debts*, pp. 60–1), and '*Sea*' / 'Yes' (*Fiacha Fola*, p. 54 / *Blood Debts*, p. 64) document the initial period of recognition, the gradual breaking of the story, the acceptance of responsibility, the setting up of help lines, the fear of AIDS, the reminder of Nazi laboratories, the desire for answers, and the descent into depression. The traumatic experience is presented as a theatre of cruelty in '*Gan Pána a Bhriseadh*' / 'Without Breaking a Pane' (*Fiacha Fola*, pp. 64–5 / *Blood Debts*, pp. 74–5), and the fear of contamination pervades the intimate spheres of family life ('*A Ghasúir*' / 'Dear Children', *Fiacha Fola*, p. 61 / *Blood Debts*, pp. 70–1; '*Piontaí*' / 'Pints', *Fiacha Fola*, p. 66 / *Blood Debts*, p. 69; '*A Leannáin*' / 'Lover', *Fiacha Fola*, p. 67 / *Blood Debts*, p. 76). Typical of the juxtapositions that add force to de Fréine's poetry is that of a reading by American feminist author Grace Paley (the sound of her New York accent conjuring up detectives Simone and Sipowicz from the television series *NYPD Blue*) and the image of the dying Brigid McCole, whose case was to fuel the national campaign to compensate the victims of the Anti-D contamination ('Grace', *Fiacha Fola*, pp. 68–9 / *Blood Debts*, pp. 78–9). Here, as the speaker's mind strays from Paley's voice in the lecture theatre to the minister in the Dáil chamber to the image of Brigid McCole's twelve children at her death-bed, the individual woman is seen as embedded in a web of relationships and responsibilities:

Tá a fhios ag an dáréag atá cruinnithe thart ar a leaba
nach gcloisfidh siad gáir mholta uaithi
an lá a mbronnfar céimeanna orthu

nach mbeidh sí ansin le barróg a bhreith orthu
lá a bpósta, nach bhfeicfidh sí
a loirg ar cheannaithe a ngasúr siúd.

Déanaim iarracht m'intinn a dhíriú ar bhlas Grace Paley
blas a aithním ó chaint Sipowicz is Simone,
faoistiní á dtarraingt acu as a gcoirpigh.

Ach ní leor mo smaointe ar Sipowicz is Simone
nó scéalta siopaí mangarae Nua Eabhrac
nó comharsanachtaí Giúdacha

le m'aird a tharraingt ó shaol ghasúir na mná seo
mar a bheidh sé is mar ba chóir dó a bheith.
Feicim ina leaba í, feicim í á haerscuabadh

ó ghrianghraif albam an teaghlaigh.
Leanann blas Nua-Eabhrac air. Leanann duine
de na banscríbhneoirí is suimiúla ar domhan

is ní féidir liom smaoineamh
ach ar dhuine de na mná is misniúla ar domhan
atá ag fáil bháis in ospidéal sa chathair
agus ar an Aire atá á deifriú chun na huaighe.
(*Fiacha Fola*, pp. 68–9)

The twelve gathered round her now
they'll not hear her applaud
the day they graduate, realise

she'll not be there to embrace them
on their wedding day, see their likeness
etched on their children's faces.

I try to focus on Grace Paley's tone
one that reminds me of Sipowicz and Simone
as they coax confessions from their suspects.

But my thoughts of Sipowicz and Simone
tales of New York huckster shops
and Jewish neighbourhoods are not enough

> to distract me from the lives of this woman's children
> of how they will be, of how they should be.
> I see her in her bed, I see her airbrushed
>
> from the family photograph album.
> The New York tone drones on:
> one of the most interesting women writers
>
> continues and all I can think of
> is one of the most heroic women
> who is dying in a city hospital
> and of the Minister hastening her to her grave.
> (*Blood Debts*, pp. 78–9)

The social effects of the contamination are related in poems that recount particular stories. Both intimate family relationships and neighbourly social interactions have all been changed utterly ('*A Iníon*' / 'Daughter', *Fiacha Fola*, p. 71 / *Blood Debts*, p. 81; '*Íobairt*' / 'Blood Sacrifice', *Fiacha Fola*, p. 73 / *Blood Debts*, p. 83), and the poems present frightening images of blemished skin and weakened limbs ('Wise Blood', *Fiacha Fola*, p. 72 / *Blood Debts*, p. 80). The story is recounted, in turn, as: '*Scéal Eile ó Shahrazad*' / 'Another Tale from Shahrazad' (*Fiacha Fola*, pp. 74–5 / *Blood Debts*, pp. 84–5), thus associating it with impending death; as an objective account of the speaker's medical diagnosis ('*Fáthmheas*' / 'Diagnosis', *Fiacha Fola*, p. 77 / *Blood Debts*, p. 87); as a description of an entry in a book of evidence ('*An Leabhar Fianaise*' / 'The Book of Evidence', *Fiacha Fola*, p. 79 / *Blood Debts*, p. 88); and as a meditation on the significance of the compensation money ('*An Seic*' / 'The Cheque', *Fiacha Fola*, p. 80 / *Blood Debts*, pp. 90–1). By employing images of nuclear disaster, blood-letting and vampirism, de Fréine is drawing on powerful metaphors of contamination, thus placing the Hepatitis C episode within broader global political and cultural debates.

The full horror of the women's condition is revealed in '*A Dheirfiúracha Dílse*' / 'Sisters' (*Fiacha Fola*, p. 86 / *Blood Debts*, pp. 96–7), an adaptation of the poem by Marina Tsvetayeva translated as 'We Shall Not Escape Hell', already familiar to readers of Irish-language poetry through Nuala Ní Dhomhnaill's well-known version, '*Táimid Damanta, a Dheirféaracha*' ['We are Damned, my Sisters'].[15] Where both Tsvetayeva and Ní Dhomhnaill present images of women breaking free from patriarchal control but ultimately paying a social and physical price, the hell depicted in de Fréine's poem refers to the punishment meted out to those who dutifully fulfilled the domestic roles of mothers and home-makers:

Mo léan, níor éirigh linn éalú as Ifreann
cé gur ghlac muid lena raibh i ndán dúinn –
na dualgais a roinneadh orainn.

Ní sinne a mealladh
ó chliabháin ár ngasúr
chuig tinte cnámh na mbligeard.

Ag cromadh chun na gcliabhán céanna
chomh leanbaí leis na leanaí iontu
ba iad na bligeaird a théaltaigh aníos chugainne.

Is maith is eol daoibh, a bhanabhraiseacha,
gur den scoth ár dtíos is nach dúinn is dual clú
sa drochobair shnáthaide.

Cén mhaith dúinn a shamhlú
sna hoícheanta gan suan
céard a tharlódh dá mbeadh

an dara rogha againn –
dá ndamhsóimis lomnocht faoi na réaltaí
an gcinnfí an cháin chéanna orainn?

Diúgadh na deora dár súile.
Tarraingíodh an ghruaig dár gcloigne
Sracadh an fheoil dár gcnámha.

Cnaífear de shíor ár n-aenna.
Go deimhin, a dheirfiúracha dílse,
níor éirigh linn éalú as Ifreann.

(*Fiacha Fola*, p. 86)

We have not escaped hell
though we had accepted our lot,
the chores apportioned to us

nor were we lured
from the cradles of our children
to bonfires lit by vagabonds.

As we leaned over those same cradles
innocent as the children in them
the vagabonds stole up to us.

Never fear, fine spinners,
good housekeepers,
it isn't we who are renowned

for slovenly needlework;
nor is there any point thinking
during those sleepless nights

what hand fate would have dealt us
had we not accepted our lot –
had we danced naked under the stars

would we have been punished just the same?
Our eyes are dry, our livers gnawed,
hair has fallen from our heads,

flesh has been clawed from our bones.
Definitely, dear sisters,
we have not escaped hell.

(*Blood Debts*, pp. 96–7)

While the illness itself is not used as a figure or metaphor by de Fréine, this poem does associate the *treatment* of the diseased women with punishment, thus unleashing a powerful critique of Irish society as represented by politicians and medical specialists. The final poem in the collection, '*Lámhachta?*' / 'Taken Out and Shot?' (*Fiacha Fola*, pp. 87–8 / *Blood Debts*, pp. 98–9), raises the question of culpability, comparing the guilt of the medical experts to that of prisoners punished for crimes whose effects were less enduring. The poem ends, however, on a note of forbearance, a refusal to impose further suffering:

Go minic feicim fir
cúlpháirtithe i gcoireanna
nár lean iarmhairtí
chomh trom céanna iad
á sracadh as a leapacha
is á lámhach.
An bhfuil mé ag iarraidh

go gcaithfí mar an gcéanna
le dream na héagóra seo?
Nó arbh fhearr liom
go mairfidís
i liombó aicídí?
Níorbh fhearr –
ní ghuífinn a leithéid ar éinne.
(*Fiacha Fola*, p. 88)

I often see films
where men are dragged
from their beds
and shot for less
than what these did.
Would I like to see them
suffer the same fate?
Or would I prefer
them to live
in a limbo of ailments?
No.
I wouldn't wish that on anyone.
(*Blood Debts*, p. 99)

The power of this collection derives from the sureness of voice of the speaker as it moves from the position of victim to that of witness, from the story of a traumatic personal experience to a story of a process of evasion and denial of women's experience. Máire Mhac an tSaoi, in her introduction to *Fiacha Fola*, alludes to de Fréine's surreal technique and to her use of language, as bare as prose, as multi-functional as conversation. Referring to one of the shortest poems in the sequence, she says: '*B'fhiú liomsa gluaiseacht na hathbheochana ar fad ach go gcuirfí a leithéid ar fáil*' or, in *Blood Debts*: 'For me, the whole revival movement has been worth it so that its like could be provided.'[16] Certainly, the poem sequence *Fiacha Fola* can take its place beside ground-breaking works of social and political significance by other women writers in Irish, including Máire Mhac an tSaoi herself, Máiréad Ní Ghráda and Nuala Ní Dhomhnaill. As an English-language publication, *Blood Debts* may be situated alongside the work of other contemporary Irish writers who 'have turned ill embodiments into extraordinary literary material'.[17] Both collections testify to the power of narrative poetry to address issues of public concern by serving as a rich and compelling form of life writing.

In relation to Irish as her primary creative medium, Celia de Fréine has stated that she feels that the Irish language is 'better suited to the surreal nature of my poetry and that through it I can more successfully mine the stuff of my imagination'.[18] On the other hand, her dual-language publications demonstrate the potential of self-translation, which can serve as 'an editing tool'.[19] Why did she wait ten years before she published an English-language version of *Fiacha Fola*, however? Part of the answer lies in her reluctance to have the poems read as biography. Referring to questions posed by a journalist when *Fiacha Fola* was published, she said, 'I declined to answer. I had written a book of poetry about a national scandal and I wanted the focus to be on *what* the book was about rather than *who* it was about.'[20] Ten years later, when *Blood Debts* appeared, her attitude to the question had changed: 'At the time *Fiacha Fola* was published I didn't have the strength to field the questions that would have arisen had my medical history entered the public domain. Ten years later I was tougher.'[21] The story of these collections serves as a fascinating reminder of the complexities and possibilities of bilingualism in Irish literary practice. If the resources of the Irish language enabled de Fréine to document a traumatic personal experience before it had receded into the realm of memory, her powers of self-translation allowed her to faithfully reproduce that experience and make it available, as part of a growing corpus of Irish women's life writing in English, ten years later.

There are many other aspects of Celia de Fréine's poetry that are worthy of critical attention, such as the influence of visual art and film, the international and multilingual context of certain poems and poem sequences, and the use of biblical, classical or Shakespearean sources. With the work of Patricia Coughlan in mind, particularly her willingness to traverse the borders of language, culture and genre, I hope that this essay will encourage others to read de Fréine's poetry, to recognise the value of her bilingual poetic project, and to engage in the kinds of close reading and analysis that the work so richly deserves.

PART 2

The Family Romance and Sibling Relations

Home Sickness

BERNARD O'DONOGHUE

Her heart was bad – or so they always said –
and she couldn't face the chapel the cold day
of her favourite daughter's funeral. But how
could they be sure that the view from the window
of the cortege passing would not kill her?
Her next-door neighbour – a midwife famous for
her tact and skill at sympathising –
would seat her with her back turned to the road
and prompt discussion of her favourite topic:
Manhattan before nineteen-twenty-nine.
Tears came to her eyes as she recalled
the skyscrapers above the narrow streets.
You'd go into Central Park on the West Side,
and it could take you half an hour and more
before you'd come out by the museums to the East.
'And you should see the view from the very top
of the Empire State Building.' The minder
kept a wary eye on the hearse creeping past
and on all the friends and cousins with bowed heads
walking with sad steps along the pavement.
A smile still played about her lips; her eyes
were far away. 'I remember still the very day
of the Wall Street Crash as if it was yesterday.
Nothing else in the papers for a week.
It took everyone's mind off everything.'
The bells tolled in twos through the midday sleet.
The neighbour pictured the mourners by the grave:
the coffin lowered; the sobs of the relations.
But still Mamie nodded at the fire,
transported well beyond the reach of grief.

CHAPTER 6

Siblings: Juliet Mitchell and Malory's *Morte Darthur*

CATHERINE LA FARGE

Siblinghood in the Arthurian stories of Sir Thomas Malory is not a pretty sight. A brother may be 'the beste frende that ye have and the man that ye moste love in the worlde', but you may end up killing each other.[1] A sister might take you tenderly into her embrace as you approach death but this does not mean she has not been trying to destroy you. A young man seeking to make his name and join the Arthurian establishment alongside his big brother may feel compelled to attack that brother as soon as his identity is announced, and then to clash with him again to death's door.

Psychoanalysis was surprisingly tardy in recognising the significance of siblings. Juliet Mitchell has been instrumental in calling attention to this complex lateral bond that is fundamental to the formation of a self and to other peer relationships, heirs to the baggage of siblinghood.[2] Literary studies are now acknowledging the richness of fictive siblings as a theme in medieval culture. Carolyne Larrington has provided a taxonomy of sibling relationships in a broad sweep of medieval European narratives, usefully referring to psychological and psychoanalytic as well as historical findings.[3]

The purpose of this essay is to delve further into the psychic meaning of sibling relationships in Malory, foregrounding Mitchell's work and how it illuminates *Le Morte Darthur*, considered here in its characteristic narrative reflexes and textual habits. The doom-laden nature of kinship in general in Malory has been well established. In his narrative, as Kate McClune cogently shows, 'blood relationships offer little alternative but chaos and destruction'.[4] Larrington invokes Mitchell's work but is nevertheless fairly upbeat about brothers and sisters; she sees a progression in Malory whereby 'sibling relationships are assimilated to other kinds of affective ties', a gradual movement from what she considers 'the more easily negotiated sphere of fraternal sameness' to its accommodation alongside heterosexual love.[5] I argue here that siblinghood, never easy, remains crucially unresolved in Malory, that major turns in the plot depend upon this lack, and that this psychic difficulty underlies the text's preoccupation with sight and recognition. At a basic level, something is missing in the way people in Malory relate to each other. The double-edged sword of sibling elimination, both longed for and dreaded, propels the text.

In *Siblings: Sex and violence*, Juliet Mitchell argues that siblings, actual or potential, are our first encounter with death. Siblings reinforce the initial trauma involved in being born, facing the subject with a black hole. This apprehension of being annihilated can only be remedied initially by hate. At this stage the subject sees the sibling not as another in any proper sense but as 'me over again', a repetition that usurps her place in the world. Murder would seem to be the only solution.[6] The subject may, in what at first glance appears to be an extreme alternative, embrace the sibling as 'more me', a wondrous extension and intensification of the self. Sibling incest, in which the subject subsumes the sibling into the self, is a ploy to sustain this illusion by obliterating the sibling's otherness. Only a blurred line runs between sibling incest and sibling murder; in both the subject strives to snuff out the threatening autonomy of the sibling. If siblinghood is to be safely negotiated, the subject must learn the rule of 'seriality': the sibling is both the same as the self and other than the self. Taking seriality on board involves the demise of infantile narcissism, the death of His Majesty the Baby. This resolution is unstable; later crises and perceptions of being displaced may return the subject to sibling trauma and build upon it. While sibling hatred can be transmuted into healthy competitiveness with peers, war represents its de-repression. Seeing and recognition, literal and figurative, play major roles. The subject initially experiences the sibling as a mirror; learning to see oneself from the perspective of one's sibling represents a major achievement in the resolution of sibling trauma. The motif of a shifting viewpoint arises frequently in Mitchell's discussion, perhaps most strikingly in her treatments of twins and of the common fantasy 'A Child Is Being Beaten'.

Siblinghood gets off to a bad start in Malory. The duke of Cornwall and his wife Ygrayne have three daughters, Morgawse, Elayne and Morgan le Fey. Uther, king of England, takes a fancy to Ygrayne and arranges for Cornwall's death so that he can sleep with her and marry her. King Arthur is conceived at once. Arthur's half-sisters are then married to three kings who initially oppose his accession to the throne. Soon after Arthur becomes king, and before he or many others know the facts of his parentage, he sleeps with his sister Morgawse.[7] The text says that Morgawse's husband, King

Lot of Orkney, was hostile to Arthur because of this event – a plausible enough claim in the circumstances – but in fact the other sons-in-law of Lot and Uther were already against Arthur's kingship, and their hostility is not immediately allayed once his parentage is generally known (61.13–15; 11.28–13.23).[8] There are underlying structural reasons for enmity between Cornwall's daughters and Uther's son. Not only had Arthur's father had theirs killed, but the half-sisters' father was less illustrious than Arthur's. A late-medieval gentry reader would have interpreted Arthur's birth as, among other things, the successful arrival of a male child after a series of girls. Morgawse, Morgan and Elayne have been trumped in multiple ways by their new boy sibling; this much is clear even before acknowledging the basic psychic disturbance of siblinghood. And this is only a preamble.

Morgawse's sibling gaze is that of a sister who seeks to defend herself by way of a takeover that engenders death.[9] We are not told what she does or does not know of Arthur's parenthood when she sleeps with him, but as she has come to spy on him – an addition to the source – she exudes a general aura of hyper-seeing and knowingness which contrast with Arthur's blindness to the facts (33.30–34.8).[10] The disparity is deepened by the sense in Malory and elsewhere that women may be privy by mysterious means to knowledge unavailable to men, especially where malevolence is afoot, and by the perennial tendency of Arthur, along with many other men in the text, not to see or know things they would rather not.[11] After the event Arthur has a nightmare that is trying to tell him something; he dreams that griffons and serpents have invaded his realm and are burning and killing all his people, but upon awaking he goes hunting to 'putte hit oute of thought' (34.14).

Arthur at this stage is poignantly unestablished. Not only does he have no sword and not know how to run a kingdom, but he does not even know who he is. In the next tale, by which time his parentage has been revealed, he unwisely entrusts another sister, Morgan, with his scabbard, that feminine accoutrement which Merlin has told him is more valuable than Excaliber itself. Morgan makes him a fake one and gives the real one to her lover. Morgawse has already conceived the child with Arthur who will effect the destruction both sisters desire. While the name of the child, 'Mordred', lacks any etymological link with it, 'murder' is too close in sound for comfort. His mother's and his more prominent aunt's similar names draw the three together as allies in the crime.

Gawayne and his brothers are Arthur's sister's sons, but Mordred is not only his sister's son but also his own. While the intensity of the sister's son bond in late medieval culture may pale in comparison to that of the

Trobriand Islands, it is a potent relationship, accompanied by its matching taboo. The incest of Morgawse and Arthur is 'unequal' and 'malign', particularly destructive to the 'unestablished self', and experienced by the less empowered sibling as 'a break in protective boundaries, a traumatic invasion of body-mind', and presenting in clinical work in the form of 'fears and fantasies of invasion'.[12] Arthur's dream is a case in point.

Mordred, the product of this union, is effectively a monster, as is typical of incest progeny; he will destroy the kingdom, try to marry his stepmother, and kill his father.[13] Following the pattern of heroes, Mordred miraculously survives Arthur's attempt to do away with him as an infant, and is then fostered by a 'good man'. The text promises to 'reherse' Mordred being brought to court at his maturity; one expects the traditional scene accorded to such moments, but it never comes (46.17–19).[14] His brother Gareth, however, most beloved of all Arthur's sister's sons, is the centre of a very elaborate and extended scene of this kind in his own tale, a story for which no source has been found. The failure of his uncle Arthur or any of his brothers to recognise Gareth, the dubious hospitality he receives, and the consequent anger of Morgawse with Arthur may all owe something to Gareth's role as a substitute for the less favoured half-brother and to the textual repression of a similar coming-of-age arrival scene for him. The heated conversation between Morgawse and Arthur about Gareth's treatment is heavily interlarded with acknowledgements of their siblinghood.[15] Perhaps this unpleasant surrogacy is the reason Gareth is moved to specify that he is Gawayne's brother 'of fadir syde and modir syde' (229.11–12). The unwritten 'Tale of Sir Mordred' haunts the 'Tale of Sir Gareth'.

Arthur has barely got his sword, and the accompanying tutorial from Merlin on the superior merit of its scabbard, when 'Balyn le Sauvage' begins. As Larrington notes, this tale is characterised by an 'excess of brothers', though in it a sister, Morgan, also presents striking sibling behaviour.[16] It is typical of Malory's narrative to repeat like a broken record when it hits a psychic snag. Complex pairs of siblings will crop up at crucial moments throughout Malory, variations on a theme, with differing degrees of logical or purely harmonic connection to the plot. One feeble gambit the text makes by way of trying to get beyond the impasse is to have one brother be good and the other bad, as in the case of Pellam and the unredeemable Garlon.[17] The central brotherly duo of the tale, with their almost absurdly similar names – Balyn (also spelled 'Balen') and Balan – cannot be so readily organised. They are inordinately symbiotically related.

Balyn is the most pathetic of Malory's ingénues. Like a child with a displeased father, he desperately wants to regain Arthur's favour but seems doomed to find himself standing beside a corpse every time he tries. The exception is the occasion upon which he is joined by his brother Balan in fighting off Nero, brother of Royns. Elsewhere in the tale, Balyn is conspicuously alone other than during the brief period when he has in tow a man and a lady whose respective wrongs he means to put right, which he does with very limited success. His encounters with other people's intimate relationships are disastrous. Having killed Lanceor, the Irish knight, he fails to act fast enough to prevent Lanceor's lady from committing suicide; he vows to convey Herleus safely to court only to have him killed by Garlon and Herleus' lady destroyed by the Dolorous Stroke, and he ham-fistedly thinks he can cure Garnyssh of his amorous obsession by escorting him to view his lady *in flagrante delicto*, thereby inspiring Garnyssh to murder the couple and himself on the spot. Herleus' lady functions as a sort of false ID for Balyn in gaining him admission to Pellam's feast where a female companion is required. Balyn certainly does not understand sexual desire, but the crux of the matter is that he is not in a position to form a relationship with another person. Yet, for a text so thin on displays of late medieval interiority, we are granted an unusual degree of knowledge of Balyn's feelings, motives, and perceptions; his introduction, in particular, is infused with narrative sympathy (48.30–49.6; 67.1–4). His experience of prison may have had a personal resonance for the knight prisoner Malory, and his speech on the subject of inner gentility gives him a moral authority that sits oddly alongside his string of failures (49.18–22).[18]

Balyn and Balan remain in the early, sibling-as-mirror phase up to the moment of their deaths at each other's hands. They are 'empty of themselves'.[19] Such people, as adults, cannot be alone; 'the other is needed but not as another separate person because they have not been represented as such'.[20] Left to his own devices, Balyn is incomplete; when he and Balan are together they are not convincing as two separate people. Malory's language is redolent of the mirroring and reflexive viewpoints of a primary level of development. Twice in his brief appearance in the tale, Balan answers questions meant for Balyn. When the brothers are asked which of them is responsible for the deaths of Lanceor and his lady, Balan jumps in with 'Whereby askist thou?', defiantly countering one question with another, but also as if to protest that it makes no difference (56.4). On its own this would be an unremarkable example of doing 'as a brothir ought to do', but in context his retort suggests a more fundamental ignorance of otherness (55.31–2). Significantly, when King Mark asks for Balyn's identity, it is Balan who replies (57.33–4).

The verbal detail of their fatal battle scene confirms their baby level of psychic development (70.22–73.11). Fleeing from the bodies of Garnyssh and his lady 'lest folke wold say he had slayne them', Balyn is conspicuously and vulnerably solitary. He comes to a cross upon which he finds the legend 'it is not for no knyght alone to ryde toward this castel'. Continuing despite this and a further warning about his borrowed shield – ignoring both in the manner with which he has treated dire predictions throughout the tale – Balyn learns that he will have to fight the knight who guards the island that lies beyond. As it turns out, this knight is none other than his brother Balan. The odd way this revelation is made and the mercurial varying of viewpoints bespeak the brothers' radical interdependence. The scene begins from Balyn's perspective: 'And thenne he loked on his armour and understood he was wel armed, and therwith blessid hym and mounted upon his hors. Thenne afore hym he sawe come rydynge oute of a castel a knyght, and his hors trapped all reed, and hymself in the same colour.' The narrative then abruptly switches to the visual experience of the stranger knight instead of directly telling us who he is: 'Whan this knyght in the reed beheld Balyn *hym thought it shold be his broder Balen* by cause of his two swerdys, but by cause he knewe not his sheld he demed it was not he.' It is as if Balan has his perception of his brother instead of a name. The blur of combatants is traditional in epic and romance battle scenes – 'he smote him, and he ...' and so on – but given the tale's other indications of symbiosis the fusing of Balyn and Balan in the fight that follows has a particular resonance. In their inevitable, too-late verbal exchange, the narrative gives Balyn's full name but for Balan, once again, brotherhood is self-description: 'Thenne said Balyn le Saveage, "What knyghte arte thow? For or now I found never no knyght that matched me." "My name is," said he, "Balan, broder unto the good knyght Balyn."' The idea of being 'matched' – common enough – has extra freight for two siblings who so perfectly mirror each other. Apprehending the situation, Balyn faints, and Balan crawls forward to take off his helm so that he can see who he is, but is still unable to 'knowe hym by the vysage' because it is so injured and covered in their shared family blood.[21] Shared blood, which poses a difficulty in the making of the self, is also a hindrance to genuine knowledge of a sibling as another person.

The extent of the brothers' lack of autonomy is neatly spelled out by the rules of the fatal game they have had to play: Balan has come across an earlier keeper of the island, and has been compelled to fight him to the death.

Having won, he has had to take the keeper's place. (This unlucky adventure is presumably why he has disappeared from the narrative for so long.) If Balyn had killed him but survived, he would similarly have been forced to take up this solitary post; he would have become Balan. There is only room for one of them, but neither can function adequately on his own. Nothing throws one back on one's own resources more starkly than an island, and neither brother is psychically well qualified for the job. The solution is that they both must die. Mitchell writes that 'death has a double dominion with siblings – they arrive from non-existence and they threaten non-existence. Womb and tomb are equivalents', or, as Balyn, still embracing his sibling as indivisibly the same as himself, puts it, 'we came bothe oute of one wombe, that is to say one moders bely, and so shalle we lye bothe in one pytte'. His statement echoes Lanceor's lady's words just before she takes her own life: 'A, Balyne! too bodyes thou haste slayne in one herte, and too hertes in one body, and too soules thou hast loste.'[22] This earlier double death, for which he is also responsible, raises the spectre of his own fatal interdependence with his brother. Psychically speaking, Balyn is not far from the 'other one Balyn' stage of development.[23]

Does the passionate attachment of Balyn and Balan – which Mitchell would term 'rampant' and inherently unstable – protest too much?[24] On the surface, the story appears to be an attempt to represent the fifteenth-century English ideal of brotherhood.[25] Malory's French source describes Balan's near-recognition of Balyn as an instinctive, almost telepathic surge of feeling. Malory rejects this slant in favour of an entirely rational mental process (that knight has two swords, so maybe he is Balyn, but he has a strange shield, so no), perhaps in order to free this early story from the blood-based emotiveness of which the text will become increasingly suspicious. The failure in recognition is a failure to grasp otherness. Balan expects Balyn to have remained the same, not to have had separate experiences that will have changed him. Even at this stage, there is a gap between the text's ostensible intention and its latent pattern of meaning. Like Arthur with his nightmare, Malory's tale, at its less conscious level, tries to tell itself things it would rather not know. As selectively deaf as the men who ride through it, the narrative is perhaps able to afford this single, mutual fratricide because it will insist upon its entirely accidental nature and will not consciously explore the ways that it suggests a darker side to siblinghood. A hint is given, moreover, of the symmetry between a tragically incomplete negotiation of siblinghood and future relationships: the sword with which Balyn kills Balan – 'the man that [he] moste love[s] in the worlde' – will be used by Launcelot to kill Gawayne – 'the man in the worlde that he lovith beste' (50.3; 74.12–13). The point is made in the aesthetic manner that Jill Mann detects in this tale.[26] The focus is not upon logical connection or the psychological development (or lack thereof) of Balyn as an individual, but rather upon the terrible continuity whereby sibling rage will lead to the ravaging of Arthur's quasi-fraternal fellowship.[27]

The mirror version of sibling relations encountered in the case of Balyn and Balan does not obtain elsewhere in *Le Morte Darthur*. The text's most complex sibling is Gawayne, whose envious nature and sorrow at the killing of his brother Gareth drive him forward towards his own death and the destruction of the kingdom. His exchange with the informant who gives him the news of Gareth's death is perhaps the most arresting of all Malory's conversations, not least because of the usual stubborn deafness (887.9–35). Mitchell suggests that sibling death is a greater cause of psychosis than the death of a parent, arousing a storm of grief fuelled not by loss alone but also by guilt, the repressed desire for the sibling's annihilation. Gawayne is carried away on a tide of crazed fury that exceeds his behaviour in either Malory's French or his English source.[28]

The relationship between Gawayne and Gareth provides scant evidence that the text has advanced in resolving the issue of siblinghood, although one might say that this time the pieces are out on the table. Gawayne does not recognise Gareth when the younger brother arrives at court, but, unlike the case of Balan, a subconscious magnetic force springing from shared blood causes him to be kind to the stranger. The narrative, in one of its very rare analytical passages, makes it clear that Gawayne's generosity is inferior to that of Launcelot, which springs purely from his courteous nature, free of genetic impulse (225.27–30).[29] Significantly, as Gawayne says, it is Launcelot whom Gareth loved more than he did his own blood brothers.

Gareth himself exudes the ambivalence of adolescence. He boasts of his family and yet treats it as a secret. He is in flight from his relatives, but wants them to look for him. He intends to make his own name before his name is revealed. Three times he lashes out at his older brother, Gawayne. On none of these occasions does the narrative comment upon the situation or provide explicit information about Gareth's motives; in fact, compared with Balyn, Gareth is generally sealed off from narratorial interior analysis. Perhaps, while the guilelessness of Balyn made him an attractive access point for comment, the more evidently mixed sibling feelings of Gareth require him to be held at arm's length. The first blow is struck when he meets Gawayne 'by fortune' in the tournament, and tellingly contrasts with his recognition of Launcelot immediately beforehand and his resolve not to hit him (275.24–8). The second is occasioned by the announcement of Gareth's familial identity. Raising the question of intention, Gawayne says to Gareth, 'I wente ye wolde not have smyttyn me so.'[30] This is evidently hard for Gareth to take: 'Whan he herde hym sey so, he thrange here and there, and so with grete payne he gate oute of the pres' (277.18–21). His infringement of brotherly allegiance is plain and more than an embarrassment. As soon as he can, Gareth goes back into hiding, with Gawayne searching for him in vain. In a couple of ways the third blow resembles the Balyn and Balan battle. As in the case of Balyn approaching the island, the narrative slows and we are invited to take note of Gareth's solitariness: 'So the deuke departed, and sir Gareth stoode there alone. And as he stoode he sey an armed knyghte on horsebak commynge towarde him' (282.10–12). As with Balyn, aloneness in this context acts as a foil for the approach of a second 'me'; it also raises questions about the autonomy of the solitary knight. Once again the drama initially unfolds according to the eyes of the main player himself, and once again the quantity of familial bloodshed is emphasised. Gareth's question could be taken as axiomatic of what Mitchell calls 'the pinhead of ambivalence': 'What ar ye ... that ryght now were so stronge and so myghty, and now so sodeynly is yelde to me?'[31] Gawayne's own statement echoes the ambivalence: 'I ought of ryght to worshyp you, *and ye were nat my brother*', which could equally mean that he would feel the urge to honour Gareth *even if he were not* his brother, or that he would feel the urge to honour him *if only he were not* his brother (282.24–34). It is not possible to go on living on a pinhead; we are soon told that, for all their kind words, Gareth made it a habit to keep away from Gawayne because 'he was evir vengeable, and where he hated he wolde be avenged with murther, and that hated sir Gareth' (285.31–2). The ostensibly cheerful 'Tale of Sir Gareth', an attempt to depict things at Arthur's court when all was as it ought to be, has an ominous undercurrent. The murderous Mordred, that present absence in the tale, is not its only sign of siblinghood's destructive potential. In sum, while the perils of brotherhood were denied in the babyhood fraternity of 'Balyn', they are spotlighted in the teenage 'Tale of Sir Gareth'.

The case of the sisters Lynet and Lyonesse is controlled by a different kind of schematic trajectory, one that depends not only upon perennial ways of organising siblinghood but also upon issues of gender. Lynet is the active guide and companion to the hero Gareth; we witness her coming to know him and revising her first impression of him over time. Lyonesse is the pattern of the peerless beauty whom the hero loves in an instant, desires from afar, and will attain with difficulty. The narrative shows some impatience with this inherited stereotype, but the traditional division between the women remains.[32] One could look upon the duo as mapping out the psychic lives of sisters, an example of difference generated as a defence against sameness and interchangeability.[33] Families, schools, communities, and siblings themselves – not to mention the biblical story of Mary and Martha – seek to contain the perils of sibling sameness by assigning roles: one sister is the good one, another the smart one, one the pretty one, the other the practical one. Medieval romance indulges in a version of this stultifying reflex. In Chrétien's *Yvain*, the hero's resourceful and constant friend Lunete will not be the one he marries; he will fall for her lady, the less intelligent, more beautiful, highhanded Laudine.[34] Unwilling to deny the hero a relationship with a capable woman who knows him and spends time with him, but also unwilling to combine these qualities with sexual desire, Chrétien's text, like Malory's, solves the issue with two women.

Malory's Lynet and Lyonesse, then, are informative about siblinghood, about the construction of 'woman', and about ideals of marriage and friendship in late medieval gentry culture. There is, in addition, a matter of literary genre to consider. While Malory's tale is not an allegory, one contributory model for Lynet and Lyonesse would seem to be the psychomachia or its medieval descendants in such works as the *Roman de la Rose*, where the figures that act and speak are interrelated aspects of the one woman whose complexities are thereby analysed.[35] Elements of psychomachia, in more limited and localised passages, are employed in romance to examine conflicts of feeling in male as well as female characters, but the use of the form in more sustained cases is particularly prevalent for women.[36] To a degree, the key to this gendering is the idea of woman as a difficult puzzle for the male glossator. Multiple female figures in such works are not afforded individuality but are in fact all aspects of Woman; femininity is seen as such an overriding marker that, ultimately, the features which distinguish one person from another are fused, leaving the one iridescent and perplexing archetype. The pattern is not confined to early literature; latter-day examples include Robert Altman's 1977 film *3 Women* and Marion Zimmer Bradley's 1983 Arthurian blockbuster *The Mists of Avalon*.

A literary inheritance, however, works in myriad ways. The analysis of the inner life by way of a plurality of fictional characters representing aspects of a single person – a kind of allegory of the emotions – had a special appeal for a cultural period when psychological nuance was becoming crucial to spiritual life, law and literature.[37] Increasingly, true gentility and sophistication demanded that individuals be versed in the complexities of their own and other people's emotions. From at least the twelfth century on, women are seen as having the edge in the perfection of this art. It is no accident that it is '*donne* ch'avete intelletto d'amore' (*ladies* refined and sensitive in love) to whom Dante addresses *La Vita Nuova*.[38] Inner complexity itself came to be seen as more typical of women than of men, and in some instances to be taken as a positive sign of the true *gentilesse* to which men also should aspire.[39] In this regard, the tendency of the psychomachia tradition to focus upon women rather than men displays one way that the late medieval era, despite its notorious misogyny, prized the feminine. For this reason, it is not a surprise that it is Lynet and Lyonesse rather than, for instance, Balyn and Balan who function, to a degree, as aspects of a single person. The results of this gendering in the psychomachia tradition are not always inhibiting of feminine agency and expression. For instance, Lynet plays the role of superego in curbing the lovers' sexual activity before marriage; she operates as, among other things, Lyonesse's *danger*. Her existence in the text frees Lyonesse to show, with impunity, not only sexual desire but also the courage to defend her clear intention to satisfy that desire – a rare achievement in a medieval romance concerned with gentry propriety. Subcontracting the necessity for the beloved to say no allows Lyonesse to declare, when caught in the middle of the night at her lover's bed: 'I woll that ye wete I shame nat to be with hym nor to do hym all the plesure that I can' (262.1–3).

Balyn and Balan were barely able to say where one of them ended and the other began. Gareth and Gawayne demonstrated the ordeal of balancing sameness with difference. Lynet and Lyonesse display no symptoms of such a tension. Insofar as Lynet is legible as an aspect of Lyonesse, however, this is not the unmitigated symbiosis in which Balyn and Balan seem to float but precisely the opposite: a differentiating impulse which, while sustaining stereotypes of separate feminine roles, also allows for a corrective to the prevailing courtly ideal of the female beloved as an angelic creature, unmarked by earthly affections.

Malory's Maiden of Astolat has received considerable critical attention; here I will confine my remarks to a few examples of how Mitchell's work illuminates Elayne and her rhyming brother Lavayne.[40] Elayne has many of the hallmarks of the hysteric, her extravagant performance of death being the major example. A recalcitrant subject, she does not want to get better, and rejects the intervention of her confessor, that late medieval close equivalent to a therapist. Mitchell finds that in order to understand hysteria one has to examine the role of sibling trauma.[41] As Lavayne points out, he and his sister are identical in their inability to leave Launcelot (826.35–827.2). While Lavayne's gender, however, unproblematically affords him a readymade role as Launcelot's junior companion in arms, Elayne, having failed to secure Launcelot's love and, due to his recovery, having lost her position as his nurse, elaborately wills and arranges for her life to end. She has been 'unable to take [her] place in a social series'.[42] Mitchell argues that, between a sister and a brother, gender functions as a defence against sameness. Perhaps, despite how little we see of the interactions of Elayne and Lavayne in the story, Mitchell's approach gives us another way to understand them, albeit one that points to the limits of that defence; it could be that in her hysteria Elayne is 'using the only form of protest available [to a woman] under patriarchy'.[43]

In certain ways, however, when all is said and done, Elayne defies the lot of the hysteric. Far from suffering the malady's classic symptom of aphonia, Elayne finds language in performing her death. She embodies the conclusions of Phillipe Ariès about medieval death as a final, dignifying act, her fatal hysteria inflected by culturally specific ideology and practices in which gender loses its inhibiting grip.[44] The speaking spectacle of Elayne's barge may have 'rubbed and rolled too and fro a grete whyle or ony man aspyed hit', but this may have less to do with the limitations upon Elayne's ability to communicate after her death than with the prevailing inattentiveness of all the main players to anything that they would rather not see (828.23–4).[45] This is not to downplay the fact that Elayne has to die in order to be seen and heard, or the irony whereby her brother's career flourishes immediately following her death (830.33–5). Elayne's body, floating on the surface of the Thames, is a symptom of the irresolution of siblinghood in *Le Morte Darthur*; she is what is left over.

The final example I will discuss is Sir Urry, whom I view as a sib-equivalent of Launcelot. It will not be my purpose here to detect a continuity of psychic history springing from Launcelot's childhood or his relationship with his brother Ector, but instead to consider elements of the healing scene in 'Sir Urry' itself in the context of Launcelot's position at court at the time.

It has not escaped scholars that Malory's description of Launcelot's celebrated weeping in 'The Tale of Sir Urry' – 'as he had bene a chylde that had bene beatyn' – coincides with the wording of a common autoerotic fantasy recorded by Freud: 'a child is being beaten' (868.1–2).[46] Spectacle, onlooking, and the shifting of viewpoints and roles are intrinsic to this fantasy, which Mitchell suspects is universal.[47] In the first stage the subject is watching a child being beaten. This is very likely to be a sibling, whether or not the subject recalls an actual scene from his childhood or makes a conscious identification of the child as such. The second stage involves a change of viewpoint: now it is the subject himself who is being beaten. In the third stage the subject is witnessing a number of children being beaten, all of them standing for the subject. This stage combines the sadism of the first and the masochism of the second for the sake of the total orgasmic pleasure in which the fantasy then culminates.[48] Freud's daughter Anna, who was among his patients, tried to repress this fantasy; she transmuted it, not always with total success, into 'nice stories', and finally into a written, quasi-medieval chivalric narrative. The 'nice stories' 'apparently, but only apparently, contain care and affection'; in them a knight holds captive a noble youth of fifteen – Anna Freud's own age at the time – and repeatedly has him tortured to the point of death. Each time, the youth pleads for mercy, and each time the knight relents at the eleventh hour and restores him to health.[49]

Malory's 'Sir Urry of Hungary' comes at a stage when Launcelot's status as perfect knight and defender of the realm has been severely compromised. Each of the episodes that precede 'Sir Urry' in 'Sir Launcelot and Queen Guinevere' shows him maintaining his position only by the skin of his teeth. When Arthur commands Launcelot to try his hand at healing the severely wounded Urry, Arthur himself and all of the other knights of the realm have failed, not to speak of those in other parts of the world. Given his recent experience and the saintly role of healer that he is being urged to enact, there is every reason for Launcelot to be filled with trepidation. On top of that, everyone is watching.

Both the Middle English expression used by Malory and the fantasy as reported use a passive construction that leaves out the beater. This grammatical occlusion could mean either that the fantasy is more about the fantasist and the beaten, or that the beater is a repressed and significant third party. Freud concluded that the beater is a parental figure, and that the fantasy is about the subject's illicit desire for the parent, who figures in the fantasy as the one of the opposite sex but whom Freud believed to be, at an unconscious level, always the father. In his view the beaten child is the subject's sibling rival. In 'Sir Urry', God, who denied Launcelot success in the Grail quest, is an obvious candidate for the Freudian Father. Like the noble youth in Anna Freud's nice story pleading with the knight who holds his fate in his hands, Launcelot prays to the Christian deity for mercy, and offers himself to him as a passive instrument. To a degree, King Arthur, who commands Launcelot to take the test, may fill the role, at least as vicar of the divinity, although his own failure rather curtails his claim. The queen, who is conspicuously not mentioned, may also be relevant as a quasi-parental figure of the opposite sex; certainly she had a hand in Launcelot's beaten condition.

To focus exclusively on Launcelot the child and his parental figures, however, is to leave Sir Urry out of his own tale and thereby to retain the blindness to lateral relationships which has typified psychoanalysis. Emphasising the mobility of their roles within the fantasy, Mitchell suggests that beater and beaten are to a large extent the subject and his sibling or sib-equivalent. In Malory's scenario, as in the common fantasy that Freud made famous, the designation of which is unstable. Urry, replete with wounds, lies at the feet of the best knight of the world who, as it turns out, like Anna Freud's knight, has the power to save him. But, as noted, there is ample reason to see Launcelot himself as the beaten one, and to anticipate that his status as beaten might be confirmed by failure in the present adventure. Certain features of this story strengthen the sense that Urry, Launcelot's surrogate or double, is, more specifically, a quasi-sibling. In his floridly wounded condition, lying on the ground, Urry resembles a new baby, needy and the focus of care, concern and great expectations; he too is Round Table material. It is the definition of the new baby to be the most recent arrival, but Launcelot, the big brother, nursing his own neediness, has managed to stage his own dramatic, even later arrival. Like an older sibling, he is required to look after this little brother. He is under pressure to excel; indeed, he must, as the family honour depends upon him. Mitchell points out that masturbatory fantasies are by their nature wish-fulfilling; in the 'nice stories' this aspect of them is retained in the 'pleasurable gain' which the fantasist gets from 'being always the centre of attention through dramatising the self's crises'.[50] Launcelot is emphatically the centre of attention; the dramatising of his crises has become the hallmark of successive stories. The wounded Urry, ostensible wonder and focus of the scene, is effectively eclipsed, though perhaps it would be more accurate to say that he is caught up in that aspect of the fantasy whereby the fantasist, 'as in a dream ... inhabits all the characters, is beater and beaten, one child or many, observer and observed'.[51] There is a striking degree of symbiosis between Malory's narrative voice and Launcelot, its hero.[52] Increasingly anxious about Launcelot's adultery, the text indulges in its own wish-fulfilling daydream by exhibiting him as a conduit of God's grace, miraculously caring for the wounded. Malory's text is not explicitly very interested in religion, but the emotive force of the visible in this scene is informed by the ocularity of late medieval religious popular culture in which copious weeping is the outcome of a charged moment of beholding.[53] The healing of Urry, then, amply partakes of the 'niceness' of Anna Freud's attempts to transform the beating fantasy into a non-transgressive tale. Launcelot, however, retains the grandiosity that would be lost in sublimation.[54] Malory's scene is a fifteenth-century chivalric, quasi-hagiographic 'nice story'; its climax, corresponding to the orgasm of the fantasy, is that sought-after medieval stamp of God's favour, the ejaculatory 'gift of tears'.

Looking at the Urry scene according to the three stages of the fantasy, we might comment in the following way: its first step, in which the subject witnesses a child being beaten, represents the 'eradication of the other'.[55] There is reason to imagine that Launcelot, or the Malorian narrator on his behalf, might relish Urry's beaten condition. Launcelot's own beaten condition is hidden; Urry's is gratifyingly plain to behold. Launcelot's trepidation also functions as suspense for Urry and the onlookers, to the brink of power play: will he or will he not save Sir Urry? Launcelot's guilty anxiety about his own status as best knight and saviour of the kingdom's reputation is relentlessly self-involved. Such is his narcissism that pity gets no purchase. His prayer to the Trinity before touching Urry is far more about the saving of himself than about the saving of Urry (867.21–6).

The second step of the fantasy, in which the fantasist himself is beaten, represents the 'eradication of the ego', a 'prelude to auto-erotic orgasm'.[56] At this stage, the male subject becomes passive.[57] Launcelot cedes control to a force other than himself and greater than he is – 'Good Lorde, never of myselff'; he prays to be taken over and used by this other all-powerful agency as it pleases. The agenda of this second stage overlaps with that of the first; 'the obvious masochism of the beating fantasy could be seen as a sadistic attack on [siblings as] doubles'.[58] Urry is not safely other. In the final stage, the fantasist is watching a number of children being beaten. This climactic phase is characterised by vagueness; the subject is simultaneously the witness of the beatings and himself the several children being beaten. This vagueness, which Mitchell identifies both with repression and with approaching physical orgasm, speaks to the sense in which Launcelot, seeing the weakened Urry on the ground before him, is also seeing himself; the plurality of children may be suggested by the vast crowd of onlookers, including 110 knights, witnesses to Launcelot's trial and themselves a host of beaten men, having failed in this strange saintly adventure. In short, 'The Healing of Sir Urry' exhibits the hero of *Le Morte Darthur*, right before the final denouement of the larger story, as His Majesty the Baby.

Things that make a page of Malory sound like Malory coincide to a remarkable degree with the clinical signs of sibling dysfunction. As we have noted, siblinghood in the text is often represented by moments of seeing: of recognising, failing to recognise, or something between the two – the same trope that infuses the experiences and fantasies of siblinghood recorded in psychoanalytic practice. Recognition, never mind failed or incomplete recognition, is a complex process prone to psychic vicissitudes. Writing of *anagnorisis*, Terence Cave argues that 'recognition may easily turn out to be an impostor, claiming to resolve, conjoin and make whole while it busily brings to the surface all the possibilities that threaten wholeness'.[59] Not only is wholeness – that prevailing desideratum of Malory's work – not guaranteed or triggered by recognition, but recognition acts as a touchstone for destruction. Referring to Peter Brooks' work on melodrama, Cave writes that 'the "return of the repressed" is what happens at the moment of recognition', but this moment does not provide cure and catharsis.[60] The comment is apt for siblings in Malory. When Balyn recognises Balan in their fatal fight, what he is registering is not only the features of his brother but also the repressed prophecy that he would kill the man he most loved in the world (50.2–3). This determination to know only what one would like to know also lies behind another familiar symptom of the text: Malory's cross-purpose conversations. Mitchell notes, 'the first sense that the other is not the same as the self induces irritation; in clinical work one meets this as a continual, grating miscommunication'.[61] In Malory this peculiarity is an habitual way of proceeding. The failure to negotiate siblinghood pervades *Le Morte Darthur* altogether beyond the exigencies of any specific character or circumstance.

Whose are these symptoms of failed siblinghood? Whose fantasy, precisely, is the fantasy of the healing of Sir Urry? The only accurate answer, tautological though it might be, is that the fantasist is the text. The aspirations, anxieties, ambivalences, and symptoms of psychic dysfunction of *Le Morte Darthur* are those that emerged from an intricate dance of elements: Sir Thomas Malory, knight prisoner; the late fifteenth-century English gentry and their culture, both familial and literary; Arthurian traditions, and the human experience of siblinghood. The crises, tensions and factiousness of Malory's society inform the book he wrote.[62] Times of uncertainty lend themselves to idealisation, but in turn idealisation gives itself away. The text openly expresses its doubts about the sibling blood tie when compared to behaviour based upon inner virtues, but this momentary remark is only the tip of an iceberg, much of it submerged below the level of the consciousness of Sir Thomas Malory and what he wrote. The failures of siblinghood place a limit upon viable selfhood and, in turn, upon all further relationships. At its worst, the insecure transaction of siblinghood leads to its tragic de-repression: war, and, in the case of Malory's narrative, the destruction of everything the text holds dear.

CHAPTER 7

Fathers and Sons, Mothers and Daughters: The family romance in Katherine Cecil Thurston's *The Fly on the Wheel*

CLÍONA Ó GALLCHOIR

Katherine Cecil Thurston's *The Fly on the Wheel* (1908) offers a highly unusual depiction of the life of the Catholic bourgeoisie in provincial Ireland at the beginning of the twentieth century, a time of enormous social and political upheaval. In her novel, Thurston depicts a tightly controlled society dedicated to social advancement and eager to grasp the opportunities available to the swelling numbers of the middle class, a class that, according to the novel 'by right of strength has formed its huge republic, and spread like a net over civilisation – invincible, indispensable as the vast machines from which it has sucked its power'.[1] The universality of bourgeois advancement is both proclaimed by Thurston but also given a local inflection in her comment on the fact that, in Ireland, the barriers previously placed in the path of aspirant Catholics create an even more determined focus on the prize of social status and respectability: 'there is incentive in the thought of a forced passage, and the constant sight of a social Mecca stirs this section of a naturally indolent community to unprecedented action' (p. 3).

Some of the contradictions in the mentality of this class, particularly at the moment of the novel's publication (just prior to the revolutionary events triggered by the 1916 Rising) are captured in the tension between the desired 'social Mecca' and the notion of a 'forced passage'. Thurston here evokes the uneasy coexistence of the desire for social status, a concept that was in Ireland impossible to disentangle from long-standing colonial structures, with the resentment of those held in subordinate positions by those very structures. The description of Irish Catholics as 'naturally indolent' in fact reflects the pervasive presence of colonial stereotypes in Irish culture. The narrator's comment can also, however, be read in terms of desire and repression. The 'social Mecca' that is pursued requires the repression of more primitive drives and forces, hinted at in the violence inherent in the idea of a 'forced passage'. In order to overcome social inferiority and subordination, it seems, the Catholic bourgeoisie must repress destructive rage and channel it into socially sanctioned 'action'. The Freudian concepts of repression and sublimation invoked here are, I argue, vital to an understanding of Thurston's novel, which explores the Irish bourgeoisie by means of the psychosexual formation and experience of individual subjects. As I intend to show, Thurston in fact offers an unusually clear-sighted portrayal of the fundamental contradiction identified first by Freud – the fact that 'the gendered human subject ... is inherently at odds with itself' and that 'what we call our identity ... is always unstable, always at risk of sabotage from the unacceptable feelings of loss and desire which we have to repress into our unconscious in order to conform to the demands of culture'.[2]

Thurston's interest in sexuality as a force in the lives of individuals and societies is not surprising given her position as a *fin-de-siècle* writer and a 'New Woman' novelist, but *The Fly on the Wheel* is something of an anomaly in her career both because of its exclusively Irish location and also because of its stringent realism and unusually pessimistic tone. Her other work, most notably her last novel *Max*, displays what Gerardine Meaney has called 'anger, energy and passionate optimism'.[3] Tina O'Toole, likewise, discussing Thurston in the context of New Woman writers, describes how she and writers like her 'imagined new relationships and gender roles in the familiar social world' and 'sought to challenge the heterosocial *status quo*'; she also notes the affinities between New Woman fiction and Utopian fiction.[4] Meaney, in fact, effectively dismisses *The Fly on the Wheel* by noting that it appears 'to indicate a turn to social realism and pessimism' and that the publication of *Max* two years later 'can be read as an emphatic recovery from both afflictions'.[5] More recently, however, Whitney Standlee has described the novel as Thurston's 'most accomplished work' and stresses the fact that its 'portrayals and preoccupations balance precariously on the cusp between two centuries and two eras'.[6] Stylistically, the novel's realism and its meticulous rendering of the bourgeois social world make evident its roots in Victorian fiction. But the novel is also committed to exploring the characters' internal worlds and desires, in a way that lays bare the psychic costs of social conformity. Freud paradoxically described as 'normal' a process involving loss, rage and repression, and Thurston's realistically faithful Waterford location has precisely the same quality: its solid 'reality' co-exists with the acknowledgement of interior, psychic realities that house unattainable desires and violent fantasies. *The Fly on the Wheel* is undoubtedly more pessimistic than Thurston's other novels about the potential to challenge heteronormative and patriarchal constructions of gender and sexuality. However, it can also be read as a form of protest against the absence of any possibility of feminine subjectivity in the Ireland of the period outside of the role of wife and mother. Freud's theories provide a developmental narrative, but one that is – notoriously – premised on a masculine subject, a subject that is shown in the novel to be compatible with the aspirations of the rising Catholic bourgeoisie of the late nineteenth and early twentieth centuries. *The Fly on the Wheel* is an exceptional novel in that it confronts the absence of a female-centred plot and registers a protest against this absence. Thurston's novel is thus a fascinating text to consider alongside the stories of fathers and sons which dominate the literature of the revival period.[7]

In his short essay 'On Family Romances' Freud locates the act of storytelling and narration in the gap between desire and reality. In its earliest form, the family romance is the story that the child tells himself in response to anger, frustration or disappointment at the hands of his parents – he constructs a narrative in which he is a foundling, the offspring of noble and idealised parents, forced to tolerate inferior and inadequate substitutes. The family romance is described by Marianne Hirsch as 'a structure of fantasy – the imaginary construction of plots according to principles of wish fulfillment' developed in response to 'the discrepancies between *social reality* and *fantasy construction*, which are basic to the experience and the institution of family'.[8] According to Hirsch, the family romance 'combines and reveals as indistinguishable the psychological subjective experience of family and the process of narrative'. In Freud's account, the family romance undergoes a crucial modification during the Oedipal phase, when the child, with a new awareness of sex, differentiates between his parents and accepts his real mother as his mother, while continuing to fantasise about an ideal but absent father, and his status thus alters from Foundling to Bastard.[9] Freud's discussion assumes a male child, whose family romance alters and develops according to the classic male Oedipus complex. The shift in status to Bastard, therefore, is accompanied by heightened sexual curiosity and fantasy around his mother, whom the child imagines in 'situations of secret infidelity and … secret love-affairs'.[10] The family romance thus forms part of the process in the formation of male subjectivity, in which otherwise conflicting feelings of admiration and anger towards the father can co-exist through the device of the ideal but absent 'real' father and the inadequate and present 'substitute'. What makes the family romance especially interesting for a discussion of *The Fly on the Wheel* is the suggestion made by Marthe Robert as to the stylistic distinction between the narrative of the Foundling and that of the Bastard. Robert explicitly aligns the second, Oedipal stage of the family romance with realism:

> Insofar as such a writer [Balzac] undertakes to maintain his inventions within the bounds of probability and verisimilitude – which does not mean that he constructs a new fraction of reality, but only that, notwithstanding his suppressed destructiveness, he pays homage to things as they are – he submits to the subtle motivations of realism that intervene at the more advanced stage of the Family Romance's development, emulating in fact the Oedipal Bastard.[11]

In *The Fly on the Wheel*, not only is realism of form clearly allied to the 'suppressed destructiveness' inseparable from the Oedipus narrative, but as already noted, Thurston also creates a space within which to register the absence of the daughter's narrative.

The initial pages of *The Fly on the Wheel* overtly establish the novel's realist principles, and yoke them firmly to the central male character, Stephen Carey. The narrative opens with a classic realist statement of time and location – 'It was an April morning in the Irish town of Waterford' (p. 1) – and then goes on to further describe this location:

> Portion of this dusty, characteristic, sparsely-populated town is dedicated to business – the business of the shops; a second and more important portion of it is given over to the quays, from whence a constant traffic is carried on with the hereditary enemy, England; while a third part, that holds itself aloof from commerce, is to be reckoned as half residential, half professional. It is to this third quarter that the eye of the story-seeker must turn on this April morning. (p. 1)

The reference to the 'story-seeker' introduces a high degree of narrative self-consciousness into this minutely detailed realism, as does the ironic comment about the trade between Ireland and England. In the same overt manner the narrator then introduces Stephen Carey, 'hero, in so far as middle-class Irish life produces heroes, of the anticipated romance' (p. 2).

The reference to his role as hero is of course ambiguous – he is both a type of 'ordinary' middle-class hero, and also hero of the 'anticipated romance', the word romance here signalling a significant divergence from the reality so deliberately established by the narrator, and to which, we quickly learn, Stephen has subjected himself. Stephen is the eldest son of Barney Carey, a man who had made a fortune as a builder, and then lost it all. As the eldest son, Stephen takes on the responsibilities of a parent after his ruined father's death and ensures that his six younger brothers are educated and provided for as their father had wished: 'What Stephen did in that tremendous crisis, rather what he did in the long toilsome years, when the actual crisis was passed and the daily burden was still to be carried, is among the unwritten records of heroism' (p. 7).

The identification with the father that, according to Freud, is essential in order to resolve the Oedipus complex is in Stephen's case very literal and complete – he has in effect become his father. The blatant inadequacy of his father reinforces Stephen's position under the 'reality principle' as he is forced to shed childish illusions, but he receives the rewards that Freud proposes are reserved for the male child who overcomes his rage and jealousy against his father and suppresses his desire for his mother: authoritative and successful masculinity. This much is made strikingly apparent in the novel's opening chapters. The narration of events begins in the breakfast room of Stephen's house in Lady Lane, where his wife Daisy is drinking tea, discussing household matters with the servant, and opening letters. Hearing footsteps, however, she listens closely and 'with the confirmation of their sound she rose from her seat, moving so hastily that the nun's letter fluttered down' (p. 10). The house, and Daisy's life, revolve around Stephen; this is hardly surprising given that the narrator describes him as 'one of those beings to whom it is given to claim consideration by a frown – service by a single word' (p. 11). The opening pages thus establish Stephen as the central focus, and his perspective, that of a dogged determination 'to grapple' (p. 4) with reality and triumph over it, as the guiding, realist perspective. The self-consciousness of the narration and the insistence with which Stephen's authority is asserted by the narrator make it clear at the same time, however, that it is precisely these same perspectives that will be at play in the 'anticipated romance': the 'story-seeker' is invoked for a second time to fix his/her attention on:

> a man of thirty-eight – a citizen with a wife and three children – a solicitor with a growing practice – a matured, controlled, successful

> Stephen Carey, possessing but one responsibility remaining from the past – Frank, the youngest brother, the seventh son, still studying medicine in Paris in fulfillment of Barney Carey's dream. (p. 7)

The narrator thus signals to the reader that this hard-won, successful present is potentially highly unstable, threatened by a remnant of the past. The potential disruption to the realist narrative is in addition suggested by the folkloric reference to the 'seventh son'. The threat is not Frank himself – his potential for disruption is easily dispatched by Stephen – but Stephen's own repressed past, a repression that is released by his meeting with Isabel Costello, the young girl to whom Frank has become engaged.

Like Stephen, Isabel is an orphan, the daughter of Dan Costello, a minor bank official who, like Stephen's father, failed in his role as provider. Having left her convent school in Paris, Isabel now lives with her aunt, Miss Costello, who attempts to instruct her in the correct demeanour for a girl of very slender means: 'you know very well that a girl must do what other people do – 'specially if she has no money' (p. 61). Isabel's arrival in Waterford is greeted with a mixture of interest and anxiety, in a predictable response to her combination of beauty and pennilessness.[12] The impact of her arrival on Stephen is immediate and its ripples are felt even before they have met: in the interests of getting to know his enemy, Stephen decides to attend a dance to which she has been invited. His uncharacteristic decision to attend 'made a definite stir of excitement' (p. 21). Stephen's presence is unusual, because in this conservative, provincial society 'the married man hardly exists as an independent being, for he is a thing appropriated, labelled, laid irrevocably on the shelf' (p. 37).

The description of Stephen as a 'thing appropriated' is unexpected and seemingly in tension with the portrayal of his mastery and authority over his wife and family, and his status as a respected citizen. The erasure of the married man as an 'independent being' in the context of the dance thus reveals its function as a carefully staged event designed for ensuring stable social reproduction. It excludes married men, but is presided over by married women, whose presence is supposed to ensure that the sexual energy such events channel remains under control. The subjection of sexual desire to other aims and goals is also made manifest in the account of Stephen's own marriage. Faced with the social expectation that he would marry, we are told that 'it was scarcely to be expected that he would lose his heart or even his head ... and he had looked round his little world much as the Eastern might have studied the slave-market' (p. 12). Daisy is selected, 'as gossip had unanimously held' for the financial resources she and her family bring to the marriage, but also for her youth and her 'pretty blue eyes, pretty fair hair', which are to Stephen a matter of 'pride' (p. 12). In exercising control over his desires even in the case of marriage, Stephen determinedly renounces pleasure in favour of 'reality'. His ego's demands are expressed through his 'pride' in the object he has chosen, but his marriage is predicated on the continued repression and denial of desire. Having been convinced by his early experiences that his desires can never be met by reality, Stephen renounces them and takes necessity instead as his law, turning himself into a servant of civilisation.

Stephen's masculinity is here presented on the one hand as excessive: in the tellingly Orientalist simile he is compared to an 'Eastern' who regards the relationship between women and men in the light of master and slave. On the other hand, however, this hypermasculinity results in a form of self-subjection, a denial of one's own desires and thus, ultimately, a kind of emasculation – the married man as a 'thing appropriated'. Joseph Valente's discussion of manliness in Irish culture at the turn of the century provides an illuminating perspective on this paradoxical masculinity. In Valente's account, manliness (an explicitly English construct) is defined through both the possession of 'animal spirits' and the capacity to govern and channel them: 'the ideal of manhood ... consisted in the simultaneous necessity for and achievement of a vigilant, rational self-control – in *strong passions strongly governed*'.[13] The imperialistic manner in which manliness functioned in this era will be obvious: the fact of political subordination to Britain implies a lack of manliness on the part of those subordinated, the need to be governed by rulers who are defined by their capacity to self-govern. The familiar nineteenth-century images of the Irish as either simian and subhuman, or as feminised and passive, construct them as either excessive in their animal nature or as lacking in the 'passions' and 'spirits' which are also an essential element of manliness. The description of Stephen as an 'Eastern' positions him as a colonial subject, lacking in civility, but ultimately his lack of manliness lies in the *excessive* control he exercises over himself, a control that renders him servile and neutered.

The excessive nature of Stephen's self-regulation suggests the fragility of his apparently 'mature' mastery of his desires, which is then exposed upon his initial meeting with Isabel. Her first appearance, to both Stephen and the reader, is in the middle of a dance, where she is described as 'a flower swaying in the wind, a young animal stretching itself to the sun, a bird in its first flight' (p. 39): she is in other words the representative of Nature, the antithesis of the culture and civilisation to which Stephen has dedicated and subjected himself. Isabel is also portrayed as driven by instinct and desire: 'she saw nothing beyond the stirring perspective of light and colour, heard nothing but the swaying music of the waltz that swelled and faded in waves of sound' (p. 39). Stephen's erotic attraction to her is instantaneous, and its source is obvious: her unusual, uninhibited behaviour reawakens in him his own long-suppressed, renounced desires. Through its portrayal of Stephen, *The Fly on the Wheel* offers an unusually sophisticated reflection on the interplay between class, gender and nationality at a critical juncture in Ireland's history, revealing the complexity of claims to leadership and authority precisely at the time in which the contest over the legitimate governance of Ireland was reaching its decisive moment. The narrative is unusual in its focus on the self-divided nature of Irish masculinity, but it is even more unusual in its depiction of a femininity that challenges this masculinity at a point at which it was poised to assume the position of leadership which had been denied under colonial structures.

The extent to which the ideological struggles taking place in Ireland in the early twentieth century are part of the social context inhabited by Thurston's characters is revealed in a scene which anticipates both Joyce's 'The Dead' and the Christmas dinner-table scene in *A Portrait of the Artist as a Young Man*. Stephen's brother-in-law, Tom Norris, is an enthusiastic Gaelic revivalist, and he, Stephen and Fr Cunningham debate the movement over a dinner at which Isabel is also present. Stephen is dismissive of attempts to 'send Ireland back to school' in order to gaelicise it, arguing instead that the country should be 'souse[d] with modern thought – Spencer and Huxley, Haeckel and Kant' (pp. 105–6).[14] This brings him into conflict with the priest, who predictably reacts against these 'dangerous writers' (p. 106). These discussions are clearly represented as being part of the masculine domain: while the men discuss 'serious' topics, Isabel is positioned as an ill-informed, female onlooker who exclaims, 'What is it you're talking about? ... I'd simply love to know!' (p. 103). There is, however, narrative irony at work here, which undercuts the apparently hierarchical arrangement of masculine and feminine spheres that structure these scenes, and the 'world' of the novel as a whole.

Below the surface of this seemingly significant discussion of politics and ideas, libidinal currents propel the characters' actions. Tom expresses support for women's involvement in the movement, asserting at dinner that 'it's sickening to think of what women could do – and don't, just because the thing isn't fashionable!' (pp. 100–1), and he later addresses himself directly to Isabel: 'I wish, Miss Costello, you'd interest yourself in the cause. If we could only induce the educated women to take it up seriously, we could move mountains' (p. 118). This laudable and seemingly progressive stance is undermined by the fact that Tom's interest in Isabel is not simply or even primarily in her ability to contribute to the cause: he is clearly attracted to her, but his only means of gaining her attention is apparently to attempt to rouse a Gaelic enthusiasm in her. Having manoeuvred himself into the position of chaperone as she walks home, he confesses that he found Waterford 'a bit narrow' (p. 117) when he returned from university, but it seems clear that his passion for the Gaelic revival has successfully sublimated any troublesome desires. Tom's efforts are rendered comical by the fact that in his case, the Gaelic movement is an obvious strategy of containment: one of the dinner guests comments approvingly that he has 'such nice quiet tastes, instead of betting and playing cards like so many of the young men' (p. 103). This suggests that, while Tom's patriotism and commitment to the cause have formed a channel in which he can redirect his libidinal energy, the other young men, similarly frustrated in this limiting and regulated world, divert their energies in other, more potentially troubling ways. The supposedly weighty discussion of Ireland's future is also undercut by the reader's awareness that, for Isabel, the sole focus of interest at this dinner has been Stephen and her own determination to live according to *her* desires. She causes unease, for instance, among the female company over their after-dinner tea by declaring that 'If I cared, I'd marry a beggar; and if I didn't care, it wouldn't matter to me if the person was a king' (p. 110). While Mary Norris, the sister of Stephen's wife, Daisy, displays a passive resentment towards the male discourse at the table – 'What fools men are!' (p. 108) she says, the minute she and the other women are alone – she is resigned simply to grasping at whatever this world can offer her. Isabel's attitude towards the order of things, on the surface simply the naive ignorance of a girl who has recently left school, is however much more dangerous and destabilising.

Isabel's attraction to Stephen initially appears to be driven by his status as an older, authoritative man, and thus serves to emphasise his masculinity: surrounded by a group of young men competing for her hand in the next dance, Isabel unexpectedly chooses Stephen instead. Stephen's authority is further reinforced by his determination to break off the engagement between Isabel and his brother, Frank. The exercise of this authority confirms Isabel's attraction to him, as she declares to her aunt, 'I'll tell you what Frank is. He's just a shadow of his brother. Only for his brother he wouldn't be there at all' (p. 73). Frank is thus positioned as a son, with

Isabel clearly stating her attraction to the powerful 'father' she perceives Stephen to be. At this point, Isabel appears to be constructed according to a classically Freudian paradigm. Freud's account of the development of female sexuality and femininity proposes that the girl's transfer of her attachment, from her mother to her father, is motivated by penis-envy: having realised that she lacks a penis, and that her mother also lacks one and desires the father who possesses one, the girl turns to the father in search of a penis, and, ultimately (in 'mature' femininity), a baby. Isabel, however, is driven by desires which undercut this apparently conventional feminine position. She passionately rejects her aunt's ideas of what a girl 'must' do: 'I'll never – never do it! I can't cut out my life on a sort of pattern. It must be what I want it to be, or nothing at all' (p. 61). Whereas Stephen's entire sense of self has been built around an accommodation to the disappointments and disillusionments of reality, Isabel demands that the external world conform to her desire: 'it must be *what I want it to be*'. The persistence of such disruptive desires suggests that Isabel is not, after all, a textbook example of Freudian femininity.

Rosalind Minsky points out that later in his career, Freud himself arrived at the conclusion that accounts of female sexuality needed a much fuller consideration of the pre-Oedipal phase, and the girl's intense and enduring attachment to her mother. As Minsky observes, even if the switch from mother to father is made by the girl child, her desire for a penis does not necessarily indicate the erasure of the mother as the primary sexual object: 'at the unconscious level they want the penis from the father *to make them acceptable to their mother*'.[15] Much psychoanalytic theory after Freud has of course focused on pre-Oedipal experience and the mother–child dyad in ways that challenge or complicate his conclusions, and I would argue that in Isabel, *The Fly on the Wheel* offers us a representation of the disruptive force, in a tightly organised, patriarchal society, of a woman whose primary bond to her mother persists.

Isabel's mother at first seems simply to be an absence in the text. She appears to have died in Isabel's very early childhood but no concrete details are given. She is described by another character as 'a Miss Dysart of Derryvane' whose father 'cut her off without a penny' (p. 44) as a punishment for her wayward love match. Of Isabel's father we learn, in the merciless judgement of Mrs Burke, that he was 'the greatest fool that ever lived. If you made a king of Dan Costello, he'd be begging in the streets the week after!' (p. 44). Significantly, Isabel is openly contemptuous of her late father; she horrifies her aunt by saying that 'if he hadn't said so many prayers … perhaps he might have got promotion in the bank – and left me better off' (pp. 63–4). As a result of Costello's inadequacy, Isabel's mother was scorned and excluded by the Waterford bourgeoisie: Mrs Burke recounts cruelly that she 'used to have to turn Dan's old coats for herself when he was done with them! But all the Wexford people are queer' (p. 44). For Isabel, however, her mother remains ideal and unattainable. When she meets Julia, a servant who remembers her as a child, 'a new look' crosses her face and she asks if Julia knew her mother (p. 99). All Julia can tell her is that she remembers being told 'the handsome-looking lady she was, and the terrible way poor Mr Costello was broke up after her' (p. 99).

In her study of women's narratives, Marianne Hirsch has argued that the silence and the absence of the mother are preconditions for the shaping of a female narrative within the realist novel: 'the fantasy that controls the female family romance is the desire for the female's singularity based on a disidentification from the fate of other women, especially mothers'.[16] Isabel's 'singularity' is certainly allied to her disidentification from other women: she refuses to conform, to play the game, and she insists on using what she calls 'true words', but her aunt sees as 'ugly words' (p. 61). She is sharply distinguished not only from her aunt, who submissively accepts her very low place in the Waterford pecking order, but also from Daisy, the wife and mother whose calm and ordered life she throws into chaos when she initiates an affair with Stephen. Isabel's dangerous singularity could however be regarded not as a rejection of her own mother, but as retribution for her mother's fate. As we have seen, her mother was punished by her father when she chose to marry for love, and as Mrs Burke's comment makes clear, Waterford society closed ranks against her. She is dismissed as 'queer', and (in a satiric acknowledgement of Irish provinciality) as an 'outsider', from Wexford. These same attitudes are apparent in the response to Isabel, newly arrived from her school in Paris. Mary Norris describes her as 'awfully curious-looking … and a queer sort of light in her eyes, different from other people' (p. 18). She is also described by onlookers at the dance as 'nearly foreign' because 'half the Wexford people have Spanish blood' (p. 38). Isabel's singularity, I would argue therefore, *identifies* her with her mother. Based on this identification, the challenge that Isabel offers to the ordered bourgeois world around her can be read in terms of the Lacanian Imaginary and Symbolic realms, where the Imaginary 'is part of the personal, bodily, pre-Oedipal world we shared with our mothers, and is pre-verbal, whereas the Symbolic is part of the social, cultural world where we are supposed to be able to achieve an authentic identity and become independent, speaking human subjects'.[17] According to Lacan, however, there is no escape from the Symbolic, and no possibility to articulate an alternative to it, since it is only through entering the Symbolic that we become speaking subjects. In spite of the fact that women have no subject position as such within the Symbolic, they must nonetheless enter into it, 'as the "other", a defective version of a human subject'.[18] This dilemma is apparent in *The Fly on the Wheel* in the fact that much of Isabel's significance as a character is founded on her position as the object of male desire.

In the novel, the Symbolic, the realm of culture, law and language, can clearly be associated with Stephen, the authoritative father who is characterised by his confrontation with the 'realities' of life. However, the fact that his position within the Symbolic is predicated on the repression of desire is illuminated by a glimpse into his childhood memories in a scene which is located in the text, significantly, immediately prior to his first meeting with Isabel. Stephen walks alone towards the house where the dance is to be held, and looking out from the crest of a hill recalls 'the years of his youth' when he would climb the scaffolding of his father's construction works, and 'looked out over this same city of roofs and spires, weaving with a child's imagination picture upon picture of the world beyond the confines that formed his home' (pp. 34–5). Stephen's decision to take his father's place has however determined his path in life and means that he has 'grown to manhood without sight of that great Beyond' (p. 35). The fact that Stephen's 'manhood' is in fact conditional on his renunciation of desire for the 'great Beyond' is further suggested by the view that appears to him, which is not one of roofs and spires, but a 'vaporous mist' (p. 35), out of which 'the phantom rose with its train of stifled hopes pressing up against him, whispering inaudible words, proferring [*sic*] intangible embraces' (p. 35). The emphasis on formlessness is strongly suggestive of the Lacanian concept of the Real, '*that which has not yet been symbolized*, remains to be symbolized, or even resists symbolization',[19] and the way in which this is linked to desire and Stephen's 'stifled hopes' indicate his imperfect subordination to his place in the Symbolic order. As we have seen, Stephen is on the one hand the epitome of authoritative masculinity, and on the other a colonial subject whose authority relies on a degree of self-regulation that in its severity threatens to compromise this very manliness. The scene is therefore set for his fateful meeting with Isabel, who becomes the object that both awakens and contains his desires. The question that remains is whether the text constructs any possibility of a subject position for Isabel outside of her function as Stephen's 'other'.

This question might usefully be considered by comparing *The Fly on the Wheel* to another text that features a 'Stephen Hero', Joyce's *A Portrait of the Artist as a Young Man*, at the end of which Stephen Dedalus determines to do what Stephen Carey has not, to leave Ireland to embark on an artistic project that is the very definition of grand ambition. As we have already seen, the milieu of *The Fly on the Wheel* is very similar to that which we find in Joyce's fiction. Like the characters of 'The Dead' and *A Portrait of the Artist as a Young Man*, Thurston's characters are positioned in a very particular historical moment – after the fall of Parnell and the collapse of the Land League, and immediately prior to the events of 1916, in which political radicalism and cultural nationalism combined to change the course of Irish history. Both writers are concerned with what it means to inhabit this particular moment, and with the precise ways in which this reality cramps and pinches. They differ in (at least) two significant ways: Thurston's realism contrasts with Joyce's increasingly experimental modernism, while Thurston's depictions of sexuality and gendered identity are more complex and arguably more radical. These differences can be further teased out by considering each writer's use of the family romance.

A number of critics have drawn attention to the relevance of the family romance to readings of *A Portrait of the Artist as a Young Man* and *Ulysses*.[20] Stephen's quest to become an artist, and thereby discover his 'true' identity, is very evidently a quest for origins, but in the manner of the child constructing his family romance, he rejects his biological father and seeks instead for alternative and ennobling origins. Referring to Rank's *The Myth of the Birth of the Hero* (the text in which Freud's 'Family Romances' was first published), Jean Kimball points out that 'the basic wish of the ego-hero is to break out of the cycle entirely, to beget and be begotten once for all: both only begetter and only begotten', and that in this quest Stephen Dedalus 'embodies the creative ego of the artist as hero'.[21] Writing however from a feminist perspective, Cynthia Lewiecki-Wilson describes *A Portrait* as 'a Family Romance constructed from the point of view of a young, immature man who rejects the body, materiality, the female, and seeks mastery in an isolated spiritual quest for the real'.[22] Although Lewiecki-Wilson is certainly right to point out that the novel's 'unstable irony' and 'continual displacement of ordering systems' means that a statement such as this can never be made without admitting that the text also contains its negation, it is undoubtedly true to say that origin in *A Portrait* is conceived of as male and that, in his call to 'old father, old artificer' Stephen 'as rightful inheritor of patriarchal structure ... invokes its power to see him through the creation of a new, better, improved human story'.[23]

For Joyce, therefore, unlike Thurston, the alternative can be realised – or if not realised, at least glimpsed and aimed for – and this realisation is enmeshed with a concept of origins and creativity that is based on male genealogies. *The Fly on the Wheel* ends on an entirely different note, with Stephen Carey's renunciation of the liberation that he had sought to access through Isabel. Thurston's novel begins with an image of an inescapable net, the bourgeois society that has 'spread like a net over civilization' (p. 2); in *A Portrait*, on the other hand, Stephen Dedalus famously asserts that 'when the soul of a man is born in this country there are nets flung at it to hold it back from flight. You talk to me of nationality, language, religion. I shall try to fly by those nets.'[24] Stephen's rejection of his own origins in the maternal body, noted by Lewiecki-Wilson, are evident in his Cartesian division of mind and body, made even more explicit in the sentence which immediately precedes his famous declaration: 'The soul is born ..., first in those moments I told you of. It has a slow and dark birth, more mysterious than the birth of the body.'[25] In Thurston's novel Stephen Carey similarly represses his maternal origin (his mother is entirely erased; she is not mentioned even once in the text, which is notable given the extended account of his father's death and the burdens placed on him as a result) but, as I have argued, Isabel's maternal origins *are* present in the novel, and unlike many heroines of realist texts she can be argued to be identified with her mother. Isabel's fixation on Stephen, however, seems to suggest that she accepts the (inevitable) position of women in the Symbolic: 'being what the phallus needs and signifies, a substitute for the mother'.[26] The only way for Isabel to 'be' is to be what Stephen desires within the phallic economy, which is not hers. The fact that Isabel commits suicide at the end of the novel could therefore be read as her inability to sustain an existence following Stephen's rejection. I would argue, however, that her act of suicide constitutes in fact an articulate statement and a resonant challenge to the crippling limitations of her world.

Having brought his respectable existence to the very brink of destruction, Stephen is recalled to his role by an idealised father, the priest, Fr James. The confrontation between Stephen and Fr James revolves around competing definitions of both subjecthood and masculinity. Asserting that Fr James has never known him, Stephen insists that in contrast to his 'industrious, sensible' exterior, 'far down – fathoms down' he has been 'something quite different': 'I tell you I have had big dreams – I am my father's son!' he exclaims (p. 281). Using images of repression – 'I've kept it under' (p. 281) – Stephen announces his intention to abandon these restraints and reclaim both his status as self-determining subject and as a man. In his efforts to persuade Stephen, Fr James tells him the story of his own life, shaped as a very Catholic morality tale denouncing pride and ambition and advocating humility – having been denied preferment in the church in spite of his acknowledged ability, Fr James now proclaims his gratitude for the simplicity and truth he finds in his poor, rural parish. The priest's 'last arrow', the one that finally succeeds, however, is his reminder to Stephen of his duty as a father, expressed by his own words after Barney Carey's death: 'by God, if ever I have sons of my own, they'll never have a hell of their father's making!' (p. 288). The priest's victory is represented as Stephen's defeat: 'haltingly, unsteadily, after the manner of a man who has suffered a long illness, he walked back to the table, seated himself at his old place, and, throwing his arms out across the scattered papers, let his head fall forward into his hands' (p. 289). In Stephen's world to be a father is, it seems, to submit to powerful restraints.

The intensely ambivalent nature of Stephen's reabsorption within the patriarchal order allows for a more radical reading of Isabel's suicide. In her encounter with Stephen after his painful recall to duty, Isabel is passionate and eloquent, while Stephen is 'silent' and turns from her 'inarticulately' (p. 297), but when she grasps that his settled determination is to resume his stultifying married life, she reaches the end of her ability to verbalise her feelings: 'I wish I had words enough to tell you all I feel. To say that I hate you is nothing – nothing –' (p. 301). Her first impulse is to murder Stephen but at the very last minute she takes the glass of wine she has poisoned in order to drink it herself. Thus, the perspective at the end of the novel is with Isabel, rather than with Stephen, and her suicide is presented as an act of mingled defeat and triumph: 'The glass rattled against her teeth, the touch of the ice chilled her lips, but, looking down into the wine, her eyes caught the warmth, the redness, the glory of the sun' (p. 327). Significantly, she expresses herself not in words, which have already been declared inadequate, but in an act, a gesture. The symbolic force of this act should not be overlooked, because in drinking the wine, Isabel subversively repeats the sacrifice of Christ – a figure who is for Otto Rank an archetypal hero of myth. Thus, although Isabel's suicide on one level signals the impossibility of her becoming a 'speaking subject' within the current order of things, her gesture is nonetheless a clearly articulated statement. Although transformation cannot be realised within the world of the novel, Isabel's final act ultimately allows us to glimpse an alternative to the reality she has rejected.[27]

The Fly on the Wheel is a novel that deserves a much wider readership. It is not simply a detailed portrayal of the aspiring Catholic middle classes at a critical moment in Irish history, it is a devastating critique of the complex and painful manoeuvres involved in maintaining claims to authority and respectability within a stratified and self-divided society. As Thurston reveals, these divisions begin in the formation of the self and are constitutive of the bourgeois 'normality' her characters inhabit. Both women and men are victims of these processes, but my reading of the novel suggests that the repression of the mother and female origins is at the root of the painful deformations demanded by 'reality'. Moynagh Sullivan's exploration of psychoanalysis in relation to Irish culture and its institutionalisation has also focused on the 'inability to relate to the mother as a subject' as a characteristic of Irish culture, and she proposes that 'the continued and repeated reinvestment of the father–son plot is central to the production of canons and "traditions" within Irish Studies'.[28] My discussion of *The Fly on the Wheel* in terms of mothers and daughters as well as fathers and sons offers the potential to read the novel in a dialogue with some of the most celebrated and canonical texts of this period, and as a contribution to the narratives of origin which have particular importance in the period of the revival and the literature of modernism in Ireland.

CHAPTER 8

'Now in the city there are two worlds': Maeve Brennan's Dublin sequences

EAMONN HUGHES

Introducing the short story collection *The Springs of Affection*, Anne Enright notes that Maeve Brennan is 'described as either silent or voluble and it is hard to reconcile the two'.[1] This is only one of the contradictions in Maeve Brennan and her work. She was a child of privilege whose writing is frequently about lack and deficiency.[2] She was a stylish, highly visible career woman in New York who dwelt on one house in Dublin and its insecure inhabitants. She was the intense writer of a specific place who never lived long in any place. She was precocious, educated and travelled, and claimed her position in a male-dominated world and yet refined herself out of existence in her writing. That writing itself comprises contradictory strands. There are the stories of Dublin life, some seemingly autobiographical and others about variously unhappy women and men. There are the Herbert's Retreat stories supposedly about rich, cultured New Yorkers which are more often than not about their (mostly) Irish maids. This opposition poses pointed questions about the status of women. The frugal suburban lives of Rose Derdon and Delia Bagot afford them control of a domestic space though answerable to their husbands. The Irish domestic servants, although accountable to employers, have powers of subversion, a sense of community, and ultimately a degree of autonomy, hence Margaret Casey's panic as she realises what she will lose by marrying ('The Bride' (1953), *The Rose Garden*, pp. 153–8).[3]

Acknowledging Brennan's third and largest strand of writing – 'moments of recognition' ('Author's Note', *The Long-Winded Lady*, p. 3) – about New York complicates this further as does the fact that the various aspects of her work are intertwined throughout her career. Brennan's oeuvre consists of around 100 separate pieces written between the 1940s and the 1970s: the

Long-Winded Lady essays and about forty short stories. A notable feature of the work is how few stand-alone pieces it contains. Publishing ephemerally, revising frequently (for example, 'A Young Girl Can Spoil Her Chances' published in 1962 was probably started in 1941–2), and working across several strands, Brennan kept tight control over the various sequences.[4] The house on Cherryfield Avenue was one way of doing this, though it was for Brennan a malleable space, not least because it accommodates three separate, and distinct, families.

Descriptions of the house are consistent, but there are variations in its social and psychological aspects. In 'The Beginning of a Long Story' (1961) it is 'a very ordinary house, a regulation uniform for the lives of certain families ... better than a workingman's house but not good enough for a successful man and his family' (*The Rose Garden*, pp. 204–5). Although not part of the sequence, this is close to the Brennan stories and accurate about their social standing when they first lived in the house. For the Derdons the house occasions financial strain; Hubert's awareness of this is part of his difficulty with Rose's unhappiness in the house ('A Young Girl ... ', *The Springs of Affection*, p. 75, p. 90). The Derdons' neighbours are rarely mentioned but we sense that Hubert looks down on them. By contrast, the Bagots seem to occupy the house without financial strain and fit in with their neighbours: 'Schoolteachers, shopkeepers, and minor civil servants ...' ('The Twelfth Wedding Anniversary' (1966), *The Springs of Affection*, p. 216). The house also varies psychologically, particularly in the changing perspectives of the Bagot stories. Delia, pregnant with her first child, can see it as a 'kingdom' ('The Eldest Child' (1968), *The Springs of Affection*, p. 266), while Martin thinks of it as cramped and 'full of people' ('The Twelfth Wedding Anniversary', *The Springs of Affection*, p. 226), though he can also view it as large enough for them all to be separate ('Christmas Eve' (1972), *The Springs of Affection*, p. 304). The bishop in 'Stories of Africa' (1968), a rare intruder into the space, provides an external perspective on it. Delia and the children's views of the house also vary as their psychological and emotional states change. Even though the house is an enclosure – sometimes a trap, sometimes a refuge – the awareness of the public spaces of the city beyond is nearly always present, though for female characters in particular, access to those spaces is challenging, requiring 'the ceremony of walking down the street' ('The Carpet with the Big Pink Roses on It' (1964), *The Springs of Affection*, p. 233).

Although memory expands the timeframe in each sequence, the events in each happen within a defined period. The stories of childhood cover the period between when Maeve was about four and when she was thirteen; these stories also contain a rare, if not unique, reference (in 'The Day We Got Our Own Back') to an external event which allows us to confirm the historical context by reference to Brennan's biography: the Brennan stories, broadly, occur in the 1920s. The Derdon stories depict scenes from various points in their 'more than forty years' ('The Drowned Man' (1963), *The Springs of Affection*, p. 196), from their courtship in 'A Young Girl ...' and 'A Free Choice' (perhaps the most irony-laden phrase in all of Brennan's writing) through to Rose's death and Hubert's failure to mourn her. By contrast, the events in the lives of the Bagots span only about three years. We can be confident of chronologies within the walls of the house because we are given information about the ages of characters and the lengths of marriages. As with the stories of childhood there are constant indications in the Derdon and Bagot stories of time passing. Indeed 'A Young Girl ...' makes an elaborate temporal knot out of Rose's age as, on this 'forty-third anniversary of Mrs Derdon's father's death' she realises that 'I'm exactly the same age today that my mother was the day I was married' (*The Springs of Affection*, p. 63, p. 65). This makes it all the more noteworthy that with the available internal evidence we cannot establish the time at which they are set.[5] The stories begin in the 1920s, though given the period at which they are written and the span of the marriages in them it is likely that they extend into the 1960s or even 1970s and Brennan seems to think of the Derdons, Bagots, and Brennans as spectrally co-habiting. If the Brennans remember the Civil War in 'The Day We Got Our Own Back', what is remarkable about the Derdons and Bagots is that no public events impinge upon them: Hubert reads the newspaper as 'camouflage' ('The Drowned Man', *The Springs of Affection*, p. 203), and the only external occasion noted by the Derdons is a funeral (*The Springs of Affection*, pp. 97–8). While such military metaphors as 'uniform' and 'camouflage' point to a state of warfare, it appears that, remarkably given the political activism of her parents, Brennan has made Cherryfield Avenue almost completely history- and politics-proof.

However, to say this is to overlook the paradoxical nature of the family identified by Anne McClintock:

> ... as a metaphor [it] offered a single genesis narrative for national history, while ... as an *institution* [it] became voided of history ... [it] was figured as existing, by natural decree ... [and] thus became ... both the organizing figure for national history, as well as its antithesis. ...

> [it] offered an indispensable trope for figuring what was often violent, historical change as natural, organic time … enabl[ing] what was often murderously violent change to be legitimized as the progressive unfolding of natural decree.[6]

Brennan's 'family' home, for all its realist specificity, is therefore at the epicentre of history and politics.

Brennan's novella *The Visitor*, completed 'in the middle 1940s' ('Editor's Note', *The Visitor*, p. 84, p. 85), is the place from which all the strands of her work diverge. It is about a young woman, Anastasia King, rejected by her grandmother and comforted, to a degree, by the servant Katherine. A verbal echo near the start, 'Ireland is my dwelling place …' (*The Visitor*, p. 6), signals the Joycean quality of Brennan's work.[7] This overlap with Joyce is most obvious not simply in the choice of Dublin as setting but in their shared concern with it as urban. Brennan makes a radical point about the nature of cities, one that challenges the conventional division of cities into public and private spaces and the equally conventional gendering of those spaces. In this view, cities are constituted largely by their public spaces, and private and domestic spaces exist as if invisible behind their public facades. Brennan insists on the equal importance of the two worlds of the city:

> Now in the city there are two worlds. One world has walls around it and one world has people around it. The second world is outside … This world has a sightless, malicious face, which is the face of the crowd … [which] shows itself in wondering side-long looks and sharp glances … There is no patience for solitary aimless wistful hangers-on who want to sit and watch … One is … sent scurrying back to the … other world … the one with walls around it.
>
> This is quite different. It is a standstill … There is no compulsion at all. The slow-turning malicious sightless eye of the crowd is not here. One can spend hour upon hour here … there is no further step to be taken, except perhaps … out again onto the street. (*The Visitor*, pp. 62–3)

The Visitor is an equivalent to Joyce's *A Portrait of the Artist as a Young Man* in that Anastasia, like Stephen Dedalus, is learning to live in the city; her discomfort and disorientation in public recall those moments when the 'gloomy foggy city' escapes Stephen's perception, discernible only as 'dim fabric'.[8] Stephen's trajectory is from various forms of enclosure into the public spaces of Dublin. Anastasia, with less purpose, alternates between the two kinds of space. The passage just quoted breaks from a narration focalised through Anastasia to an analytical and already urban-educated voice, just as Stephen's urban education is filtered through the street-smart voice of Joyce. At the end of the novella, Anastasia, having moved to a hotel, stands outside her grandmother's house neither staying nor yet quite leaving. Brennan's move beyond this novella is not towards a Joycean flight into exile or to an attempt to represent the totality of the city. Instead, she takes the two spaces she has established in *The Visitor* and considers them largely in terms of how female characters interact with them.

A number of seemingly autobiographical pieces introduce the domestic space in *The Springs of Affection*. These seven stories, published initially between February 1953 and January 1955, represent Brennan's single most concerted effort; by contrast the six Derdon stories appear over a twenty-year period and the eight Bagot stories are published over eight years. Brennan's writing habits, the *New Yorker*'s publishing routines, and the 'sometimes unfortunate order' in which the stories appeared in book form, mean that there is no definitive arrangement for any of her sequences.[9] None of this diminishes the importance of the sequences. The childhood stories can be read, setting internal evidence against Brennan's biography, within a fixed timeframe (roughly 1920–30). This leaves us with a question about how we might read not simply the individual stories but the sequence as a whole. Joyce's *Dubliners* is, again, an obvious point of reference for the ways in which Brennan connects her stories, but so too are Turgenev's *Sportsman's Sketches*, or even William Carleton's *Traits and Stories of the Irish Peasantry*.[10]

The childhood stories in *The Springs of Affection* appear after the publication of 'The Joker' (1952, *The Rose Garden*, pp. 52–69) in which, as Ellen McWilliams has noted, the male Irish writer is '… presented as … a self-aggrandizing, hard-drinking cliché … It is against such bombastic mythmaking and self-aggrandizing ambition that privacy – and, to a point, obscurity – for the Irish woman writer takes on a new value as both a strategy of self-defense and a means of escaping the sensationalist excesses of a clichéd version of the Irish writer abroad'.[11] The childhood sequence can then be read as the education of a female writer. In 'The Morning after the Big Fire', Maeve learns both about the power of story-telling and how easily public stories can be appropriated by male voices. 'The Old Man of the Sea' demonstrates how stories help her to make sense of the world. As the mother's act of kindness becomes an inexorable obligation, Maeve understands how an apparently frail old man can become 'the old man [with] cruel, talonlike hands [that] dug into Sindbad's shoulders' (*The*

Springs of Affection, p. 23). In 'The Barrel of Rumours', Maeve's questions about religious life are unanswered. She is therefore exasperated when her infant brother, Robert, is able to pass into the enclosed world of the Poor Clares, especially as on his return she 'could make no sense of his language' (another Joycean echo) and the story ends with her acceptance that 'He never would be able to tell me what the inside of the convent looked like' (*The Springs of Affection*, p. 36). Religion is then followed by politics in an account of two raids by Free Staters on the Brennan household. The five-year-old Maeve is initially 'spellbound with gratitude, excitement, and astonishment' at being included in the raid when she is questioned, though the mother forestalls this ('The Day We Got Our Own Back' (1953), *The Springs of Affection*, p. 39). A second, more disruptive raid involves 'a pollution of the sacred space of home' and ends with one of the raiders covered in soot.[12] Although it would be 'a long time before she got the house neat again' (*The Springs of Affection*, p. 40), the mother ends the story 'laugh[ing] as though her heart might break' (*The Springs of Affection*, p. 41). Religion returns in 'The Lie' in which the consistency of Maeve's minimal penance at Confession becomes a bond between mother and daughter. When Maeve confesses that in a fit of temper she had broken Derry's favourite toy sewing machine and lied about it to her mother, she receives a harsher penance. The father, making a rare appearance, questions her about the penance and responds jokily, 'you're going up in the world'. However, the mother's saddened reaction is 'my poor child, why couldn't you have kept your mouth shut?' (*The Springs of Affection*, p. 46). 'The Devil in Us' complicates this emerging pattern of female injunctions to silence in the face of male questioning. Maeve and others are wrongly accused of failing to sing in a choir and, as punishment, are made to replace the choir one Sunday; despite their willingness they can 'only caw' (*The Springs of Affection*, p. 53). Here, silence is not so much enjoined as enforced, and the double bind of silence as both a form of appropriate female behaviour and a form of insolence is made clear. While the other stories work with an aptly childlike perspective, 'The Clever One' is an adult and explicitly retrospective story. Maeve is staying in Deirdre's house in Washington DC. Deirdre is married, with young children, and still sewing despite the loss of her childhood sewing machine. (That the accusation of silence in 'The Devil in Us' came during a rendition of 'The Spinning Wheel' is simply another example of how carefully Brennan stitches the stories together.) Maeve's memories of childhood are shaped by her apparently natural dominance over her younger sister until the moment at which Derry reveals that she had faked her childhood illness. Brennan is 'thunderstruck': 'Derry's delicate health had loomed as importantly in my childhood as the Catholic Church and the fight for Irish freedom' (*The Springs of Affection*, p. 57). The upsetting of what Brennan has taken to be the natural hierarchy between them is here immediately linked to those larger, extra-domestic issues that her stories touch on. Derry's 'duplicity' and her ability to carry 'through such a black and complicated plot, and of *not speaking* about it to anyone' (*The Springs of Affection*, p. 58; emphasis added) rouses Brennan's admiration and causes her to remember 'that this was not the first time she had set me back' (*The Springs of Affection*, p. 59). The structure of Brennan's childhood and of her identity were shaped by the relationship with Derry; where Derry was frail, Brennan was hardy, where Derry had the beauty, Maeve had the brains (*The Springs of Affection*, pp. 58–9). But now she remembers a moment when she revealed her ambition to be a famous actress, only to be met with Derry's withering 'Don't go getting any notions into your head' (*The Springs of Affection*, p. 60). The story, and the sequence, ends with 'I was astounded, and I was silent. I had nothing to say. For the first time, it had occurred to me that little Derry had *brains*. More brains than I had, maybe' (*The Springs of Affection*, p. 60; emphasis in the original). Everything that has shaped Brennan's memories and in turn the stories has been undercut here: Derry's illness has been revealed as fakery, with the Catholic Church and the fight for Irish freedom implicated by being immediately linked. The relationships predicated on those matters, and the memories shaped by them, have all been cast into doubt. If this is an autobiographical sequence we can no more trust it than Brennan can trust either what she thought was serious or her own memory.

By this point then Brennan has mocked and dismissed a public version of the Irish male literary voice, and has also examined both forms of speech and silence as practised by women, most particularly herself. The rejection of a performative and public role as a 'notion' leaves her silenced and unsure, but the actual contemplation of these issues has itself set her going as a writer. The slightly uncertain start to her career derives from these contrary impulses – *The Visitor*, abandoned on completion in the mid-1940s, was followed in 1950 by 'The Holy Terror' (already a story about the power of knowing when to speak and when to keep silent) and another two years would pass before 'The Poor Men and Women' (the first of the Derdon stories) appeared. In the next few years she would complete the childhood stories, develop the Herbert's Retreat stories, and begin to write the *Long-Winded Lady* pieces. That last point in particular must be kept in mind, for, as we turn to the Derdon and Bagot stories, we must remember the 'two worlds' of the city as the lives in Cherryfield Avenue are partly defined by the urban pressure of the public world of Dublin outside the door.

In one way, we can trace this back to the writer rather than the characters: Maeve has already learned that public events, such as a big fire, can be appropriated by others. At another level, of course, Brennan has taken as her subject one of the central subjects of post-independence Ireland: the family. As Bourke points out, Brennan witnessed the same thing happening twice in very different contexts: 'After the Civil War ... women who had been articulate and active in the nationalist and feminist movements for years, working and facing dangers as equal with men, found themselves relegated to the home in much the same way as American and British women would after the Second World War.'[13] Brennan growing up would have seen this attack on women's rights happening at state and church level.[14] After she had been living in Washington with her family for three years, Brennan received Dorothy Macardle's pessimistic prognosis about her then planned return to Ireland: '... how I hope you won't encounter heartbreak and frustration when you come back here ... If you find you can't do your best work here I think you'll just have to go where you <u>can</u> do it – but you'll want, I know, to stay in Ireland and hope you'll continue to'.[15] Macardle's own novel of 1942, *The Uninvited*, can be read as an allegory of how the supposedly 'good' (that is, domesticated) mother, who conforms to all the approved Marian virtues, is a dangerous, limiting presence and must be displaced by the supposedly 'bad' (that is, undomesticated) mother.[16]

Heartbreak and frustration are the keynotes of Brennan's stories of family life in Dublin. In the Derdon stories the two worlds of the city appear initially as clearly divided and gendered. For Rose Derdon the house is her territory and she 'didn't like to have to go off and leave [Hubert] in the house by himself' ('A Young Girl ...', *The Springs of Affection*, p. 66). In turn, Hubert responds to his wife's rare public outings with dislike: 'In the presence of strangers, she sometimes took to smiling ... a grimace of absurd condescension on her face ...' ('An Attack of Hunger' (1962), *The Springs of Affection*, pp. 150–1). Rose does not have the ability, necessary to the urban citizen, of being able to make 'believable appearances before strangers'.[17] But once again things are not as they seem, for this passage begins with another Joycean echo from the opening of *Dubliners*: 'There was no hope for her inside the house' (*The Springs of Affection*, p. 150).

If this suggests that Rose is not at home in the house, only there because '... it's my duty to stay here and keep your house' (*The Springs of Affection*,

p. 169), then we must bear in mind that Hubert, although inclined to believe that Rose's discomfort outside the dwelling is due to her being a 'simple girl from her simple country town' (*The Springs of Affection*, p. 72), is not himself at ease in the city. One lunchtime, wandering aimlessly, he takes a memory walk the co-ordinates of which are Stephen's Green and the nearby house that he and Rose had rooms in after their marriage, though he actually avoids both. These locations are linked by more than proximity and memory:

> Stephen's Green ... had been their favorite place, the favorite place of all. They were always there on Sunday afternoons ... During those first weeks together they lived ... in two small rooms at the top of the house ... The day they left Somerville Street, Rose cried. ('A Young Girl ... ', *The Springs of Affection*, pp. 74–5)

At this moment public and private are not separated, and nor are Rose and Hubert. It is when they move to the suburban privacy of their own house in Cherryfield Avenue that everything, including them, becomes separate. Marriage therefore, far from being a union, is a separation, and places as much as people are subject to this. In consequence, the two worlds of the city are hostile places: Hubert is uneasy in public and wary at home, while Rose rarely ventures out of the house but is trapped within it by duty.

Hubert is not an admirable figure, but he is not a monster. Brennan's typically dry, free indirect discourse allows for mockery of Hubert when he thinks of himself as 'a sensitive, kindhearted man' (*The Springs of Affection*, p. 196) but our response must also be tinged with sympathy for someone who has done what his society has demanded of him. If Rose's 'delirium of loss' (*The Springs of Affection*, p. 154) is dwelt on, this does not mean that Hubert himself is complete. Examining the remnants of her life after her death Hubert sees her makeshift efforts to achieve coherence, and recognises that he had looked to her for his completion. Her '... mind [was] given over entirely to trivialities and makeshift ... wasting nothing except her time and her life and his time and his life. Even so ... he had had hopes that she possessed and would reveal to him the common secret that had been given to everybody except him' (*The Springs of Affection*, p. 205). It is Hubert who diagnoses the problem facing both:

> When had all this obedience begun and who had marked out the appointed way where men and women walked without protest and most of the time without complaining? (*The Springs of Affection*, p. 169)

Looked at from the point of view of family as endorsed by the Catholic Church and enforced by the 1937 constitution – arguably the twin sources of 'this obedience' – the Derdons are the perfect family: a dutiful, enduring, and frugal marriage, which produces a son who becomes a priest, makes them almost too good to be true (not least in their echo of the Holy Family). The family that Brennan depicts is no longer an image of union so much as of civil war. Nowhere is the satirical edge of Brennan's writing about this more evident than in her grisly parody of Molly Bloom's resounding final affirmation:

> And Rose had said, 'Yes.' 'Yes,' she said, and the one word came out quickly, like a sigh or a laugh, like a sound of recognition and acceptance and mockery. 'Yes,' she said, but only once, as though she was finally giving into something that she had not wanted to give in to or accept yet. (*The Springs of Affection*, p. 208)

The contrast between Molly's willing and sensuous affirmation and Rose's unwilling but necessary 'Yes' (she is dying and wants a doctor) is a sign of just how these stories function as an excoriating critique of the family as defined in the 1937 constitution: 'the natural primary and fundamental unit group of Society ... a moral institution possessing inalienable and imprescriptible rights' such that 'The State, therefore, guarantees to protect the Family ... as indispensable to the welfare of the Nation and the State'.[18]

In its very attempt to naturalise it as antecedent to state law, the constitution constructs a particular ideological version of family which may work for the nation and the state but which does so by sacrificing the individuals who constitute the family, the nation, and the state. This is what will come to be called the nuclear family. In these stories Brennan was in line with what Mary Corey states about the *New Yorker*'s distinctive attitude to family in its 'refusal to glorify the nuclear family ... The *New Yorker* ... did nothing to promote domesticity, extol the charms of marriage, or present a coherent womanly ideal'.[19]

Even so, Bourke, and others, are probably correct in their assumption that Brennan's interest in family was piqued by the conundrum of her own background: how her parents' marriage had led to her mother's retreat from activism.[20] However, this is to overlook the attention given to Hubert. Rose's mother says 'a young girl can spoil her chances' but she continues that 'a young man can spoil his chances just as easy' (*The Springs of Affection*, p. 81). It is clear that Hubert had been looking for the wrong thing in Rose: 'Her walk, her step, had been brave and free and definite, and it occurred to him now, as it had before, that he had fallen in love with her for the exact qualities that were not hers at all. It was not Rose's fault that he had been mistaken in her' (*The Springs of Affection,* p. 209). That 'brave and free and definite' walk, allied to her name, suggests that he was, misguided by ideology, looking for something more symbolic than actual. Rose too recognises that she has been diminished: 'she could barely bear to look in the mirror because the face she saw there was not the one that was sympathetic to her but her own face … the face of one whose courage has long ago *been* petrified into mere endurance … (*The Springs of Affection*, p. 150; emphasis added). It is then this sense of outside forces working on both of them that requires us to read these as not simply realist stories about a marriage, but rather as stories about the institution on which the 1937 constitution is predicated.

Compared to the bleak ferocity of the Derdon stories, the Bagot stories have a gentler tone partly because of the presence of the children Lily and Margaret (echoing Maeve and Derry), who have not yet lost their potential and so mother and daughters can be mutually affirming: 'Mrs. Bagot wanted to … always have them before her as she had them now – alive and confident in their independence, and seeing her. They saw her. She knew they did' ('The Sofa' (1968), *The Springs of Affection*, p. 259). The different tone of these stories may also be because, as Heather Ingman suggests, Brennan's anger with her mother, evident in the Derdon stories, had dissipated with her mother's death and she was 'trying to … reclaim the authentic voice of her mother and affirm the strength of the mother-daughter bond'.[21] Additionally, Martin Bagot is less present than Hubert in the Derdon stories; he works later and more irregular hours than Hubert and is more openly mocked by the narrative voice: 'He was a solitary man, not an ordinary family man … his loneliness came from a deep source in his nature, and … made him more sensitive than other men, and at the same time stronger – a visionary of a kind' ('The Twelfth Wedding Anniversary' (1966), *The Springs of Affection*, p. 230).

Delia retains a consciousness of the dangers of loss of self: 'It was not right to let yourself get so lost in your children that you could find no trace of yourself when they were gone' (*The Springs of Affection*, p. 241). Because of this she is also aware of the dangers that lie in wait for her daughters: 'The children were safe. There was no one near to cut them down, or to put them in their place, or to … tell them they were too sure of themselves' ('The Sofa', *The Springs of Affection*, p. 258). What is strange here, by comparison with the Derdon stories, is that Lily and Margaret are completely visible to Delia 'out in the open' (*The Springs of Affection*, p. 257), suggesting that the gendering of spaces is a factor in that process of socialisation that will attempt to contain and constrain them. The fragility of their potential is paradoxically marked by the way that the word 'safe' resonates through the Bagot stories:

> She wanted the children to have their privacy and, beyond that, she wanted them to be safe. She didn't really know what she meant by safe – respectable, maybe, or successful in some way that she had no vision of. ('Christmas Eve' (1972), *The Springs of Affection*, p. 299)

The paradoxical sense of 'safe' here – finding a secure place in the social order and being removed entirely from the social gaze – suggests the impossibility of what Delia wishes for her children. It also establishes a family pattern different from the Derdons. Here too however a son has been lost, but this time only three days after his birth, though during this pregnancy Delia developed strength and confidence: 'The house became a kingdom, significant, private, and safe' (*The Springs of Affection*, p. 266). This confidence does not survive the death of the child, but traces of it remain. Through the voice of the bishop in 'Stories of Africa', Delia finds herself being recalled to a time before her marriage and therefore to a more complete sense of self: '... she was amazed to find how much there was to be said about this person, herself' (*The Springs of Affection*, p. 289). The sense that a real if insubstantial aspect of Delia somehow survives – in the double bind of her children 'seeing' her, in the stories of the bishop, in her own flickering sense of herself – separates the Bagot stories from the sense of loss and dissolution that marks the Derdon stories: Rose's loss of her father and her son, the Derdons' loss of their initial, transient idyll, Hubert's loss of Rose all point to loss as the central condition of the family. The Bagot stories are less focused on the family and more on the matrilineal component of it, so Delia's response to her mirror image is to find in it a sense of reinforcement and continuity rather than the self-cancelling that Rose experiences:

> Mrs. Bagot ... was surprised to see how like a mirror the big naked window in the back room was, but like a mirror that you could see through ... she could see herself ... [In] the children's room ... She looked closer and at that moment, as it [her shadow] bent its head, she knew what she was looking at. That was her mother's shadow there on the wall. (*The Springs of Affection*, pp. 251–3)

Despite the continuity of identity offered here – the mirrored self, the shadow of her mother identical with her own seen in her daughters' room – and although their tone is gentler than the Derdon stories, the Bagot stories offer at best only ambiguous consolation. Where the two sequences differ most significantly is in the distance between the finality of the Derdon stories and the more open ending of the Bagot stories. The sense that Margaret and Lily have more access to the public spaces of the city and that they may have a future is a significant counterbalance to the Derdons' narratives of loss. That possible future is paradoxically strengthened after the deaths of Delia and Martin as the children vanish from Min Bagot's continuation of the narrative. 'The Springs of Affection' (1972) is best seen as a coda to the Bagot sequence rather than a culmination since it turns to a different variation on family. Martin's twin sister Min (having looked after Martin in the wake of Delia's death) takes what she wants from the house and leaves the city to return to her small-town life. There, she re-asserts what are for her proper family values: 'out of them all she was the one who was always faithful to the family. She ... hadn't gone off and got married' (*The Springs of Affection*, pp. 308–9). For Min the marriages of her sisters and, worse, of her twin Martin made them 'like animals. It was disgusting' (*The Springs of Affection*, p. 309). The story pursues the logic of the constitution's idea of family as a 'fundamental unit' of society into absurdity. Min's attitude may seem merely bitter and resentful. She despised Delia and hated her for 'stealing' Martin, but Min is adhering to the idea of family as a 'fundamental unit' which leads logically to the idea of the family as sealed and complete within itself. For society to reproduce itself, however, the family must in every generation break itself apart and this paradox is not one that Min can accept; for her to have the shelter of the family is to be sealed within it. Her loyalty to her birth family is absolute and any move outside it can only be seen as a betrayal. This certainly is how Min regards her siblings' marriages. Her fidelity to family as she sees it means that the children of the marriage of Delia and Martin must vanish, since for her they are the illegitimate inheritors of treachery. In 'I See You, Bianca' Brennan makes the point, almost a plea, that 'It should not be a problem to have shelter without being shut away' (*The Rose Garden*, p. 256), but her stories of family life prove how difficult if not impossible this is. Men such as Martin may find an escape from this both through their life in a public world and by internal withdrawal but this is not available to women. So, when Rose or Delia wish, however fleetingly, to breach their claustrophobic environment they must give up 'shelter'.

Brennan establishes her writerly voice initially by moving outside the house, but she develops it by returning to it:

> Home is a place in the mind. When it is empty, it frets. It is fretful with memory, faces and places and times gone by. Beloved images rise up in disobedience and make a mirror for emptiness. Then what resentful wonder, and what half-aimless seeking. It is a silly state of affairs. It is a silly creature that tries to get a smile from even the most familiar and loving shadow. Comical and hopeless, the long gaze back is always turned inward. (*The Visitor*, p. 8)

The other major component of her work – her *Long-Winded Lady* pieces – are founded on the opposite of that last phrase: her gaze here is at the present moment and very much turned outward as she practises 'the ceremony of walking down the street'. In her last published piece in her lifetime she appears to find a moment of grace, a respite in this ceremony:

> Yesterday afternoon, as I walked along Forty-Second Street ... I saw a three-cornered shadow on the pavement in the angle where two walls meet ... I recognized it at once. It was exactly the same shadow that used to fall on the cement part of our garden in Dublin, more than fifty-five years ago. ('A Blessing' (5 January 1981), *The Long-Winded Lady*, p. 267)

This is a return to Cherryfield Avenue and is yet another of those links that tie Brennan's writings together. We are reminded of Delia seeing her mother's shadow, and that connection to the Bagot stories is reinforced by the fact that the final word before the sign-off here is 'safe'. We might also, of course, be reminded of *The Visitor*: 'It is a silly creature that tries to get a smile from even the most familiar and loving shadow' (p. 8). It is typical of Brennan's subtlety that we cannot be sure if we are to be glad that she has in some sense found her way home or whether we are 'silly creatures' who have been misdirected yet again.

CHAPTER 9

The Law of the Mother and the Sibling World: Leeanne Quinn's queer ecologies

MOYNAGH SULLIVAN

> I expect to see some body flung
> far from itself, broken to a new form –
>
> Leeanne Quinn, 'The Impact'

> Little did we know how the sun would burn
> every last cord between us, leaving us battling
> through insect-thick nights for a bigger patch
> of the sibling world.
>
> Leeanne Quinn, 'Mosquitoes'

Poet Leeanne Quinn attends to the interdependence of all life, 'every last cord between us', on this planet and beyond. Born in Drogheda in 1978, she is an award-winning and critically acclaimed, Munich-based poet. This essay explores her writing through psychoanalytical and eco-critical perspectives and feminist literary cultural research that highlight the damaging dominance of the father–son model of inheritance and influence in Irish cultural critique. The molecular and cellular granularity of Quinn's vision, 'wrapped in particles of winter/light', is perceptually entwined with the existential threat of climate emergency.[1] My critique is informed by the path-making ecocritical work of Nessa Cronin, Christine Cusick, Derek Gladwin, Maureen O'Connor, and John Wilson Foster among others.[2] I use neuroscientific and evolutionary biological research to explore the sensorial detail in Quinn's work.[3] I also draw on key work by Susan Cahill, Claire Bracken, Margaret O'Neill and Michaela Schrage-Frueh, and Margot Backus and Joseph Valente, all of which read 'between the lines of twentieth-century Irish culture' by employing psychoanalytical perspectives to re-orientate our attention to the personal and psychosocial body.[4] Tina O'Toole's linking of diaspora to an analysis of translocation and queer subjections across national borders additionally shapes my reading of translocated bodies intertwined with other-than-human life in Quinn's oeuvre.[5] I consider how the interconnectivity of body, planet, and art is expressed in Quinn's acclaimed first volume *Before You* (2012) through the holding metaphor of the 'sibling world', an emotional ecosystem so painstakingly painted in the sister poems 'Imprints' and 'Mosquitoes'. *Before You* poignantly explores the death of her beloved older sister, Caroline, and the memories and loss of this precious relationship are embedded in a wider relational aesthetic that encompasses the globalised infrastructural and economic systems of late modernity, what Jason W. Moore has termed the 'capitaloscene'.[6] The 'sibling world' is interpreted via Juliet Mitchell's work on the law of the mother and sibling relationships, which I use to build on Patricia Coughlan's and Gerardine Meaney's work on siblings in Irish culture.[7] Taking my cue from Quinn's poem 'Peculiar Alphabets', I attune to the recurring images that wash like waves of grief through the volume, to argue that coming to 'know the patterns / of their changing' ('Peculiar Alphabets', p. 29) and mapping the collection's queer ecology can create a welcome for new perspectives in an evolving and diversifying Irish culture.

Before You explores the links between social upheaval, personal loss, and 'the earth's irreproachable / response' to this ('Naples', p. 45) and was described by Lucy Collins as 'a debut of considerable depth and maturity'.[8] Quinn's signature focus on relatedness as a central theme and a formal imperative is also developed in her second volume, *Some Lives*.[9] Niall McMonagle deemed it a 'beautifully orchestrated collection' in which the 'handling of rhythm and repetition is pitch perfect'.[10] The formally accomplished musicality he notes, where 'narrative and lyric poems are in counterpoint, as are past and present', is a feature too of *Before You*, which invites us to think not only about the texts themselves, but how poetry and poets become linked in the making of literary, personal, and visual history more broadly.[11] The second half of *Before You* comprises four sequences that function as a coda for the first section; under the headings of 'Storms', 'Houses', 'Water', and 'Accidents', they offer a formal variation of the first in a series of prose poems intertextually linked to selected letters from Elizabeth Bishop's travels. The threading of relationship, loss, home, displacement, tradition, and writing across the volume disrupts our notions of seriality, phrase, and harmony, and asks us to read backwards, across and forwards again and yet again. The exosystemic architecture of each collection is a formal echo of her own environmentalist sensibility; each poem chromatically opens the ear and eye multi-directionally, each sense intensification emphasising multiple interconnections across aural, oral, and visual environmental planes.

This interweave between lyric and narrative, ear and eye, affords a reconceptualisation of the procedural shape of Irish literary history, notoriously inhospitable to women, queer, and racially diverse writers coming from a range of backgrounds and abilities. *Before You*, in its very title, relationally locates itself in the poetic non-linear time of the unconscious and the conscious practices of the inter-relational through intertextual conversations with the letters, notes, and poetry of Bishop, and with poets such as A.R. Ammons, Mary Oliver, W.S. Merwin, and Medbh McGuckian providing deep ecological and aesthetic roots. Effectively, Quinn's work appears to decolonise and de-binarise the masculinist canon to which she does not want to belong, even as it engenders a new pattern of inclusion that encodes interrelationship at its core. *Some Lives* links with writers Jakob van Hoddis, Anna Akhmatova, Marina Tsvetaeva, Osip Mandelstam, Nadezhda Mandelstam and, crucially, the cultures of support and collaboration that enabled their writing, a key dimension to Quinn's understanding of creative life.

Olga Tokarczuk's assertion in her 2019 Nobel lecture, that it takes more than one person to write a book, is an orienting principle for Quinn, and she highlights the importance of co-creativity in her own practice, describing her wife Georgina as 'fundamental to her writing', much as she honours Virginia Woolf's partner in 'Letter to Leonard Woolf'(p. 20).[12] Relationally focused intertextuality also extends to the intervisual. The volume's intermedial interplay illumes the shadow places of hetero-patriarchal tradition as it:

> disrupt[s] the illusion
> that what is hidden is the depth of the surface,
> not the depth of what we cannot see. ('Accidents', p. 61)

In 'Gertrude Stein Poses for Man Ray', she continues to draw our attention to 'the depth of what we cannot see' (p. 21), by playing with Man Ray's now famous 1922 photographic portrait of Alice B. Toklas and Gertrude Stein, surrounded by their art collection which, in the absence of the legal recognition of their 'Boston marriage' was intended to provide security for Toklas after Stein's death. In the event, Stein's relatives left Toklas destitute, so she went without both a material legacy that would have vouchsafed her a home, and due recognition of her co-generativity in cultural value systems that consider the term 'singular' an expression of high praise. Stein 'sits in opposition to the lens' and knows the 'right angle for genius / is darkness' ('Gertrude Stein Poses for Man Ray', p. 21). The hetero-patriarchal construct of 'genius' becomes the focus of the poem rather than the Picasso on the wall, when 'genius sits / like a noun in limitation', and the fetishisation of creative individualism is shown as the way that 'one name / makes a phantom of another' ('Gertrude Stein Poses for Man Ray', p. 21).

The co-relationship between legacy, text, and visuality is further signalled by the title of Quinn's first published poem 'In Paint', which she describes as 'the first poem I wrote that felt different to what I had been writing previously'.[13] The importance of visual culture for Quinn is further exemplified by the amplification of the Irish artist Nano Reid in her palette. Her stratified symbolic work shares aspects of Reid's 'intuitive artistic practice', which Quinn has described as the 'building up of layers in her paintings'.[14] For Reid, 'there was no point in trying to paint a place she had no feeling for', and Quinn 'feels the same way about poetry'.[15] Her work, 'safe and earthed' ('Peculiar Alphabets', p. 29), like Reid's, 'is tangible and grounded in recognisable landscapes'.[16] The poem 'Nano's Dream Castle', in which Reid is imagined speaking to her friend and fellow painter Gerald Dillon from the space of the fantastical painting, also called 'Nano's Dream Castle' (1940s), that he painted for her, invites us to see how the co-creative relationship between the poet and painters not only visibilises an important and understudied Irish woman artist – 'I surface where the dream begins, oiled / in autumn you've made me visible' (p. 28) – it likewise blends visual and textual poetries for personal and public memorialisation and elegising. The untimely death of Quinn's only sister, which happened unexpectedly when Quinn was in her late teens, is at the heart of *Before You*, and an earthed connecting thread to Caroline is spooled through the co-creative elaboration of Reid's art and life.[17] Reid, Caroline, and Quinn share a powerfully grounded symbolic lineage. Quinn's father was 'a publican and proprietor of the Dublin Gate Bar, the pub formerly owned by Nano Reid's family in Drogheda', and when Quinn's family took ownership of it in the 1970s, a 'mural Nano painted for the bar still adorned the walls'.[18] Quinn grew up with stories of Reid, who became a family friend, and Quinn's father collected Reid's work. As a result, Quinn was 'lucky enough to be familiar with Reid's paintings from a very young age' and both she and Caroline loved Reid's paintings. For Quinn, memories of Reid and

Dillon coming to 'paint the Drogheda environs of Louth and Meath, and Monasterboice, where we subsequently moved as a family in the nineties' provide a bridge to Caroline who is buried in the Monasterboice graveyard where Reid and Dillon liked to 'sketch the High Crosses'.[19] Quinn's elegiac elaboration of an artist's rendering of this ancient landscape with its pre-Christian and early Christian markers of life and death lies side by side with her intercourse with Bishop's letters – a writer who had famously objected to Robert Lowell's use of his ex-wife's letters, and whose commitment to abstraction seemed to prove an obstacle to her own successful creation of elegies. The volume self-consciously explores the braiding of lives through art, with Quinn's Reid telling Dillon from the dreamscape that he brought to life for her, 'you've made a chameleon / of my mind and called it my own' ('Nano's Dream Castle', p. 28).

This interweave can be parsed through the relational paradigm advanced by Juliet Mitchell in *Mad Men and Medusas* and *Siblings: Sex and violence*.[20] Elaborating on her earlier work in *Psychoanalysis and Feminism*, Mitchell proposes a nodal map of formative connections via siblings which she notes are 'everywhere in psychoanalytical accounts – even though they are absent from the theory and clinical practice'; this is superintended by the 'law of the mother', which can be brought into 'conjunction' with the over-dominant Oedipal 'law of the Father' to 'open up several perspectives'.[21] This has applications for reshaping literary lineages over-influenced by the Oedipal father–son model which result in, as feminist scholarship has noted, cultural 'traditions' that masquerade as either 'human' or 'neutral', but which are heteronormative and patriarchal in reality. As Bracken so brilliantly shows us, the limitations of the Oedipal model itself have been mistaken for the limits of culture.[22] Mitchell writes that 'the law of the mother operates both vertically between herself and her children and laterally to differentiate her children one from each other', and can thus set maternal legacies alongside these vertical father–son lineages, as well as opening up the sibling strata to make interpenetrating 'horizontal/vertical' connections legible.[23] In other words, by highlighting the importance of *new* (non-Oedipal) maternal vertical links, and by extension horizontal sibling ties, it widens the cultural field to reshape the well-worn but incomplete story of masculinist seriality, influence, and lineage with its core practice of exclusion. Coughlan and Meaney have deepened their early critiques of the gendering of Irish literary tradition by studies of sororal and fraternal connections and disruptions in Irish cultural studies, unearthing a rich metaphoric seam in Irish writing. Coughlan has highlighted sibling relationships in Bernard O'Donoghue's poetry as an aesthetic and psychoanalytical device for exploring Irish migrant experience, dramatically enlarging our critical lexicon.[24] Likewise, Meaney's psychoanalytic and postmodernist exploration of Antigone in the context of Irish cultural criticism represents one of the most radical paradigm shifts in theorising Irish cultural identity for several decades.[25] Her essay 'Waking the Dead: Antigone, Ismene, and Anne Enright's narrators in mourning' models lateral relational mapping as a more inclusive frame for Irish studies when she 'proposes a reappraisal of Antigone's relationship with her sister, Ismene, so often dismissed as a cypher for conventional femininity' and highlights that Ismene's 'loyalties are to her living sister rather than her dead brother'.[26] These arguments pave the way for reading Quinn's multiple concerns through the painful and passionate weave of sibling bonds.

Part I of *Before You* illuminates the shadows of the personal 'sibling world', while Part II evolves this powerfully imprinted relationship into a wider and non-chrononormative aesthetic and symbolic imaginary. The collection is opened by 'Imprints', a poem about the formative somatic imprint of the sibling relationship in the growing psyche, and the deep symbolic impression made by an oft-invoked poem in the Irish cultural imaginary: Seamus Heaney's 'Digging' (1966).[27] This has to be one of, if not *the* most widely recognised Irish poems of the later twentieth century, which Heaney famously opened his readings with because it represented for him his first 'feeling into words'.[28] 'Digging' eschews the view of singularity by linking to a tradition and to the past, but as Coughlan argued in her much-anthologised essay 'Bog Queens', the speaker's links to tradition are fraught by Oedipal anxieties.[29] This well-known 'scene' in Irish poetry dramatises an act of symbolic repatriation to the land. This Oedipal shift is facilitated when the paternal shafts of the pastoral spade become poetic pen (and gun), ensuring a patrilineal inheritance flowing from mother earth via the ritual transferral of phallus from father to son. Coughlan points out that this particular physical drama between father and son, via an unrealised maternal presence figured as earth, is also to be found in Montague's work. These fêted expressions of patrilinear logic form part of the cultural template that has normalised illusions of monadic disconnection from the environment.[30]

Continuing cultural investment in hetero-patriarchal articulations of singular poetic voices as widely representative of genius, impedes attunement to the multiple and intersectional sets of relations in which we are all embedded on this planet and universe. *Before You* retunes us by amplifying the lateral sibling axis to make interdependence and connection culturally available as an enabling metaphor. The patrimonial spade is replaced by a children's spade in 'Imprints'; the toy spade does not dig back or in but is sideways swung by her sister, delivering a 'smack' to the poet that leaves an acoustic and cellular 'imprint' on her psyche, recalled in the soft assonantal accenting with which Heaney so beautifully patterned his work:

> you stunned me
> with the smack of the spade
> on skin already sun-burning
> among soft accents. ('Imprints', p. 13)

With a sideways swing of a spade, Quinn quietly references how those who resist the status quo are caricatured as excessive, or as 'making a scene', and creates a lateral connection between siblings, while the poem 'breaks into' one of the most famous Oedipal 'scenes' in the Irish cultural imaginary: 'when too young to care / about scenes we broke into one' ('Imprints', p. 13). Because the tradition of Irish poetry has remained so resistant to including women, breaking and entering appears the only means by which to introduce the 'sibling world' to the self-enclosed sphere of masculine lineage; the recent publication of *The Cambridge Companion to Irish Poets* (2017) was a shocking reminder of how masculinist values are still uncritically mistaken for the norm; here, this mistaken impression is displaced by the imprint of the beautiful, wild, and passionate love and hate of siblings for each other and is concentrated in the image of the spade, figured through the cellular memory of hot and cold skin.[31] When the speaker fails to run cold water over a burn, she hears her sister's voice tell her she will 'never get the sting from it', much like this still 'hot' memory burned into her very being ('Imprints', p. 13). The still 'smarting' smack of the spade and 'sting of the burn' ('Imprints', p. 13) illustrate what Mitchell argues is the enduring imprint of the sibling complex, with its unmediated intense fraternal and sororal rivalries likely the source for quickly ignited enmities and the 'mysterious speed' with which hostilities spring up between neighbouring tribes and cultures. Mitchell proposes that the law of the mother 'operates between siblings or between siblings and peers' as a means of regulating these feelings, and without this law, murder and incest would prevail.[32]

However, unlike the law of the father, which can be internalised, Mitchell argues that the laws governed by the mother have had to be externalised 'because cultural conditions do not allow for their internalisations, such as happens with the law of the father'.[33] Thus while the burning heat of the unmediated and unselfconscious devotion and fury in the aggressive love between siblings is captured in the wonderfully evocative image of the wild energy of a child running for her survival, it also describes the psychic cost of externalisation:

> you ran for cover
> quick as a rock-lizard
> leaping jellyfish
> that lurked like landmines
> on the taut wet sand. ('Imprints', p. 13)[34]

Because a patriarchally inflected culture struggles to perceive this dimension of psychic life and its cultural correlatives, intense horizontal rivalries persist throughout life in peer and other groups, in which seriality, place, and sequence have to be repeatedly assured in the re-enacting of sibling scenes such as seen in inexplicable and irrational flashpoints and competitions that arise within organisations and groups. The final line of the poem is left unpunctuated and open; thus, running for cover, her sister is left without the formal closure of a full stop, without containment, into an external environment that threatened the hurtful psychic sting of further explosion. Mitchell argues that this oscillating, passionate love-hate is a key aspect of how we differentiate the self from the other, but it has been obscured by an over-emphasis on separation from the mother. Personal growth also takes place through mediating our place among siblings (or sibling substitutes) and is crucial for understanding our role within larger structures, modelled first for us by family. She writes that:

> hate for the sibling enables the first move to be made: I hate you, you are not me, is the precondition of seriality. The mother restricts this hate — enjoins the non-enactment. Children's games — musical chairs, oranges and lemons, pig in the middle and all the spontaneous play — are about seriality ... the lateral relationship itself instigates its own processes of managing sameness through constructing difference.[35]

Without metabolising symbolisation and ritual, it remains 'a scar we cannot yet see, nor heal' ('Berlin', p. 34). 'Mosquitoes' (p. 14), like its companion poem 'Imprints', explores the repeated and damaging externalisation of the 'law of the mother' by 'acting out' the differentiation process of 'I hate you, you are not me', while concurrently seeking modes of internalising 'the law of the mother': while a smack burns externally, a mosquito bite burns internally. 'Imprints' is set in early childhood in which unconscious feelings towards a sibling are *physically acted out*, while 'Mosquitoes', set in adolescence, *acts out* via a speech-act, and demonstrates the inherited lack of means to internalise this law while simultaneously providing them:

> you swam in from your rage
> and casually, as if requesting the time, asked me,
> *Do you think I am a good person?*
> I answered honestly but you took it as truth
> and swam back to sea – a cerulean blue
> I have never known. ('Mosquitoes', p. 14)

No epistemological or symbolically enabling lexicon was available in that moment to transform the friction from negotiating selfsame difference into an empowering epistemology: '– a cerulean blue / I have never known'. A new blueprint, an imprint in blue, is suggested in the play on 'unknown' and 'cerulean blue', a colour used by painters as a cool highlight to offset hot hues. The differentiation needed, yet 'not known', is hummed into being when the individual names of the siblings are applied as a calming agent to 'rage' that had nowhere symbolic to go for as long as it was generated under the 'law of the father'. The sisters' names are articulated from the patriarchal 'name of the cultural father'. 'Cerulean' contains an acoustical cue in its smooth assonantal emphasis of low-noted vowels that alerts us to a double play on names: cer-rule-ean is homophonically revealed as both the poet's name – at least when conjoined with the perceptions that come from 'answering honestly' in a culture without transformational supports, 'cruel Leeanne' – *and* the name of her sister, Caroline. The complexities of the sibling world along with the personal physical cost of the lack of its symbolic presence become audibly visible in this synaesthetic picture, where the tones and timbre of the cerulean blue sky and sea bring our interdependence with human, other-than-human, and elemental life into focus.

The sibling world is thus washed into the liminal landscape of horizon and coastline, with the sea both raging and calm from which a sibling swam in and out. The patterns of coastlines across all scales of composition have been described as having a 'fractal selfsimilarity', a term that recalls Mitchell's description of sibling-like 'selfsameness'. Artist and cartographer Tim Robinson writes that the 'general characteristics of coastlines are the same, roughly speaking, as all scales from the whole side of a continent down to a rockpool', and he delineates fractals as forming the building blocks of 'many natural entities, such as coastline, systems of geological faults, cloud forms, even the pattern of distribution of the 200 billion galaxies in space'.[36] Such shapes were first named by mathematician Benoît Mandelbrot as 'selfsimilar', a term that aims to describe the natural tessellations unrepresentable by linear geometry.[37] In *Before You*, sublunary, 'selfsimilar' fractal patterns are intertwined with those of selfsameness in the sibling world. Fractal is parsed into the fractiousness that is a key part of the sibling process of attachment and disattachment; actions more often than not hushed-up, deflected, and denied. Far from distracting from sibling disputatiousness, *Before You* opens with it, and in the oscillation between affiliation and difference the 'selfsame' yet 'differentiating' movements of the sibling world are fractally extended across the collection to highlight how these human patterns resonate universally. *Before You* is fractally self-repeating, the amoebic iterations of 'burn', 'smart', 'rock', 'rage', 'sand', and 'sun' in 'Imprints' and 'Mosquitoes' creating a language to allow for the non-linear law of the mother to be internalised. In 'Mosquitoes', the coast becomes fractionalised as an oceanic womb contained within the poet's sibling world:

> I hid from a sea that smarted every part
> of my home-sickened body
> as if I were the rocks that contained it. ('Mosquitoes', p. 14)

This geological image of a gestational inner sea symbolises an imaginative space where the sibling relationship can be metabolised – named and experienced. 'Mosquitoes' opens with a symbolic search for 'places big enough to hold us both / together', for when 'spinning maps on the axis of [the] globe', they find that 'soil', 'rock', 'cartographic shape', and 'name' are unlinked by experiential knowledge:

> Geography was soil and rock until we landed
> With two fingers upon the cartographic shape
> I knew in name only. ('Mosquitoes', p. 14)

Here, geography is first known as the physical matter of soil and rock 'until' they make a leap into the symbolic: the word geography denotes applying writing (graphia) to the earth (geo), highlighting Quinn's poetic act of integrating matter and making. Two fingers, implying one from each sister, find an external 'cartographic shape' together, which while already named, had yet to be *internally* mapped, an imperative that recurs in a later migration poem, 'Berlin':

> Without the maps of our known lives, we feel
> Our way through others' histories, seeing
> Neither past nor present. ('Berlin', p. 34)

The image of the 'two fingers', evoking as it does the colloquial use of the phrase, symbolises the pivoting axis of sibling love and hate – and also, specifically here, the precious relationship that ended before these complexities could be teased out together. Instead, the poet is thrown into grief and must continue to map the inner and outer world without her sister. The poem 'brings us full sphere and becomes / a sleeping kiss' ('Permafrost', p. 31) when the journey begins with a globe, not a flat map, and proceeds by limning rondures, spheres, and the curves that reveal the shape of lost love. The poet's ranging sensibility imaginatively '[a]nchors the blood' in 'the floor / of existence'('Accidents I', p. 60), and her bereft body is interwoven with the conjugated effects of the capitalocene. The shock and ensuing high alert caused by sudden bereavement are intertwined with the infrastructural impacts of globalisation and the existential threats of climate emergency and multiple extinction. Poems such as 'The Impact' (highly commended in the Forward Prize for Poetry 2012, and published in *The Forward Book of Poetry 2013*) show how, in Quinn's symbology, the military-industrial complexes that have driven climate crises are intertwined in the human nervous system like 'memories' that 'wake you like a gun going off in the night' ('Accidents', p. 62).

Before You elaborates the evolving awareness that we are far more sensate, and that other life forms are more conscious than human-centric sciences have hitherto allowed for; the experiential threat of the capitalocene is set against an expanded understanding of consciousness, which is shown to belong to both organic and inorganic matter: 'like you were wood or stone, waiting / to be something made from wood or stone' ('Before You', p. 47). Wood and stone, seemingly inert materials, are described in a state of anticipation, suggesting a form of organisational intelligence impelled by an elaborating imperative: 'something in the cells say yes when our mouths say no' ('Accidents I', p. 60). Research in evolutionary biology and quantum physics has discovered signs of plant and particle intelligence and challenged rationalist and human-centric beliefs about consciousness. Not only is intelligence a feature of other-than-human life forms, but many levels of intelligence co-exist in the ecology of our very own being, with our individual cells and the microbiomes which we host exhibiting discrete signs of attunement: 'the cells go on' ('Accidents I', p. 60).

The metabolising intelligence of the material world that 'goes on' is shown in the rising energies of the earth, in rivers that carve new pathways through the landscape as needed: 'new water / turned to sea' ('Chorus', p. 22). The propelling, transformative forces of the planet are shown to be beyond the human will but part of human nature; our connection to ecological regulation evident in salt and water: through our tears. Salt is the signifying component of tears, which have unique chemical compositions according to the triggering event, and a purifying and ritual significance in many cultures; humans are the only documented life form that weep and sob. Weeping melts the neurological freeze instantiated by sudden trauma; crying 'salt tears', as the saying goes, facilitates a nervous system reset when this discharge unfreezes a nervous system arrested by intolerable pain, helping to integrate unprocessed feelings, and transforming a sea of loss into an ocean of recovery: 'one sea became another' ('Water', p. 59). Oceanic salt is transferred to the 'salt that covers ice, stark / and stubborn, on the pavements below' ('Accidents III', p. 62), and as the reader moves through 'Storms', 'Houses', 'Water', and 'Accidents' in Part II, it is breathed in 'the 'air' that 'tasted of salt' ('Houses IV', p. 58), and physically expressed in 'forehead beaded sweat' ('Storms III', p. 53). The profound materiality of neural and affective connections is shown when salt is transferred between bodies: 'the skin damp under your hand' ('Houses III', p. 57). In 'Chorus', the title of which implies more than one voice, the salinating flux of colliding icecaps is blended with the unfreezing of the polyvagal system, when consonants are 'knocked together' like 'blocks of / frozen sea' (p. 22), evoking the clunk of ice floes and the transformation of frozen continental plates of language to fluid sea, 'breaking' to a 'new form'. Detached icebergs, harbingers of ecological disaster, and rising sea levels mirror how melting into love can *also* throw a shocked nervous system back into high alert. The poem invites the reader to be first 'all ears' – to a text full of plosives and glottal stops, sounds that mimic attack.

Our neural system first detects threat and pre-cognitively ascertains our level of security – not through the *content* of speech but via tone, volume, and flow: *neuro*ception is a primary mode of orienting us to our environment which precedes *per*ception, and depends on hearing.[38] Further, nerve sensation – felt as intense fluctuation between cold and heat – is registered through the skin, such as we see in 'Imprints' and 'Mosquitoes'; in 'Siesta', the 'skin knows' ('Siesta', p. 27). In 'Absence of Memory', the 'thin-skinned sky' (p. 40) suggests extra sensitivity to the overheating earth and the fragility of its thinning ozone, where traumatised individual systems are mirrored in a distressed anthropocenic ecosystem. In theory, all poetry affects us neuroceptively through tone, rhythm, and pattern, but Quinn's work also *symbolises* this neuroceptive process at work. Quinn has described the affects of reading the works of other writers as so potently physical that she often needs to 'recover' after such an encounter.[39] *Before You* recounts her unfolding *per*ception of the sympathetic system response (freeze, flight, or fight) to traumatic loss, and how a chronic state of 'Permafrost' (p. 31) can be melted – albeit not without challenge – by art and love. The poetry 'nurture[s] a body you cannot see' ('Siesta', p. 27), meaning both the inner neural workings of the personal body and the psychic connections of the psychosocial body. By making the slow, imperceptible, elemental, and healing processes of cellular awareness, renewal and recycling of matter *perceptible* in this 'peculiar alphabet', Quinn's work counters the dromological logic of the capitalocene with quite another ethical space and speed, which comes close to philosopher Luce Irigaray's aim 'to restore an embodied materiality' to the western 'philosophical tradition'.[40]

Irigaray identifies this as a feminine dimension and the 'repressed and hidden underside of metaphysical construction'.[41] How this can be coded as 'feminine' is worth briefly exploring in the context of queer theory, social justice movements, and eco-feminism. Trans activism and feminist and gender theory have alerted us to how masculinity and femininity are manifested on an oppositional binary by patriarchal systemising as a precondition of its own power. Attributing feminine and masculine characteristics to people, places and objects serves to further damage and exclude those marginalised – that is, feminised – by patriarchy. 'Feminine', although a complicated and evolving term, has been strategically recuperated by activists seeking to mitigate and reverse the toxic effects of hetero-patriarchy, and in this context it is increasingly used to describe corrective qualities and practices cultivated by those historically feminised. Values that have arisen from 'feminised' lives lived in care for and adjacent to bodies and the earth are increasingly consulted to model an ethics and economics of care and sustainability.[42] This 'feminine' affective relationality of the 'repressed underside' links to what Irigaray calls a 'sort of tetralogy, tackling the problem of the four elements: water, air, fire, earth, applied to philosophers nearer our own time'.[43] Quinn reworks how water, fire, earth, and air have been codified in classical and common-sense arrangements of time, space, and form – 'the wind warps words, earth, sky' ('Ode to Memory', p. 35), disrupting the body–mind and human versus nature dichotomies of metaphysical philosophy: 'leaves hang on like flames / resisting extinction' ('Accidents IV', p. 63). The human body is shown to be part of planetary bodies: water simultaneously inside and outside the human body; fire a weapon and an inner heat, a life-giving and obliterating sun; earth 'soil-skin' and ground, and air which 'above the sea / reaches the horizon' ('Houses IV', p. 60) is particulate. These four elements, which do not strictly correspond to the elements of matter, are here not only placed 'before us', but also *as* us recalling diatomic pairing, the interlinking atomic bonding that forms the building blocks of matter – the 'floor of all existence'. The interface between the intelligence of material life and the human's capacity for abstraction is symbolised by the elusive horizon, when 'earth and sky / mark the apparent, below' (p. 60) and the liminal links between sea and land.

Thus, the word 'strand', which calls up not only shores but also fibres and hair, gestures to human movement across the globe, emotional ties, and material links between beaches in England, Brittany, Haiti, Italy, Japan, New England, and beyond. The 'furious brawl' of the two sisters on a Brittany beach in 'Imprints', leaving them emotionally stranded, summons the Western Front as well as the expansionism of imperial wars in Africa and South-East Asia which transformed the resourceful earth into a menacing nightmare and blew relationships apart. The jellyfish that 'lurked like landmines' ('Imprints', p. 13) evoke the death-dealing corms of modern western warfare, planted in the agricultural soils of embattled and colonised lands. Objects and actions from the modernised safety of the northern hemisphere hearken to a violent and destructive cost elsewhere, when a tray of coffee is carried 'like a bomb' ('Graffiti on the Plant Store', p. 16) and a forest 'burn[s] like paper' ('Imprints', p. 13), foregrounding the escalating ecological and human cost of the capitalocene. The scorching sun and rising water levels of a dysregulated climate system are echoed in the overheated nervous system and flooded emotional world; each is enmeshed in the other, the natural world infected by the destructive explosive force that humanity exerts upon the earth, where market demands generate populations of low-paid workers. The powerful elegy 'Cockle Picker (Morecambe Bay)' is written to honour the undocumented Chinese workers whose economic precarity forced them to work so close to a turning tide that, in the most awful way, they lost their lives at Morecombe Bay on the north-western coast of England in 2004:

> the blood explosion –
> bursting, gave yourself up, naked, poorer –
> your body brimming, full as the sea. (p. 23)

The 'brimming body' of the person so shamefully exploited and betrayed foreshadows the climate displacements to come. Filled with the natural destructive yet recycling force of 'the sea', this collection sets her body alongside the 'body flung far from itself' ('The Impact', p. 17) linked to heat and fire, and 'broken to a new form', when it is metonymically replaced by the impact of a young boy's lit cigarette against an oncoming windscreen.

In this rehearsal of catastrophe, the speaker watches her own expectation of disaster unfold; she expects to 'see some body flung / far from itself, broken to a new form—/ but the cars only ever move on'. In reality, the fatal collision is diverted by 'tyres [that] break / to a dead halt', bringing the car into sharp focus, while the line break between 'break / to' functions as a linguistic brake applied to the accelerating capitalocene, which veers the speaker onto a new vector of possibilities where the 'unexpected beauty' of the impact can be contemplated ('The Impact', p. 17). This explosion in part 'disarm[s] us' ('Graffiti on the Plant Store', p. 16) and without the weapons, the poem leads back to the natural world which metabolises what has been broken by violent impact, explosion, or detonation; its healing processes transform damage so that a new form will be created – but this is not a simple romantic opposition of the natural and the industrial. Instead, these are connected in the potential of 'a sudden impact' to 'reduce us both / to steel and glass' ('After Violence', p. 19). Impact deconstructs the human body back to the very natural matter exploited by the fossil industry: the sand used to make glass, and the iron, carbon, manganese, silicon, phosphorus, sulphur, and oxygen in steel. The collision between modernity's narrative of poisonous progress and virtual reality is symbolised in the scattering of the toxic tobacco flashpoints against a 'screen'. The broken body is 'broken to', the preposition in the verb phrase compelling us to see how planetary survival depends on valuing interdependence: on us seeing a 'new form'.

A visual clue to interconnectedness, in the em-dash that connects the enjambment 'form—/but', is in harmony with another, aural clue to the sympoietic new form this poetry seeks; 'form/—but', homophonically connects to 'the butt of [a] cigarette' that a small boy flicks at the 'windscreen/ of an oncoming car', creating a fire show in which 'the embers flare / magnificently' ('The Impact', p. 17). Voices '[l]ike a splay of bullets, from the bloated sky', evoke the shadow of a haunting rifle butt, and when 'a cheer goes up', like a flame, into the 'bloated sky', the 'display' is linked to the dysregulated capitalocene, with its toxic food products and investment in violence through gaming and sport. The simmering city violence palpable on this hot summer's night speaks once more to material and symbolic poverty. We internalise our relations to our environment not only through language, but also by how we play. Symbolic play is both a precursor and a companion to language, and in time language is substituted for behaviours that are acted out in early childhood, when we learn to 'use our words'. Here, the symbolic play is dis/play, an externalised dis/placement, substituting *acting out* for the inner and outer symbolic relating which have not been nurtured by the culture.[44] With no symbolic playground in or outside, this dis/play shows children dysregulated by the social and political bodies that have dis/placed them in toxic urban habitats: they 'splay bullets', and 'shoot footballs, bottle tops / hot chips'. Along with the 'small boy' who smokes, this highlights the structural failure of the state to nurture and safeguard children across all socio-economic strata, both inside and outside the home – a 'home' that has been, in the Irish constitution, defined by the imperatives of hetero-patriarchal capitalism, colonialism, and nationalism.[45] Ownership of the privately defined home was the economic imperative that grossly propelled the building industry that inflated the Celtic Tiger – an industry that largely built (and continues to build) high-density housing without supporting infrastructure for families.

Quinn's is also a poetics of the late-Celtic Tiger years and the spectacular and sudden recessionary implosion that followed the economic expansion; *Before You* is marked by the sense of structural precariousness and temporariness, and by the concussive cuts that attended the end of the Tiger years in Ireland. The links between housing insecurity in Ireland, global homelessness, and climate migration are witnessed in shock, and the coterminousness of house and home is broken by transposing houses into permeable structures, ruined, unbuilt, floating, always on the verge of being 'broken to a new form' ('Rubble', p. 26). The collection de-couples house and home, re-placing the ideological bricks of patriarchal heteronormativity with the individual body, substituting a home in the bones for the privatised house where the value of reproductive labour and children are diminished and where desire is circumscribed into national service. In this articulation of home, women have been conflated with family and shelter and emotional labour has largely fallen to them without external support, to the ongoing detriment of a meaningful and state-supported care policy for all. The 2021 Citizens' Assembly Report on Gender Equality recommended that article 41.1 be amended so that diverse forms of kinship are recognised, women are no longer defined by their place in the home, and care becomes the paid and valued responsibility of all, not just women.[46] *Before You*'s 'peculiar alphabet' queers the hetero-patriarchally defined 'home' through its elaboration of 'Houses' in Part II, showing how it engendered shame.[47] The speaker's 'body' is 'home-sickened' ('Mosquitoes', p. 14), dis-eased not by queerness, but by the social body derived from the template of the heteronormative home, an isolating and lonely space in which 'bare walls made bad companions'; and 'windows made promises they couldn't keep' ('Houses I', p. 55). In this inhospitable world the speaker 'built walls around a scream but it grew louder' ('Houses III', p. 57), to the point where it became a prison in which the speaker could not recognise herself:

> you knew how to name the things you saw and in what order they should be named. You waved to yourself from a height, but you were looking the other way when you waved back. ('Houses IV', p. 58)

Looking an 'other way' is explored in 'Rubble', a poem written in response to the 2010 earthquake in Haiti, when the poet saw news footage of bodies being carried from the rubble of their homes in blankets; as victims make their way out from the wreckage, they are also 'made out' by the digital eye of 'photographs and footage taken by news crews'.[48] These images, 'sold to accompany reportage feeding an intense global interest that inevitably waned', are themselves framed by the poem, which recounts the poet's discomfort with the 'unseemliness of photographing and filming tragedy', and by extension her 'own unseemliness in writing a poem about it'.[49] Here, the global communication network functions like an over-aroused nervous system, of which, the poet acknowledges, she is, in some way, a part. And, much like when adrenaline retreats and the nervous system collapses, the poem counters over-activation with a slower impulsion of renewal and sustainability. The poem looks in multiple directions, and the speaker's grief and discomfort as bystander are transferred to another register, an erotics of visibility, that extends to all lives occluded by the paradigmatics of salacious storytelling; the speaker asks for the house to be removed from/as her so that she can be 'made-out': 'take this house from my body, brick from my bones'. Here, being 'made out' also refers to 'coming out', creating oneself from the rubble, and seeing and being seen in the ruins of a structure that was designed to hide queer lives. 'House in the Ocean' (p. 18) was written after the 2011 Tōhoku earthquake and tsunami in Japan, when the poet saw a photo of a house floating in what looked like the middle of an ocean:

> Half-submerged, a house floats
> on the ocean. Its roof and second story
> protrude from the surface—a curious island. ('House in the Ocean', p. 18)

The house becomes 'a curious island' saturated by the salt water necessary for biological life, like a child in a womb.[50] In this elegy, the waters of the sea wash through the house like breaking waters in birth.[51] 'Story', meaning narrative, not floor level, cues us to the 'second story' told here of healing by coming home to one's own body, within the oceanic body of another, two cohabiting stories. The illusory self-containment of inherited ideas in masterful aesthetic forms has to be both flooded and 'rearranged', in order to bear witness and give birth: 'rearranged what you could do to fit yourself inside, like one body fitting itself to another's' ('Houses II', p. 56). This amniotic flooding is also connected to the transformative effect of salt water in the act of weeping which facilitates new pathways to intimacy, connection, and awakening sexual desire, through naming and mourning the imprint of sibling love and loss. The privatised land-based and defended home is replaced by what Eavan Boland called 'an origin like water'.[52] Ireland becomes Ire-sea/see, when the 'ire' can become seen, visible, and processed, and an integral part of our psychosocial history. Because of the persistence of homophobic violence, being visible is not always safe for queer folk; thus the poem also plays on 'in' and 'out', showing how 'in' can be safer than 'out' and visibility can be life-threatening, and how taking a place in the polis can prompt a neuroceptive response of terror. It is up to us, the readers, the culture, whether this becomes life-affirming rather than life-threatening.

The speaker's imperative is addressed to the reader as well as her partner; we are directly called to witness in the 'stork's gift' a new erotics of poetic form, when we are asked for help, to 'make her out':

> Oh make me out.
> prose me. Poem me. Put flesh on these blanketed bones.
> Bundled compare me to the stork's gift.
> ('Gertrude Stein Poses for Man Ray', p. 21)

Not only are we beseeched to witness, but we are also called into co-creation. As we read, we read in the first person, simultaneously asking to be newly made out too. We are invited to 'make out' what we are saying from the rubble of the culture. Our co-perception is brought into sharp focus as crucial partner in bringing 'in-out' house-bodies into focus and seeing and feeling the beauty of an interconnected life outside the limits of heteronormative and patriarchal description. We are invited to 'make out' the 'cords', 'threads', and 'ties', the many weaving materials used to show the myelinated map of internal neural imprints and external interconnections via neuroception – the first embodied register of sensation that precedes both seeking and language. We are invited to help the speaker 'make her way out' of the pain by weaving this new world with her, and by attuning our eyes and imaginations to the connectors. 'Ode to Memory' is parsed by 'Absence of Memory', in which 'ties' and '[h]ome-spun sentiments' connect to the speaker's desire to 'comb the world for facts', while the comb links to the 'strand of hair / woven to the collar' in 'Winter Coat' (p. 44). The garment, although '[p]ast meaning' and 'out / of season', still 'retains her [sister's] shape', but 'holds nothing', that the speaker 'can touch', save for this 'strand', which links to the shorelines on which their sibling scenes were played, and to her poetic, environmental strata. Thus, although it is 'a reminder that marks / only absence', on 'this coat that is no longer coat' ('Winter Coat', p. 44), the hair that 'glistens still', an image of fine light vibrating into stillness, calls a chord to mind, and connects us to the short poem 'Chorus' which, Lucy Collins notes, 'expresses the power of the auditory in visual terms'.[53] Such *per*ception of the *neuro*ceptive affect of sound on our bodies is also emphasised in 'Rubble', when the speaker asks to be 'decomposed'; here de-composition links to 'cells going on' – when new life emerges from the compost of decomposing matter. It also suggests being un-composed and returned to a foetal-like state held within the 'dirty threads' of the 'heroic sheet' in which she asks to be wrapped: 'how my spine curves to these dirty / threads' ('Rubble', p. 26).

The dirty threads of the 'sheet' relate us once more to the sheet music at the heart of Quinn's ecosystem – and the lyric. Body, language, song, and world are synaesthetically intertwined when we and/as the speaker become the lyre from which the tradition of the lyric originated: 'loot me, Lyric me. Pick at my bones'. The earliest lyres were made from animal bone, the command to 'pick the bones' not only inviting us to 'choose' unsung bodies from the past, but also reminding us that first we *feel* music, sound, resonance, in the hollows from which our bones are made, in the air inside us. Bringing air inside us, from an atmosphere that permeates and precedes us, we expand and contract, and our opening and closing are like a fractal of the expansion and contraction of the uterus as it brings forth a new body, or a flower as it responds to the sun, in 'a cacophony of flames' ('Permafrost', p. 31). Through the atmosphere, we take in the matter of mother earth, in 'air' that 'was breathable then' ('Before You', p. 47).

The lyric is of course the public-private, the 'in-out' poem, that echoes the expansion and contraction of breath. Breathing in, we internalise the law of the mother; breathing out, she is 'made out'. Also constructed from sheep's gut, the lyric song relates us to our guts, which have more neurons than our brains. In 'singing our guts out', we release the held breath that physiologically freezes the nervous system; in singing it deliquesces: 'and with that life / Was in the wings, beating a silent drum / Before you' ('Before You', p. 47). Flow is restored through 'taking in' and 'giving out' – 'it took from you / and was returned / unblemished' ('Before You', p. 47) – a physical process already familiar to our cells from when we vibrated with and bathed in the first music, the drumbeat of a mother's heart. The lyric poet is at once the amniotic sea, and the uterine rocks through which it flows: 'I hid from a sea ... as if I were the rocks that contained it' ('Mosquitoes', p. 14). The enteroceptive restoration of the elemental, atmospheric, and material to metaphysical traditions vibrates in the lines 'I wait as the current resounds / in me, whirring like the engine of the world' ('Letter to Leonard Woolf', p. 20). The re-sounding electrical and tidal current 'makes out' through the poet, existing *before* and in her, much as mother, earth, and atmosphere do.

Thus a binary of human and habitat is resisted to advance an ecological sensibility in which humanity can be made out as one species among many; our special gift is our complex nervous system that allows us to cry, sing, craft, and symbolise – to 'make out' and 're-sound' matter through the instruments of our making through the 'beat of our talk' ('Peculiar Alphabets', p. 29). The lines that divide human 'soil-skins' ('Letter to Leonard Woolf', p. 20) from the atmosphere of the 'thin-skinned sky' are shown to be illusory:

> Before us there is only horizon,
> the clean line signalling the apparent
> meeting of sky and earth. ('After Violence', p. 19)

The horizon that stands in for an existential and material encounter we cannot cleanly map is embedded in lines that illuminate the permeable particularity of matter, and the larger ecosystem of phylogenetic strands of DNA through which all life is linked in 'some in-between hour' ('Graffiti on the Plant Store', p. 16), the interstitial time that re-sounds as 'our'. In this in-between 'our' space, flowering, pollination, oceans and flight are connected in this beautiful image of the butterfly effect: 'the sea / rose and dipped, butterfly waves' ('Cockle Picker', p. 23). The permeable co-being of environmental and interpsychic renewal flows from a gestational darkness that is different from the shadow cast by the hetero-patriarchal tradition of genius: 'darkness bodies us without shadow', and from this darkness feeling is restored to sight: 'now nothing / can be seen that is not felt – / here where our bodies / are once again enough' ('Rhapsody Blackout', p. 25). The original meaning of genius, a spirit attendant on a person, reveals its early iteration of attention, care, and attunement. *Before You* supplies us with 'the right angle for genius' through an alphabet queer enough to speak of the law of the mother and the ongoing effects of the sibling world: 'it makes us. make out. acting out'. Sympoietically, it parses this fundamental set of correlations, initiating us into a co-creative, reciprocal ecology of meaning-making, following the 'beat of our talk' ('Peculiar Alphabets', p. 29) to where 'the new heart unfurls / unmasks memory' ('The New Heart', p. 38). *Before You* leads us across time and space into the 'stratosphere // of hereafters' ('Absence of Memory', p. 40).

PART 3

Rethinking Femininity/ Masculinity

The Lionhearted

PAULA MEEHAN

Sometimes, she said, with massage things come up.
Your tears do not worry me. Stuff lodges
In the body. Feel free. To weep. To shed.

Like a snake its skin; like a crab its shell.
The tears run down my face into my ears.
I am stretched, a starfish on a blue sheet

Under the shade of the tamarisk trees
The surf pounds the rocks below, cicadas
Are bowing their tune again and again.
Again. Chrysacheira above me

Pressing on my limbs with her palms
Pressing, pawing like a big red cat.
Suddenly my mother, emissary

Of the underworld, a great big red cat,
Her paws kneading my child body, my paws
Kneading her breasts, nuzzling towards her nipple

Hungry mouth searching through the stink of her,
The fog of nicotine that wreaths her head.
She – a big red cat; I – a small grey mouse.

Timid inside the wardrobe, hiding from her rages,
Her grief, the belt with the silver buckle.
I'll beat that accent out of you. Common.

Common as muck. You little guttersnipe.
Big red cat with her sharp claws unsheathed.

* * *

There is a place inside of me where you
Are always walking up the avenue.
I see you from the front seat of the bus.
I am heading into college. I'm late

For a lecture: The Origins of Myth.
Some lessons I will have to learn over
And over and over again. I should

Have quit the bus, I should have run to you
And taken the heavy bags from your hands,
I should have smoothed your cramped and blistered hands

Finger by swollen finger, I should have stood
Shoulder to shoulder with you, I should have walked
The road with you – even into hell.

* * *

Seventy seven and then some light years
Away – I place you now, beloved mother,
In your own starry constellation fixed

Between Virgo to the east and Cancer
To the west, crouching over the sun this
Peaceful morning like a cat with your ball

Of light. I will raise my face to you, lion
In your cave of dreams; I will stand my ground:
Herculean mouse, my first labour done.

City Without God

THOMAS McCARTHY

Without its Friday morning crush of people
The city is all nakedness and vulnerable bones.
How will it sin again and be sinfully inimitable
If it doesn't have adulterous men on mobile phones,

Phoning on the off-chance that husbands are
Not at home? Like the poet who was more than
Past his sell-by date who I met at the corner
Of Grattan Street: how I annoyed him on

So many inopportune corners, him excusing
Himself as quickly as possible. I would linger
Just to watch him become annoyed. Nothing
Is more sinful, though, than this meagre

Habit I've inherited from my father of wanting
To annoy clever people, of frustrating ambition
In my betters. It must be a country thing,
Or perhaps just an Irish thing; or Augustinian

In a city that was always in the grip of Franciscans.
The devil needs a people to flourish in
But the pandemic has washed these streets clean
And nothing immoral can flourish. Walking

In the dead quiet of the Marsh I come upon
Another scene of dereliction, a whole street
Of unpeopled houses, falling down, broken
Sash windows and a rain-shattered sheet

Billowing repeatedly. Time sweeps the city centre
Clean of people, as if time were a disease
To which town planning has succumbed. A letter,
A stiff letter about this lack of vice, I must compose.

CHAPTER 10

Female Personal Names in Old English

ELISABETH OKASHA

In this essay I discuss, and question, the general principle, long accepted by Anglo-Saxon scholars, that the grammatical gender of an Old English personal name is a clear indicator of biological sex.[1] That is, this principle suggests that one can look at an Old English personal name and unerringly say that it belonged to a woman or to a man. Anglo-Saxon scholars, as discussed below, have almost all accepted this general rule of thumb, with the notable exception of Fran Colman who has consistently expressed grave doubts about it.[2] Her work has been a source of great inspiration to me.

This principle is predicated on the belief that there was gender specificity in Anglo-Saxon personal names. If asked, most people today would say that modern English given names are gender-specific, citing examples like Mary, John, and so on; this opinion may then be quickly modified by the recall of names like Lesley or Frances, although with the proviso that of course the spelling is different. To the majority of the population of Anglo-Saxon England, the spelling of names was not a gender issue, or indeed any other sort of issue, since they were of course non-literate. Nevertheless, as today, most given names seem to have been recognised as at least more suited to one sex or the other.

Most of the Anglo-Saxon personal names discussed in this essay are di-thematic and are those that belonged, or probably belonged, to Anglo-Saxon women. Di-thematic names are composed of two elements; the name Alfred, for example, consists of *aelf-* plus *-raed*. According to the accepted principle, the second element *-raed* is a grammatically masculine noun and therefore Alfred is a male name. Now of course nobody doubts that King Alfred the Great was a man, but in many other instances where personal names appear in texts, the extra historical evidence indicating the sex of the owner is lacking.

I start by presenting the evidence in favour of the principle, then set out the evidence against it, and draw the conclusion that the principle does not hold true in every case. I then examine three instances where we should, I suggest, be revising or reconsidering our opinions about the sex of the person or people in question.

The evidence in favour of the principle that we know someone was a woman because of the grammatical gender of her name is accepted in part because this rule of thumb often seems to work, and in part because so many eminent Anglo-Saxon scholars over the centuries have accepted it unquestioningly. These include some notable scholars from the nineteenth century whose work is still used today, for example J.M. Kemble and Henry Sweet; they include famous early twentieth-century name-scholars such as Mats Redin and Olof von Feilitzen; and they include people currently producing important work on the place of women in Anglo-Saxon society such as Carole Hough, Gale Owen-Crocker, and Barbara Yorke. I myself have also accepted this principle in the past. Can we really all have been wrong?

In an effort to consider this question systematically, I collected 289 names of Anglo-Saxon women from historical sources, where there was evidence other than the form of their names to indicate their sex.[3] That is, these names were only included in this work if the source referred to the person as 'she', or included a title such as 'queen', or 'wife', or 'abbess'. Since then, two or three further names have been brought to my attention. Most of these 290-plus names are di-thematic and almost all are formed with a noun or an adjective as the second element. Where the second element is a noun, these nouns are indeed very largely grammatically feminine, for example *burg* 'dwelling', *thryth* 'might', and *guth*, assuming this last to be a variant of *gyth*, 'battle'. These grammatically feminine nouns, used as second elements, form over 70 per cent of the di-thematic names I recorded. That is, the principle often works. What then, one might enquire, is the issue?

The issue lies of course in the 30 per cent of the names that are formed with second elements that are not grammatically feminine nouns. Some are grammatically masculine nouns, such as *wulf* 'wolf'. Some are grammatically neuter nouns, like *cild* 'child'; indeed the neuter nouns *laf* 'remnant' and *noth* 'boldness' form di-thematic names of both men and women. Sometimes the female names are formed with an adjective as the second element, for example *swith* 'strong'. In Old English, adjectives are genderless, taking their inflexions according to the grammatical gender of the noun they qualify. Perhaps even more interesting is the second element

-mund: in Old English this noun is grammatically feminine but it never forms female names, only male ones.

Further examples could be given but this is perhaps sufficient to demonstrate that the evidence presents a fairly confused picture. However, one thing is crystal clear: there is not a one-to-one relationship between the biological sex of the person named and the grammatical gender of their name.

The Anglo-Saxons seem not to have been confused by this. And why should they have been? If in conversation today a third party is named as Ashley, or Vivian, or Robin, the hearer can only know whether a man or a woman is being referred to if they are acquainted with the person in question, or if the sex is made obvious from the context, or if a clear indication is given by the use of a word like 'she' or 'he'. We cope with this perfectly well and no doubt the Anglo-Saxons did too. It is necessary not to jump to conclusions too quickly, either today or with reference to Anglo-Saxon England. Carole Hough once pointed out the depressing fact that, when in doubt, Anglo-Saxon scholars generally tend to interpret personal names as those of men, not women.[4] This is not the sort of position that we should wish to be emulating.

There now follow three cases where I suggest that some re-evaluation of the generally accepted conclusions is required.

CASE STUDY ONE: TWO INSCRIBED FINGER-RINGS

The first of these rings was found at Steyning in Sussex and is now in Worthing Museum.[5] It is a gold ring, probably dating from the ninth century, with a diameter of *c.* 20mm. The text stands out by the use of plain lettering on a pounced background and is in Old English. It reads: *aescwulf mec ah*, 'Aescwulf owns me'. The name Aescwulf is well recorded as a male name and finger-rings were worn by both men and women at this date.[6] However, there is a problem: the ring is most unlikely to have been large enough for a man's hand, unless the owner was of particularly fine bone structure and wore it exclusively on his little finger.

With this in mind, I once suggested that the name Aescwulf should be read as an error for an unrecorded female name *Aescwylf, where the second element **-wylf* was formed from the Old English feminine noun *wylf* 'she-wolf'.[7] I have revised this opinion, since finding that the name Eadwulf appears as the name of an undisputed woman in a tenth-century charter.[8] It now seems to me more probable that the second element *-wulf*, although it usually forms male names, could on occasion have been used to form female names, and that this is the explanation of the Steyning ring.

The second of the inscribed finger-rings is unprovenanced but has been in the British Museum, no. AF 459, since 1897.[9] It is a decorated gold ring, of ninth- or tenth-century date, with a diameter of *c.* 30mm. The Old English text is picked out in niello and reads: *eawen mie ah s petrus stan ces*, 'Eawen owns me; may St Peter the rock choose [her/him]'; the final pronoun is not given, as is quite usual in such Old English texts.

The problem here is the reverse of that concerning the Steyning ring. The name Eawen has usually been taken, including by myself , as that of a woman, with the name being a variant of the recorded name Eawynn.[10] However, the ring is much too large for a female hand, unless it were worn on the thumb; moreover, the reference to St Peter, the rock on whom the church was to be built, is rather more appropriate to a man than to a woman. So perhaps the second element of the name, *-wynn*, could be used occasionally for a male name; alternatively, the element could be an unusual spelling of the common element *-wine*, which is always recorded as forming male names.

These two finger-rings demonstrate how, if we are not fixated on the idea that we can always tell the sex of an individual from the grammatical form of their name, some difficulties disappear. In this case the vanishing difficulties are the apparent mismatches between the size of the hoop of the rings and the presumed sex of their owners.

CASE STUDY TWO: THE INSCRIBED NAME-STONES FROM HARTLEPOOL, COUNTY DURHAM

Ten inscribed name-stones have been found during building work and excavation in and around Hartlepool from 1833 until the present, most of them before the middle of the nineteenth century.[11] In addition, two new stones, as yet unpublished, have recently been found from nearby Hart. Most of the Hartlepool stones came from the site of the eighth-century monastic graveyard at Cross Close, a graveyard that no longer exists, and others were found nearby. The exact position of the name-stones in relation to the graves and to the existing skeletons is not known.[12] None of the texts on the stones indicate the sex of the person commemorated.

Now, we know from written sources that the eighth-century monastery at Hartlepool was a double monastery, with both male and female religious in it, presided over by an abbess. The graveyards contain both male and female skeletons, but there are more skeletons than there are name-stones, so clearly choices were made as to who was to be given a name-stone. The ten stones from in or near the Cross Close cemetery yield nine fairly legible names, one of which is the monothematic Abba. It has always been assumed that six of these were the names of nuns, those ending in *-gyth*, *-swith*, and *-thryth*, and that three were the names of monks, those ending in *-mund* and *-wine* as well as the monothematic Abba. Of course this may indeed be so and, in this case, some nuns and some monks could have been commemorated with a name-stone in the same Cross Close cemetery.

However, in the light of what I am suggesting about the relationship between grammatical gender and sex, it is possible that some of the apparently male names were in fact those of females. For example, the name Aethelwine, on Hartlepool III, appears to contain the common masculine noun *-wine*, and indeed names with this second element have always been taken to be those of males. However, I have come upon the names Beorhtwine and Herewine both of which appear in charters where the person is stated to be female.[13] It has indeed been suggested that the Hartlepool graveyards were divided according to sex, with nuns in one, and monks, lay people, and children in another.[14] The Cross Close graveyard could have been a monastic graveyard where only nuns were buried and where some, but not all, were commemorated by a name-stone.

I am not suggesting that abandoning the principle that grammatical gender indicates sex necessarily solves the problems of the Hartlepool monastic graveyards. What it does do is alert us to the fact that the issue cannot be resolved solely on the basis of the personal name-forms, as has been suggested in the past. Moreover, further name-stones continue to be found, and further archaeological and historical evidence may be forthcoming in the future to shed light on this question.

CASE STUDY THREE: SOME NAMES IN THE DURHAM *LIBER VITAE*

The third case study concerns a well-known manuscript, the Durham *Liber Vitae* (BL MS Cotton Domitian A. VII).[15] Folio 43r contains some of the original entries in this manuscript, dating from the ninth century. In column one, lines seventeen to twenty-one, there are five names which appear to be those of females. Indeed, all these names appear elsewhere in the manuscript, some more than once, under the heading *Nomina reginarum et abbatissarum*, 'Names of queens and abbesses'. However, here in folio 43r, they are in the middle of a large set of apparently male names, under the heading *Nomina monachorum*, 'Names of monks'. The names in question are Cynethryth, Eadu, Eardgyth, Hildegyth and Wilburg. Cynethryth is a well-recorded female name, including that of the (later) Anglo-Saxon queen who issued coins in her own name. The other three dithematic names, despite consisting of well-known name elements, are not certainly recorded as female names except in this manuscript, the Durham *Liber Vitae*.

There are several possible explanations for the placing of these names. One, perhaps the most obvious, is simple error: this is the view taken by David and Lynda Rollason in their edition of the manuscript. They simply refer to the names as 'feminine', adding that their appearances in this folio 'presumably represent a misplacing'.[16] An alternative, if less likely, explanation might be that the heading *Nomina monachorum* could be taken to mean 'Names of monks and of nuns'.

However, there is a further piece of evidence from this manuscript: on folio 20r, under the heading *Nomina abbatum*, 'Names of abbots', there appears the name Maeswith. The other abbots' names do look unquestionably to be male, in that they are almost all recorded elsewhere as the names of men and never as the names of women. Maeswith is a rare name but *-swith* is a common second element, always forming female names. Is this name also misplaced? Rollason and Rollason do not comment. It would seem an odd error, to place the name of one abbess among the abbots, not the abbesses, but it is of course not impossible. However, if gender exclusivity is a principle to be abandoned, then it is possible that in this instance the name Maeswith belonged to a man. Perhaps then one could argue that the five apparently misplaced female names on folio 43r are rare examples of what look like female names but which, in fact, belonged in these cases to men.

CONCLUSION

Unfortunately, there are no existing texts from Anglo-Saxon England that set out for us the principles of Old English nomenclature. Moreover, there exists no list of all (or indeed of any) possible names to choose from, and only occasionally do we even know who actually decided on the given name for a child. All we can do is try to work out some general principles from the existing examples.

If we were to accept the principle that the grammatical case of the second element of a personal name had to fit the sex of the child, then at least three further assumptions would have to be made. The first assumption would be that there is complete gender specificity in Old English names, which I hope I have demonstrated is not the case. The second would be that the Anglo-Saxons recognised in speech, as they did in writing, that there were different sorts of nouns with different endings: while this is the case in many Old English written texts, we have no possible way of knowing how far it was true in speech, particularly in the speech of those who were non-literate. The third assumption would be that these different types of nouns were labelled as 'masculine', 'feminine', and 'neuter'. Of course Aelfric the Anglo-Saxon grammarian, a literate and educated classicist, recognised and used these labels in both Old English and Latin, as his extant work makes clear.[17] Most mother-tongue speakers of Old English, however, were non-literate, uneducated, and knew no Latin.

It is possible, but hardly very likely, that one Anglo-Saxon habitually said to another, 'Oh, no, you cannot call her Aelfred because *-raed* is a masculine noun.' It seems inherently more probable that, then as now, convention, fashion, and the names of other family members were more important factors.

I would suggest that the principle that the sex of an individual is definitively indicated by the grammatical case of the second element of his or her name was not a principle that the Anglo-Saxons themselves would have recognised. Rather, I think that it is a modern construct, given respectability and weight by the fact that it has been, and continues to be, widely accepted, and that it often works. It has remained a principle unthinkingly endorsed by Anglo-Saxon scholars for far too long. In my view it is now time for it to be jettisoned.

CHAPTER 11

Writing Irish Women in South America

LAURA IZARRA

Margaret Mac Curtain observes that the personal letters of the great are 'a source of temptation to the historian. Like faith, they are the evidence of things not seen, and provide proof of intangible qualities of personality.'[1] She affirms, 'if they were written by a great man over a number of years to the one person ... such a series of letters succeeds in establishing more concrete facts than transitory emotions'.[2] Personal letters, memories, fictionalised autobiographies, sketches, and chronicles are part of the cartography of the nineteenth-century Irish diaspora around the River Plate in South America. The focus of this essay is not the 'letters of the great'; it is the personal letters of unknown immigrants written over a period of ten to twenty years, recording their struggle to keep the family united and the hope of reunion alive in spite of geographical distance, but mainly to share with their relatives the social, economic, and political life in the new land.

Histories of the Irish diaspora are male-defined and seem to neglect women's experiences. Patricia Coughlan notes the critical attention paid to the importance of feminist recovery work for the field of Irish studies but adds, '[T]here remains, however, a need for persistent intervention in the canon to redress the occlusion, omission and marginalisation of women writers by those male-focused metanarratives which still dominate perceptions of Irish literary tradition.'[3] This is specifically the case of the literature of the diaspora in general, and of the Irish diaspora in particular. Patrick O'Sullivan applies Gerda Lerner's feminist insights to Irish migration studies and challenges researchers to 'build up a history of women "functioning in that male-defined world on their own terms"'.[4] This essay raises some examples related to both issues and shows that some types that have received more attention at home, like 'the patriarch's wife', or abroad, like 'the emigrant gentlewoman', do not represent the pattern of the Irish community in South America.

In order to complete the cartography proposed by O'Sullivan in *Irish Women and Irish Migration* and Irish South American historiography, I shall focus on the Irish-Argentine diaspora space and analyse some women's letters: those written by Sally Moore, Kate and Fanny Murphy to their cousin in Australia between 1864 and 1875 compiled by Edmundo Murray in *Becoming Irlandés*, and Maria Elena Walsh's grandmother's letters (1872–99) published in *La abuela Agnes*.[5] Then, in the light of these letters that make us weigh the invisible role of immigrant women confined to their homes, I shall discuss their self-figuration in Marion Mulhall's travel writing (1881), the autobiographical novels *Tia Barbarita: The memories of Barbara Peart* (1932), and Kathleen Nevin's *You'll Never Go Back* (1946).[6] My argument centres on three issues: the aesthetic arising from the experience of the unknown and a social apprehension of the physical environment and its people; the moral and religious beliefs of the time; and a political perception of the quotidian which creates a transatlantic network of information.

Personal and fictional representations of the late nineteenth and early twentieth centuries reveal that language is the main protagonist in women's '(self)figuration'.[7] 'Self-figuration' implies a 'figure' as form, such as the shape of a person, but it is also connected to the verb 'to figure out', meaning to 'imagine', or something that is 'imagined'; it is a construction that represents the image of the self within the context of the author. It is worth mentioning here the great gap between the image of 'the symbolic woman, woman as ethereal ideal, woman as personification' and 'what many Irish women have experienced'.[8] Life-stories, letters, and narratives of the quotidian help to bridge that gap and to weigh the socio-political dimension of female 'invisibility' in the historiography of the Irish immigrant community in Argentina.

In *The Story of the Irish in Argentina*, Thomas Murray (1919) focuses exclusively on men's deeds.[9] Irish women are not mentioned directly, though it is understood that they have the same function as Argentine women in the society of the time. He writes, '[h]er sphere in the olden time seems to have been mostly in the home and attending to her charitable and religious duties'.[10] Thus, he only extols very briefly the piety, generosity, and patriotic spirit of Irish women as the wives of important social figures within their community, or as members of Irish charitable societies. He also praises the Sisters of Mercy for being 'courageous volunteers' who came to Buenos Aires to work in the Irish Hospital, which then became the first Irish convent in Buenos Aires and later the Irish orphanage. In his writings in *The Southern Cross*, William Bulfin, the Man of the Pampas as he was called in Ireland at the turn of the twentieth century due to his prominent nationalist voice among his compatriots in Argentina, also portrayed life in the camps and in the city from a male perspective. Bulfin wrote that the 'boys, having established themselves fairly well in the camp, came into Buenos Aires to look for wives'.[11] Fr Fahy was their friend and was acquainted with 'all the marriageable girls in the city, knew where they came from at home, knew the particular kind of boy for whom each would make the best possible wife'. William McCann laments the lack of women in the first decades of immigration as three quarters of the Irish in Argentina were men.[12] For the Argentinian historians Juan Carlos Korol and Hilda Sábato, it was not difficult for Irish women who ventured to live in these lands to 'find a husband of the same nationality with whom to share their future', which suggests an endogenous community.[13] Bulfin writes that the morning after the marriage 'the honeymoon tour started and in the bullock-cart, besides the bridal pair, were stowed away some necessary articles of furniture for the new housekeeper ... The expedition reached its destination in two or three or five weeks, according to the weather, and the hero and heroine lived happy for ever after.'[14] Bulfin's representations of Irish women in the camp or in the city place them in the traditional role of housewives / 'housekeepers' and mothers. Although, according to Maria Luddy, women in Ireland were seen in symbolic terms in literary and political writings, in real life they participated in secret societies throughout the nineteenth century and became publicly active in all types of political organisations in the early twentieth century.[15] Yet, the male-oriented Irish-Argentine diaspora story constructs an image of women as obedient to 'the societal authority of the church', while confined 'in a patriarchal family unit'.[16]

However, photographs and letters of the time offer different reflections of that image as they also throw light on the women's silenced desires and the gender-specificity in the social structure. Women register family events, either in the camp or in the city – births, marriages, and deaths; but they also refer to their perceptions of the mysterious unknown when they are on the move or already settled; they reveal their love expectations, sexuality, compatriots' behaviour, the strange habits and external appearance of the natives, and the disastrous political and economic effects of the wars in the country. The paradox is that Irish women, while invisible to men's eyes, prove to be active observers and critics of their context.

In her autobiography *You'll Never Go Back*, Kathleen Nevin writes in the first person and struggles for a genuine narrative autonomy as if her text were an ethnographic study of the host society and culture. Her dreams and expectations about the new country are shattered on board ship before she even arrives. She points out that 'the gentlemen, as usual, were very discouraging when they spoke of the town, and, indeed, of the whole country. '"A very unhealthy place," they said, "when they are not suffering from cholera they are dying of yellow fever" ... "During the yellow fever epidemic ten years ago, people fell dead in the streets and were flung into nameless graves. They had cholera the year before last and died like flies – not that anyone wishes to alarm you, young ladies, but you had better be on your guard"' (Nevin, p. 13). The imperial eye dehumanises the inhabitants of the city, deprives them of their names, and describes how they are victimised by diseases due to their primitivism.

On reaching the port of Buenos Aires, her perception of the unknown city resembles the first unfavourable impressions registered not only by men but by many immigrant women before, such as Agnes Walsh and Marion Mulhall. Kathleen describes the flooded streets, 'the queer dark shops under the arches', the horses under the trams, the passers-by looking very solemn, 'mostly men in dark suits with very black beards and mustaches (*sic*)' and a few ladies handsomely dressed with very white faces and black eyes (Nevin, p. 18). The outside world becomes significant when contrasted with the already known. However, the unknown raises an implied prejudice that has to be immediately denied by the narrator herself:

> And then I saw a nigger! A tall black woman with a woolly head. She was carrying enormous peaches in a basket. I had seen peaches once; they came from the hot-house at Heatherstone Court, but I had never seen a nigger. I leaned over to Bessie all excitement. When she had looked, however, she only held her handkerchief to her nose and said: 'Wasn't it disgusting!' I gaped, not knowing what she could have against the poor black creature, till I saw that we had not noticed the same thing. After a second, my cousin's shuddering and a peculiar, nasty smell drew my attention to a dead dog that lay on the edge of the pavement, covered with flies. It was disgusting, of course. (Nevin, p. 18)

The description of the first encounter with the unknown other, carrying a basket of peaches, has aesthetic echoes of naturalist paintings, but the experience of colonial relations of perception, of looking and being looked at, is reified when the narrator compares the black woman with the enormous peaches. Moreover, there is an ethical disjunction here in the act of enunciation when her excitement is counterpoised with Bessie's reaction of disgust. I believe that the tension created by the narrator between the individual experience of the first racial encounter and its representation raises the shame of colonial racism, as Timothy Bewes affirms: 'Shame is an event of incommensurability: a profound disorientation of the subject by the confrontation with an object it cannot comprehend, an object that renders incoherent every form available to the subject.'[17] Kathleen is caught in a 'shame spiral' trying to provide 'an explanation that does not explain' in referring to the 'poor black creature'.[18] However, an implied racism underlines this experience of incommensurability because the awareness of a postcolonial shame comes about 'between the I as experienced by the self and the self as it appears to and is reflected in the eyes of the other' – in this case, a double other: the black woman being observed and the reader realising how embedded the eurocentric gaze is as a constitutive element of these diasporic subjects.[19] Thus, the above excerpt proves what Bewes contends, that in postcolonial shame, 'subject and object coincide'.[20] Emotional stability seems to be regained by the protagonist with the nasty smell of the dead dog. In the coexistence of both kinds of representation, meanings are deferred in a Derridean way to be countersigned by the readers according to their knowledge of the eurocentric experience of the unknown. In the transfiguration of an individual experience into an aesthetic form, Bewes argues, 'the very presence of shame raises questions concerning the ethical, political or representational adequacy of the text', and 'shame appears overtly, as the text's experience of its own inadequacy' in the semantic approximation of the black woman, the peaches, and the dead dog.[21]

While in the United States Irish women 'provided the largest ethnic group of domestic servants', in Argentina they were housekeepers, governesses, and nursemaids.[22] In *You'll Never Go Back*, Kathleen Nevin tells how Miss Honoria Brady, who welcomed her, her cousin Bessie, and her friend Nancy on their arrival in Buenos Aires, mentioned that there were three kinds of jobs: domestic service, 'places for nursery governesses, and finally there are sometimes positions to be had in one or two select schools' (Nevin, p. 26). The first alternative was not appropriate for them as they came to Argentina to 'make some money, as quickly as possible and go back and be independent' (Nevin, p. 26). They were looking for what Luddy and McLoughlin describe as 'the possibility of an economically productive life, the fulfilment of personal aspirations, such as control of their own finances, the choice of a marriage partner, or indeed, the choice of not to marry at all, and the promise of a certain level of independence' in their adoptive land.[23] In this way, women's migration is understood as a metaphor for change, and their writing and experience of migration are both a product and a cause of change that varies according to the host place. However, the reverend who welcomes them reaffirms the traditional role of women in a patriarchal society: '"women don't make money, in this country or in any other. They leave that to their husbands"' (Nevin, p. 34). This is reaffirmed by their hostess, who dismisses their dream of making money and returning home: 'she had no doubt that [they] should all get married and settle down in the country which was what happened to most of the young ladies from Home' (Nevin, p. 27).

Though Kathleen Nevin had not been told about the presence of black people in Buenos Aires, she is warned about the natives by the captain of the ship and later by their hostess, who says: '"... you don't know the native! ... Extremely violent and passionate ... You must on no account touch any of them"' (Nevin, p. 23).[24] A racist prejudice towards the natives and their language thus permeates the first chapters: '"Life in this country has many snares and pitfalls; and the native, my dear, is not to be trusted. My first and last word to you must ever be: Beware of the native!"' (Nevin, p. 23).

The figure of the rural native is the opposite of the urban native described above. The character of the 'gaucho' is generally romanticised in the words of women immigrants. In a letter of 1868 published in *Becoming Irlandés*, Kate Murphy tells her cousin John James Pettit who moved from Argentina to Australia with his father that 'the grandest time for the natives in the camp', is the shearing at the '*estancias*'. Men and women shear together for a whole month and every night they have '*bailes*' (dances): 'their favourite instrument is the guitar and almost all of them play a little, they have great taste for music so for them it is a time of great joy, people coming out from England do be greatly amused at their dances' (Edmundo Murray, p. 106). Though the point of view is from the outside, there is an appreciation of their enjoyment of music. Marion Mulhall's translation of Sarmiento's categorisation of the figure of the 'gaucho' also refers to the '*payador*' and his great musical and intellectual skill (Mulhall, p. 23).

In Marion Mulhall's own writings in the 1860s, she registers the everyday life and economic progress of the countries she and her husband visit. Her descriptions of the pampas when she visits Mr Shennan's '*estancia*' refer to the constant exposure to danger of people living on the frontier of civilisation, although she explains that Indians seldom interfered with them. She portrays herself as an adventurous English woman in the wilderness of South America. Her word-portraits of the 'gauchos' celebrate their activities in the camps and confirm that 'the contact of civilization is fast changing the semi-Bedouin semi-Indian character of the rude inhabitants of the plain' (Mulhall, p. 21). She translates the four distinctive types of 'gauchos' from Domingo Faustino Sarmiento's book *Facundo*: the '*Rastreador*' or tracker, the '*Baqueano*' or guide, the '*Payador*' or wandering minstrel, and the '*Gaucho Malo*' or outlaw (Mulhall, pp. 21–5). However, in other passages, the last example is reversed, and the native's wit counterpoises the corruption of the political class. For example, she recalls an amusing occurrence in the region of Azul in which a shopkeeper, who was also the justice of the peace for the district, made a bargain with a 'gaucho' named El Cuervo (The Crow) to bring him cattle hides for a few dollars each. When he found out that the hides were from his own cattle, the shopkeeper said furiously:

> 'You scoundrel, you have killed and skinned some of my cattle'; to which the gaucho replied, 'Master! whose cattle did you want me to kill unless your own?' The shopkeeper, being Justice of the Peace, did not dare to punish El Cuervo, and wisely said no more about it, seeing that the gaucho had outwitted him. (Mulhall, p. 27)

Marion Mulhall's example shows a woman's perception and admiration of the native's shrewdness and imagination. It subverts the prejudiced views of Sally Moore, Kate Murphy's cousin, about the illiterate, uneducated natives as registered in her letters to her cousin John James Pettit in Australia (1864–75), published by Edmundo Murray in *Becoming Irlandés*. Sally describes the gaucho's dark skin, black hair, and eyes negatively, saying that 'most of them are very ugly ... they are like savages, in the line of education very few of them know how to read or write and those that do are looked up to with respect, this is the very lowest of them' (Edmundo Murray, p. 98). Her superior position makes her devalue them with regard to their different physical appearance and attitudes when compared to the educated Europeans.

In addition to family events, Irish immigrant women wrote about their thoughts, religious beliefs, morals, and desires. In Maria Elena Walsh's *Novios de antaño*, Agnes Walsh's letters to her father and sister-in-law depict her status as housewife, fully dependent on her husband. Agnes explains to them her long-postponed desire to visit her family in Britain: 'David hasn't told me yet whether he will let me travel home, but I trust he will' (Walsh, p. 296). She had travelled alone to Buenos Aires a year after the yellow fever outbreak, which killed so many people in the city. She travelled on board

The Boyne in 1872 to work as a governess of the Austrian consul's children, and after four years she married an Irishman who came from Boston to work for the Anglo-Argentine Tramway.[25] She left her job as it was not socially acceptable for a married woman to work; only unmarried young women, widows, or spinsters continued in employment till middle age. In that period, confessional differences posed more of a challenge than they do today. Agnes was an English Protestant and wrote to her sister-in-law that she would have preferred to tell her family in person about her fiancé's Irish Catholicism. They would have married six months earlier but 'had innumerable problems and lots of expenses due to difference of religion. David is Irish and Roman Catholic. Fortunately we could overcome inconveniences of time and money' (Walsh, p. 285).

But religion was also a source of spiritual strength for women when they had to face death in the family due to cholera and yellow fever. Sally Moore's letters in 1867 and 1868 refer to the great suffering of the people seeing their family dying. People were frightened and 'flocked to the camp in the thousands which makes the town look very dull, three thousand in Buenos Ayres alone' (Edmundo Murray, p. 100). The 'dreadful cholera ... made fearful ravages' and Moore lost many members of her family (children and adults); in 1874, the cases get worse and more violent (Edmundo Murray, p. 112). Kate Murphy writes to their cousin in Australia in a religious mood saying they 'must be awful sinners' as 'the Almighty punishes' them with so many deaths in their family. Sally was more pragmatic and she writes that, when the cholera commenced in the family,

> most of the members living apart went to Uncle James to live or die together, it was a fearful time so many sick and dying in the same house, but we felt very grateful to God that so many have recovered, there have been whole families carried away not leaving a single person behind ... everything came together, war, plague and locusts. ... The hand of God seems to be on our poor country, no one ever saw such times here before. (Edmundo Murray, p. 102)

Religious feelings, impatience, and the trial of faith are also the focus of the letters of Kate's sister, Fanny Murphy, to their cousin in Australia. She writes, 'I find it harder to resign myself to the will of God' (Edmundo Murray, p. 103). However, Kate Murphy stresses that 'all the goods of this miserable world are transient', a very Catholic consolation (Edmundo Murray, p. 108).

Cases of what we now recognise as postnatal depression within the family were also the subject of some letters. Kate Murphy writes to John about her brother Robert who is married and has five children, whose wife Mary Daly suffers a breakdown. She 'lost her reason quite suddenly'; they brought her into town and

> after a few days trial we found it impossible to keep her here she was so troublesome so we took her to the lunatic asylum, the poor fellow was in such trouble that Mama went out to stop with him for a short time and to bring some of the children in, but thank God she recovered sooner than we expected and is now at home again quite well. Mama remains until she thinks Mary strong enough to take care of the family for she was not able to recover her reason. (Edmundo Murray, pp. 96–7)

Affliction after childbirth and also concern for members of their own community who had problems with alcohol lead women to reflect upon the causes of such madness. In her letters, Agnes Walsh states that 'drinking is the worst misery of a large number of English-speaking people' (Edmundo Murray, p. 298). She worries about the miserable state that provokes this inebriation when they are in Buenos Aires: 'it happens mainly with the Scottish, though there are exceptions; however all who speak English receive the nickname of drunkard even if they don't drink a drop' (Edmundo Murray, p. 290). Sally Murphy refers to the common saying '*Inglés borracho*' (English drunkard) and affirms 'I don't know the reason but it is a fact that a great number of young men coming from Europe get lost here, they turn to drink and it is not from the natives they learn it, for it is scarcely ever seen in the respectable classes, amongst the poor gauchos' (Edmundo Murray, p. 101). There is an implied moral judgement and a demonisation of the country; its hostile landscape and nature are what make Europeans 'get lost and turn to drink' (Edmundo Murray, p. 101).

While questions concerning the family, fellow countrymen, household management, and motherhood are openly discussed in the letters, issues of sexuality, intimate desire, and psychological unrest are not. In the period of modernisation at the beginning of the twentieth century, there were great changes of values in Argentine society. The critic and writer José Ingenieros (1877–1925) attacked the hegemonic morality of the time. In *El imperio de los sentimientos* (*The Empire of Feelings*), Argentinian critic Beatriz Sarlo shows that Ingenieros in his posthumous book *The Treaty of Love* proposed a new sexual morality based on scientific data which provoked a tension between 'a deterministic biologist perspective and the will of founding a new ethics'.[26] He attacks institutional forms that conceive sexuality as 'oppressive of the instinct'. He criticises the monstrous contract of an exclusive and indissoluble marriage that eclipsed the individual right to love. According to him, each party is condemned to continue making children with the first person chosen, under the most inexperienced conditions possible. In order to maintain the actual family system, 'human beings are obliged to subordinate their individual feeling of love to the conveniences of the family'.[27] Social morality is based on this subordination, which is necessary for reproduction and is opposed to all kinds of love, whether suitable for domestic harmony or not. Every feeling that is guided by sexual instinct is deplored as it has no domestic end and is banned by society. Love outside marriage is immoral since it fails to attend to social convenience; it is a sin according to religious dogmas aimed at establishing moral law; and it is a crime since the law protects men's possession of their wives and daughters. Those who loved outside these social norms were outlaws. Ingenieros writes that those who loved with no intention of getting married were seen as robbers and their actions described as seduction, kidnapping, or adultery.

However, the constraints of domestic life render unconditional love impossible, so it can only be part of fictional narratives. Passion is antisocial and collective morality causes 'passion to be only interesting for literature'.[28] Sarlo confirms that passion, as it was understood by Ingenieros, only appears when there is an obstacle in its path. Social rules defending marriage and domestic life are the antithesis of passion, which rebels against the status quo and fights to overcome obstacles that do not allow it to live up to the true ideal of a lover rather than of husband or wife; in this way 'passion draws its tragic character and greatness from resistance'.[29] The aesthetics of passion that represents the fight between love and Christian morality in the literature of past centuries functioned as a social ideology leading to moral transformation in a still traditional society. Narratives that represent those transgressors of Christian morality resist and react against the social hypocrisy imposed by the political, cultural, and religious system and pave the way for a future Argentinian society. Supporting Ingenieros' *Treaty*, Sarlo insists that the aesthetics of passion is one of the ways of legitimising change in society as great passions shape 'aesthetic emotions, elevate the intellectual level and enable [us] to act with heroism' and make a difference to social ideology.[30] The true story of Camila O'Gorman's love affair with a native priest Uladislao Gutiérrez was condemned during the Rosas dictatorship (1835–52) because the lovers defied the rigid norms of social behaviour that banned passion and suppressed all kinds of feelings.

They were shot by order of Juan Manuel de Rosas on 18 August 1848 when Camila, who belonged to a very prominent aristocratic federal family and was a close friend of Rosas' daughter, was twenty years old and eight months pregnant.[31]

In Barbara Peart's *Tia Barbarita*, the protagonist gets married in order to become independent of her family. However, she 'accepted [her husband] on the distinct understanding that she would be allowed to ride horseback in the Argentine as often as she liked', a symbolic way of asserting her freedom to govern her own acts (Peart, p. 32). Peart uses a third-person narrator because she finds she can be 'much more revealing under the faint disguise of the third personal pronoun' (Peart, p. 16). Thus, her sexuality is represented through her narrative, disclosing secrets which go against the collective morality of the time; she blames the social norms and openly confesses there is no love in her marriage: 'Horse-riding she had bargained for when she married and came out to the Argentine, but not for love' (Peart, p. 133). When she leaves the convent where she was raised, she has not been told about husband–wife sexual relations. She is trapped on the first night, subjected to sexual violence, and 'damned' to have children, recalling Ingenieros' words. She reveals herself to be openly against the Victorian ideal of motherhood when she confesses that she never liked children very much, even though she has had five and loved them all. Peart may be said to be suffering from the 'ordered hypocrisy' of traditional Irish morality in modern times. She had no idea as to how babies came into the world, and whenever she asked a question about it, especially after leaving the convent, she was told 'she ought to be ashamed of herself for asking such questions' (Peart, p. 35). More recently, in *Tréboles del Sur* (*Southern Shamrocks*), Juan José Delaney, a contemporary Irish-Argentine writer, fictionalised the correspondence exchanged between two recently married female cousins, disclosing their fears and reactions with regard to their respective wedding nights.[32]

The economy of the country is an ever-present backdrop in women's letters and novels, which contain references to the closing of banks and constant complaints from natives about the scarcity of money. Many realist narratives, whether written from an urban or a rural viewpoint, represent the causes of the diaspora, forcing people either to return home or to move elsewhere to pursue their utopian dream of constructing a 'New Ireland' abroad. The letters by Sally Moore, Fanny Murphy, and Kate Murphy to their cousin John James Pettit (1864–75) published by Edmundo Murray represent a set of translocations because many presences and territories are inter-connected over space and time, revealing 'the world-wide-ness of ... Irish migrations'.[33] There is an encounter of three distant locations, Ireland, Argentina, and Australia, John Pettit having emigrated with his father to the latter continent. The spatial and temporal axes intersect when the women comment on the newspapers they exchange: *The Standard*, a newspaper founded in 1861 by the Irish unionists Edward and Michael Mulhall, was sent to John by his cousins in Argentina; they also received Australian papers, while the ones from Ireland went to both destinations. Sally wrote in 1865:

> Your papers I receive regularly, they are very interesting. I think that country is far in advance of this but I would not admit this to an Englishman, they are always finding fault with this country and the people, and although we mix very little with the people of the country I like them better than I do the English perhaps it is because they are Catholics that we have more sympathy with them. (Edmundo Murray, p. 87)

Thus, the letters are not just a product but an act of enunciation with a signifying effect; their discourse produces a specific meaning in a particular situation. The writers create an intersubjective space and stand doubly removed from their own selves to reveal their ideological position in the political interrelationships between 'home' and 'homeland' and to establish a network of translocations.

The immigrant women sent letters and newspapers to their family to give them an idea of the Argentinian context in which they were living. Agnes Walsh sent her father *The Standard* and *The Southern Cross*, the Irish Catholic newspaper founded by Fr Patrick Dillon in 1875, to which her Irish husband was an appreciative subscriber. These women bridge the Atlantic, creating a virtual space with words, constructed not only through their letters, but above all through newspapers which authorised and empowered their personal views of their adopted land. Their letters refer to places that, according to Marc Augé, 'can be defined as relational, historical and concerned with identity'; however, the regular flow of letters, together with the newspapers from the three countries, create a space in words, a 'non-place' which preserves the temporalities of all three places.[34] Augé describes such non-places as 'meaning spaces which are not themselves anthropological places and which, unlike Baudelairean modernity, do not integrate the earlier places: instead these are listed, classified, promoted to the "spaces of memory", and assigned to a circumscribed and specific position'.[35]

The writers create an intersubjective space and stand doubly removed from their own selves to reveal their ideological position in the political interrelationships between 'home' and 'homeland' and to establish a network of translocations. Sally's letters are politicised and concerned with the economic and political problems of the country. She feels that Argentina is 'her' country, though her superior point of view is sometimes very clear. She describes the Triple Alliance War in which Brazil, Argentina and Uruguay united against Paraguay (1864–70), and the civil war of 1874 when Arredondo led a rebellion in the city of Córdoba. General Mitre supported the rebels but they were beaten by forces loyal to the federal government. She reveals her own political position when she writes that 'the revolution that had broken out here after so many years of peace, it has been fortunately put down, as it would be a bad example for the future if the rebels had triumphed, although the present government is not as good as it might be' (Edmundo Murray, p. 113).

The Triple Alliance War was very violent, resulting in the deaths of thousands of Paraguayans.[36] However, the victory of the allied forces in Yatay in 1865 failed to bring peace, and Sally comments in her letter: 'it is difficult to say when we shall have peace and the soldiers are suffering very much for want of food and other necessaries. Our boys thank God are yet unmolested about the services but if the war continues they will be in want of more men so they are not by any means out of danger' (Edmundo Murray, p. 91). Military service was a big concern for the sons of immigrants because it was compulsory for native Argentines; the 'gauchos' were the first to be called up, but British foreigners living in the country could also be conscripted. There was an order that all men born in the country had to enlist, but 'very few were caught as they went to the camps and nobody finds them' (Edmundo Murray, p. 109). This was an ambiguous situation; they were supported by the British consuls if they assumed British nationality and renounced their Argentine one (Edmundo Murray, p. 199). Sally describes the disastrous effects of the war and affirms that 'the native people are disappearing little by little, one meets in the street about ten foreigners to one native among the male population and so many families in mourning, and from all accounts no sign of its termination. You cannot appreciate fully the blessing of peace until you have passed a while in a country like this' (Edmundo Murray, p. 93). When the end of the Paraguayan war was declared in May 1870, Sally wrote that there was a revolution in Entre Rios and 'General Urquiza who has ruled there with a strong hand for something like twenty years has been assassinated and also two of his sons' (Edmundo Murray, p. 109). She condemned the rulers of the country for its instability and the suffering of its people.

Ten years later, in a letter dated 14 July 1880, Agnes also described the economic effects of a civil war when the central party fought against the federal party in the streets of Buenos Aires, and Carlos Tejedor and Bartolomé Mitre were defeated by Roca: 'hard battles were fought near here. There is a scarcity of goods: what cost $6 before the war, now it is $60' (Edmundo Murray, p. 294). She also refers to women's fashion, stressing that the colour of their clothes accorded with their political beliefs. Women wore black dresses with red ribbons on their skirts and in their hair. The black dresses meant war and the red ribbons represented support for Roca, the new president (Edmundo Murray, p. 296). The 1880s was a period of modernisation in Argentina. It was called 'La Pampa Gringa' (1870–1929) because immigrants played a key role in contributing to the growth of the host land. However, in the 1890s there was political and economic decline, high unemployment and a rise in prices, due to speculation and the overvaluation of gold.

The act of writing down one's feelings, impressions, and undertakings in an unknown place far from home reduces distances metaphorically and creates a virtual space of shared experiences. In Argentina, women did not generally work in factories, as happened in the United States, which was an 'astute move in relation to market demand, and also a rejection of traditional family life and its inherent male power structure'.[37] In Argentinian social circles, men and women alike believed that work was inappropriate for women. Sometimes widows enjoyed a privileged position, and several managed their holdings as *estancieras*, becoming a target for Irish bachelors even when they were not well off.

However, the self-figurations in the autobiographical narratives in Barbara Peart's *Tia Barbarita* and Kathleen Nevin's *You'll Never Go Back* present the reverse side of the story. Their narratives subvert the traditional figure of the woman in a society that prescribed the family home as the primary site of women's work, leading women, at home or abroad, overtly or silently, to challenge the nineteenth-century gender order. The publication of letters and autobiographies brought to light the unseen/unheard narratives of those women who chose jobs as governesses, or did not work at all, and then built a family of their own after getting married.

In conclusion, these narratives of the self by women well settled in a non-English-speaking country may be seen as metaphors of change within local struggles for inclusion – inclusion in their family unit, in their Irish diasporic community, and in the host society. The female protagonists are ordinary people seeking to assert themselves within male social and moral rules. The enunciating subjects write their own narratives to construct the significance of the outside world. They tell of the place where they live, the city of Buenos Aires and the camps, the events that take place, the myths that motivated their move (such as the country's wealth), and even the history of their adopted land. The immanent elements present in the grammatology of their texts represent the coexistence of different places which converge in a virtual space made of words that is an intersection of moving bodies and moving memories. The attitudes of Irish women in the South American diasporic space, whether in the camps or in the city, are representative of a culture of survival that is linked with Ireland, though in an emancipatory way. They reveal not only an aesthetic sense of their experience and a passion for family independence but also the construction of a transnational and transdisciplinary understanding of 'New Irelands' across physical boundaries.

The historiography of Irish-Argentine women is a rich resource and should be extended to cover the twentieth and twenty-first centuries to allow inquiry into how the new generations position themselves within their adopted community, and to find out if they are still connected with the later generations of relatives in Ireland. New questions emerge now, due to recent and current Argentinian economic and political crises: who are the protagonists of recent reverse labour migration to Ireland, their ancestors' motherland? Why do they claim Irish citizenship? Do they apply for Irish passports to cross to Europe or to remain in Ireland? The new generations born in Argentina have an idealised vision of the arrival of their ancestors and have shaped their understanding of women's role in a changing, non-English-speaking society enduring war and disease, interfaith or interethnic marriages, making efforts either to preserve their endogenous community or to be integrated and accepted by the indigenous. Sarah O'Brien's *Linguistic Diasporas, Narrative and Performance: The Irish in Argentina* (2017) is an interesting source of men's and women's memories of their ancestors' roles as well as of their own present role within the Irish-Argentine community and provides a model for future research into this subject.[38]

CHAPTER 12

'All I am is feeling': Samuel Beckett, aesthetics, and the matter of mother

SEÁN KENNEDY

On revient toujours à ses premières amours

In the early works of Samuel Beckett, the matter of misogyny is the matter of mother. It was at his mother's house, in his mother's room, that he had the great epiphany of 1945 – dramatised in *Krapp's Last Tape* – in which he discerned that the darkness he had been holding at bay was, in fact, the proper stuff of his artistic vision. And a significant amount of that stuff, he realised, pertained to mother. He had been trying to mine his life for art but was being too clever about it: 'Molloy and the others came to me the day I became aware of my own folly,' he told Gabriel d'Aubarède. 'Only then did I begin to write the things I feel.'[1] Russell Smith has pointed out the dearth of attention given to this statement in Beckett studies.[2] Yet, it occasioned the great masterpieces that made his reputation. The implications of this great realisation were worked out in stages. First, there was an autographic turn: Beckett learned to say 'I'.[3] Then, an affective one: he learned to say 'I feel'.

THE MATTER OF MOTHER

In aesthetic terms, Beckett's affective turn inverted the common sense of things. Since Immanuel Kant's *Critique of Judgement* (1790), at least, restoring classical order in an age of sensibility, aesthetics had meant *an*aesthetics. Aesthetic reactions were subjective and so, for Kant, they were not judgements. Rather, judgement is what happens when we cease to feel altogether. In *Under Representation*, David Lloyd traces this determination to redeem judgement from the vagaries of emotion. Kant displaced

Edmund Burke's 'pathological sublime' with a 'capacity for disinterested contemplative pleasure'. For Burke, aesthetics was a 'discourse about the sensible body'.[4] Kant rendered it sensible by divorcing it from bodily sensation altogether. Kantian aesthetics, G.F.W. Hegel observed later, went 'far beyond the *feeling* of the beautiful'.[5]

Is man a reasonable creature or is he in thrall to his senses? Beckett had studied the debate in Wilhelm Windelband's *History of Philosophy*. At stake was what it meant to be (or feel) human. For rationalists, like Kant, passion was a problem. For the sensualists, like Thomas Hobbes and John Locke, 'knowledge and morality grow upon the soil of sensibility'.[6] But they were all of one mind on the problem of necessity. For Locke, freedom and necessity are mutually exclusive categories. Facing 'that which he cannot avoid, a man, in respect of that act of *willing*, is under a necessity, and so cannot be free'.[7] Kant agreed. And if necessity is the condition under which consent lapses in Locke, it is also the condition under which aesthetic judgement becomes impossible in Kant. Only when man is free – not just *in* his person, but *from* his need – says Kant, can he make aesthetic judgements. We cannot love something – *aesthetically* – if we need it. There may be an art of necessity. But not an aesthetic of need.

It was at this intersection (of aesthetics and necessity) that Beckett's epiphany of 1945 took place. And the matter at hand was the matter of mother. A main problem in Kant's formulation was economic in the sense of that term used by Sigmund Freud. After the First World War, Freud discovered the economic problem of masochism. He had built his model of the psyche on the pleasure principle: the idea that pleasure is produced in the release of tension: 'The psychic apparatus is geared to minimizing the quantity of excitation [and] anything tending to *increase* that quantity is bound to be experienced as unpleasurable.'[8] How, then, to explain masochism? The masochist's pursuit of pain baffled the logic of Freud's first topography and pushed him beyond the pleasure principle. Kantian aesthetics faced a similar conundrum. Arthur Schopenhauer, Kant's great disciple in these matters, remarks upon it: 'how is it possible for us to take pleasure in an object when this object has no kind of connexion with our desires?'[9] In 'affairs of state, in war, in finance and business, intrigues of every sort', Schopenhauer observes, 'the *will* must first of all, through the vehemence of its desire, compel the intellect to exert all its energies'.[10] Yet art produces quantities of excitation divorced from the domain of the will. How? Schopenhauer's solution is Kantian (after Plato). In art, we cease to apprehend reality and apprehend its ideal forms: 'The true work of art leads us from that which exists only once and never again, i.e. the individual, to that which exists perpetually.'[11] In the process, 'the individual is transformed from a willing subject into a purely knowing subject'.[12]

In *The Will to Know*, Michel Foucault suggests that a main objective of this idealist quest for pure knowledge, from Plato onwards, was to contain the threat of contamination by sexual desire (figured as female).[13] In *Manhood and Politics*, Wendy Brown relates it back to Aristotle's theory of the political sphere (or *polis*) which he designates as the realm of manly action, in contrast to the realm of the home (or *oikos*) traditionally the province of women and slaves.[14] Manliness is achieved only in withdrawal from the *oikos*.[15] Since masculinity is defined in opposition to – repudiation of – the *oikos*, no accommodation between the two spaces is possible.[16] To labour means to be enslaved by necessity, and free men refuse to submit to necessity. In fact, being a man is only possible beyond the realm of necessity. Moral conduct, in particular, is impossible.[17] For Brown, this betrays the fragile basis of masculine autonomy, conceived in reactive contempt for that realm of necessity which is its necessary precondition.[18] By way of the familiar binarisms decried by Hélène Cixous and others – self/other, culture/nature, idea/matter – the subject of patriarchy distorts itself into a self-generating paragon of pure reason.[19] In Hegel's view, this solved the problem of man's 'finitude':

> Man, on the particular and finite side of his needs, wishes, and aims, stands primarily not only in a *general* relation to external nature, but more precisely in a relation of *dependence*. This relativity and lack of freedom are repugnant to the ideal, and man can become an object for art only if he is first freed from this labour and distress, and has cast off his *dependence*.[20]

Patriarchy as a system for male domination doubled as a fantasy of autonomy, of masculine self-actualisation, beyond the realm of dependence: beyond the realm of the *oikos*. 'What's true,' says Hegel, 'is the Idea.'[21]

Freud's discovery of infantile sexuality would puncture this fantasy. In *Three Essays on the Theory of Sexuality*, he proposed a model of desire as inherently retrospective. Freudian man (the presumptive male subject of his theories) lives forwards but desires backwards. His discovery, at puberty, of the sexual object is always, Freud suggested, a rediscovery.[22] And the object that is rediscovered is the maternal body. Condemned to abandon mother under the threat of castration, Freud's manchild rejoins the game of desire at puberty in a fraught quest for viable substitutes. It is a sticky business, especially for the *would-be-autonomous* subject of patriarchy. How to conjure autonomy from the matter of mother? One way, Freud suggested, was by splitting. Splitting is the psyche's 'crafty' attempt to have it both ways in circumstances of catastrophic disruption: the subject seeks both to 'reject reality' by continuing to seek satisfaction from the object, but also to acknowledge (and overcome) the loss of the object as source of satisfaction.[23] The result, says Freud, is ambivalence: a kind of 'to-ing and fro-ing between denial and acknowledgement'.[24] As Karen Horney remarked in 1932, 'man feels himself drawn to the woman and, side by side with his longing, the dread that through her he might die and be undone'.[25] For Luce Irigaray, it is a kind of blindness on man's part about their mothers.[26] In patriarchal societies, it is the mother – the matrix – that is both obfuscated and venerated – obliterated and adored – as a function of man's enduring anxieties about her. From this overdetermined perspective, she is simultaneously re-cognised (idealised) and de-scribed (repressed): split into an idealised *Mother* and a repressed *mOther*. The one nourishes man's fretful pre-eminence while the other menaces his very existence.

For Irigaray, this woman is a substratum: 'a reproductive body in the pay of the polis'.[27] Nancy Fraser points out that, in fact, social reproduction is usually unpaid: is an 'indispensable background condition' to capitalist accumulation.[28] The maternal function underpins the social order, says Irigaray, yet it 'remains in the shadows of our culture'.[29] If infrastructure is the 'unthought known' of the *polis*, the *oikos* is the infrastructure of patriarchy.[30] As Irigaray notes, women are both repudiated by men and, simultaneously, condemned to 'be their bodies': guarding corporeality on their behalf while providing access to it on patriarchal terms:[31]

> You have no current? I said. No, she said, but I have running water and gas. Ha, I said, you have gas. She began to undress.[32]

This is the double standard that structures masculinist autonomy: the economic problem of patriarchy. In Kant's search for a supersensible basis for judgement – 'a life independent of animality and even of the whole sensible world' – it would become the economic problem of aesthetics.[33] For Beckett, meanwhile, it was a problem of character.

THE MATTER OF MISOGYNY

Beckett's female characters have long dismayed critics, in the early works especially, and have been variously condemned as 'disturbing', 'regrettable', 'exuberant' and 'cruel'.[34] Susan Brienza highlights a 'totally gratuitous' instance of misogyny in 'A Wet Night', from *More Pricks than Kicks* (1934):

> Throttled gazelle gives no idea. Her features, as though the hand of an unattractive ravisher were knotted in her chevelure, were set at half-cock and locked in a rictus. She had frowned to pencil her eyebrows, so now she had four. The dazzled iris was domed in a white agony of entreaty, the upper-lip writhed back in a snarl to the untented nostrils ... It was impossible to set aside the awful suspicion that her flattened mammae, in sympathy with this tormented eructation of countenance, had put forth cutwaters and were rowelling her corsage. But the face was beyond appeal, a flagrant seat of injury.[35]

The problem here is that the overflowing energy of the description 'encourages the male reader to enjoy and share' it.[36] And invitations of this kind pervade the early work.

Overall, the contention has been that Beckett's men are Cartesian creatures for whom women embody 'the dark side of humanity, the realm of physicality and feeling'.[37] Characterising the logic of this position, Jessica Benjamin cites Herbert Marcuse:

> Self-sufficiency and independence of all that is other and alien is the sole guarantee of the subject's freedom. What is not dependent on any other person or thing, what possesses itself, is free ... Having excludes the other ... Relating to the other in such a way that the subject really reaches and is united with him counts as loss and dependence.[38]

For Susan Brienza, Beckett's work exhibits this logic with such 'uncanny clarity' that it takes on the character of a 'monomaniacal genealogy' consigning woman, time and again, to the subordinate role: as 'a clod of earth that impedes intellectual man'.[39] So perfect is the fit, however, that one might wonder if it is not, perhaps, too perfect. For a body of work that so often eludes characterisation, can the issue of misogyny in Beckett be so easily formulated?

A complicating factor all along, as Patricia Coughlan suggests, is that Beckett offers 'equally virulent denigration' of the misogynists themselves.[40]

'Ding-Dong', also from *More Pricks than Kicks*, openly betrays Belacqua Shuah's pretensions:

> He did not fatigue himself, he said: on the contrary. He lived a Beethoven pause, he said, whatever he meant by that. In his anxiety to explain himself, he was liable to come to grief. Nay, this anxiety in itself, or so at least it seemed to me, constituted a break-down in the self-sufficiency which he never wearied arrogating to himself, a sorry collapse of my little internus homo, and alone sufficient to give him away as inept ape of his own shadow.[41]

Here is a character whose story just does not add up. We see him – his actions and convictions – discredited from within the narrative.

'First Love' is often cited as the 'worst' instance of misogyny in Beckett, containing the most ignoble of his protagonists:[42]

> She began stroking my ankles. I considered kicking her in the cunt. You speak to people about stretching out and they immediately see a body at full length. What mattered to me in my dispeopled kingdom, that in regard to which the disposition of my carcass was the merest and most futile of accidents, was supineness in the mind, the dulling of the self and of that residue of execrable frippery known as the non-self and even the world, for short. But man is still today, at the age of twenty-five, at the mercy of an erection, physically too, from time to time, it's the common lot, even I was not immune, if that may be called an erection. It did not escape her naturally, women smell a rigid phallus ten miles away and wonder, How on earth did he spot me from there?[43]

Here again, with a neatness that might serve to put us on our guard, the problem is amply demonstrated: man consigns woman to the realm of matter and then both desires and resents her.

In December 1933, Beckett entered psychoanalysis with Wilfred Bion at London's Tavistock Clinic. He had been suffering 'sweats & shudders & panics & rages & rigors & heart-burstings'.[44] His relationship with his mother quickly came to the fore. The 'speechless infant' of psychoanalysis is born twice, he discovered, first physically, then psychologically.[45] Both are normatively traumatising: vulnerable to all the vagaries of what Jean Laplanche terms 'the fundamental anthropological situation' (an infant in its mother's arms).[46] Alongside his sessions, Beckett immersed himself in the literature, taking copious notes. In *New Introductory Lectures*, he learned, Freud had characterised birth trauma as prototypical. The entire range of morbid anxiety phenomena stand in intimate relation to the actual birth event as archetype: it is 'our model for the anxiety state'.[47] Psychoanalysis with Bion consolidated this belief.[48] Mothering is a rapport. Beckett's individuation had been frustrated by it. 'Birth was the death of him.'[49]

This diagnosis was unsettling, but also clarifying. Beckett's first love, and the prototype of all his subsequent anxieties, was *Mother*. His feelings, as far as she was concerned, were ambivalent in the precise sense given to that term by Freud. He both loved and hated her. He was in love with *Mother* but terrified of *mOther*. As Charles Rycroft notes, ambivalence assumes the existence of 'contradictory attitudes [that] derive from a common source and are interdependent'.[50] For Beckett, the source was mother. The trigger for his neurosis was need of her but, to the precise extent that he needed her, he was in thrall to terror of her. He saw his symptoms fluctuate as a function of proximity to her and took this to confirm the diagnosis. Indifference to her – autonomy – was inconceivable. Hence psychoanalysis. He understood now that ambivalence had become the prototype for his subsequent relationships, and had also structured sexual relations in his early work.

THE MATTER OF CHARACTER

Here, then, was the problem of character. Schopenhauer saw that people were very different but held the reasons why were 'a mystery'.[51] Character is both innate and unalterable, he suggested, and a good deal of his pessimism stems from this view: 'in innate character, in the actual kernel of the whole person, lies the seed of all his virtues or vices'.[52] Freud, for his part, highlighted the role of infantile sexuality. Beckett read about it at the time of his analysis. From Ernest Jones, he learned that experiences of deprivation cause regression to points of fixation that, in turn, are determined by inherited disposition as well as infantile experiences and fantasies.[53] An important source for 'First Love' would be Jones' 'Anal Erotic Character Traits':

> Interest in the act of defaecation itself often leads to interest in the site of defaecation – i.e. in the anal canal itself ... This may manifest itself in many different ways: in marked curiosity about the opposite

> or back side of objects and places – e.g. in the desire to live on the other side of a hill because it has its back turned to a given place ... Another curious trait of the same origin is a great fascination for all underground passages, canals, tunnels, etc.[54]

This provides the setting for the encounter with Lulu:

> I met her on a bench, on the bank of the canal, one of the canals, for our town boasts two though I never knew which was which. It was a well situated bench, backed by a mound of solid earth and garbage, so that my rear was covered.[55]

Beckett also took notes on the act of defecation as a power struggle with mother.[56]

> One day, on my return from stool, I found my room locked and my belongings in a heap before the door. This will give you some idea how constipated I was, at this juncture. It was, I am now convinced, anxiety constipation. But was I genuinely constipated? Somehow I think not. Softly, softly. And yet I must have been, for how otherwise account for those long, those cruel sessions in the necessary house?[57]

In psychoanalysis, Beckett learned, character is an overdetermined product of childhood: an intimate archive of first and lost loves:

> But what kind of love was this, exactly? Love-passion? Somehow I think not. That's the priapic one, is it not? Or is this a different variety? There are so many, are there not? All equally if not more delicious are they not? Platonic love, for example, there's another just occurs to me. It's disinterested. Perhaps I loved her with a platonic love? But somehow I think not. Would I have been tracing her name in old cowshit if my love had been pure and disinterested? And with my devil's finger into the bargain, which I then sucked?[58]

Here was Freud's rejoinder to Kant. Desire has a maternal hangover. There could be no disinterested contemplation of the matter. The maternal body is the material limit of man's fantasy of autonomy: it brings him back to earth.

In 'Just Rage', Adam Phillips offers a psychoanalytic account of man's resentment of dependence that can be indexed to this perception of humiliation by the mother. We are humiliated, in Phillips' view, whenever someone exploits our dependency on them: whenever we *need* someone and they weaponise the fact. And humiliation, says Phillips, is the usual experience of the child. In 'Family Romances', Freud had pointed out how the feeling of being 'slighted' was a major source for the child's counterfactual fantasies about the provenance of their 'real' parents.[59] Our real parents are found wanting, so we invent preferable substitutes. And patriarchal family structures gender this dynamic, inevitably. Children resent their mothers more as a function of proximity: of dependence on them. Whereas fathers – being more remote – are more easily idealised. Familiarity breeds contempt for mother, while father remains something beyond them, albeit an important something. In this model, patriarchal rage sees woman scapegoated as a function of man's (disavowed) dependency on her. In manly self-fashioning, going back to the Greeks, what cannot be tolerated is *need*.

For Phillips, however, the more fundamental problem is the masculine aspiration to autonomy in the first place: 'it is not the need that is tyrannical,' says Phillips, 'but the fantasy of self-sufficiency'.[60] Beckett's early works replay this dynamic constantly. Murphy's 'troubles had begun early', we are told. 'To go back no further than the vagitus.'[61] Like Belacqua Shuah before him, he is constantly in thrall to women, hence constantly enraged by them. He hates his London landlady, for example. She is a presumptuous boor with a body odour problem. But he loves tea. And she brings tea: 'Choicest Lapsang Souchong'. This is a comic version of the classic double-bind: *mOther* (whom he hates) has something man loves (which he resents). The solution is to drink the tea while abjecting its source: a Miss Carridge.[62] The hateful aspect of this abjection occurs in Murphy's mind where, in the first of its three zones, he behaves like the typical Freudian fantasist (whose daydreams 'are a corrective of unsatisfying reality'):

> In the first were the forms with parallel, a radiant abstraction of the dog's life, the elements of physical experience available for a new arrangement. Here the pleasure was reprisal, the pleasure of reversing the physical experience. Here the kick that the physical Murphy received, the mental Murphy gave. It was the same kick, but corrected as to direction. Here the chandlers were available for slow depilation, Miss Carridge for rape by Ticklepenny, and so on. Here the whole physical fiasco became a howling success.[63]

There is no anger, says Phillips, that is not revenge.[64] Murphy is beholden to Miss Carridge for tea and lodgings, is aroused by the smell of her, and so he fantasises about having her raped. This is just rage. And women are justly terrified by it.

THE MATTER OF NEED

Much has been made of the prevalence of prostitutes in Beckett's writing, and they have been taken as further evidence of his need to denigrate women.[65] Most often, however, they are the only characters to emerge with any degree of dignity. Beckett uses them to explore this problem of need: the economic problem of autonomy. He knew Schopenhauer's essay 'On Women', which decried the institution of monogamy because it necessitated the existence of sex workers. 'There are 80,000 prostitutes in London alone,' says Schopenhauer, 'and what are they if not sacrifices on the altar of monogamy?' Because men must marry and honour one woman only, Schopenhauer suggests, prostitutes are a necessary reserve army for 'the gratification of the male sex'.[66] In effect, he makes a moral case for polygamy. Beckett tells a different story. 'First Love' is not a feminist text in any obvious sense, but it does lay bare the spurious fantasies of its protagonist:

> I did not feel easy when I was with her, but at least free to think of something else than her, of the old trusty things, and so little by little as down the steps towards a deep, of nothing. And I knew that away from her I would forfeit this freedom.[67]

This freedom implicates him at another level of indebtedness, however, as Anna makes clear:

> I was more seriously disturbed by other sounds, stifled giggles and groans, which filled the dwelling at certain hours of the night, and even of the day. I had given up thinking of her, quite given up, but still I needed silence to live my life ... So a fat lot of help it was when, having put the question to her, I was told that they were clients she received in rotation ... So you live by prostitution, I said. We live by prostitution, she said.[68]

Here, in one swoop, the subject of pure knowledge, the *would-be autonomous* subject of patriarchy, is revealed as a sham. It is only by way of the room provided by Anna that he can ever hope to be free, but free only in continuing dependence on her. He is trapped in need for, hence resentment of, the female domain of the *oikos*. And economic dependence here (itself disavowed) figures all of the deeper dependencies that structure patriarchal autonomy: *oikos* as infrastructure (as reproductive body, as mother). Beckett's prostitution problem is precisely not the one described by Schopenhauer: the terms of dependency are reversed.

Murphy was an important precedent in all of this, written before Beckett learned to say 'I'. It documents the life of another hard-working prostitute, Celia, funding the spurious fantasies of another man, Murphy, who wishes only to 'come alive in his mind'.[69] Again, there is an economic problem – autonomy has to be funded somehow – and, notoriously, Murphy refuses to work. His horoscope says it is not time. The 'only system outside his own in which he felt the least confidence', we are told, was 'that of the heavenly bodies'.[70] In the absence of his contribution, they separate. Murphy is not unhappy with this arrangement, so long as it allows him to rock himself into a delirium of Schopenhauerian 'will-lessness'.[71] But the problem of necessity persists. For Locke, we recall, freedom meant freedom from necessity. 'Unless [they] can consist together', he remarked, in which case 'a man can be free and bound at once'.[72] Beckett was intrigued, and Murphy in his rocking chair had explored this possibility. But 'it was not enough and showed no signs of being enough'.[73] And the problem again was need: Murphy's 'deplorable susceptibility' to Celia.[74]

In his *Critique of Judgement*, Kant sought to 'emancipate the aesthetic from its dangerous subordination to physical gratification or affects'.[75] A capacity for aesthetic judgement was an index of human development: 'a means of discriminating a savage subordination to immediate pleasure'.[76] Central to this formulation was the belief that savages are too sensual to be objective. Lloyd calls it the racial regime of aesthetics. For his part, Schopenhauer made an analogous case against women: as 'a kind of intermediate stage between the child and the man'. Their 'entire vocation', he says, is 'propagation of the race', and they have no feeling or receptivity for art.[77] They are, in fact, 'the *unaesthetic* sex'. By this, he means incapable of aesthetic discernment: too given to emotion to take a '*purely objective interest* in anything whatever'.[78] Only men 'clouded by the sexual drive' could find them beautiful, he concludes, yet only judgements unclouded by the sexual drive could be aesthetic in the Kantian sense.[79] For Schopenhauer, then, woman is not aesthetic but neither is the man who desires her. *Murphy* and 'First Love' both read as parodies of this position:

> As to whether it was beautiful, the face, or had once been beautiful, or could conceivably become beautiful, I confess I could form no opinion. I had seen faces in photographs I might have found beautiful had I known even vaguely in what beauty was supposed to consist. And my father's face, on his death-bolster, had seemed to hint at some form of aesthetics relevant to man. But the faces of the living, all grimace and flush, can they be described as objects?[80]

In 'First Love', however, the Cartesian man of *Murphy* has been displaced by the Freudian 'I' of the autographical turn.

Theodor Adorno's critique of the Kantian subject (of both reason and morality) condenses the issues at stake. Kant had centred all on the 'antithesis between sensualism and rationalism'.[81] For Freud, there could be no such antithesis. Reason would always have to contend with the senses of the subject. His work on infantile sexuality demonstrated the impossibility of any purely rational understanding. This was the matter of mother. As to morality, Kant, in his *Critique of Practical Reason*, had gestured towards the stars, intimating their creator as the source of the categorical imperative: 'Two things fill the mind with ever new and increasing admiration and reverence, the more often and more steadily one reflects on them: *the starry heavens above me and the moral law within me*'.[82] Freud demurred: 'the stars are undoubtedly magnificent,' he said, 'but as regards conscience God has done a careless and uneven piece of work'.[83] Beckett recorded this critique in his psychology notes.[84] In psychoanalysis, as Adorno has it, one becomes moral to the extent one becomes subject to fretful surveillance by the superego. Our moralities are not transcendent: they are 'internalizations of actual power, internalizations of dominant social norms'. We 'appropriate them by identifying them with father figures'.[85]

'First Love', we might say, depicts a Freudian subject who professes to be a Kantian: 'I felt nothing.'[86] For Freud, there could be no such transcendence, only the to-ing and fro-ing of ambivalence. This is the narrator's real predicament – 'stumping to and fro' – in 'First Love':

> Precautions would have been superfluous, there was no competing with those cries. It must have been her first. They pursued me down the stairs and out into the street. I stopped before the house door and listened. I could still hear them. If I had not known there was crying in the house I might not have heard them. But knowing it I did. I was not sure where I was. I looked among the stars and constellations for the Wains, but could not find them. And yet they must have been

> there. My father was the first to show them to me. He had shown me others, but alone, without him beside me, I could never find any but the Wains. I began playing with the cries, a little in the same way as I had played with the song, on, back, on, back, if that may be called playing. As long as I kept walking I didn't hear them, because of the footsteps. But as soon as I halted I heard them again, a little fainter each time, admittedly, but what does it matter, faint or loud, cry is cry, all that matters is that it should cease. For years I thought they would cease. Now I don't think so any more. I could have done with other loves, perhaps. But there it is, either you love or you don't.[87]

Kant's observations about the starry heavens had contained their germ of truth, Freud suggested. Cosmology was an early domain of the Father who, 'in his great disembodied wisdom', Beckett's narrator projects onto the stars.[88] The insistence of the vagitus betrays continuing desire for communion with the maternal body (projected onto the specific constellation of the Wains). The tale's stark conclusion – either you love or you don't – fails to obscure this problem of ambivalence (he both loves and does not). Unlike Murphy, who has no parents, Beckett's autographical 'I' is haunted by the father while remaining ambivalently attached to the matter of mother.[89]

But otherwise, 'First Love' is a mere repetition of *Murphy* (the stars, the prostitutes, the vagitus). Not unlike the Freudian subject, Beckett realised, he was stuck. In the wake of his analysis, he had clarified the matter of mother rather brutally in one direction: 'I am what her savage loving has made me.'[90] This, he realised now, was scapegoating. It occasioned a 'radical reconsideration of the nature of feeling' in his writing – the affective turn – and *Molloy* was the result.[91] It went straight to the source. The motherlode:

> I called her Mag, when I had to call her something. And I called her Mag because for me, without my knowing why, the letter g abolished the syllable Ma, and as it were spat on it, better than any other letter would have done. And at the same time I satisfied a deep and doubtless unacknowledged need, the need to have a Ma, that is a mother, and to proclaim it, audibly.[92]

It is a classic – and classically analysed – case of an ambivalent relation to mother.[93] The difference is the affective turn: Beckett has learned to say 'I feel'. And what he feels is *need*: 'Need of my mother!'[94] This short-circuited the problem of autonomy – of freedom from necessity – at the heart of

Kantian aesthetics. How to feign indifference to the prototypical source-object of all desire?

Kant thought aesthetics meant freedom from feeling. After 1946, Beckett reverted to an art of the sensible body. He rejected the philosophical antithesis of rationalism and sensualism altogether: 'I wouldn't have had any reason to write my novels if I could have expressed their subject in philosophical terms,' he told d'Aubarède: 'All I am is feeling.'[95] This had first occurred to him in his mother's room and *Molloy* returns to the scene: 'I am in my mother's room. It is I who live there now. I don't know how I got there ... I was helped.' This admission of vulnerability – of need – was crucial. He was home. The *oikos*. It was Ma(g) and Da(n). Ma and Da. The Oedipal relationship finally consummated. Beckett saw that, in order to go on, he needed to go back. What had been triangulated previously – through lovers and landladies –must be confronted directly. He would 'sweep, with the clipped wings of necessity, to ... mother'.[96] This would put an end to scapegoating, to just rage, to spurious autonomy. In 'First Love', regression had been everywhere admitted but Beckett had not confronted the source. *Molloy* would be different:

> What a rest to speak of bicycles and horns. Unfortunately it is not of them I have to speak, but of her who brought me into this world, through the hole in her arse if my memory is correct. First taste of the shit.[97]

Molloy accepts what Beckett himself had been resisting: that it was into that 'old mess' – the matter of mother – that he must 'stick [his] nose' if he was to get anywhere, aesthetically.[98] It was a matter of taste – but also of need – and the results would be sensational.

CHAPTER 13

'Mind Our Men': Fragile masculinity in post-crash Irish men's writing

ANNE MULHALL

Concerns about 'masculinity in crisis' are by no means new.[1] Forebodings about the perceived threat to the position of (generally white) men tend to intensify during economic crises and periods of social, cultural, and economic change.[2] 'The 'mancession' narrative was one dominant popular mode of narrativising the 2008 economic crash and subsequent recession. This narrative has two basic elements: first, the claim that men were most severely affected by the recession, and second, the attribution of responsibility for this disproportionate suffering to women, who were conversely represented as benefiting from men's suffering. Borrowing from a well-established trope of 'white male injury', 'the perception that the recession affected males and females quite differently, and to different degrees, quickly gained prominence', as Suzanne Leonard argues in the US context.[3] The fact that the effects of the crash first manifested in the nosedive in the housing market and the largely male-dominated construction industry, both in the US and in Ireland, gave a further appearance of self-evident truth to this understanding of the recession as a mancession and offered some 'a convenient opportunity to recirculate and revalidate misogynist tropes about how feminist ideals have hurt boys and men'.[4]

In this essay, I want to explore how some key works of post-crash Irish fiction published in the midst of the last economic recession borrowed from and recirculated the 'mancession' narrative that took hold during that time in both the US and Ireland. In the bleak dystopian Irish landscapes found in the post-crash writing of Donal Ryan, Colin Barrett and Kevin Barry, these dominant common-sense truths about the redistribution of gendered precarity in recessionary Ireland are strongly evident. In referring to these works as post-crash Irish fiction, I intend to foreground their status as epochal texts published in the course of the last recession as well as their explicit aesthetic and narrative addressing of the 2008 economic downturn, its causes and its consequences. The fictions that I focus on, Barry's *City of Bohane* (2011), Ryan's *The Spinning Heart* (2012), and Barrett's *Young Skins* (2013), were quickly (I would suggest) canonised as key literary representations of the crash. The reception of these publications as landmark texts inaugurating the explosive emergence of a new Irish writing that spoke to the realities of twenty-first-century Ireland lends an additional significance to their recirculation of mancession tropes of (post) feminist emasculation and crisis masculinity.

Pat Coughlan's '"Bog Queens": Representations of femininity in the poetry of John Montague and Seamus Heaney' demonstrated why in 1991 'the persistent demystifying of representations of women in men's work must continue' alongside the analysis and recovery of writing by women, not least because of what continues to be true, 'that even able and serious contemporary work is deeply and dismayingly reliant upon old, familiar and familiarly oppressive allocations of gender positions'.[5] Coughlan's essay, a landmark in Irish feminist literary criticism, has (along with her entire body of work) been a key influence for me as for so many feminist critics and scholars, an influence that is, I hope, legible here in the demystification of the representations of women and the recirculation of masculinist gendered tropes in influential male-authored fiction. Coughlan's critique of the work of Heaney and Montague remains relevant now, thirty years after it was written. Feminist cultural initiatives such as *Waking the Feminists* in theatre, *Fired* in poetry, and *Fair Plé* in traditional Irish music have highlighted, decades on, the structural, material, and intrapersonal effects of unaddressed patriarchal domination in Irish cultural institutions. As Coughlan points out, such effects extend to literary representation. In the post-crash period, representations of social and economic collapse in key male-authored Irish fiction relied heavily on a re-entrenched and powerfully insistent gender binary and heavily stereotyped representations of women.

The statistical facts of austerity map the devastation suffered following the 2008 economic crash. In 2012, at the peak of recessionary unemployment, 18 per cent of men in the labour force were out of work, an increase of 300 per cent from 2007 levels. Young people were particularly badly hit. The employment rate for men aged 20–24 years fell 30 per cent during the years 2008–12. For women in the same age cohort, the employment rate fell 16 per cent in the same period. So-called structural adjustments implemented as emergency austerity measures inflicted intergenerational as well as class violence. State supports for 20–24 year olds were cut by 50 per cent between 2008 and 2015. Unemployment benefit was slashed from €204.30 to €100 per week for people 18–24 years old and to €144 for 25 year olds, and the full rate was not restored for people under 25 until January 2020.[6] In 2011, minister for social protection Joan Burton blamed soaring youth unemployment on young people opting to sign on as a lifestyle choice.[7] This narrative of workshy welfare dependency became the popular government line, with for instance then Labour tánaiste Eamon Gilmore infamously commenting that the 'place for any young person is not permanently in front of a flat screen TV'.[8] Despite the received narrative of uniquely male recessionary suffering, the gutting of the welfare infrastructure and the increased precaritisation of work in the wake of the 2008 crash did not target men so much as all people on low incomes – a demographic disproportionately comprised of women. As Alison Spillane and Ursula Barry have both noted, working-class women continue to bear the brunt of the fiscal adjustment well into the deeply uneven economic recovery.

In addition to the effect of cuts to child benefit, lone parent, and other vital supports, Barry observes that already existing gendered inequalities were exacerbated during the recession and into the recovery, as the gendered, unequal demands of care hurt women's earnings, with the absence of affordable childcare in Ireland particularly penalising lone parents and low-income households.[9] The mancession narrative that took hold during the recession distorted and obscured the reality of the deepening of such poverty traps for many women and families.

These are important contexts for reading the recession-era fiction of Barry, Ryan, and Barrett. In these texts, the effects of economic crisis and austerity are strongly masculinised, and readerly sympathy is likewise strongly elicited for male protagonists. As well as making powerful connections between rural and class dereliction and male suicide, these recessionary fictions reiterate mancessionary narratives about women's role in causing, and their duty to fix, men's suffering. At the height of recession and austerity cuts, between 2008 and 2012, there was a spike in suicides among young and middle-aged men. Many studies from the medical to the cultural have made the connection between suicide and the effects of austerity, particularly poverty and unemployment, clear.[10] The mental health of boys and men was of major public concern at the height of the economic crisis. This was not accompanied by a similar concern for the well-being of girls and women. As Michael Cronin has noted, Ireland had one of the highest rates of suicide among young men in the EU during the worst years of austerity. While he notes that five times more males than females aged 15–24 died of suicide from 2002 to 2012, neither he nor other contemporary analysts of the impact of austerity policies paid much attention to the fact that Ireland had the highest rate of suicide and self-harm among young women in the EU during the same period. This imbalance in attention to gendered effects was reflected in Pieta House's high-profile 2013 campaign 'Mind Our Men' and the accompanying 'Man Overboard' series in *The Irish Times*. The campaign foregrounded the crisis in men's mental health and placed a heavy burden of responsibility on women for the lives and well-being of the men close to them with no concern for the effects of this on the well-being of women and girls. The *Irish Times*' 'Man Overboard' series in addition firmly admonished women to look kindly on men's unwillingness to shoulder housework and childcare so as not to further dent their self-esteem.[11] These narratives recirculate cultural givens about the secondariness of the woman, the assumption of the self-sacrificing, self-abnegating maternal figure who bears the heavy burden of the unpaid labour of social reproduction and is responsible for the care and comfort of those around her, most especially within the heterosexual couple and heteronormative family. In the post-crash fiction of Ryan, Barrett, and Barry, a good deal of anger and resentment is directed at women characters who refuse such deeply gendered duties of care.

This family of tropes in the mancession repertoire is particularly present in Donal Ryan's 2012 novel *The Spinning Heart*. By now canonised as a seminal novelistic account of the economic crash and its effects, Ryan's novel is set in 2010 in a devastated village in Tipperary. This polyphonic text comprises twenty-one chapters each told by a different character and focalised through their interior monologue, interlinking with the narratives of other characters, clarifying some past events and connections as we read on. A local developer Pokey Burke has fled following sudden bankruptcy and his employees discover that he has not been paying employer stamps, leaving people stranded when his business goes bust. While there are several subplots in the novel, the narrative revolves around Bobby Mahon, Pokey's foreman. Bobby narrates the first chapter and his wife Triona the last, and several chapters in between are in one way or another involved in Bobby's story. The novel rehearses many familiar recessionary tropes, not least that of the authentic manliness of the ordinary working man as the panacea to the excesses of the boom and the despair of the bust. Recalling the models of ideal Irish masculinity familiar in the 'manly Gael' figure that has long animated orthodox national models of Irish manhood, it is clear that Bobby is not just the fulcrum of Ryan's novel, but also represents the kind of heroic yet humble masculinity that will lead the nation through the economic and moral wasteland left in the wake of the Tiger and the crash to a better, kinder future. Bobby and Pokey are positioned as opposite types of men: Pokey, representative of ethically bankrupt, boom-time Tiger profiteers, and Bobby, local GAA hero who keeps people's spirits up even in defeat, handsome, diffident, a man of few, but always authentically felt, words who can be relied on in times of trouble, a working man who is smart and entrepreneurial but also the salt of the earth. This opposition is articulated by Pokey's own father Josie Burke, like Bobby a hard-working, self-sacrificing, self-made man's man whose construction company Pokey has inherited (rather than built from nothing himself as a real man would do): 'I think of Pokey and I feel disgust, with him and with myself. Wasn't it I reared him? Or maybe that's what went wrong: I left most of the rearing to Eileen.'[12] Bobby's position in the narrative as a hero of the people is affirmed by various characters. A young man Rory asks what is it that makes Bobby special. He responds, 'It's a mix of imagination, balls, confidence and something else that I can't put words on. Something that makes you know he was born to give orders, not take them', while his mother proclaims, 'thank God for Bobby Mahon and the father agreed away and he said begod tis the likes of Bobby will put paid to this auld downturn and isn't he a solid sight to God altogether' (*Spinning Heart*, p. 110 and pp. 108–9). Triona, Bobby's clear-eyed wife, can see the truth about her husband even if he cannot see it himself: 'Bobby was never able to see how he affected people. People always saw what they wanted to see in Bobby. He could never see the way people reacted to him. The adoration of the young lads, the respect of the builders, the misty-eyed devotion of the old codgers who roared themselves raw from the sidelines while he led a team of committed losers to the gates of glory' (*Spinning Heart*, p. 153). It is notable that this evidence of Bobby's exemplary nature all comes from men, even if mediated by Triona. It is men's opinion of other men that counts in the tallying of 'the good man' and the masculine ideal.

The intergenerational conflict between men and the dysfunction at the heart of the father–son relationship is one of the canonical Irish literary motifs. It is also a core, recurring feature of the patriarchal family structure in *The Spinning Heart*. This dynamic is played out between Josie and Pokey Burke as well as between Bobby and his father Frank, a monster beyond redemption whose only motivation and enjoyment in life is the destruction of his wife and son and whom Bobby (with echoes of Synge's Christy Mahon in *The Playboy of the Western World*) fantasises about killing. Frank *is* killed by another character in the novel, but Bobby, already in extremis when he comes upon the corpse of his father, somewhat inexplicably takes the blame for the murder. We hear from the murdered father in the penultimate chapter, speaking from beyond death, trapped as an unquiet ghost in the house he made such a hell for his wife and son. We learn that the abuse and dysfunction are transgenerational. Frank's father was in turn a monster who used physical and psychological violence against his son: 'I wonder how is it I was able to do to Bobby exactly what was done to me' (*Spinning Heart*, p. 145).

While this transgenerational transmission of patriarchal violence is a mainstay of Irish cultural narratives, the hetero-relations between men and women in the novel are more specifically inflected by mancessionary recited truths. Many men in the narrative are depressed and harbour suicidal thoughts. For the most part, such suffering is represented as situational – men are depressed because they have lost their jobs and are struggling to keep themselves and their families afloat. This affects a range of men in the novel: Bobby, 'so suddenly useless' (*Spinning Heart*, p. 15), not even able 'to pay for the messages' (*Spinning Heart*, p. 13), ashamed, afraid, and unable to open up to his wife who puts much work into enabling him to talk about his past and his feelings, taking the same care 'as when I'd be trying not to startle a wild animal that had wandered into the garden' (*Spinning Heart*, p. 149). Seanie, a friend and former workmate of Bobby's, has lost his way in 'the blackness I feel sometimes', a darkness that has grown more encompassing since he lost his job and because of his difficulty forging a relationship with his baby son Dylan and Réaltín, the mother of his son. 'Drowning is easy, I'd say,' Seanie concludes. 'You only have to breathe in a lungful of water and you're gone, floating away to nothing' (*The Spinning Heart*, p. 96). The suffering of men is foregrounded in small details as well as in the main characters and plots. Triona's cousin, when a teenager, is driven to suicide by his evangelical mother. Denis' client, a hotel owner in Limerick, took his own life 'when it all went wallop' (*The Spinning Heart*, p. 121).

We get numerous perspectives on the characters of Kate and Denis, a married couple whose relationship is shattering under the pressure of financial struggle and shifting gender roles in a post-crash landscape. Denis is a tradesman whose construction-dependent business has been hit hard by the crash, so the couple rely on Kate's expanding creche business to stay afloat. This reversal – Denis' loss of the breadwinner role and the growth of Kate's creche – replays the 'men lose, women gain' post-crash narrative. The emasculating effect of this reversal of the proper gender order is amplified by Kate's harsh criticism of her husband. Her sympathy for him wears off as time goes on and she slips into the henpecking harpy role: 'I felt sorry for him at the start, I suppose it was weird for him, but for a finish I just wanted to slap him and tell him to take the puss off him and just get on with it' (*The Spinning Heart*, pp. 99–100). Not satisfied with her husband's symbolic castration, she threatens actual castration if his attention strays: 'I'll cut it off of him. I'll cut it. Clean. Off' (*The Spinning Heart*, p. 100). Kate's character is further undermined by her mercenary attitude to business – doubly unnatural because her business is in childcare, by nature women's unpaid vocation – and her relentlessly hostile critique of other women as filtered through her interior monologue. Her employee Nuala is 'a little bitch'; one benefit of the recession is that 'people will work for less than the minimum wage' (*The Spinning Heart*, p. 102). Four chapters later, Denis recounts his own story. Another victim of a dysfunctional relationship with his father, Denis kills Frank (Bobby's father) in a moment of hallucinatory frenzy when Frank's whispered 'you're nothing but a useless cunt' conjures up Denis' dead father (*The Spinning Heart*, p. 124). According to the logic of Frank's inner thoughts, Kate is partially responsible for the murder. Her nagging is not directly blamed but is certainly connected through proximity:

> I killed an old man. Kate wanted to know every evening how much did I get, did I send the invoices by registered post, did I call to the bank to know would they extend the overdraft, did I get back the plant? I sat there several evenings picturing myself punching her into her mouth. I sat thinking about hitting my wife, and that was the only way I could *stop* myself from hitting her. She didn't know. She doesn't know me. Then I killed a man. (*The Spinning Heart*, p. 122)

It is a mark of how naturalised and structurally intrinsic misogyny is to our society that the reader is enjoined to sympathise more with a man who murders another man and fantasises about murdering his partner than we are with the wife who is in fact holding them both afloat. The mancession narrative of the man who has lost his breadwinner status and his punishment for this at the hands of his partner is repeated in Millicent's chapter. Millicent is a young girl whose father Hughie has lost his job. The fraught relationship between Millicent's parents is focalised through her consciousness. Millicent adores Hughie, now a stay-at-home father, while her mother, who supports the family with her wages from Tesco, is portrayed as unrelentingly hysterical and abusive. The assault on Hughie is merciless as witnessed by the little girl: 'Mammy roars and shouts at Daddy over all the things Daddy done wrong to leave us without a bob to our name only what she gets from the poxy few hours that fat bitch allows her on the roster inside in Tescos' (*The Spinning Heart*, p. 119). Nothing that Hughie does is right for his partner (echoing the narratives of Kate and Denis), who criticises his ability to mind their daughter: 'I don't know what way you mind her when I do be at work, sure you're an awful eejit, you could let her run out onto the road or anything, and she kept giving out and giving out and I said Mammy, Daddy is brilliant at minding me' (*The Spinning Heart*, p. 117).

The mancession narrative is, then, a structuring presence in Ryan's novel. Ryan's account of contemporary masculinity in crisis involves a further twist that distinguishes 'normal', authentic masculinity from perverse, dysfunctional masculinity, by making a distinction between a largely situational depression on the one hand, and what is represented as pathological disorder on the other. In a strange, disorienting subplot that focuses on Trevor who has (it is implied) inherited schizophrenia from his father, Trevor enlists his online friend Lloyd to help kidnap Réaltín's young son Dylan from Kate's creche. Lloyd is also represented as acutely disturbed. He tells us he is 'alone in the universe; the universe is created by me and for me and nothing exists outside of my consciousness' (*The Spinning Heart*, p. 105). The narrative suggests abandonment by fathers or some inheritance from the father's line as causative of their mental disturbances. Lloyd's father left him and his mother while young, while Trevor's father was 'broken in two' by schizophrenia and is now dead. Trevor fantasises about kidnapping Dylan and 'saving' Réaltín from Bobby, as well as torturing and killing 'Mother' and her friend Dorothy whom he describes in terms of the monstrous maternal. Dorothy is not human, but a vampire, while he says of his mother that he sometimes catches 'a glimpse of her black, forked tongue as it flicks back in' (*The Spinning Heart*, p. 64). It is difficult to see what the inclusion of Trevor and Lloyd's story line is intended to bring to the novel, but one effect is to make a distinction between the mental suffering of ordinary, empathetic if flawed men on the one hand, and the mental disturbance of men who live in the perverse labyrinths of the dark web and their own equally dark minds on the other.

The Spinning Heart, for all the isolation and despair it charts in its male protagonists, strongly suggests that the resurgence of a traditional wholesome kind of masculinity as exemplified by Bobby is where the future of the nation lies. The post-crash literary narratives of Kevin Barry and Colin Barrett are less attached to fantasies of the heroic but deeply ordinary, demonstrably 'normal' man. These texts are more interested in outlaw masculinities and anti-heroes, even when they ostensibly critique these, as in the new gangster characters that populate Barry's *City of Bohane* and the hopeless, betrayed, paralysed young men who inhabit Barrett's bleak rural wastelands in *Young Skins*. The narratives by Barry and Barrett may intend to critique the maverick masculinities they describe, but they cannot escape some implication in what Diane Negra describes as fantasies of 'compensatory agency' in which 'men's falling status and positionality in the recession is recuperated by their symbolic mastery of power'.[13] All of these books foreground characters who are simultaneously maverick hard-men and yet stuck and powerless, hostages to this version of hegemonic masculinity. They also at the same time underscore the cultural narrative that asserts, in often subtle, even unconscious but clearly demonstrable ways, that women's accession to power involves the subordination or dereliction of men, and a corrosion of the gendered order of things.

Colin Barrett's *Young Skins* was published in 2013 to critical acclaim, winning the *Guardian* First Book Award for that year as *The Spinning Heart* had the year before. *Young Skins* is a collection of interlinked short stories, most based in Glanbeigh, a small (fictional) rural town in Mayo that could be one of many places in the peripheral, derelict landscapes of contemporary rural Ireland. The narrative point of view in all seven stories is male and the stories focus on and are focalised through men. The gendering of class is marked throughout many of the stories – 'maleness' and 'femaleness' are tacitly ascribed to particular class positions. Writing in 2018, Lisa McInerney noted that in relation to gender, class, and the Irish writer, only the male writer can be legitimately working class and in a very particular way. There is something 'legitimate, fetishized ... and ... male about being working class. All that struggle, you know. All that sweat and block-laying and emigration and stout-drinking. When one thinks of working-class communities one thinks of men in white vests, young lads in hoodies ... the feminine is there but no one seems to want to think too hard about it.'[14] Men in Barrett's stories are downwardly mobile, at the very sharpest edge of recession and rural disenfranchisement and caught in various states of arrested development – living at home with overbearing, overwrought, or barely-there mothers, unable to sustain relationships with women or with their children, unable to escape the moribund life and land that threaten to swallow them whole. This portrait of contemporary white, rural, working-class Irish masculinity resonates with Debbie Ging's analysis of the 'new gangster genre' in Irish film and television drama (notwithstanding the predominantly Dublin setting) from the height of the Celtic Tiger in the early 2000s in films such as *Intermission* through to the recession and post-crash period and the hugely popular RTÉ drama series *Love/Hate*. Ging observes that as men's place in the family as the breadwinner has eroded and as men's domination of women in the private and public spheres has been destabilised, maverick and outlaw masculinities have become increasingly prominent in popular culture and increasingly compelling for many disenfranchised young men. She notes that in the new gangster genre:

> new identities and activities are invoked to reaffirm male power and privilege, such as organised crime, joyriding, stealing horses, betting, prostitution, pornography and drug-dealing. In this context, the gangster functions as the quintessential 'fantasy of compensatory agency' for a number of reasons: his money-making is not constrained by the regular economy, he is repositioned at the centre of power while women are relegated to roles of wives or sexual objects, he revels in exclusively homosocial spaces and, because he operates outside the law, he accommodates fantasies of rebellion and counter-hegemony.[15]

The stories in *Young Skins* critique and engage with this fantasy in different ways. 'The Moon' rehearses the narrative of male stasis and female mobility that reinforces the automatic transposition of class distinctions onto gender distinctions between men and women. The story is focalised through the main protagonist, Val Neary, 'senior bouncer at the Peacock Bar and Niteclub', who falls into a relationship of sorts with his boss's daughter Martina Boran when she returns from college in Galway for the summer to work in her father's pub. She is nineteen and Val almost thirty. The asymmetry in power that this suggests is emphasised by Val's blustering, laddish boasts about his sexual exploits: 'I just pulled a wee length of pussy out of my gob', which the narrator tells us 'was a cunt hair, electric red, and it belonged to Martina Boran'.[16] Val routinely reduces women to their body parts, and this laddish bravado and the reduction of women to 'fanny' and 'pussy' are core to the maverick masculinity he aspires to: 'Fanny frequently got in without ID as long as they'd dolled themselves up to the due degree' ('The Moon', *Young Skins*, p. 34). However, the reader is persuaded into a position of sympathy for Val as the narrative unfolds and the power dynamic of his relationship with Martina shifts. This dynamic is defined not by age or gender, but by class. Martina is cool, attractive, and smart, and while we have no access to her inner consciousness, the narrative and her dialogue portray her as entitled and casually, perhaps unintentionally, cruel. She mocks men who exhibit any vulnerability. Reversing the grim, received hetero-binary of the woman trying to catch her man and the man eluding her grasp, keen to play the field, Martina ridicules her college boyfriend to Val and her sidekick Joan while the three are out bush-drinking: 'He's so excitable. Laps at my neck, like a dog. *Pants*' ('The Moon', *Young Skins*, p. 40). Martina's disposition is primarily defined by contempt – contempt for those she sees as inferior or under her control. The spotlight of Martina's scorn soon turns to Val himself. '"You like this place, don't you, Val? You like everything about it,"' she remarks. Their exchange continues:

> 'Someone has to stay put, hold the fort.'
> 'You're not going anywhere that far.'
> 'Galway's not that far,' said Martina, 'but it might as well be the moon for people like you.' ('The Moon', *Young Skins*, p. 44)

The power dynamic that is described in 'The Moon' goes beyond observation of the complex realities of small-town rural life. The tropes that are deployed in this story and others in *Young Skins* borrow from and re-inscribe received truths about the putative post-feminist subordination of men, the gendering of class and class mobility, and the belief that as women rise, men are increasingly downtrodden. In this story, the fact that Val is so much older and more experienced than the still-teenaged Martina is trumped by her class status and her mobility, all connected to her supposed sexual power over men. In contrast, Val is stuck, immobile, with no apparent way out of his situation. The misogyny that is inscribed in his language and treatment of women in the first pages of the story becomes a mark of his marginalisation, and instead of alienating the readers, we are led to feel pity for him as he makes a futile attempt to pursue a connection with Martina, who is by the end of the story the woman on top.

The tropes of women on top and the subordination of men emerge in another story in the collection, 'Calm With Horses'.[17] Once again, the main women protagonists in the story possess a socio-economic mobility denied to their male counterparts. From one angle, the story clearly intends to critique the maverick, counter-hegemonic, new gangster masculinity that the young men in the story perform. It performs this critique, however, while simultaneously inviting sympathy with the story's violent, even psychopathic male protagonists and once again sets up a correlation between women winning and men losing at the story's conclusion. The main protagonist, Douglas Armstrong, known as Arm, works as the muscle for Dympna Devers (a woman's name, indicative of the sense of masculinity crisis that pervades the collection), a young Traveller man who is the main drug dealer in the area. The story begins with Arm and Dympna exacting punishment on Fannigan, a man in his fifties who lives with his mother and cuts a pathetic figure, and who also attempted to rape Dympna's fourteen-year-old sister Charlie at a house party. Content that the vicious beating Arm subjects Fannigan to while his mother is locked in the bathroom is sufficient to make restitution for his violation of his sister, Dympna hears otherwise when he and Arm meet his uncle Hector in Lally's pub – an all-male domain. His uncle Hector is outraged, or at least feigns outrage, at what he considers Dympna's inadequate efforts at family retribution.

Arm dispatches Fannigan when he crosses his path on the way home from Quilligan's bar one evening. Shortly after, he and Dympna venture to the farm of Dympna's uncle Paudi and Hector – operating now primarily as a marijuana grow house. Arm shows Paudi the rock he used to murder Fannigan; the uncle takes this as a threat and opens fire on his nephew and Arm. Arm, badly injured, manages to escape, and drives the battered car to Ballintober, where Hector is visiting his woman-friend Maire Mirkin, referred to repeatedly as 'the widow Mirkin'. The visit is ill-fated; Arm kills Hector and presses the widow to hand over the inheritance from her recently deceased mother that Hector had been angling for. She gives him the money, rolls and rolls of old currency, and Arm orders her to drive him home. He passes out in the back of the van, and when he comes to, Maire Mirkin tells him a long story about her dead husband while, unbeknown to him, driving not to the hospital but in a circle back to Ballintober, until she is sure that Arm is dead. Just as Dympna's given name suggests a certain taint of the feminine, a fear of emasculation, so too Mirkin suggests a shifting of gender dynamics. A merkin was a pubic wig that was used on the Renaissance stage to cover male actors' genitals when they were playing female characters; it was also associated with prostitution and women attempting to conceal the symptoms of syphilis. Mirkin then carries these confused but interrelated implications of the duplicity and danger of women, of the woman's body as abject and signifying death and decay, of Widow Mirkin herself as performing a feminine masquerade that covers over her true position of power and the putative contemporary usurpation by women of traditional male dominance.

It is worth emphasising that while the male protagonist in the story makes his living from violence and intimidation and brutally murders two men, the narrative voice guides us towards sympathy for Arm while Maire, the widow Mirkin, who acts to save her own life in the first instance, is portrayed in an unsympathetic light and as a murderer by other, passive-aggressive, slyly 'feminine' means. Arm routinely dissociates from the violence he metes out: he had 'the clear head and cold-bloodedness required by the ring, the knack of detachment' ('Calm With Horses', *Young Skins*, p. 73). The reader is likewise held at a distance from the horror of his acts. For instance, when coldly instructing Fannigan to take off his clothes in preparation for his execution by the river, we are given access to Arm's interior thoughts and his rationalisation of what he is doing via Fannigan's dawning interior realisation of what is happening and why: 'The uncles, Dympna was right, Arm knew, they'd butcher Fannigan. They'd use him for sport, and take their time doing so' ('Calm With Horses', *Young Skins*, p. 98). While he impassively carries out what he perceives as his obligation, we are privy to Arm's thoughts which silently urge Fannigan to run or fight back: 'A part of Arm wanted to scream at him to take his chance. To push Arm over, or run, or smash Arm's skull with whatever conviction he could channel into his fists; just to try' ('Calm With Horses', *Young Skins*, p. 99). We also witness Arm's vulnerability and capacity for care, however stunted, in his relationships with his son Jack, Jack's mother, and his interchanges with Olivia, Jack's horse-riding instructor. The contrast with the narrative treatment of Maire, the widow Mirkin, is telling. Maire, a woman probably in her late fifties or sixties, is portrayed as a relic from a dead or dying era with a crucifix and a 'doe-eyed, winsome Christ' on the walls of her genteel, old-fashioned sitting-room, an 'old dear' who is wholesome of dress and face with a spinsterly girlishness presented as a jarring, unseemly contrast to her years. We do not have any insight into her interior life, just the narrator's externalised description of her which suggests a prudish, rural, middle-class, somewhat desiccated gentility with more than a whiff of the convent boarding school. With Hector sprawled in a bloody and moaning heap on the floor and Arm, hammer in hand, demanding that she take him to where she has hidden her money, she responds: '"The money," she giggled abruptly, scrambling to cover her mouth' ('Calm With Horses', *Young Skins*, p. 134). She 'steps mindfully' over the dying heap of her gentleman caller Hector, and 'winces in distaste' when the dying man calls her and Arm 'cunts' ('Calm With Horses', *Young Skins*, p. 134). She acts the ingenue, asking Arm in a 'small voice' what he will do if there is no money ('Calm With Horses',

Young Skins, p. 135). When she sniffs, her nose is 'prim'; her touch is 'ice-cold'. By the end of the story, four men are presumably dead, all through homicidal violence: Fannigan, Dympna, Hector, and Arm. Arm's death, however, is ambiguous. Maire fails to bring him to the hospital, but the narrative tacitly begs the question of her responsibility for his demise. The multiple male deaths are opposed to the quiet, sly resilience of Mirkin. Her holding onto the dead money that made her a target and the signposting of her bourgeois propriety against the chaotic, outlaw violence in the story speak to the recurring post-crash narrative of women benefiting and coming out on top in the face of the death of men and traditional modes of hetero-masculinity.

One much-remarked feature of post-crash recessionary media and popular cultural representations of crisis masculinity figures, young white cis hetero men especially, is seceding from heteronormativity with its associated obligations to reproduce the fantasised ideal population and/or nation for the future. Hetero men are often narratively figured as refusing hetero-domesticity, the call to reproduce, and the heteronormative life narrative structured by the injunctions to work, marriage, family, and child-rearing. In the post-crash landscape, the accepted truth goes, men have been hard done by the entwined forces of a post-feminist social and sexual economy that has emasculated hetero men, and an economic cataclysm that has resulted in the further precaritisation of men and masculinity for which women are to blame while also being its net beneficiaries. In his analysis of 'queer failure', Jack Halberstam considers this hetero-masculine refusal in relation to Irving Welsh's 1996 novel *Trainspotting*. In *Trainspotting*, Renton explicitly rejects the imperative to self-development and maturation along heteronormative lines in the post-welfare state. Ultimately, Halberstam argues, the novel's refusals do not qualify as *queer* failures (failures that might be in some way politically liberatory and transformative) because of its investments in white patriarchal power that 'cannot imagine the downfall of the white male as part of the emergence of a new order'.[18] Halberstam notes that: 'Without an elaborate vision of alternative modes, the novel collapses into the angry and seething language of the male punk from whom a legacy of patriarchal and racial privilege has been withheld. In this example of unqueer failure, failure is the rage of the excluded white male, a rage that promises and delivers punishments for women and people of color.'[19]

Similarly, the hetero-masculine refusal of heteronormative developmental trajectories is a recurring motif in *Young Skins*. This refusal is often tied to traditional tropes of the smothering, over-bearing mother, a well-worn figure in the Irish cultural and representational landscape. In 'Calm With Horses', Fannigan, in his fifties, still lives with his mother. Dympna lives with his mother and three of his sisters. Both of their fathers are dead. Ursula Dory, 'the girl, who was no longer Arm's girl' ('Calm With Horses', *Young Skins*, p. 77) and the mother of his son Jack, has lived with her parents since Jack was born, while Arm also lives with his parents and, though he spends time with his son, is fundamentally unreliable as a father and, of course, a partner. Brothers Hector and Paudi are unmarried and childless and have made their remote farm into a survivalist bunker, with a stockpile of weapons, canned goods, and unlikely hydroponic machinery. The same patterns of ambivalent refusal/failure in relation to hetero-development assert themselves elsewhere. In 'The Clancy Kid', the narrator's friend Tug Cuniffe, 'prone to fits of rage and temper tantrums', is 'called Manchild behind his back'.[20] Tug's father is ten years dead and he also lives at home with his mother, 'a sweet old ruin of an alcoholic'. Marlene Davey also lives with her mother; her father is also dead. She is, the narrator Jimmy Devereux tells us, 'the nearest thing I've had to a steady girlfriend' ('The Clancy Kid', *Young Skins*, p. 5); they still have sex occasionally even though she has had a child with the faux-heroically, satirically named Mark Cuculann, a 'manly Gael' nomenclature if ever there was one. Jimmy puts on his customary bluster and bravado when he sees the two together in the pub: they are 'playing Mammy and Daddy'; Cuculann has taken 'the paternity bullet I dodged ('The Clancy Kid', *Young Skins*, p. 7). A similar unconvincing renunciation of the bonds of heteronormative commitment is made in 'Kindly Forget My Existence', but again it is tinged not with queer autonomy but hetero-masculine misogyny: 'He splayed a hand on the counter and inspected the digits, as if in a moment of recent inattention a ring might have somehow contrived to snag itself there. "No," he continued, "I've entered the era of grand onanistic solitude, and, to be honest, that's fucking fine with me."'[21]

The refusal of marriage, fatherhood, and domesticity has been framed by contemporary pundits as a largely male rejection of the normative obligations of mature adulthood in response to the flipping of received gender scripts in a viciously neoliberal, post-feminist, feminist-centric, woman-dominated world. As Sue Leonard observes in her analysis of post-recessionary gender in the US, radical queer critiques of heteronormative life scripts notwithstanding, the perception that young men are avoiding marriage and the maturity this signifies in a heteronormative order of things repeats the familiar recessionary narrative of failing men and winning women. She notes that this recurring contention is seen in a number of accounts, most prominently Kay Hymowitz's *Manning Up: How the rise of women has turned men into boys* (2011), in which the author recognises the harm this causes for women as well as men yet focuses on the 'man-child' whose condition she attributes to 'self-infantilization rather than, say, a severely depressed job market' for people in their late teens and twenties.[22] In contrast, Leonard reports that, according to Hymowitz and the popular script,

> women are reaching their twenties with more achievements, more education, more property, and arguably, more ambition than their male counterparts. Such observations pointedly echo recessionary discourses that predict bright economic futures for women and dismal ones for men, and illustrate again the influence of popular culture products on perceptions of actual demographics.[23]

In *Young Skins*, the economic factors at play in the paralysed situation of so many of its mostly male protagonists are exacerbated by the post-crash recessionary context, but it is also clear in Barrett's stories that the marginalisation, infrastructural and economic dereliction, and demographic decline of Ireland's rural periphery pre-date the 2008 crisis and its fallout. While neither Barrett nor Ryan suggest self-infantilisation as the cause of the condition of their male protagonists, the man-child theme recurs and is problematically interconnected in the narratives with depression, mental illness, suicidality, schizophrenia, psychosis, and brain injury, almost solely associated with men and boys by both writers. Although the convergence of these varied traits and conditions reflects some very troubling problems in the depiction of mental illness, disability, and neurodiversity in contemporary Irish writing, for this essay the point is the way in which such representations are made to suggest the incapacity of men to take care of themselves and the role of women – mothers, especially – in keeping them in a state of arrested development.

Kevin Barry's *City of Bohane* was published to immediate acclaim in 2011. The novel was shortlisted for the 2011 Costa book award and won both the 2012 Author's Club Award for first novel and the IMPAC Dublin Literary Award in 2013. It is a work of speculative dystopian fiction set in 2053 in Bohane, a fictional city in the Irish west. Bohane is set in a near-future Ireland that has undergone a structural and environmental collapse whose exact nature is never spelled out but is presumably extrapolated from the context of economic, environmental, and social collapse and crisis in which the book was written and published. The city is a lawless and savage place, dominated by violence, drugs, and tribal factions. Despite references to The Authority, any semblance of state control or local government has entirely broken down, while the local 'polis' are in the pay of the gangs that run Bohane's streets. Leading out of the town is the High Boreen that crosses the Big Nothin' beyond, a bleak and forbidding wasteland including the Rez where the 'sand-pikeys' live. The infrastructure that holds contemporary Ireland together has collapsed – electricity appears to be sporadic and there is no technology to speak of, compounding the sense of ambient squalor, material dereliction, and toxic pollution that seeps into the crevices of the city and the country landscapes alike, and inhabits the bodies and souls of everyone the tainted fog touches: 'Whatever is wrong with us is coming in off that river. No argument: the taint of badness on the city's air is a taint off that river ... A blackwater surge, malevolent, it roars in off the Big Nothin' wastes and the city was spawned by it.'[24] Bohane can be seen as a kind of speculative future and periphery akin to the ghost estates haunting Donal Ryan's account of the crash and its effects and the bleak, dilapidated, rural council estates and arid, death-stalked landscapes of Colin Barrett's stories.

Bohane is run by rival gangs, the Hartnett Fancy and the Norries, and the narrator (a photographer and film buff who runs the Ancient and Historical Bohane Film Society and keeps a stock of old film reels that people pay to view while they indulge in melancholic reveries of the 'Lost Time') recounts their brutal feud and the rise to power of a teenage girl, Jenni Ching, who by the conclusion has outwitted all the men around her and takes over the town along with her followers, a gang of young girls who have been ostracised and abused by their communities, described by the narrator as Jenni's 'pack of feral teenage sluts' (*City of Bohane*, p. 255). Jenni is part-Chinese and in Bohane this adds an orientalist aspect to her fetishistic representation in the novel. For instance, we see the 'Chinkee gal' as the narrator refers to Jenni tending to Logan Hartnett: 'The girl put the flame to the [opium] pipe for him. He drew deeply. She placed a dampened cloth on his brow' (*City of Bohane*, p. 220). The orientalising objectification in the depiction of Jenni extends to other aspects of the novel's representations. As Keith Ridgway points out in his review of the novel, Bohane is peopled by different factions that function as fairly uncritical vehicles for racialised and 'underclass' stereotypes of Travellers and the urban working class. The portrayal and naming of the 'sand-pikeys' are particularly troubling; they are depicted as unremittingly barbaric and violent, and we are told later in the novel that they are of Traveller origin – a detail that makes Barry's uncritical use of a racist slur to name this Bohane tribe even more inexplicable.

One ever-present feature of the constant and extreme violence that characterises life in Bohane is an excessive and violent misogyny. While individual women have some power in this society, it is a deeply patriarchal order where brutal subordination of women is the norm. Women seem to work predominantly in the sex industry and under the absolute control of men. The Gant reminisces sentimentally about the 'stable of hoors' he ran 'as a young man' (*City of Bohane*, p. 15). In line with the stereotyping of Traveller and working-class urban cultures, the worst misogyny is ascribed to the so-called 'pikeys' and the Norries. In a 'pikey-run grindbar' in the S'town part of Bohane, a 'slave-gal lurcher' puts on a floor show. She 'had the telltale welts of captivity on her back'; 'lurchers' are girls who are held in captivity from a young age, kept in cages and chains (*City of Bohane*, p. 165). When defeated by the Hartnett Fancy in league with Prince Tubby, the Norries turn to religion: 'there was an outbreak of Sweet Baba Jay mania on the Northside Rises' (*City of Bohane*, p. 223). There are apparitions, novenas, and messages conveyed from heaven via Sweet Baba Jay flags, while sexual continence and modest behaviour become the norm among the previously rampant Norries. Women wear 'a more modest cleavage', and the reviled objects for the repressed urges of the Norrie community are 'the sluts'. Nightly 'slut parades' are held where young women are punished for attempting to seduce Norrie men by being forced to carry huge banners bearing messages from Sweet Baba Jay. Mutilation is considered: 'At holler-meetings nightly, it was argued that banner-bearing was hardly punishment enough for these Baba-denying harlot bitches and that their private parts should by force be rendered useless, with the aid of knitting needles and hot knives, but this was controversial' (*City of Bohane*, p. 226).

These 'sluts' under the leadership of Jenni become the ascendant power in Bohane nonetheless. While virtually all of the male protagonists of the novel, young and old, are dead by the end of the novel, eighteen-year-old Jenni is left standing and supreme. The two old stags, Gant and Logan, both recognise her potential and the female takeover that is coming. 'Them girls the future in Bohane,' the Gant Broderick observes, 'these young girls workin it now in the Trace' (*City of Bohane*, p. 200). Jenni Ching becomes the idol of the Back Trace girls: 'They wore white vinyl zip-ups tighter than sin, or black nylon catsuits as though fitted with a spray-can, or gym shorts worn a handful of sizes too small over sheer silver stockings, and … groin-kicker boots for the bad girls … And you did not kowtow to no fuckwad boy-chil' (*City of Bohane*, p. 207).

City of Bohane presumably intends to critique the misogyny that is etched into the bones of Bohane and the Big Nothin', and the survival of the three 'strong women' of the novel (Jenni, Macu, and Girly Hartnett) and especially the triumphant rise of Jenni and her girls are perhaps supposed to demonstrate the ascendancy of a kind of lawless girl power. *Bohane* is another version of the masculinity in crisis narrative, albeit a more anarchic, cartoonish, playful, and bloody version than we find in Ryan or Barrett, another take on the post-feminist, mancessionary story about women on top and men ground down under their variously matriarchal or dominatrix heels. The women in *City of Bohane* tend towards cyphers, true to the genres that the novel energetically draws on – the western and film noir, with echoes of Patrick McCabe's novels and the new gangster genres analysed by Ging. Macu's function in the novel is mostly as the Achilles heel of Gant and Logan and the conduit for their homosocial rivalries; Girly Hartnett, Logan's unspeakably old mother, is a classic phallic mother figure who dominates her son and even plots with Jenni to oust him from power when his jealous, obsessive love for Macu weakens his hold over Bohane and the Fancy; while Jenni's power is largely constituted by her canny use of her sexual hold on men, to the extent that she causes the death of the love-lorn Wolfie Stanners, who dreams of having children with her but who also makes his living from maiming and murder and is in fact Jenni's main contender to take over the Fancy. The novel dwells obsessively on fashion and dress, which is of paramount importance for Bohane society. Jenni's slick sense of style makes her an object of both identification and desire, and we do not get a glimpse of her unmediated by the frank male gaze of the narrator, of other male characters, and indeed of the author himself. It is important to note that while Jenni and her girls don their groinkickers, their transgressive, violent mob rule is not a feminist revolution, but the incorporation by these young women of the patriarchal condition. They become the new gangsters, at least while they are young and fresh enough to do so convincingly in the hetero-masculinist domain that is *City of Bohane*.

This points to a dynamic that is common to *City of Bohane* and *Young Skins*: the normalising of cross-generational hetero desire that at times shades in to assault and rape between invariably very young women (often teenagers and school girls, sometimes minors) and much older men. This is central to heterosexual relations in *City of Bohane*; even in the case of (the middle-aged) Gant's ongoing obsession with (the middle-aged) Macu, we are told that his desire is oriented to youth – a 'taste of Macu, in her youth, had left him with an insatiable taste for girls of that age' (*City of Bohane*, p. 200). Men leering at and targeting underage girls is also a normalised feature of *Young Skins*. This is social realism, it could be argued, but the instances of cross-generational desire and sexual violence that I have touched on above complicate the difficult line between critique and complicity in a kind of ambient misogyny in that text. Another repeated trope from the playbook of representational misogyny is the double-act of the 'bombshell' and her much less attractive friend. Thus, we have Réaltín and Hillary (who Seanie informs us 'looked liked a browny-grey blob beside' Réaltín) in *The Spinning Heart*, and Sarah Dignan and Jenny Tierney in Barrett's story 'Bait' ('lookswise, Jenny had no chance against the hogging nimbus of Sarah's beauty') as well as Martina Boran and Joan Doody ('a stout, pleasant girl') in 'The Moon' in *Young Skins*.[25]

The works I have focused on in this selective and limited account of mancessionary motifs in post-crash Irish fiction are absorbed by contemporary anxieties about the decline and fall of (white) hetero-masculinity. Male violence against other men is a marked feature of all these narratives and yet repeated representations of women as nagging, cruel, unforgiving, manipulative, mercenary, smothering, and other well-worn traditional stereotypes of femininity are explicitly implicated in this decline. Male violence against women is downplayed in both Barrett and Ryan, while in *City of Bohane* the violent misogyny of Barry's speculative Ireland of the future is for the most part a largely uncritiqued, unremarked backdrop, and women's revolt against their subjection happens only through young women themselves becoming the perpetrators of violence. In keeping with the new gangster mode in Irish film and television, there is a particular strain of post-crash Irish men's writing that uses misogyny and representations of extreme violence against women as a way of marking its edgy transgressiveness. The popularity of a particular kind of masculinist crisis narrative has, perhaps, waned for now at least. In a 2020 essay, entitled 'Emasculated', Luke Brown singled out Rob Doyle as the last man writer standing in the Anglophone world who would dare to write with what was lauded as a brave but near-extinct Rothian honesty about the libidinal drives of the embattled hetero-male despite the shrivelling effect of supposed woke domination.[26] It is also true that there are landmark works of fiction – Mike McCormack's *Solar Bones* (2016) is the key case in point – that do not conform to the mancession mode that this essay identifies. However, beyond the realms of fiction, the exploitation and extraction of women's reproductive labour – the presumption of whose availability undergirds many of the mancession tropes noticed in this essay – continue unabated. The crisis of care occasioned by the global Covid-19 pandemic has shown this in no uncertain terms, with women disproportionately carrying the burden of much-increased caring responsibilities and reduced earnings. In the post-Covid Irish fiction that is perhaps already emergent (Emma Donoghue's *The Pull of the Stars* may prove one starting point), how will the gendered realities of this, our latest crisis, be narrated?

CHAPTER 14

'a permeable membrane gives at the slightest touch': The ecopoetics of houses in the poetry of Vona Groarke and Sinéad Morrissey

MARGARET MILLS HARPER

A sort of critical perversity may explain why I first began to think of two volumes of poetry, *Other People's Houses* by Vona Groarke (1999) and *Through the Square Window* by Sinéad Morrissey (2009), as ecopoetry.[1] Despite a certain lingering fuzziness in the term ecopoetics, or even of its cousin ecocriticism, surely an engagement with the environment is at least likely for poetry that fits into the first category – or this essay to fit into the other. Yet I have no such subject matter, just like Groarke, who mis-categorises herself in the poem 'Why I Am Not A Nature Poet' (about the death of her children's goldfish) from her 2006 volume *Juniper Street*.[2] The first line of Morrissey's poem 'Our Flower Garden', from her 2002 collection *Between Here and There*, likewise begins parodically: 'Consider the flowers in our flower garden, how they rot'.[3] Gardens in Morrissey, as in Groarke, tend towards the urban patch rather than the open wild, resembling the fantastic creation described in the poem 'Jo Gravis in His Metal Garden': 'Metal the medium and metal the message'.[4] Indeed, the built and human environments engage both poets, especially in the two volumes that are my focus in this essay. *Other People's Houses* is a tightly thematised volume in which every poem is about a house, in some form or other. *Through the Square Window* preoccupies itself with themes arising from the experience of new parenthood in a city space.

Yet, both volumes of poetry are in aesthetic and political conversation with ecocritical discourse. Their contributions often involve a strikingly ironic or semi-comic tone, as in the examples cited above. The essay that follows suggests that Groarke and Morrissey adopt a position of what might best be called *play* in poetry that addresses environmental crisis and the urgent questions of human responsibility and action in the face of it. I do not intend by this word necessarily to categorise either Groarke or Morrissey as postmodern, a discourse that features *play* as a commonly used term of art, except in a general sense, or to suggest that their attitudes towards environmentalism are flippant. The opposite, in fact. The two senses of the word that suit it to my purposes are, first, the notion of what we might call 'give', a little looseness, something that can be moved a bit if pushed or pulled on. The second is as a way to describe the work of healthy children (and the young of many other species), which helps them develop complex and flexible brains, with both cognitive strengths and social skills.[5]

This poetry by Groarke and Morrissey advances ecopoetics by troubling it, that is to say, addressing issues of human consciousness and form that are persistent stumbling blocks, speaking philosophically and also structurally. In other words, if lyric poetry begins, as Joyce's Stephen Dedalus says it does, with 'the simplest verbal vesture of an instant of emotion', a 'rhythmical cry such as ages ago cheered on the man who pulled at the oar or dragged stones up a slope', something that is 'purely personal', then that form is relentlessly cultural.[6] The lyric is, after all, in Stephen's striking word, a *vesture*, not a naked expression (though as we might remember, nakedness in western tradition is always a post-lapsarian condition: to be naked is to be ashamed of being without clothing). Further, lyric form in Stephen's description has something to do with the work of a terrestrial animal moving artificially over water or hauling bits of rock uphill, presumably to build something – an *oikos* or house, perhaps, which may share an etymological root with the word *ecology* but not much else. The personal quality of the lyric poem also precludes the crying human animal from engaging with the non-personal world beyond it. The problem might seem, at first, to lie in consciousness, the sense in which a lyric is Stephen's 'cheer', which would be after all a complicated response by one person to another's work, or beyond that, the 'I' or self doing the cheering, separated from the water or the stone. Perhaps human beings exist in a prisonhouse of our own mouths or heads, or the constructs we build out of our minds, emotions, and bodies, trapped by what we tend to think of as our freedom from the world of other beings on the earth.

The trouble lies deeper than the perceived binary of subject and object, in which case we might find ourselves returning to Heidegger's influential analysis and critique of the terms in which human 'being' is understood. Both Jacques Derrida and Giorgio Agamben have addressed questions of the human relationship with animals.[7] Interestingly, each has given a prominent role in their own thought to Heidegger's project (in Derrida's words) 'to define the essence of the human otherwise than through consciousness, otherwise than through the reason that might be attributed to a certain animal ... and even less through the "I", "an ego with pure life-experiences that has been tacked on to a body"'.[8] Both Agamben and Derrida point to Heidegger's emphasis on spatiality in his thinking about animals. Derrida notices Heidegger's tendency to posit ideas in clusters of three and the overall circularity, or spirality, of his intellectual structures, so that Heidegger finds himself going around and around: 'He insists a lot on this dizziness, which, he says, is *unheimlich* ... This vertigo is that of an interrogation into the animal, and, finally, it's the concept of world itself that becomes problematic and fragile.'[9] For Agamben, Heidegger presents 'a dialectic between concealedness and unconcealedness, openness and closedness' that links the relation between human and animal to the work of art, in which the earth as an 'essentially Undisclosable' field (but not really a field, nor any other concept, because it can neither be dis-closed nor opened) can be brought to light.[10] For both, biopolitics has defined western philosophy and goes a good distance in explaining humankind's 'inhumanity' to the earth, other living beings, and itself.

For the purposes of this essay, such speculations are relevant to the collections by Groarke and Morrissey with which I am concerned. As Derrida and Agamben suggest, past a certain point, western intellectual approaches fail. Some issues can only be thought or felt beyond the limits of 'thinking'. In the conceptual universe from which I cannot escape, to understand intellectually is irremediably linked with domination. To avoid understanding, however, is a version of the same; not to think is not the Other of thinking. That Other, for want of a better term, may be approached in art, or possibly mystical awareness. At any rate, it requires the firing of other neural pathways than those that create rational structures. Thus, to return to Joyce, the poet is not the rower or hauler but in relation with them. Structures like the notions of interior and exterior, active and passive, may open in poetry to other terms that allow specificities as well as generalities, attention to the ever-presence of perspective and language as well as an active reach into a space in which human beings might be able to be with, and in, the world, while leaving it alone.[11]

I owe much to the thinking of Patricia Coughlan in pondering a pronounced strategy in the work of contemporary Irish women poets, in which distinctions between interior and exterior spaces shift in surprising ways. Groarke and Morrissey belong to a generation that has as poetic mentors poets such as Eiléan Ní Chuilleanáin and Medbh McGuckian, both of whom are intensely engaged with issues of domestic space, which is always gendered, and the space of the lyric poem. In the work of Ní Chuilleanáin, for example, as such critics as Dillon Johnston have noted, point of view often sidles around and through space, suggesting worlds that overlay each other and interact in mysterious ways.[12] Ní Chuilleanáin often represents space as both solid and shifting, attending to architectural features and areas that impede free movement or vision: corners, closing doors, blocked-up windows. Travel across bridges, up alleyways, or along roads or paths leads to scarcely recognisable destinations. Entrances are often blocked, but places from which there seems to be no exit may suddenly shift into wide space. Sometimes, as Patricia Coughlan has noted, enclosures result in 'contented containment [that] can, paradoxically, enable an opening-out within the experiencing self'.[13] At other times, obstruction, or potential obstruction, is deeply unsettling. For example, in 'The Flood', from her 2009 collection *The Sun-Fish*, the poet desires 'the neutral ground' but finds herself 'Skirting' on a road and bridge into an unknown landscape.[14] She cannot escape the 'cry' that has sent her out looking for something at a tangent: 'Did I try this angle before?' she asks herself. She finds herself unable to avoid the full rush of perception:

> I call on the muscles to shift,
> Choose, focus, as if I had found
> A crack with a spiral glimpse,
> And what lies within. But it comes
> Full against me like a motorway –
> I can look nowhere else. (*The Sun-Fish*, p. 26)

Only human grief, 'singular' and 'Repeated, the protest of the mother / By the bed where her daughter lay dead' (*The Sun-Fish*, p. 26), opens the poet at the end of the poem into a state beyond her own resistance and into momentary participation in an alien world. Supported by structures of alliteration, internal rhyme, and assonance, the poet goes beyond herself into what she described in an earlier line as 'A pure pouring':

> The eye can only
> Relax, distended:
> The heart hammering, the danced tangle
> Of light on the sliding depths. (*The Sun-Fish*, p. 26)

Fluctuations in a recognisable time/space equation in Ní Chuilleanáin certainly speak about a shift in that Cartesian subject, the 'I' that troubles Medbh McGuckian's poem 'Harem Trousers': 'A poem dreams of being written without the pronoun "I".'[15] Ní Chuilleanáin has for many years been interested in how the movement between inside and outside mirrors the way that women in particular are defined, by cultures or myths, by others or by themselves. Thus, shifting how a door in a convent wall is positioned or functions with regard to the people on either side, describing what happens at a shoreline when a wood-encased saint washes up on a strand, or watching how a stone face representing a woman causes the whole scene around it to come to life, are part of an ongoing effort by Ní Chuilleanáin literally to shift the subject – to attend to the fact that the western subject does not reflect or serve the purposes of the people whom it is meant to reflect and define.

McGuckian's poetry shifts not so much the subject but the poetics that supports it. Her radical undermining of the 'I' of the poetic voice is arguably the result of the collapse of more general poetic structures that prop up that construction. The emptying out of the subject in McGuckian has been compared to religious ecstasy, vatic possession, or a kind of antenna picking up radio waves of language (a metaphor that surfaces especially in the volume *Marconi's Cottage*).[16] McGuckian's refusals to play the role of poet as authority extend to her well-documented practice of recycling texts from a host of sources, turning the *techné* of a well-crafted poem into a kind of palimpsest or bird's nest of collected quotations from other writers.[17] This composition as citation changes the meanings of source and destination texts as well as generating new resonances between them. McGuckian also transgresses other underlying ground rules for lyric poems, such as relationships between grammatical structures and meanings (or other structures: her poems typically appear in orderly stanzas on the page but defy the ways of making meaning that stanzaic structures imply). Her insistence on privacy, to which she paradoxically draws attention in interviews and readings that claim outré and inconsistent sources for allusions, also subverts conventional relationships between 'inspiration' and work. As the poem 'The Time Before You' asserts,

> The secret of movement
> Is not the secret itself
> But the movement
> Of there being a secret. (*On Ballycastle Beach*, p. 43)

In other words, McGuckian's radical poetics destabilise not only representations of space but the spatiality inherent in the lyric itself.[18]

To some degree, of course, these phenomena in Ní Chuilleanáin and McGuckian may be (and have been) explained in terms of second-wave feminism. Both poets came of age in association with this movement, and feminist re-imaginings are some of their major concerns. However, something is missed when Ní Chuilleanáin and McGuckian, as well as other poets of their generation like Nuala Ní Dhomhnaill or Eavan Boland, are read too exclusively through the lenses of Anglo-American, British, or continental feminisms. There is a sense of something escaping, some way in which the subject and the poem were not as tied down as we might have thought to begin with, or at least not in the same ways the critical models suggest. This something may be connected with the fact that these poets are Irish, from circumstances that, while varied, have led them to artistic responses to particular kinds of uneven globalisation (and thus its redefinitions of space and time).[19]

Thus, a sense of literary history (and my own position as a female critic who came of age feeling the last bit of spray from the second wave) is to some degree responsible for my interest in the two poets that will occupy me for the rest of this essay, who belong generationally to a time well after any second-wave moment. If poets who came of age during the women's movement in Ireland are doing something different with the subject, something that is not finally explained by their prominent feminisms, what about poets in mid-career such as Groarke and Morrissey? In the readings that follow, one motivating question concerns the implications of coming next – of being able in the field of contemporary Irish poetry by women to take a subject with a complex and potentially shifting relation to objective space, or indeed to lyrical structure, for granted. The practices of poets like Ní Chuilleanáin and McGuckian in particular are enabling forces for formal and ideational issues in Groarke and Morrissey.

Vona Groarke has been writing about the problem of dichotomising interior and exterior since her earliest volume, *Shale* and *Flight and Earlier Poems*, in poems like 'For the Unkept House'.[20] This is a deceptively simple lyric, consisting of five highly repetitive quatrains. The reader expecting a poem describing an interior space is immediately unsettled by the first stanza:

> Fill the bucket with water.
> Fill the coffin with stones.
> There's a full moon over the river
> and there's no going home. (*Flight*, p. 19)

We might hear a nod to Auden's 'O where are you going?' in the uneasy joining of ballad metre and an uncanny or even threatening tone. The entire poem is an injunction, alternating between imperative and indicative mood as if the second two lines in each stanza explain the command in the first two lines. A full moon reappears in every stanza, but it is unclear if the moon, or the unnamed person being ordered in the five quatrains to 'Fill', 'Make', 'Sweep', 'Break off', and 'Pick', is outside – from where 'there's no going home' or 'there's no going back' in the first two stanzas – or inside – from where 'there's no place to go' or 'there's no time to leave' in the last two stanzas. The places over which the moon is suspended, river, meadow, kitchen, gatepost, and threshold, feel as if they are a sequence. If so, some sense of movement is suggested towards increasingly liminal zones, from an exterior space ('over the river') to the centre of a house (its hearth, possibly in its kitchen) and then outwards again, or rather just to an edge:

> Pick the stones from the meadow.
> Pick the weeds from the grave.
> There's a full moon over the threshold
> and there's no time to leave. (*Flight*, p. 19)

Yet to posit a sequence seems to push things too far: the movement is only suggested, spatial form inside the rigid poetic form neither affirmed nor denied. Movement in time is also an issue with which the poem seems concerned but leaves unsolved, though the time of personal activity seems linked, in some unexplained way, with the 'natural' or elemental time suggested by the simple nouns: water, stones, moon, stars, dust, weeds. Seemingly purposeful activity is enjoined upon someone, yet the purpose is unclear: what, for example, will it avail both to 'Break off the branches that withered' and, in the next line, 'Break off the flowers that grow' (*Flight*, p. 19)?

The title 'The Unkept House' points to some of the questions raised by this little *unheimlich* lyric. Certainly, the poem takes for granted the problematic nature not only of order, in the sense that 'housekeeping' is about maintenance of a domestic space, but also of possession. If a house, or home, is not kept, it seems to ask, what is loosened or unleashed?

Groarke's second volume, *Other People's Houses*, published in 1999, is wholly centred on such questions about space and consciousness. As is obvious from a first glance at the Table of Contents, which reads like a list of sorts of houses or expressions with the word *house* in them (from

'Open House' to 'House-bound', 'House Wine', 'The Lighthouse', 'The Slaughterhouse', and even 'House Style'), the volume is thematically preoccupied with the ways in which people and things are imagined in terms of structured domestic spaces. I like to think of this as Groarke's Celtic Tiger volume, responding not only to her personal moment, a woman of home-buying age, when she was writing these poems, but also the moment when Ireland began to go house-mad. Some poems examine phenomena like housing estates and the buying of houses, rooms, or furniture. Many suggest, in a style that combines lightness of touch and a hint of orality, that neither houses nor the inhabitants of them are as solid as they might seem.

Consider, for example, the poem 'House Rules' (*Other People's Houses*, p. 12). The formal structure in this poem suggests haiku or at least a zen-like reflection in its six three-line stanzas, with a triple rhyme scheme, separated from each other by a repeating typographical ornament. The house, which is described in the meditative structures and white space on the page, turns out to be as much about the world beyond its structure as the structure itself. The poem begins comparing a solid physical base to a chess move, suggesting that intellectual and material 'rules' by which houses are measured or purposed are perhaps equally risky:

> The foundation is the opening gambit;
> what's added are storeys or rooms. But
> its premise is the open ground, unbuilt.
>
> * * *
>
> The walls are true, impregnable and straight.
> They break the rain, contain the family fight,
> cleave what's outside in, and inside out.
>
> (*Other People's Houses*, p. 12)

Each stanza ostensibly describes an architectural element – foundation, walls, windows, doors, floors, and roof – suggesting certainty and order. Yet, each stanza undercuts this sense with third terms. Walls, in a phrase that takes advantage of a word that Groarke has said she likes for its doubleness (meaning 'both to split or cause to split and to adhere. I like a word that can look two ways at once'), 'cleave what's outside in, and inside out' (*Other People's Houses*, p. 12).[21] Windows 'are transparent, yet what surfaces / is ... the stranger's dour face' (*Other People's Houses*, p. 12). The last stanza presents, in a suggestion again of sound logic, the roof:

The roof straddles the house.
Yet for all its confinement and poise,
it is, in turn, preoccupied with skies.
(*Other People's Houses*, p. 12)

This structure, which is simultaneously an intellectual and built topos, has as its 'premise' in the first stanza and its 'preoccupation' in the final stanza the 'open ground' and 'skies' of what is not a human construction at all.

This house is also the structure of poetry. The tight form of the poem on the page, with typographical breaks between the clean lines of stanzas (and we might recall that the term *stanza* is derived from the Italian word for standing or stopping place and room), suggests solidity and purpose, as if it can contain and order meaning since the house seems to enclose space and human activity. Yet the 'confinement and poise' of the poem on the page do not in fact confine, or define, its linguistic space. Nor does the poem weigh or balance human experience, measure it out with *gravitas* or style, as suggested etymologically and connotatively by that unusual word *poise*. Instead, these house rules unmake rules: in the striking line at the end of the second stanza the outside and inside are cloven 'outside in' and 'inside out'. Similarly, the cognitive category of difference is itself opened into a different register by doors that are both 'points of entry and deliverance' and which 'look both ways at once'. Floors offer support but, in a lovely pun, 'subversively'. A 'stranger' surfaces at the windows in the centre of the poem, unsettling the mood and the solidity of the house, the inhabitants, the meaning of the ordinary impulse to live in houses, and art's ability to comprehend and express that meaning. Each stanza is not foursquare like right-angled rooms but comprised of three lines, as if one wall is open to the outside. (Groarke has suggested in spoken remarks about poetry that one of the most important aspects of reading is to pay attention to the white space on the page around the words: this poem, with what might be a final fourth line of every stanza replaced by a nonlinguistic symbol, repays such notice.) The neat division of space into interior and exterior, like the clean division of human beings into family and stranger, opens into an unknown. The rules by which the house of poetry operates include acute awareness of their own provisionality.

Groarke often describes a moment like this, when the expected sensation or perception or story turns inside out, as it were. In the synaesthetic climax of 'The Lighthouse' (*Other People's Houses*, pp. 34–5), one of the best-known poems in the volume, the triumph of rural electrification in Ireland proves the mixed blessing of heedless modernity. The poem turns attention from the public space to a private one, from the male-gendered village centre and speeches by the parish priest to a kitchen in which three women rest after their day's work. The loud messianic rhetoric of official discourse – 'light in the darkness / and the dawn of a new age' – is set against the quiet 'music / of the room when it was still', the harshness of utopian cliché in opposition to the light touch of a nonverbal present:

> the rustle of the fire in the grate;
> the single held note of a teaspoon
> from which the knitting needles took their cue;
> the steady flutter of the carriage clock
> that kept their breath in check.
>
> (*Other People's Houses*, p. 34)

A meta-narrative at which the poem hints, in the opening line ('I heard her tell the story another way') and the second stanza ('She told it / so we would listen ...'), suggests history and the evocation of space (*Other People's Houses*, p. 34). The poem is alert to the ironies of a house perceived as comfort by the breathing creatures within it becoming isolated by the very technology that connects it to a modern electric grid, leaving history for a vague 'new' no-time and a space transformed into what Marc Augé calls a 'non-place', a node on a filament flung from an urban centre.[22] Thus,

> ... in the length of time
> it took to turn a switch and to make light
> of their house, three women saw themselves
> stranded in a room that was nothing like
> their own, with pockmarked walls
> and ceiling stains, its cobwebs and its grime:
> their house undone and silenced
> by the clamour of new light.
>
> (*Other People's Houses*, pp. 34–5)

It might be argued that all poetry finds the new in the ordinary, that this may even be its defining characteristic. Groarke, perhaps because of the freedom allowed her by her generational ability not to have to dismantle the master's house in the same ways her predecessors did, does not so much undo the 'I' as allow this revelatory moment to shift the experiencing self in a more traditional manner than Ní Chuilleanáin or McGuckian might have done (we could argue that the effect here is something like Keats' 'negative capability').

But Groarke is doing something else too, and it is this other effect that interests me. The poet's voice is not effaced into the experience, her agency subsumed into structure, inside displaced into outside. Nor does it master the experience, transforming it into poetic power. Something else is happening, a sign of which is the punning quality of the end of the poem, in which a structure is 'undone' by technology as a switched-on light 'make[s] light' of the house it illuminates – as well as by the surprise of the synaesthesia, in which light can 'clamour' and a house be 'silenced' by it. A hint of humour on the part of the poet's voice reminds the reader of the distance and agency that occupy this space as well as the helplessness and victimisation (like a rape, the invasion of electric light leaves the women 'undone' and 'silenced'). After all, the *mise-en-scène* crucially has this story being made, voiced, and passed on to the poet, as if the connections forged in time and space by women across generations in Ireland survive, even if they are changed by such reality-altering events.

Groarke's poetry is almost always singular, narrated by an 'I', but that 'I' seems intent on allowing into itself the motility of the world it encounters. In her 2009 collection, this lightness of touch, of self and world in mutual relation, is symbolised by 'spindrift', a word used in several poems and also for the title of the volume.[23] Near the end, the title poem, in forty-five sections, is a haiku-like series of short evocations, or maybe eco-cations, that work less like consciousness acting upon nature and more like a voice aiming for the lightness of sea foam, a little spray over the page. These moments may form themselves into the shape of compassionate relation: 'Spindrift' is dedicated to Groarke's children. A two-line poem entitled 'House Style' suggests the possibility of lyric as response to the question of what humans build for their habitation. The poem never mentions houses except in the punning title, but it suggests (in the image of eyes, in the exploded chiasmus of the three generations, as well as in the pun) that awareness of time as well as human connections structure a poetic space that allows something to be built that does not at the same time destroy:

> When my grandmother looked into my mother's eyes
> she saw what I see in my daughter's. (*Spindrift*, p. 46)

A similar gesture is made visually by the portrait of the author on the cover of Groarke's memoir/essay about frames and framing, *Four Sides Full*.[24]

The portrait presents the back of the author's head: the poet facing away from the viewer/reader in a square of golden colour, dark hair and exposed neck over black cowl-necked garment. What we look at is not the author posing for public viewing but something seen by a daughter's eyes, since Groarke's daughter Eve O'Callaghan made the painting. The book is itself such a portrait, revealing self by suggesting that autobiographical writer and readers are both watching something else entirely:

> Though scarcely a confessional poet I write about my life. Impossible not to, really, since it's what puzzles me most. The lyric voice permits me to acknowledge that, when I write about frames, I may also be writing about my life and, conversely, though I write about what looks like my life I might as well write about any object that is both discrete and amenable, cordial and solitary. Much as any person is. Much as a frame tends to be.[25]

Like Groarke, Sinéad Morrissey might seem an unusual choice of poet to address in terms of aesthetic response to environmental issues. She is for the most part an urban poet. Her 2009 volume *Through the Square Window* contains a number of poems that register the transformations of pregnancy and giving birth, and witnessing the development of a young child. Like Groarke's *Other People's Houses*, the aptly titled collection *Through the Square Window* draws attention to the ambivalences of houses and built space in terms of what they enclose, keep outside or in (or fail to), and with what consequences. Like Groarke, Morrissey is highly alert to questions of form and aesthetics, and like Groarke, the consciousness that is expressed in her poetry is both grounded in intimate space and able to take as given the claims of postmodern as well as late-feminist discourse. Morrissey attends to the political and aesthetic stakes of what is on one side of a window or other limit, and what is outside, as well as the liminal space of the window itself. To quote from another poet from Belfast, Morrissey is unusually likely to ponder what it means that 'There is more than glass between the snow and the huge roses'.[26]

Morrissey's poem 'The Invitation' begins almost as if alluding to MacNeice's 'Snow': 'You think you're safe? You think all this can stay? / The solid success of a high-banked fire, a February at bay / beyond the window?' (*Through the Square Window*, p. 33). The three-part poem advises the 'You' it prods with the direct addresses that start the two questions in the first line to make a leap from the familiar into somewhere else. The poet's puckish voice narrates the journey in the first two sections. The recommended jump begins with noticing 'the fault-line under the armchair ... a hairline crack' and then (as if the 'hairline' were a 'hareline' and we were in a scene from *Alice in Wonderland*), by means of close attention to the 'emptying grace' of afternoon light, into 'A hole, a portal' through which the 'you' is told to 'Jump' (*Through the Square Window*, p. 33). In the second section, 'you' will fall down a 'lift- / shaft' or 'rabbit-hole or well' and find 'Circles within circles' and a mysterious landscape (*Through the Square Window*, p. 34). This place, where items occur without context, a farmyard, perhaps a building, a statue of Narcissus, hints at a psychosexual surrealism but is crucially different in that it is impersonal, less redolent of a journey into the interior space of the subconscious and more 'absolute black' – a state that, riddlingly, 'can have a blacker heart ... lodged within its centre' (*Through the Square Window*, p. 34). This location is there, although neither exterior nor interior but elsewhere, and also elsewhen, as it were. 'You' must travel there by taking 'light's sure paradoxes with you', finding the place precise but unknowable ('A nineteenth-century farmyard. The intimation of a building.'), the time equally so ('Perhaps it's morning – what light there is is surely compromised / – or dusk') (*Through the Square Window*, p. 34). This poem's Alice finds by her armchair travel an awareness of a world that is active and other, 'darkness turned autonomous, in love with its own wild deft / capacity / to take light's definition of each working day and render it senseless' (*Through the Square Window*, p. 34).

'The Invitation' is dedicated 'for/after' the contemporary German-Northern Irish artist Benjamin de Burca, who produces witty visual engagements with traditional representation. For example, a group of nine paintings entitled *The Journey's End*, mounted in a group show in the Belfast Golden Thread Gallery in 2006, borrowed from modernist collage as well as postmodern pastiche in canvases that cut out, painted over, and rearranged elements from reproductions of older works, inserting blank white or black space and geometrical frames or holes into familiar images. In her review of the show, Slavka Sverakova describes the canvases:

> In one painting, oblong composition is split into white and black strips through which protrudes a tree, roof, road, cottage, bush, boys at a well, hat and some plants from the obliterated image. Drawing with white pen covers most of another image, allowing cows, a bridge and two figures to stay as remnants of the reproduced image. Men in hats are silhouetted by smooth white paint. A group wears masks. A large, nightmarish moonlit landscape has details that may or may not

> be left over from the 'original' reproduction. A horse is painted over by a skeleton in white. Pale blue almost masks over a Dutch landscape, with a windmill and dancing peasants. Scenes redolent of happy compositions, now separated from their context, are foregrounded by suppression of the rest into an abstract field of one hue.[27]

The playful titles of two solo shows imply de Burca's interest in decoupling binaries like old and new, reproduction and original, familiar detail and empty space, in spatial and temporal terms: *The Trouble with Context* (2009) and *Things Will Always Be the Same, Again* (2007). His art does not negate the forms, but it does insist on denaturing context and identity (that entity created by performance and repetition). Noticing the qualities that this poem shares with the visual art it honours and adapts allows us to note again that Morrissey's seeming surrealism or postmodern pastiche actually creates the possibilities for political engagement, although that engagement occurs with a world that is nonetheless insisted upon as ungraspable.

The method for remaining in the state of productive irresolution required by this poem (and perhaps also the art that inspired it) involves the seeming contradiction of owning or being responsible to only the openness of light and sky outside the windows: 'The single thing to catch / ... is the light. That wintry, five o'clock light. Its emptying grace' (*Through the Square Window*, p. 33). 'You' can carry only one bag on this flight: 'Take light's sure paradoxes with you. Jump' (*Through the Square Window*, p. 33). Like any responsible advisor, the voice names herself in the third section of the triptych, which begins, 'Who am I? You've met me twice before' (*Through the Square Window*, p. 35). The two embodiments of a 'tricksterish deity' were encountered in statues of a fox in a Shinto shrine and a Cupid in a Dutch museum, and the wild god is the knowledge of permanent consequences: 'I am what cannot be appeased / by wine, rice cakes, prayer, entreaty, I am what cannot be undone' (*Through the Square Window*, p. 35). With this naming, readers realise that the 'you' is the same as the 'I', and the poem is recommending that journeys into wider fields can only be undertaken by opening cracks in interior life. Heightened awareness will remain after the return journey:

> Yet something strange will stay. Remember Alice?
> *Toothscomb – Fury – Ambleweed – Frost –*
> Once broken through, a permeable membrane gives at the
> slightest touch. (*Through the Square Window*, p. 35)

The references to Lewis Carroll's Alice are typical of the poems in *Through the Square Window*, in many of which the words and stories of childhood highlight the strangeness of being human. Many of the poems play with a doubled consciousness of adult-in-child and child-in-adult, and the blurring of what might be mistakenly taken to be a bright distinction between two temporal or developmental states becomes a correlative to other invalid dichotomies, such as the one between interior and exterior space. Two striking poems that take this approach are 'The Clangers' (*Through the Square Window*, pp. 38–9), which retells plot lines from a children's television programme, and the concrete poem 'The Hanging Hare' (*Through the Square Window*, pp. 51–2), which hangs on the page like the dead animal that is the subject of a childhood memory. Both poems might be read as allegories, 'The Clangers' as a tale in which the adventures of small beings on another planet teach a lesson about how children (and adults) might regard 'curious and conciliatory' Otherness, very much including the Otherness of other species, here on this one (*Through the Square Window*, p. 38). 'The Hanging Hare' hearkens back to George Herbert, the figure of the crucified Christ replaced by the carcass of a hare. It might be analysed as an indirect condemnation of the violence during Morrissey's youth in Northern Ireland, a place hardened by 'the sunken playground, hacked-out stumps of trees / & blackened mattresses where a fire had been', or an examination of the fascination of martyrdom, with its sacralisation of an imagined purity that requires violent destruction to come into being (*Through the Square Window*, p. 52). The hare 'hung there / motionless, impaled upon its own / frozen direct line of perfect martyrdom' (*Through the Square Window*, p. 51).

However, neither poem is comfortably explained by such readings. 'The Hanging Hare', for example, points to the legitimate mystery (in the shortest lines of the hanging stanzas, across the stanza breaks) of the 'legacy // of unimpeded air … spaces / where a hare // might flourish' (*Through the Square Window*, p. 52). The 'perfect martyrdom' in the longest line of one stanza turns at mid-stanza and retreats to much less 'direct' lines (then breaks just where the skin does, at 'abdomen'): 'its eye an abyss, its foxglove fur / unblemished bar the torn / & matted abdomen // where the shot / went in' (*Through the Square Window*, p. 51). The poem's final pronouncement by the girl who was Morrissey could only be read unambiguously if the relation between girl and woman, speaker and poet, were clear. But the degree of irony on the page is unknowable: 'Look, I said to a ring of children / & pointed. *It's gorgeous*' (*Through the Square Window*, p. 52). Similarly, 'The

Clangers' ends with the poet sending the Clangers to bed, as she might send the child to whom she is reading the poem as a bedtime story. It is impossible to know to what the 'stretched and iridescent shawl / of stars and dark between your world and ours is beckoning ...' nor who is being called – Clangers, poet, child, or readers (*Through the Square Window*, p. 39). Perhaps the distinctions between the beings created through the miracle of stop-motion animation, teller of poetic tale, and auditors are anything but neat (what is happening when readers, for example, are in the position of children being sent to bed?).

The reason for the inadequacy of allegorical readings of these two poems brings me to a final point. Such readings assume that an exterior, social context may be understood by virtue of its being represented in the interior space of the poem. This essay has argued that Groarke and Morrissey participate in a lineage of contemporary Irish women poets in complicating the poetics and politics with which inner and outer realities are represented, and imagined to be related. Morrissey's poems, like those of Groarke, refuse such bipolar interpretation. By this refusal, they not only demonstrate the fallacious logic that would have art contribute to social betterment by depicting a ready-made world, a logic that still has a remarkable purchase in a number of arenas. More importantly, this poetry also suggests a different path of engagement, trying consistently to express that which cannot be perceived or articulated by starting, as it were, at home. The best thing to do, these poems suggest, may be to focus on the act of seeing. One of Morrissey's most interesting poems in *Through the Square Window* is almost pure description of a view of Belfast Lough; it is entitled 'A Device for Monitoring Brain Activity by Shining Light into the Pupil' (*Through the Square Window*, pp. 11–12). The poem 'Lighthouse', from the 2013 volume *Parallax*, blurs the poet's young son's and her own memories of childhood by means of a seeing lighthouse: on sleepless nights, it 'starts its own nightlong address / in fractured signalling; it blinks and bats / the swingball of its beam, then stands to catch, / then hurls it out again beyond its parallax' (*Parallax*, p. 188). The route into this valid engagement, as my readings have, I hope, suggested, begins on the level of form. In form, the lyric enacts a possibility of moving outside binaries of self and Other, subject and world, passive expression or active rhetoric, all of which cripple humankind from addressing grave and complex issues of our relationship to the environment in which we live.

That relationship is highly structured, in ways that outstrip human abilities to understand or change. Readers can, however, engage, an activity that is itself structured. Thus, to make a last observation, it is worth taking into account also the external form that is performativity in Groarke and Morrissey. For both of these poets, the setting or performance of poetry is a significant determinant of meaning. Besides insistence upon the orality of poetry in general, Groarke's 2008 translation of *Caoineadh Airt Uí Laoghaire* deepened her involvement with questions of oral composition as well as the negotiations of identity and style that accompany a new version of one of the most often-translated poems in the Irish canon.[28] Morrissey's distinctive reading style, including her memorisation of all her poems, is one of her trademarks. Nothing human is unstaged, both of these poets seem to suggest. The irony inherent in this position is related to the lightness of tone with which both approach their serious work. That irony is also, of course, related to deep structures of gender that are for both of these poets powerful enablers of art and (dare I say it) love.

CHAPTER 15

Alienated Subjects: Post-feminist control and contemporary Irish femininity

CLAIRE BRACKEN

'Yet, in Irish postmodernity women's liberation is an incomplete project.'
(Patricia Coughlan, 'Irish Literature and Feminism in Postmodernity')

Patricia Coughlan's incisive, influential, and indispensable scholarship on Irish literature is far-reaching, spanning as it does the twentieth and twenty-first centuries and incorporating ground-breaking and paradigm-shifting analyses of Samuel Beckett, Elizabeth Bowen, John Banville, Seamus Heaney, John Montague, Alice McDermott, Nuala Ní Dhomhnaill, Edna O'Brien, Peig Sayers, and Edmund Spenser, to name just a few. The astonishing range of her work is marked by an always inspirational scholarly rigour, as well as the beauties of a precise and formal literary criticism. My first encounter with her critical writing was as an undergraduate in UCD, when Moynagh Sullivan assigned '"Bog Queens": Representations of femininity in the poetry of Seamus Heaney and John Montague' as reading for a seminar on gender and poetry. The article stopped me in my tracks with its powerful unveiling of abstractions of femininity that rehearse problematic stereotypes. The ramifications of that crucial piece, which provides a powerful critique of the gendered and Oedipal dynamics of two canonical Irish poets (and by extension the field of Irish poetry more generally), are still felt to this day, as the article continues to make its indelible mark on the future spaces of Irish poetry criticism.

Coughlan's voice is vital to both critical discussions of the ways in which literature intervenes in the social and cultural changes of modern Ireland, and analyses of representations of women's bodies and the politics of gender and sexuality. I was lucky enough to have her as supervisor of my master's dissertation in UCC and she expertly guided me through a study of the poet Catherine Walsh, encouraging me to think through the complexities of contemporary feminism in our many enlivening conversations. Since then, her influence on my scholarship has been immense. In this piece, I would like to engage with her 2004 essay 'Irish Literature and Feminism in Postmodernity', connecting some of its ideas about contemporary feminism and women's writing to a specific analysis here of representations of post-feminism and girlhood in Celtic Tiger culture. Coughlan's excellent essay focuses on four novels from the early Tiger period, namely Anne Enright's *The Wig My Father Wore* (1995), Anne Haverty's *One Day as a Tiger* (1998), Eilís Ní Dhuibhne's *The Dancers Dancing* (1999), and Mary Morrissy's *The Pretender* (2000). It is a thoughtful and comprehensive analysis of gender politics and feminism in Irish postmodernity, examining the various playful performativities, inter-subjective connectivities, as well as alienated isolations, at stake in the representation of selfhood in these literary postmodern novels. In a comprehensive overview of the liberalisation of Irish society since the 1970s, Coughlan acknowledges the enabling effects of cultural change on the material realities of women's lives. However, she also reflects on how constructions of subjectivity in postmodernity, characterised by alienation and an 'internalized self-regulation', can be prohibitive to women's freedoms. Here, 'individualism is the dominant mode of selfhood' and 'the drive towards style, affluence, success, and a guise of self-sufficiency places new obligations – including, ironically, the obligation to achieve pleasure – upon increasingly isolated subjects'.[1] Drawing on the work of Zygmunt Bauman, Coughlan importantly charts a crucial contradiction of contemporary Ireland whereby postmodernity both liberates and isolates the self. This essay will reflect on the complexities of postmodernity that Coughlan's essay explores and analyses in such depth, engaging ideas of alienation with a focus on representations of girlhood and post-feminism in the Celtic Tiger period.

Critics note that the popular rhetoric of post-feminism, a discourse that subtly undercuts feminist relevancy by championing women's full equality in late-capitalist Irish society (primarily based on their capacity to consume), was prevalent during the hyper-consumerist years of the Tiger.[2] In what follows, I explore the problematic effects of this popular discourse on contemporary constructions of subjectivity, making explicit links with the Tiger's neo-liberal mindset. Coughlan's perceptive comments on 'internalized self-regulation' and isolation are particularly apt when considering the mechanics of post-feminist discourse in Tiger culture, where it operates 'dividually' (a term I draw from the philosophical work of Gilles Deleuze), instigating as it does both alienations within the self as well as fracturing affinities and shared connectivities between the self and others.

These alienations have particular resonances when considering representations of girlhood in the Tiger period, as late-capitalist postmodernity intensifies body image pressures for young women and increases problematic processes of objectification and sexualisation. This all happens in a culture that pathologises girlhood, a culture that – to quote Susan Cahill – inflicts a 'Tiger shaming and blaming of the girl as too closely tied to the commodity'.[3] The vulnerability of girls and their bodies in such a context is both temporally preceded and succeeded in pre- and post-Tiger eras respectively by such cases as Ann Lovett's tragic death (1984), the X case (1992), Slane Girl (2013), the Y case (2015), and the Belfast rape trial (2018). In an important essay, Cahill explores an upsurge in the post-Tiger period of dynamic feminist representations of 'teenage girls' voices, visibility, energy'.[4] While the Tiger period was not as fervently or intensely marked by activist feminist politics, this essay will unpack – through a harnessing of Coughlan's conceptualisations – both the dynamics of post-feminist alienating constructions of girlhood, as well as subtle representations of relational resistance in texts by women writers.

In what follows, I analyse two important Celtic Tiger texts that focus on teenage girlhood and stage a critique of the restrictive representative structures of post-feminism: Anne Enright's short story 'Natalie' (2008) and Leanne O'Sullivan's poetry collection *Waiting for My Clothes* (2004). Both 'Natalie' and *Waiting for My Clothes* present a complex portrayal of the vulnerabilities of girlhood and the damage alienation can inflict on the subjectivities of young women, revealing the contradiction at the centre of post-feminism itself: while it trades on conceptions of women's agency and individuality, its mechanisms of control rely on configurations of the feminine as an always-alienated and incomplete subject of desire. Enright's 'Natalie' presents dividuation as key to post-feminist control through a narrative about a teenage girl and her friendship with Natalie, who represents (from the protagonist's point of view) an 'ideal' and isolating construction of femininity. However, the story dislodges the primacy of the unattainable 'ideal' through a creative engagement with the mechanics of dividuation itself, revealing how desire can be re-routed towards connectivity. Similarly, Leanne O'Sullivan's collection explores relationality as a vital mode of subjectivity that is produced because of, rather than in spite of, alienating conditions. Detailing the traumas of an adolescent eating disorder, O'Sullivan's first poetry collection draws on gestational and inter-uterine imagery to describe ways of being in the world that are alienating and dividual. However, as the collection progresses these same images shift towards the connective. Thus, by configuring selves that are intensely situated, O'Sullivan stages wide-ranging ethical interrogations of contemporary Irish culture in the Celtic Tiger years, which include critical observations of twenty-first-century constructions of femininity, all the while re-establishing inter-subjective relationalities, what Coughlan terms 'personal ties and emotional connectedness', which can be lost in post-feminist times.[5] 'Natalie' and *Waiting for My Clothes* figure the vulnerabilities of those subjectivities, all the while rerouting dividual mechanics so as to offer complex, and at times more hopeful, representative imaginings for the configuration of girlhood(s) in postmodernity.

POST-FEMINISM AND CONTROL SOCIETIES

In their book on the subject, Stéphanie Genz and Benjamin A. Brabon locate post-feminism as a heterogeneous term, arguing that it has multiple contexts, and multiple meanings, and while in some arenas it holds negative and regressive connotations, in others it can be progressive.[6] They critique scholarship that presupposes 'a distinction between a more "authentic" and unadulterated feminism on the one hand and a suspect, usually commercialised postfeminism on the other'.[7] However, feminist critics make the point that it is exactly this type of commercialised post-feminism, articulated in popular venues such as media, advertising, film, television, and music, which dominates representations of femininity in the West.[8] While there is no doubt that other, perhaps more enabling, instances of post-feminism are in place in social and cultural life, the ideological power and reach of neo-liberal configurations of contemporary womanhood, which trade on the language of 'choice', cannot be discounted. In *The Aftermath of Feminism*, Angela McRobbie makes the point that women are 'offered a notional form of equality' that is 'concretized in education and employment, and through participation in consumer culture and civil society', with the resultant sense that there is a wealth of opportunity available in the free market economies of neo-liberalism: career choice, education choice, romantic and sexual choice, and (perhaps most crucially) consumer choice.[9] Differences in class, race, sexuality, gender identity, and age are completely elided in the popular post-feminist paradigm, which constructs an image of heteronormative, cisgendered, young, middle-class whiteness. A philosophy of individualism integrates the concept of 'woman as empowered consumer' with all other aspects of professional and personal life.[10]

If the primary figuration of popular post-feminism is the 'empowered' choosing (and consuming) woman, its dominant assumption is that the time of feminism has passed. McRobbie defines post-feminism as a type of ideological thinking fundamentally regressive in terms of women's rights, arguing that it operates to insidiously adopt feminism's language ('empowerment', 'choice') in a way that assumes its very demise, hence subtly undervaluing it as a mode of organisation. She identifies post-feminist discourse as being in the service of a patriarchal symbolic where

> The dynamics of regulation and control are less about what young women ought not to do, and more about what they can do ... What seems to underpin these practices is a suggestion that young women have now won the battle for equality, they have gained recognition as subjects worthy of governmental attention and this has replaced any need for the feminist critiques of ... hegemonic masculinities. This abandonment of critique of patriarchy is a requirement of the new sexual contract.[11]

McRobbie demonstrates the interconnection of two important elements of post-feminist discourse here: a rejection of feminism and the access of subjectivity. As Diane Negra puts it, there is an 'assumption that feminism has disturbed contemporary female subjectivity. Over and over again the post-feminist subject is represented as having lost herself but then (re) achieving stability through romance, de-aging, a makeover, by giving up paid work, or "by coming home".'[12] Supposed post-feminist agency is connected to the relinquishment of feminist thought, re-generating an 'essential' and coherent identity for women. As McRobbie clearly identifies, this functions as a mechanism of patriarchal restriction and control.

Reading post-feminism as a mechanism of control invites reflection on how bodies are managed and inscribed by the cultures in which they participate. Speaking of contemporary, late-capitalist society, philosopher Gilles Deleuze notes: 'We're in the midst of a general breakdown of all sites of confinement – prisons, hospitals, factories, school, the family ... *Control societies* are taking over from disciplinary societies.'[13] Deleuze claims that in late capitalism subjectivity functions in 'dividual' terms: divisions are constructed between self and others, as well as internally within the self. The neo-liberal cult of individuality, of being different and unique, ultimately separates. Deleuze identifies this as a mechanism of control generated by what he terms a system of modulation: 'controls are a *modulation*, like a self-transmuting molding continually changing from one point to the next, or like a sieve whose mesh varies from one point to another'.[14] Deleuze uses corporate business as an example of how modulation works, where wages are in constant processes of variation, and 'healthy competition' between employees structures the workplace.[15] As such, the self is constantly divided from others in late capitalism through a system predicated on shift and change, presenting alternative images to the subject so as to imbue them with a sense of 'unique' difference. But the contemporary self is not in any way a coherent entity. In control societies, nothing is ever complete; the fetish for individuality, which processes of modulation establish and maintain, paradoxically creates internal instability and epistemological instability, 'dividing each within'.[16] As such, late-capitalist modulation works to construct an experience of selfhood as fundamentally alienated and alone. In a required contradiction, ongoing processes of division from others (presented positively as generative of individuality) simultaneously work to configure divisions within the self: modulation maintains that the subject's work is never done, and the ongoing desire to be different creates an experience of selfhood that is split.

Reading this theoretical perspective into the discourse of post-feminism, it is evident how dividuation is a prevalent effect. Post-feminism, with its focus on self-fulfilment, appearance, and beauty, necessarily divides women from other women, as competition becomes a marked feature of inter-feminine relationships. Of course, there is nothing new in such a pitting of women against women; the 'virgin–whore' dichotomy has long structured the patriarchal gendering of the feminine.[17] However, what is different about rivalry between women in the Celtic Tiger context is that it is said to be *post*-feminist, coming after feminist movements of togetherness, which sought to connect rather than divide women. Deleuze's point that in 'control societies you never finish anything' also speaks to how internal dividuation works: constructions of post-feminist womanhood are never quite complete.[18] As a discourse, post-feminism has the effect of self-alienation: the goal of perfect and ideal beauty is always unrealisable, and the related emphases placed on professional and personal 'opportunity' sets up a marketplace of desire and endless 'choice'. Fulfilment, it seems, is a never fully attainable goal, but rather something that must be continuously sought. Thus, while post-feminism visibly trades on the concept of individualism and identity, which functions as a modulating and dividual mechanism of control, it also manages to restrict feminine potentiality by invisibly tapping into what psychoanalysis has identified at the core of psychic life: the absence of coherent identity as generated by never-ending processes of desire.[19]

'NATALIE' AND THE POST-FEMINIST IDEAL

Post-feminist narratives – whether in the form of beauty industry publications and advertising, gossip magazines, Hollywood romance films, or women's popular fiction – all function to promote competition. This structural arrangement is explored in Enright's story 'Natalie', from the 2008 collection *Taking Pictures*, which represents a fractured relationship between two young girls, what the narrator calls 'the tangle between Natalie and me'.[20] The unnamed narrator and the eponymous Natalie are both teenage girls (about seventeen years old) and the story tells of their complicated friendship, their relationships, and of how these relationships intersect with the illness of the mother of Natalie's boyfriend, Billy. Elke D'hoker makes the point that the narrator is distinguished in the text through the use of idiosyncratic youth-speech, which compounds the narrative's desire to tell a story about a girl on the cusp of becoming woman.[21] The story reflects on the past year, as the narrator wakes from sleep feeling unsettled (she initially thinks) by an argument she had had with Natalie on the phone. The narrative unspools in non-linear memory, as she thinks back trying to make sense of the 'tangle' of events at the recent Debs dance.[22]

In popular post-feminist discourses, the emphasis placed on self-fulfilment is invariably tied to appearance and the ability to shop, manicure, and beautify – and crucially, that it is a *choice* to do so. Thus, the most prevalent and popular form of post-feminist discourse embeds contemporary femininity in the consumerist domain, marking women's bodies and their appearance as primary. In the Celtic Tiger era, this fashioning and managing of the body became all the more insistent, evident in the marked increase in beauty salons and plastic surgery clinics, not to mention the availability of expensive designer fashions. Natalie functions as the epitome of this, as she is consistently presented to the reader (via the narrator) in terms related to the grooming of her body. While the narrator is 'gabbling on about some day' getting her legs waxed, Natalie 'just does things', making decisions, such as for example getting her 'eyelashes dyed professionally' (p. 46; p. 42). She is determined, self-assured and confident, a clear representation of the post-feminist subject as constructed in the texts of popular culture. For the Debs she wears a white dress, which the narrator states is 'very Renée Zellweger' (p. 47). Natalie operates in terms of the 'ideal' feminine (the narrator states that she 'should be a star. When she grows up'), the image of perfection that women are encouraged to unrealistically aspire to in an age where practices of beautification are configured as markers of feminine activity, agency, and control (p. 41).

Natalie's investment in her body and appearance is constructed in the story in dividual terms: hers is a body that is in marked differentiation from the world around her. Post-feminist practices of grooming are presented in terms of separation. Natalie's nail polish (she is a '*Rouge Noir* sort of girl') does not flake or scrape, it 'stays put', maintaining itself as a distinguishable cover (p. 42). Moreover, the narrator notes that she doesn't have a 'single open pore' (p. 42). It seems that even the permeable membrane of skin is, in this body, impermeable to the outside world. On seeing the narrator dressed and ready for the dance, 'Natalie jigs up and down and screams, and she hugs me from four feet away, not to muss' (p. 48). This desire for impermeability can be linked to Natalie's aversion to relations of any kind, part of her continuous attempts to keep herself divided and separate from others. As the narrator notes: 'Because that is what Natalie is saying, isn't it? That we are alone. That there is no connection between me and her, or between Billy and me, or between any of us ... Between human beings' (p. 50).

If Natalie functions as symbol of the 'ideal' promoted by popular post-feminist discourses, then the nameless narrator is the subject of desire, encouraged to dividuate-to-perfection, while never feeling quite finished or complete in this regard. Enright's story interrogates just what that might mean. Throughout, the narrator repeatedly compares herself negatively to Natalie, highlighting how her attempts at performing femininity never quite live up to the standards set by her friend. Describing herself as 'the fat, jokey one with the flaking nail polish', she is 'on the strictest possible diet' (p. 42; p. 47). Moreover, the narrator identifies Natalie as an object of desire: 'I really admired her, that's all. I began to see how beautiful she is close up and I started asking her advice on chip-proof nail polish, even though these things don't interest me as much as I think they do' (p. 46). However, she never achieves the closeness to Natalie that she desires, as she is continually kept at a distance. Natalie's distance emphasises the control mechanisms functioning within post-feminist discourse, as the narrator attempts to deploy the correct passwords ('chip-proof nail polish') so as to get closer to her.

The story opens: 'So Natalie put me straight', figuring Natalie's embodiment of post-feminism as a heteronormative one. Moreover, the story's critique of gender normativity is implied through the narrator's attempt to reconstruct her boyfriend's rigid masculinity – offering him hand cream and recommending he use hand soap – something that he resists (p. 43; p. 47). As identified, Natalie is an object of desire for the narrator throughout and the story registers the possibilities of her queer desire: 'Apart from anything else, it's so *gay* – this trailer fantasy I had of me and Natalie swapping mascara, and spraying each other's hair and fixing the boy's ties', with the pejorative construction of 'gay' quickly dissipating, as the narrator notes 'it isn't hairspray that makes you gay, it's sex' ... 'and I don't even like hairspray' (p. 50). The structuring principle of dividuation is that systems of control require ongoing enactments of dividuation, which contributes to the presentation of Natalie as an object of unattainable desire within a heteronormative frame.[23] Furthermore, the narrator's statement, 'even though these things don't interest me as much as I think they do', signals her own self as a divided one, constantly splitting her position as an epistemological, knowing subject.

However, the narrator ultimately rejects this model of separation and embraces a sense of self that values connectivity, unsettles post-feminist dividuation, and opens up space for inter-subjective relations between others, especially other women. Enright herself states in interview that 'the girl ... is highly connected and obviously Natalie isn't and that is a problem and question for her'.[24] Her desire for connection signals a resistance to dividuation and this takes the form of a literal embodied reaction. For example, the narrator's experience of incoherence, of not being quite complete or perfect enough, is signalled through the motif of nail painting: 'You can tell by the way the stuff jumps off me that I don't really mean it' (p. 36). The painting of the nail can be read as a dividual process, which marks and separates the body from the world around it. However, the image of 'polish' jumping off the liminal site of the nail signals an interesting resistance to complete division. The narrator's desire for connection works while in the very process of dividuation, highlighted even more given that she does not 'really mean it'. Furthermore, the narrator's attempts to dress her body up in beauty (with consumer coverings that will mark her distinction from the world) are actually performed from the space of connection itself. Trying to find a dress for the Debs dance, she brings her little sister into town: 'Between us, we solve everything with a sub-Westwood, sub-goth bustier and my mother's long silk skirt, and a gorgeous second-hand – or should I say vintage – lamé shawl' (p. 47). The use of the word 'between' here signals the possibility of connection as dividuation is processed. In a sense, it highlights the multiple places from which dividuation comes, the multiple possibilities which are dividing, via systems of control. Interestingly, what is constructed most clearly here is a connective multiplicity of feminine relationships – mother and sister are part of this process along with the narrator, as connectivity and dividuation combine in this creative configuration. Thus, the post-feminist separation of women, of 'sisters', is not just refused, but reworked, in Enright's story.

Coughlan's perceptive readings of Enright's novels *The Wig My Father Wore* and *The Pleasure of Eliza Lynch* identifies inter-subjectivity as a thematic concern, integral to the ethical fibres of both texts.[25] 'Natalie' continues such an interest, as the narrator refigures alienation as a structuring principle of selfhood. It is her desire for connections of multiplicity – the messiness of love, desire, and care – that changes her focus in the story, as she recognises the need for mutual affinity and togetherness, emotion and the empathy of affect: 'And I think that Billy's mother will live or die whether or not we get in a fizz. So I say *fizz away*. You might as well play it as it feels, *Natalie*' (p. 50). Natalie's aversion to 'fizz' constitutes an aversion to any form of embodied leaking or 'muss' – emotive or physical (p. 48). The narrator's body, however, is constructed in a 'muss' and 'fizz'. She wakes up in a 'sweat' and realises, at the end of the story, that what woke her was a memory of 'the sheets':

> It was the sheets. When I lay down, just for a second, on Mr and Mrs Casey's moss-green sheets. Before the dance, when I was all dolled up in my silk skirt, and I pushed my hands along them and put my cheek against the dark cotton, just for a second. It was the smell of those sheets – cool, unwashed; like something I really wanted, going stale. That is what woke me up. (p. 48)

The imagery demonstrates the narrator's desire for connection, and this is again articulated from the space of dividuation. It is 'before the dance' and she is all 'dolled up', yet she decides to lie down on the sheets and allow her body the 'muss' of sensation and embodied 'smell'. The smell of the 'unwashed' sheets points towards bodily remnants, the excretions, and leakings of the permeable body. This can be linked to the mother – the bed belongs to Billy's mother and the fear of her death pervades the narrative.

Essentially, what wakes the narrator up is her desire for the multiplicity of embodied inter-generational (Billy's mother, the narrator's mother) and cross-generational (the narrator's sister) relationships between women which are cancelled out in dividual mechanisms of control.[26] It is in this way that dividuation is disrupted from within. 'Natalie' is not suggesting an *a priori* truth or unity to the feminine self, nor is the story attempting to perform a utopian move of freedom from the reality of systems of control. Rather, it is identifying the positive potential of desiring connection that can be found in the process of dividuation, thus reading post-feminist discourse against itself, and opening up inter-subjective configurations for the feminine. The story's ending, where the narrator articulates a desire for 'something I really wanted, going stale' refers at once to the multiplicity of desires for relationships the narrative has marked as waning: for her boyfriend, for Billy, for Billy's dying mother, and – most importantly – for Natalie. The representations of these desires provide a new affective marker of relationality that Enright's story constructs in resistance to the dominant heteronormative post-feminist narrative for girls.

EMBODIED RELATIONALITY IN LEANNE O'SULLIVAN'S *WAITING FOR MY CLOTHES*

Relationality is also a key feature of Leanne O'Sullivan's poetry collection *Waiting for My Clothes*.[27] O'Sullivan has four collections of poetry published to date, with *Waiting for My Clothes* being the first, published in 2004 when O'Sullivan was twenty-one years of age.[28] Throughout this collection, the poems' speaker reflects on growing up as a young woman in Ireland, confronting the debilitating and traumatic experiences of an eating disorder head-on. In an insightful analysis of the collection, Luz Mar González-Arias notes how Eavan Boland's poem 'Anorexic', with its religious themes and undertones, can be traced as a crucial influence.[29] Moreover, she identifies an important theme to be a 'critique of the oppressive beauty myth that imprisons Western women'.[30] This is something powerfully articulated in the poem 'A Thing of Beauty':

> We become sculptors. Beauty is the shape of love.
> A skeleton as prone to worship as a Goddess
> Is by many called beautiful, or worse,
> a hunger that teaches power.
> We look; she's gone. Brutally perfect. (p. 26)

Constructions of 'perfect' 'beauty' here are marked by an absence of self ('We look; she's gone') that is most extreme in terms of its alienating effects. In her discussion of gender constructions in twenty-first-century Ireland, Debbie Ging notes how the intensification and rampant proliferation of consumerism, and of accompanying beauty fantasies, start early with 'the blatant sexualisation of girlhood in child-directed advertising'.[31] *Waiting for My Clothes* provides a poetic account of a young girl growing up in this context: the alienations, anxieties, and the traumas, in addition to the powers of healing.[32]

Like Enright's story 'Natalie', O'Sullivan engages a particular configuration of selfhood that runs throughout the poetry, which is one of embodied relationality – a type of 'productive inter-subjectivity' – that Coughlan notes as an alternative to the alienations of postmodernity.[33] In this collection, which focuses thematically on bodily denial and denigration, images of the embodied self in connection, in conjunction, in engagement, permeate. One particular image of embodied relationality (figuring in over twenty poems) is that of gestation, both in terms of inter-uterine experience and pregnancy. In her positive review of the collection, Belinda McKeon astutely observes the 'theme of the womb'.[34] Variously constructed, there are configurations of the speaker as pregnant, as foetus, and as pregnant-foetus. The representation of selfhood in these terms is the embodied site through which the poems' speaker negotiates her surrounding personal and societal worlds, her complex position as both twenty-first-century young woman and poet.

Psychological studies have identified how an 'internalization of sociocultural standards of beauty mediated the links of sexual objectification experiences to body surveillance, body shame, and eating disorder symptoms'.[35] One of the most powerful poems in the collection, 'Mirror', captures this:

> The image grew there,
> just as a child would grow,
> a private hope in that tunnel skin
> of my mind. I saw I existed.
> I saw two where there should
> have only been one. Divided, the image
> climbed into my head
> and that foetus flooded my guilt, until nothing explained
> my life better than these clothes falling to the floor. (p. 16)

The speaker's eating disorder is imagined as a 'foetus' housed in her mind, an alienating parasite of dividuation, that separates the speaker into 'two where there should / have only been one'. Such negative forms of affect are powerfully traced throughout O'Sullivan's collection, signalling the ways that contemporary post-feminist ideology actively promotes women's bodily shame and self-hatred through a 'broad promotional rhetoric' of 'bodily perfectionism'.[36] 'Mirror' reflects this process, as the speaker experiences 'the image' of such perfectionism climbing into her 'head', with the post-feminist imaginary operating as a Lacanian mirror of alienation. This alienation is compounded as the poem progresses, as the speaker considers the internal division constructed by 'The skinny saint', 'the beautiful bitch': 'Then she took my real eyes / and made them hers. / I could barely name myself. / I wear black, because black / is what she wants to see'. The devastating loss of self that is being described here – much more intense than the narrator's reflections in 'Natalie' – is compounded in the poem's final lines: 'Woman, I know you not'. And this traumatic experience is refracted through gestational imagery. This imagery correlates the sense of being two with a dividuated, doubled self of alienation, which marks the subject's experience with anorexia and bulimia throughout the collection.[37]

Incorporation is a key image in O'Sullivan's construction of alienated selfhood. In 'Mirror', the dividuated 'image' is incorporated into the 'mind' and the speaker affectively constructs this in terms of a 'foetus that flooded my guilt'. In another poem, 'Famine', a young woman who 'sits at the dinner table' refusing food imagines her stomach to be 'swelling / with the heat like bread'. She 'folds her arms over the guilt that is filling her' (p. 14). In the action of folding her arms, the subject of the poem is withdrawing from others into herself, an isolating gesture of dividuation. The affective incorporation of guilt, rather than food, is again imagined in terms of a pregnancy, the 'swelling' stomach which becomes a marker of shame. In her reading of Anne Enright's *The Wig My Father Wore*, Coughlan notes how 'Enright finds an inspired language for this whole underlying anxiety about incorporation', which she observes is an anxiety about loss of self.[38] This is a similar feature of O'Sullivan's poetry, where experiencing a loss of selfhood in 'Mirror' and 'Famine' is figuratively represented as an unwanted pregnancy in a time when abortion was still unavailable to women in Ireland.[39] The incorporated foetus figuratively operates as a mechanism of infiltrating sexual and gendered post-feminist ideologies that alienate the self from others and parasitically disturb the subject's sense of self.

Simultaneously, however, gestation imagery is fostered in O'Sullivan's collection as a means to move beyond this alienation and establish connections and inter-subjective ties.[40] Like in 'Natalie', where the dividuated space becomes retranslated as a connective one, O'Sullivan's collection reworks the connective possibilities of the gestation metaphor. Many of the poems, the later ones especially, reveal a receptive and connected openness to others, particularly family members: brother, sister, mother, and father. In 'The Journey', her sister asks, 'Where does the baby go? ... I said it grows behind your tummy, in your womb' (p. 54). The speaker then watches a metamorphosis occur, as she 'took it in', 'the light fibres being spun behind her tummy' and then 'curled up'. Inhabiting both pregnant space and foetal curling, her sister is at that moment processing the idea of being-two, while the condition of being in-transit is emphasised in their figuration on a moving train. By infusing connective selfhood with a moving form of existence, the poem marks the possibility of change in a poetic dialogue that connects women and sisters, rather than alienating them from each other.

This is also the theme of 'Graduating', the penultimate poem of the collection. The speaker is getting into a taxi, about to embark on a journey and its potential of change, as she turns to look at her mother. What follows is a meditation on the mother–daughter relationship that is refracted through 'this love of the womb' (p. 63). Leaving her mother, she considers what she has 'taught' her, which is a way of living-in-connection. She acknowledges 'the old topography of her belly where / I once lay my entire small body, / egg-curled in her palms. Or the nights I went to her as she wept, climbing / over her into the bed, without a word, / and drew her into my chest'. The speaker alternates between the positions of gestated and gestating, and it is the doubleness of this condition, of 'taking me into you', where the 'me' and 'you' are fluidly interchangeable, that is ultimately at stake in the collection's figuration of being in the world, a world that the speaker used to believe was 'flat' before 'my mother / taught me it was round' (p. 63).

Writing in 2007, Ivana Bacik makes the point that, in contrast to the feminist activism of the 1970s and '80s, no 'identifiable "women's movement" exists in Ireland' during the Tiger period, something that she attributes to 'the failure of younger women to identify themselves as feminist, and to their tendency to view feminist ideology as a relic of the past, outdated and irrelevant'.[41] The post-feminist co-optation of the language of 'choice' plays a large role in this process, since the presentation of women as having agency and independence is calculated to render feminism immaterial. As the analyses of 'Natalie' and Leanne O'Sullivan's poetry have shown, post-feminism works via complex processings of dividuation which are intensely alienating. However, if post-feminist thinking works to instil bodily self-doubt, even hatred, through a relentless inward introspection, Enright's 'Natalie' and O'Sullivan's poetry refigure this way of living in/with the body and these texts imagine a feminist perspective into post-feminist ideologies. Thus, they demonstrate how it is possible to subvert post-feminist practices of control, and reconfigure inter-subjectivity and relationality as paradigmatic markers of contemporary femininity.

Bacik's point about the absence of feminism during the Celtic Tiger period, in contrast to the 1970s and '80s, is echoed in other sources.[42] Moreover, it has become commonplace in Ireland to contrast the vibrant feminist and queer activisms of the post-Tiger era, which culminated in landslide referendum victories for both marriage equality and abortion, with the more subdued Tiger period, thus suggesting potential links between economic climates and political activism more generally. Needless to say, online activism has especially intensified during the post-Tiger era, with hashtags #ibelieveher (support for the woman at the centre of the Belfast rape trial), #wakingthefeminists (reaction to the marginalisation of women in Irish theatre), and #hometovote (people returning to support the marriage equality and abortion referendum) just a few examples of the active harnessing of digital spaces. However, while there is no doubt that feminist activism was not as visible in the Tiger period, activism was of course taking place, despite pronouncements to the contrary.[43] And while comparisons between the activisms of the recessionary periods of the 1970s and '80s and the post-Tiger period are necessary, valid, and fascinating, it is important to remember that the post-Tiger momentum also grew, directly, from the Tiger period. As work like that of Enright and O'Sullivan demonstrates, the alienating dividuations of neo-liberal post-feminism produce a desire for connection, a desire that can be said to explode in its intensity in the subsequent post-Tiger activisms. Moreover, their work provides a model of subtle post-feminist resistance, still vitally necessary in a contemporary moment in which, despite an intensification of feminist activism, post-feminist ideology persists. It is crucial that feminist voices, in all their differences, are heard and listened to so as to counter post-feminist discourses where control masquerades as choice in a system that touts 'ideals' of femininity that are both unrealisable and *unreal*. The prototypical and stereotypical post-feminist construction of the young, white, middle-class, heterosexual, cisgender woman does not even begin to speak to the diverse experiences of women in Ireland, and does nothing to address systemic gendered inequalities (particularly in terms of class, race, and sexuality) in Irish social life. For this reason then, continued and ongoing destabilisations of the mechanics of post-feminist discourse are needed, to quote Patricia Coughlan, in 'contemporary feminisms' that 'afford spaces of action and reflection within several disciplines, including psychoanalysis and literary criticism, as well as showing themselves in women's creative work'.[44]

Notes

(All online links are active at time of publication)

PREFACE

1 Patricia Coughlan (ed.), *Spenser and Ireland: An interdisciplinary perspective* (Cork: Cork University Press, 1990), pp. 46–74 (pp. 46–7).

2 Patricia Coughlan, '"Cheap and common animals": The English anatomy of Ireland in the seventeenth century', in Thomas Healy and Jonathan Sawday (eds), *Literature and the English Civil War* (Cambridge: Cambridge University Press, 1990), pp. 205–23 (p. 206).

3 Ibid., p. 206.

4 'Introduction', in Henry Burkhead, *A Tragedy of Cola's Furies or Lirenda's Miserie*, Angelina Lynch (ed.) (Dublin: Four Courts Press, 2009), pp. 9–32.

5 Patricia Coughlan. '"Fold over fold, inveterately convolv'd": Some aspects of Mangan's intertextuality', in Birgit Bramsback and Martin Croghan (eds), *Anglo-Irish and Irish Literature, vol. II (Acta Universitatis Upsaliensis)* (Uppsala: University of Uppsala, 1988), pp. 191–200 (p. 198).

6 Patricia Coughlan, '*Entre le galet et la mer*: Reading a Beckett poem between two languages', in Stephen Boyd and John C. Barnes (eds), *Cross Currents in European Literature* (Dublin: UCD Dept. of Italian, 1996), pp. 69–79 (p. 70).

7 Boyd and Barnes (eds), *Cross Currents*, preface.

8 Patricia Coughlan, '"The poetry is another pair of sleeves": Beckett, Ireland, and modernist lyric poetry', in Patricia Coughlan and Alex Davis (eds), *Modernism and Ireland: The poetry of the 1930s* (Cork: Cork University Press, 1995), pp. 173–208 (p. 176).

9 Patricia Coughlan, 'An Léiriú ar Shaol na mBan i dTéacsanna Dírbheathaisnéise Pheig Sayers' ('The Representation of Women's Lives in the Autobiographical Texts of Peig Sayers'), in Máire Ní Chéileachair (eag.), *Peig Sayers, Scéalaí, 1873–1958 (Ceiliúradh an Bhlascaoid 3)* (Baile Átha Cliath: Coiscéim, 1999), pp. 20–57 (p. 21).

10 Patricia Coughlan, 'Rereading Peig Sayers: Women's autobiography, social history, and narrative art', in Patricia Boyle Haberstroh and Christine St Peter (eds), *Opening the Field: Irish women, texts, and contexts* (Cork: Cork University Press, 2007), pp. 58–73 (p. 63).

11 Coughlan, 'An Léiriú ar Shaol na mBan', p. 21.

12 As Moynagh Sullivan notes, the 'complicated questions of gendered ambivalence raised in Coughlan's pioneering essay have since been largely ignored and instead commuted into quietist considerations of perplexed and interlinked Irish and poetic identity'; see Sullivan, 'Treachery of Wetness: Seamus Heaney, Irish studies, and the politics of parturition', *Irish Studies Review*, vol. 13, no. 4, 2005, pp. 451–68 (p. 452).

13 Patricia Coughlan, '"Bog Queens": The representation of femininity in the poetry of Seamus Heaney and John Montague', in David Cairns and Toni O'Brien Johnson (eds), *Gender in Irish Writing* (Milton Keynes: Open University Press, 1991), pp. 88–111 (p. 88).

14 Patricia Coughlan, '"The whole strange growth": Heaney, Orpheus, and women', *Irish Review*, vol. 35, 2007, pp. 25–45 (p. 30).

15 Patricia Coughlan, '"Killing the Bats": O'Brien, abjection, and the question of agency', in Kathryn Laing, Sinéad Mooney, and Maureen O'Connor (eds), *Edna O'Brien: New critical perspectives* (Cork: Cork University Press, 2006), pp. 171–95.

16 Ibid., p. 182.
17 See the April 2013 video interview with Pat Coughlan, accessible at http://www.youtube.com/watch?v=G_I7yiXhaiM
18 A revised and shortened version of this essay appeared in Claire Bracken and Susan Cahill (eds), *Anne Enright* (Dublin: Irish Academic Press, 2011), pp. 107–26.
19 Patricia Coughlan, '"Chipped and Tilted Marys": Two Irish poets in their contemporary contexts', in Britta Olinder and Werner Huber (eds), *Place and Memory in the New Ireland: Irish studies in Europe, vol. 2* (Trier: WVT Wissenschaftlicher Verlag Trier, 2009), pp. 71–100 (p. 74).
20 Coughlan, '"Chipped and Tilted Marys"', pp. 74–5.
21 See http://research.ucc.ie/profiles/A014/patcoughlan/Research
22 Coughlan, 'The Whole Strange Growth', p. 41.
23 Patricia Coughlan, '"For nothing can be sole or whole / That has not been rent": Torn motherhood in Máire Mhac an tSaoi's "Love has pitched his mansion ..."', in Louis de Paor (eag.), *Míorúilt an Pharóiste: Aistí ar fhilíocht Mháire Mhac an tSaoi* (Indreabhán, Conamara: Cló Iar-Chonnacht, 2015), pp. 41–62 (p. 61).
24 Patricia Coughlan, '"An t-éitheach; is an fíor? ...": A note on two late poems by Máire Mhac an tSaoi', in John Carey, Kevin Murray, and Caitríona Ó Dochartaigh (eds), *Sacred Histories: A festschrift for Maire Herbert* (Dublin: Four Courts Press, 2015), pp. 103–14 (p. 104).
25 Patricia Coughlan, 'The Poetry of Máire Mhac an tSaoi and the Indivisibility of Love', in Ailbhe Darcy and David Wheatley (eds), *A History of Irish Women's Poetry* (Cambridge: Cambridge University Press, 2021), pp. 255–69 (p. 266).
26 Patricia Coughlan, 'Hard Times and Sibling Songs: Sibling relations in contemporary Irish literature', in Luz Mar González-Arias (ed.), *National Identities and Imperfections in Contemporary Irish Literature* (London: Palgrave Macmillan, 2017), pp. 67–82.
27 Patricia Coughlan, 'Elizabeth Bowen', in Heather Ingman and Clíona Ó Gallchoir (eds), *A History of Modern Irish Women's Literature* (Cambridge: Cambridge University Press, 2018), pp. 204–26 (p. 209).
28 Patricia Coughlan, '"We get all sealed up": An essay in five deaths', *Irish University Review*, vol. 51, no. 1, 2021, pp. 9–23.

INTRODUCTION

1 On the rights of survivors and adoptees to their identity, see Catriona Crowe, 'The Commission and the Survivors', *The Dublin Review*, vol. 83, Summer 2021, pp. 60–83. See also Caelainn Hogan, *Republic of Shame* (London: Penguin, 2019).
2 On the attributes of this phase of feminism, see R. Clarke Snyder, 'What Is Third-Wave Feminism? A new direction essay', *Signs*, vol. 34, no. 1, 2008, pp. 175–96. For an overview in which she argues that the third wave of feminism is more politically adept and at ease with contradiction than post-feminism, see Sarah Gamble, 'Postfeminism', in Sarah Gamble (ed.), *The Routledge Companion to Feminism and Postfeminism* (London: Routledge, 2006), pp. 36–45.
3 For an assessment of this campaign, see Emer O'Toole, 'Waking the Feminists: Re-imagining the space of the national theatre in the era of the Celtic phoenix', *Literature, Interpretation, Theory*, vol. 28, no. 2, 2017, pp. 134–52.
4 See Ailbhe Darcy and David Wheatley (eds), *A History of Irish Women's Poetry* (Cambridge: Cambridge University Press, 2021), and Maria Johnston and Conor Linnie (eds), *Irish Women Poets Rediscovered: Readings in poetry from the eighteenth to twentieth century* (Cork: Cork University Press, 2021). On the exclusion of women poets in twentieth-century Irish literary history, see Anne Mulhall, '"The well-known, old, but still unbeaten track": Women

poets and Irish periodical culture in the mid-twentieth century', *Irish University Review*, Special Issue: Irish Poetry Cultures, 1930–1970, Lucy Collins (ed.), vol. 42, no. 1, 2012, pp. 32–52, and Kathy D'Arcy, 'Why Uncomplicated Recovery Isn't Enough: Rhoda Coghill, her letters, and the Fired! movement', *The Honest Ulsterman*, June 2020, n.p., https://humag.co/features/why-uncomplicated-recovery-isn-t-enough

5 For a keen-eyed analysis of the problems facing women writers from the 1950s onwards and the liberatory effect of second-wave feminism, see Éilís Ní Dhuibhne, 'Introduction', in Éilís Ní Dhuibhne (ed.), *Look! It's A Woman Writer: Irish literary feminisms, 1970–2020* (Dublin: Arlen House, 2021), pp. 13–33.

6 Linda Connolly, *The Irish Women's Movement: From revolution to devolution* (London: Palgrave, 2002), pp. 3–55.

7 Ailbhe Smyth, 'The Obvious Explanations of How Power Is Held and Exercised Over Women Are Very Basic', in Una Mullally (ed.), *Repeal the 8th* (London: Unbound, 2018), pp. 129–42 (p. 130).

8 Anne Enright, 'Call Yourself George: Gender representation in the Irish literary landscape', *No Authority: Writings from the laureateship* (Dublin: UCD Press, 2019), pp. 69–88.

9 Ibid., p. 86. On the pervasive assumption that women have less expertise than men, see Mary Ann Sieghardt, *The Authority Gap: Why women are still taken less seriously than men* (London: Doubleday, 2021).

10 Henri Lefebvre, *The Production of Space*, Donald Nicholson-Smith (trans.) (Oxford: Blackwell, 1991 [1974]), pp. 229–91.

11 See Tina O'Toole, *The Irish New Woman* (London: Palgrave Macmillan, 2013).

12 Samuel Beckett, 'First Love', in S.E. Gontarski (ed.), *The Complete Short Prose, 1929–1988* (New York: Grove Press, 1995), pp. 25–45 (p. 45).

13 Rita Felski, *Hooked: Art and attachment* (Chicago: University of Chicago Press, 2020), p. viii.

14 Ibid., p. x.

CHAPTER 1. *'Gente Blanca'* in the Green Atlantic: Selfhood, victimhood, whiteness, and early modern Ireland

1 Whitley Stokes (ed.), *The Saltair Na Rann: A collection of early middle Irish poems edited from Manuscript Rawlinson B502 in the Bodleian Library* (Oxford: Clarendon Press, 1883), quoted in John Carey, 'Ireland and the Antipodes: The heterodoxy of Virgil of Salzburg', in Jonathan M. Wooding (ed.), *The Otherworld Voyage in Early Irish Literature* (Dublin: Four Courts Press, 2000), pp. 133–6.

2 Patrick McKenna, 'Irish Migration to Argentina', in Patrick O'Sullivan (ed.), *Patterns of Migration* (Leicester: Leicester University Press, 1992), p. 62.

3 Patricia Coughlan, '"Without a blink of her lovely eye": *The Pleasure of Eliza Lynch* and visionary scepticism', *Irish University Review*, vol. 35, no. 2, 2005, pp. 349–73 (p. 350).

4 What we call the Irish overseas in the early modern period – 'exiles', 'migrants', 'refugees', 'aliens', 'immigrants' – carries its own ideological baggage. For a related discussion, see Mary Hickman, 'Migration and Diaspora', in Claire Connolly and Joe Cleary (eds), *The Cambridge Companion to Modern Irish Culture* (Cambridge: Cambridge University Press, 2005), pp. 117–36.

5 R.F. Foster, *The Irish Story: Telling tales and making it up in Ireland* (London: Allen Lane, 2001), pp. xv–xvi; Sara Ahmed, 'The Phenomenology of Whiteness', *Feminist Theory*, vol. 8, no. 149, 2007, pp. 149–68 (p. 150).

6 Colm Lennon, *Archbishop Richard Creagh of Armagh, 1523–1586: An Irish prisoner of conscience of the Tudor era* (Dublin: Four Courts Press, 2000), p. 9.

7 On the early-modern writing of selfhood, see Peter Burke, 'Representations of the Self from Petrarch to Descartes', and Jonathan Sawday, 'Self and Selfhood in the Seventeenth Century', in Roy Porter (ed.), *Rewriting the Self: Histories from the Renaissance to the present* (London: Routledge, 1997), pp. 17–28, pp. 29–48; Michael Schoenfeld, *Bodies and Selves in Early Modern England: Physiology and inwardness in Spenser, Shakespeare, Herbert, and Milton* (Cambridge: Cambridge University Press, 1999).

8 Francis Baker, *The Tremulous Private Body* (London: Methuen, 1984), p. 56.

9 'Padre Toma Pildi, irlandés de nación, hombre de muy madura edad y rara virtud', in Ruiz de Montoya, *La conquista espiritual del Paraguay*, Ernesto J.A. Maeder (ed.) (Asunción: El Lector, 1996 [1639]), p. 54. Unless otherwise stated, translations in the text are mine.

10 Aubrey Gwynn, 'Fr Thomas Fihilly, SJ (1549–1625)', in F.J. Sheed (ed.), *The Irish Way* (London: Sheed & Ward, 1922), p. 150.

11 Lennon, *Archbishop Creagh*, p. 74. Through the genealogical miasma, we glimpse Muiris and Domhnall Ó Fithcheallaigh, both Oxford graduates who, in the early sixteenth century, wrote, respectively, commentaries on Duns Scotus and a now lost 'Irish Annals'; see Séamus Ó hInnse, *Miscellaneous Irish Annals* (Dublin: Dublin Institute of Advanced Studies, 1947), p. ix. 'Carolus Fildius' and 'Philippus Fildius, pauper, Hibernus' appear on the register of the University of Louvain in April 1565; Brendan Jennings, 'Irish Students in the University of Louvain', in Sylvester O'Brien (ed.), *Measgra i gCuimhne Mhichíl Uí Chléirigh* (Dublin: Assisi Press, 1944), pp. 74–97 (p. 76).

12 Guillermo Furlong, *Tomás Fields S.J. y su 'Carta al Prepósito General' (1601)* (Buenos Aires: Casa Pardo, 1971), pp. 9–12 (p. 12). 'para evitar los peligros de la herejía', in Nicolás del Techo, *Historia de la Provincia del Paraguay de la Compañía de Jesús*, 3 vols, Manuel Serrano y Sanz (ed.) (Madrid: Uribe, 1897 [1673]), vol. 1, p. 181.

13 Furlong, *Tomás Fields*, p. 10.

14 Techo, *Historia de la Provincia*, vol. 1, p. 81.

15 Furlong, *Tomás Fields*, p. 12.

16 Brother Foley, *Records of the English Province*, 8 vols (London: 1882), vol. 7.i, p. 253.

17 Francisco Mateos includes it in his *Historia General de la Compañía de Jesús en la provincia del Perú*, 2 vols (Madrid: CSIC, 1944), vol. 2, pp. 433–7. Printed in Ramón J. Cárcano, *Primeras luchas entre la Iglesia y el estado en la gobernación de Tucumán* (Buenos Aires: El Ateneo, 1929), pp. 296–300.

18 Pedro Lozano, *Historia de la Compañía de Jesús en la provincia del Paraguay*, 2 vols (Madrid, 1754), vol. 1, p. 23.

19 Lozano, *Historia de la Compañía*, vol. 1, p. 25; Techo, *Historia de la Provincia*, vol. 1, p. 140.

20 Mateos, *Historia General*, vol. 2, p. 436.

21 Lozano, *Historia de la Compañía*, vol. 2, p. 27.

22 'Upon Appleton House', in *The Poems of Andrew Marvell*, Hugh MacDonald (ed.) (London: Routledge & Kegan Paul, 1952), ll. 771–2. On Patricia Coughlan's work on Marvell, see 'Classical Themes in the Non-Satiric Poetry of Andrew Marvell', unpublished PhD thesis, University of London, 1980.

23 Serafim Leite, *História da Companhia de Jesus no Brasil*, 2 vols (Lisboa: Livraria Portugália, 1938), vol. 1, p. 351.

24 'à los ultimos terminos del dominio de la Corona de Castilla'; Lozano, *Historia de la Compañía*, vol. 1, p. 61.

25 'un lago interminable, ò un pielago inmenso, desde donde solo se descubria agua y Cielo ... pantanos ... cienagas, en que se atollaban las mulas hasta la cabeza'; Lozano, *Historia de la Compañía*, vol. 1, pp. 250–1.

26 Lozano, *Historia de la Compañía*, vol. 1, p. 68.

27 'innumerables Infieles, puliendo lo bronco de sus genios, y domesticando lo cerril de sus naturales'; Lozano, *Historia de la Compañía*, vol. 1, p. 253.

28 Lozano, *Historia de la Compañía*, vol. 1, p. 59.

29 'hicieron un Catecismo breve en el cual se contenia sólo lo que es precisamente necessario para salvarse'; Lozano, *Historia de la Compañía*, vol. 1, p. 70.

30 Bartomeu Melià y Liane Maria Nagel, *Guaraníes y Jesuitas en tiempo de las misiones: una bibliografía didáctica* (Asunción: CEPAG, 1995), p. 160. See also Bartomeu Melià, *La lengua guaraní en el Paraguay colonial* (Asunción: CEPAG, 2003), pp. 74–7.

31 'retratos vivos de la muerte, o esqueletos animados'; Lozano, *Historia de la Compañía*, vol. 1, p. 59.

32 Coughlan, '"Without a blink"', p. 354, p. 357.

33 Furlong, *Tomás Fields*, p. 52; Leite, *História da Companhia*, vol. 1, p. 353.

34 Coughlan, '"Without a blink"', p. 357.

35 'Invictos Campeones à pelear las batallas del Señor ... como Soldados esforzados, que bolvian triunfantes, y ricos con los despojos de tanta Gentilidad rendida al Evangelio'; Lozano, *Historia de la Compañía*, vol. 1, p. 56, p. 63.

36 'como dos gotas de agua, en un campo seco'; 'dos Angeles venidos del Cielo ... volando de una parte à otra como Angeles veloces'; Lozano, *Historia de la Compañía*, vol. 1, p. 250, p. 254.

37 Lozano, *Historia de la Compañía*, vol. 1, p. 459.

38 Furlong, *Tomás Fields*, p. 70. Subsequent quotations are shown parenthetically in the text.

39 *A Facsimile Edition of the First English Translations of Miguel de Cervantes Saavedra's El Ingenioso Hidalgo Don Quixote de la Mancha (1605–1615)*, compiled and introduced by Anthony G. La Ró (Chapel Hill: University of North Carolina, 2002), p. 4. On Shelton and his translation, see Edwin B. Knowles, 'Thomas Shelton, Translator of *Don Quixote*', *Studies in the Renaissance*, vol. 5, 1958, pp. 164–75; J. George, 'Thomas Shelton, Translator, in 1612–14', *Bulletin of Hispanic Studies*, vol. 35, 1958, pp. 157–64. On other Hiberno-Cervantine connections, see Patricia Palmer, 'Flights of Fancy: Journeying into the miraculous', in David Finnegan, Éamonn Ó Ciardha, and Marie-Claire Peters (eds), *Flight of the Earls / Imeacht na nIarlaí* (Derry: Guildhall Press, 2010), pp. 75–83.

40 Coughlan, '"Without a blink"', p. 350.

41 Thomas G. Mathews (ed.), 'Memorial Autobiográfico de Bernardo O'Brien', *Caribbean Studies*, vol. 10, 1970, p. 91. All subsequent parenthetical references to the original come from this edition.

42 Joyce Lorimer (ed.), *English and Irish Settlement on the River Amazon, 1550–1646* (London: Hakluyt Society, 1989), p. 125; Lorimer translates O'Brien's petition; unless otherwise indicated, that is the one used here (referenced parenthetically).

43 Coughlan, '"Without a blink"', p. 362.

44 On that tradition, see Abby Wettan Kleinbaum, *The War against the Amazons* (New York: McGraw-Hill, 1983). On its early-modern English deployment, see Mary Villeponteaux, '"Not as women wonted be": Spenser's Amazon queen', in Julia M. Walker (ed.), *Dissing Elizabeth: Negative representations of Gloriana* (Durham: Duke University Press, 1998), pp. 209–25; on the colonial inflection of Spenser's Amazonphobia, see Patricia Palmer, *The Severed Head and the Grafted Tongue* (Cambridge: Cambridge University Press, 2013), pp. 88–9.

45 Coughlan, '"Without a blink"', p. 353.

46 The heretics, of course, had equipped him with beads, bracelets, knives, mirrors, whistles, and combs, rather than the *ex votos* carried, as we will see, by the Jesuits.

47 Nini Rogers suggests that the young Tupi was, in fact, O'Brien's slave. As she notes perceptively in another context, '[n]eedy and marginalised, [the Irish] could on occasion find themselves forced into unexpected equality with those whom, in more prosperous moments, they sought to dominate'; see Nini Rogers, *Ireland, Slavery, and Antislavery: 1612–1865* (Basingstoke and New York: Palgrave Macmillan, 2007), pp. 30–1.

48 Lozano, *Historia de la Compañía*, vol. 1, p. 57.
49 Ibid., vol. 1, p. 41.
50 Ibid., vol. 1, p. 52.
51 Cárcano, *Primeras luchas*, p. 297.
52 Mateos, *Historia General*, vol. 2, p. 436.
53 David Richardson and Filipa Ribeiro da Silva (eds), *Networks and Trans-Cultural Exchange: Slave trading in the South Atlantic, 1590–1867* (Leiden: Brill, 2015), p. 6.
54 The echo here is with Peter O'Neill and David Lloyd (eds), *The Black and Green Atlantic: Cross-currents of the African and Irish diasporas* (Basingstoke: Palgrave, 2009), though their metaphor of 'cross-currents' indicates their investment in finding 'overlap and cooperation' as much as 'competition and exploitation' in the nineteenth-century US context on which they focus, p. xvi.
55 Paul Gilroy, *The Black Atlantic: Modernity and double consciousness* (London: Verso, 1993), p. 17; Peter Linebaugh, 'All the Atlantic Mountains Shook', *Labour / Le Travailleur*, vol. 10, 1982, pp. 87–121 (p. 109).
56 Ernesto Muñoz Moraleda, *Fray Francisco de Vitoria: Primer obispo del Tucumán* (Buenos Aires: Junta de Historia Eclesiástica Argentina, 1998).
57 In addition to the cargo inventoried by the agent, the *San Antonio* carried significant quantities of episcopal contraband: there was Peruvian silverware hidden under bales of cassava and textiles. See Elena Phipps, Johanna Hecht, and Cristina Esteras Martín, *The Colonial Andes: Tapestries and silverwork, 1530–1830* (New York: Metropolitan Museum of Art, 2004), p. 212. Cárcano, *Primeras luchas*, p. 299.
58 In the event, the Peruvian authorities prevented the sale since Victoria did not have a trading licence; see José Luis Cortés López, *Esclavo y colono: Introducción y sociología de los negroafricanos en la América española del siglo XVI* (Salamanca: Universidad de Salamanca, 2004), p. 99.
59 Lozano, *Historia de la Compañía*, vol. 1, p. 66.
60 Furlong, *Tomás Fields*, p. 74.
61 Lozano, *Historia de la Compañía*, vol. 1, p. 57.
62 Lorimer, *English and Irish Settlement*, p. 303; text in square brackets translated from Matthews, 'Memorial Autobiográfico', p. 96.
63 Lorimer, *English and Irish Settlement*, p. 265, p. 303; Matthews, 'Memorial Autobiográfico', p. 91, p. 96. Lorimer's observation that the Irish were more 'efficient' at 'exploiting' Amazonia (p. 125) should be considered alongside accounts of Ireland's one *de facto* colony, Montserrat; see Donald Harman Akenson, *If the Irish Ran the World: Montserrat, 1630–1730* (Buffalo: McGill-Queen's University Press, 1997).
64 Cárcano, *Primeras luchas*, pp. 298–9.
65 I am deliberately echoing Gilroy's formulation, 'innocent modernism', in *Black Atlantic*, p. 44.
66 Matthews, 'Memorial Autobiográfico', p. 90, Lorimer, *English and Irish Settlement*, p. 264; I have rephrased Lorimer's translation slightly.
67 The oblique reference is to Noel Ignatiev, *How the Irish Became White* (London: Routledge, 2012).

CHAPTER 2. Transformational Transactions: Eochaidh Ó hEodhasa's poem (1603) to James I

1 Patricia Coughlan, '"Some secret scourge which by her shall come unto England": Ireland and alterity in Spenser', in Patricia Coughlan (ed.), *Spenser and Ireland: An interdisciplinary perspective* (Cork: Cork University Press, 1990), pp. 46–74 (p. 46); Patricia Coughlan,

'"Cheap and common animals": The English anatomy of Ireland in the seventeenth century', in Thomas F. Healy and Jonathan Sawday (eds), *Literature and the English Civil War* (Cambridge: Cambridge University Press, 1990), pp. 205–26 (p. 206).

2 Marc Caball, *Poets and Politics: Reaction and continuity in Irish poetry, 1558–1625* (Cork: Cork University Press in association with Field Day, 1998), p. 1.

3 Eleanor Knott (ed. and trans.), *The Bardic Poems of Tadhg Dall Ó Huiginn (1550–1591)*, 2 vols (London: Irish Texts Society, 1922–6), vol. I, p. xxxvii.

4 Mac Craith, 'Gaelic Ireland and the Renaissance', in Glanmor Williams and Robert Owen Jones (eds), *The Celts and the Renaissance: Tradition and innovation. Proceedings of the Eighth International Congress of Celtic Studies 1987* (Cardiff: University of Wales Press, 1990), pp. 57–88 (p. 60).

5 Louis de Paor, '*Do chor chúarta ar gcridhe:* Léamh ar dhán le hEochaidh Ó hEoghusa', *Saoi na hÉigse: aistí in ómós do Sheán Ó Tuama*, ed. Pádraigín Riggs, Breandán Ó Conchúir, and Seán Ó Coileáin (Baile Átha Cliath: An Clóchomhar, 2000), pp. 35–53 (p. 36).

6 Breandán Ó Buachalla, 'James Our True King: The ideology of Irish royalism in the seventeenth century', in D. George Boyce, Robert Eccleshall, and Vincent Geoghegan (eds), *Political Thought in Ireland Since the Seventeenth Century* (London: Routledge, 1993), pp. 7–35 (p. 8). On national consciousness, see Caball, *Poets and Politics*.

7 Like other Irish learned men, Ó hEodhasa applied for and received pardons, as well as significant grants of land in 1610–11 (Caball, 'Ó hEódhusa (O'Hussey)', *Dictionary of Irish Biography* (Cambridge: Cambridge University Press, 2010), https://www.dib.ie/biography/o-heodhusa-ohussey-eochaidh-a6374

8 Text edited and translated by Breatnach in 'Metamorphosis 1603: Dán le hEochaidh Ó hEódhasa', *Éigse*, vol. 17, 1977–8, pp. 169–80. This translation is employed herein with occasional modification and amplification; archaic spelling is retained, but macrons are silently transcribed as fadas. Breatnach dates the poem to soon after James I's accession, but its tone and internal references, as well as its possible association with the land grants Ó hEodhasa received, may suggest a date of between 1605 and 1610, as John Minahane proposes in 'Hiding Ireland', *The Dublin Review*, vol. 31, 25 March 2013. See https://www.drb.ie/essays/hiding-ireland

9 Breatnach, 'Metamorphosis', p. 169; Ó Buachalla, 'James Our True King', p. 9.

10 Ó Buachalla, 'James Our True King', p. 11.

11 Ibid., p. 13.

12 Ó Buachalla, 'Poetry and Politics in Early Modern Ireland', *Eighteenth-Century Ireland*, vol. 7, 1992, pp. 149–75 (p. 163).

13 For Mac an Bhaird's poem, which was probably written in the early 1580s on a visit to Scotland, see Lambert McKenna (ed. and trans.), *Aithdioghluim Dána*, 2 vols (Dublin: Irish Texts Society, 1939–40), vol. I, pp. 177–80 and vol. II, pp. 104–6.

14 Breatnach cites the Ovidian reference in 'Beag mhaireas do mhacraidh Ghaoidheal' ('Few live of the sons of the Gael'), 'Metamorphosis', pp. 169–70.

15 *Suirgeach sin a Éire ógh*, printed in Damian McManus and Eoghan Ó Raghallaigh (eds), *A Bardic Miscellany: Five hundred bardic poems from manuscripts in Irish and British libraries* (Dublin: Department of Irish, Trinity College Dublin, 2010), pp. 619–21.

16 Colin Burrow, 'Re-embodying Ovid: Renaissance afterlives', in Philip Hardie (ed.), *The Cambridge Companion to Ovid* (Cambridge: Cambridge University Press, 2002), pp. 301–19 (p. 301).

17 Perry Curtis, *The Making of Jacobean Culture: James I and the renegotiation of Elizabethan literary practice* (Cambridge: Cambridge University Press, 1997), p. 37.

18 See Curtis, *Making of Jacobean*, pp. 15–49.

19 James himself lauds Caesar Augustus in the *Basilikon Doron*, declaring that 'of all the Ethnick Emperors, or great Captaines that ever were, he hath farthest excelled, both in his practise, and in his precepts in martiall affairs'; in Neil Rhodes, Jennifer Richards, and Joseph Marshall (eds), *King James VI and I: Selected writings* (Aldershot: Ashgate, 2003), pp. 243–4. For James' biography, see Jenny Wormald, 'James VI and I (1566–1625)', *Oxford Dictionary of National Biography*, http://www.oxforddnb.com/view/article/14592

20 In Giraldian manner James called the highlanders 'all uterly barbares, without any sort of shew of civilitie' (Rhodes et al., *King James*, p. 222).

21 Coughlan, '"Cheap and common animals"', p. 207.

22 See Hiram Morgan, 'Giraldus Cambrensis and the Tudor Conquest of Ireland', in Hiram Morgan (ed.), *Political Ideology in Ireland, 1541–1641* (Dublin: Four Courts Press, 1999), pp. 22–44, and Sarah McKibben, 'In their "owne countre": Deriding and defending the early modern Irish nation after Gerald of Wales', *Eolas: The journal of the American Society of Irish Medieval Studies*, vol. 8, 2015, pp. 39–70. On violence, see David Edwards, 'Beyond Reform: Martial law and the Tudor reconquest of Ireland', *History Ireland*, vol. 5, no. 2, 1997, pp. 16–22, and David Edwards, 'Tudor Ireland: Anglicisation, mass killing and security', in Cathie Carmichael and Richard C. Maguire (eds), *The Routledge History of Genocide* (London: Routledge Press, 2015), pp. 23–37.

23 The poet's choice of author may also bespeak his consciousness of the contemporaneous English literary fashion for Ovid; see Burrow, 'Re-embodying Ovid', pp. 304–5. Mícheál Mac Craith demonstrates that the poet was '*au fait*' with the fashion for the answer-poem, perhaps having heard of it from patron Rudhraighe Ó Domhnaill, recently returned from London; see 'Fun and Games among the Jet Set: A glimpse of seventeenth-century Gaelic Ireland', in Josephy Falaky Nagy (ed.), *Memory and the Modern in Celtic Literatures, CSANA Yearbook 5* (Dublin: Four Courts Press, 2006), pp. 15–36 (p. 35).

24 On Spenser's obverse, settler-colonial use of Ovid to sanitise historical memory, see Patricia Coughlan, 'The Local Contexts of Mutabilitie's Plea', *Irish University Review*, vol. 26, no. 2, 1997, pp. 320–41 (p. 326).

25 See Wormald, 'James VI and I (1566–1625)'.

26 Heather James, 'Ovid and the Question of Politics in Early Modern England', in Yvonne Bruce (ed.), *Images of Matter: Essays on British literature of the middle ages and Renaissance. Proceedings of the Eighth Citadel Conference on Literature, Charleston, South Carolina, 2002* (Newark: University of Delaware Press, 2005), pp. 92–122 (p. 98); Burrow, 'Re-embodying Ovid', p. 301.

27 Ó hEodhasa's *Ionmholta malairt bhisigh* ('A change for the better is to be commended') reflects ironically on the shift in Irish poetic norms. For text and translation, see Osborn Bergin, *Irish Bardic Poetry*, compiled and edited by David Greene and Fergus Kelly (Dublin: Dublin Institute for Advanced Studies, 1984), pp. 127–9 and pp. 270–1.

28 Ó Buachalla, 'James Our True King', p. 7.

29 See, for instance, the 1600 poem lamenting Maguire's sufferings and celebrating his flamelike insurgency, *Fuar liom an adhaighsi dhÁodh* ('Too cold I deem this night for Hugh'), in Bergin, *Irish Bardic Poetry*, pp. 124–7, pp. 268–70.

30 Tadhg Ó Dúshláine, 'Dál na mBeach a Bharamhail: An dúlra mar dhlúth faoi inneach shaothar an fhile, Eochaidh Ó hEoghusa', *Léachtaí Cholm Cille*, vol. 11, 1980, pp. 97–119 (p. 107).

31 Clare Carroll, *Circe's Cup: Cultural transformations in early modern writing about Ireland* (Notre Dame: University of Notre Dame Press / Field Day, 2001), p. 100. Caball notes, 'Ó hEodhusa intimates obliquely that accelerated English expansionism has hardly been propitious from an Irish viewpoint' (*Poets and Politics*, p. 88).

32 On 'spiritual light' that banishes 'the darkness of ignorance' in a poem by another Ó hEodhasa, Giolla Brighde (aka Bonaventura), see Ailbhe Ó Corráin, *The Dark Cave and the Divine Light: Verses on the human condition by Giolla Brighde Ó hEódhasa* (Oslo: Institute for Comparative Research in Human Culture, Novus Press, 2016).

33 See David Edwards, 'The Escalation of Violence in Sixteenth-Century Ireland', in David Edwards, Pádraig Lenihan, and Clodagh Tait (eds), *Age of Atrocity: Violence and political conflict in early modern Ireland* (Dublin: Four Courts Press, 2007), pp. 34–78.

34 Peter McQuillan, *Native and Natural: Aspects of the concepts of 'right' and 'freedom' in Irish* (Cork: Cork University Press in association with Field Day, 2004), p. 196, and pp. 211–12.

35 Nicholas Canny, *Making Ireland British, 1580–1650* (Oxford: Oxford University Press, 2001), p. 181; Minahane suggests that the poet references Chichester's 1605 proclamation in 'Hiding Ireland' (n.p.).

36 See Peter Mack, *Elizabethan Rhetoric: Theory and practice* (Cambridge: Cambridge University Press, 2004), p. 170.

37 On the silencing of Irish voices in English representation and in criticism, see Patricia Palmer, *Language and Conquest in Early Modern Ireland: English Renaissance literature and Elizabethan imperial expansion* (Cambridge: Cambridge University Press, 2001), and 'Missing Bodies, Absent Bards: Spenser, Shakespeare, and a crisis in criticism', *English Literary Renaissance*, vol. 36, no. 3, 2006, pp. 376–95.

38 See Mícheál Mac Craith, 'The Political and Religious Thought of Florence Conry and Hugh McCaughwell', in Alan Ford and John McCafferty (eds), *The Origins of Sectarianism in Early Modern Ireland* (Cambridge: Cambridge University Press, 2006), pp. 183–202; and Carroll, *Circe's Cup*, pp. 124–34.

39 The dramatic image also foregrounds Ó hEodhasa's exquisite poetic decorum in employing grand classical figures particularly favoured by James, as in his poem 'The Furies', in *His Maiesties poeticall exercises at vacant hours* (Edinburgh: Printed by Robert Waldegraue, printer to the Kings Maiestie [1591]), n.p., https://quod.lib.umich.edu/e/eebo2/A04260.0001.001/1:11?rgn=div1;view=fulltext. I thank John Minahane for drawing my attention to this.

40 Carroll, *Circe's Cup*, 101.

41 Sarah McKibben, *Endangered Masculinities in Irish Poetry, 1540–1780* (Dublin: UCD Press, 2010), pp. 52–5.

42 See eDIL: Electronic Dictionary of the Irish Language, http://www.dil.ie

43 On this image, see Kenneth Olwig, *Landscape, Nature, and the Body Politic: From Britain's Renaissance to America's New World* (Madison: University of Wisconsin Press, 2002).

44 Discussed in McKibben, *Endangered Masculinities*, p. 23.

45 Of course, not all the Irish were rebellious, and Ó hEodhasa's reference to a collective 'anxiety' allows for this.

46 Canny, *Making Ireland British*, p. 181.

47 Ernest Renan, 'What Is a Nation?', Martin Thom (trans.), in Homi K. Bhabha (ed.), *Nation and Narration* (London: Routledge, 1990), pp. 8–22 (p. 11).

48 Adrian Hastings writes that nationalism 'arises chiefly where and when a particular ethnicity or nation feels itself threatened in regard to its own proper character, extent, or importance, either by external attack or by the state system of which it has hitherto formed a part' (*The Construction of Nationhood: Ethnicity, Religion, and Nationalism* [Cambridge: Cambridge University Press, 1997]), p. 4.

49 'Pobal' derives from the medieval Latin loanword signifying 'a people, tribe, nation' (See *eDIL: Electronic Dictionary of the Irish Language*, http://www.dil.ie, s.v. 'popul'). On 'pobal' and emergent concepts of nationalism, see Peter McQuillan, '"Nation" as *Pobal* in

Seventeenth-century Irish', *Early Modern Ireland: New sources, methods, and perspectives*, ed. Vincent P. Carey, Valerie McGowan-Doyle, and Sarah Covington (Milton: Routledge, 2019), pp. 113–29.

50 Coughlan, '"Some secret scourge"', p. 46.

51 'Transformation is an Elizabethan preoccupation', remarks Patricia Palmer, 'and, in a colonial context, transformation meant degeneration'; 'Irish [Gaelic] was ... transgressive and contagious and threatened the colonial self with defilement and transformation' (*Language and Conquest*, pp. 97–8).

52 Ó Buachalla, 'James Our True King', pp. 10–11.

53 From the 1599 dedicatory 'sonet' (See Rhodes et al., *King James*, p. 199).

54 James reminded his son in the *Basilikon Doron* that he was 'rather borne to *onus* [burden] than *honos* [honour]'; 'a lawfull good King' understood 'himselfe ordained for the people, having received from God a burthen of government, whereof he must be countable' (Rhodes et al., *King James*, p. 200, p. 218). In *The Trew Law of Free Monarchies*, first published anonymously in 1598 and reissued several times in London in 1603, James referred to 'the mutuall duetie, and alleageance betwixt a free and absolute *Monarche*, and his people' (Rhodes et al., *King James*, p. 260).

55 Bart Jaski, *Early Irish Kingship and Succession* (Dublin: Four Courts Press, 2000), p. 47.

56 Carroll, *Circe's Cup*, p. 101.

57 For instance, James urges his son: 'Use Justice, but with such moderation, as it turne not in Tyrannie: otherwaies *summum Jus* is *summa injuria*' [Law taken to extremes is extreme injustice] (Rhodes et al., *King James*, p. 240).

58 See James Stewart, 'How the Eagle Cools It: An apologue and its analogues', *Éigse*, vol. 25, 1991, pp. 165–72. James himself refers to the 'royall Egle' in 'The Furies'.

59 Philip O'Leary, 'Foreseeing Driver of an Old Chariot: Regal moderation in early Irish literature', *Cambridge Medieval Celtic Studies*, vol. 11, 1986, pp. 1–16; Peter McQuillan, 'Courtesy and Civility in Early Modern Irish Literature', XIV International Congress of Celtic Studies, Maynooth, 4 August 2011, conference presentation.

CHAPTER 3. The Ghost Comes to Town: Le Fanu and the urban gothic

1 Accounts of the form include Julia Briggs, *Night Visitors: The rise and fall of the English ghost story* (London: Faber, 1977); Jack Sullivan, *Elegant Nightmares: The English ghost story from Le Fanu to Blackwood* (Athens: Ohio University Press, 1978), and Andrew Smith, *The Ghost Story, 1840–1920* (Manchester: Manchester University Press, 2010). On the lingering power of gothic in the nineteenth century, see Deborah Lutz, 'Gothic Fictions in the Nineteenth Century', in John Kucich and Jenny Bourne Taylor (eds), *The Oxford History of the Novel in English. Vol. 3: The nineteenth-century novel, 1820–1880* (Oxford: Oxford University Press, 2011), pp. 76–89.

2 Patricia Coughlan, 'Doubles, Shadows, Sedan-Chairs and the Past: The ghost stories of J.S. Le Fanu', in M. Allen and A. Wilcox (eds), *Critical Approaches to Anglo-Irish Literature* (Gerrards Cross: Colin Smythe, 1989), pp. 17–39.

3 The classic account of his literary career is still W.J. McCormack's *Sheridan Le Fanu and Victorian Ireland* (Oxford: Clarendon Press, 1980).

4 'Death of Mr Lefanu', *Freeman's Journal*, 10 February 1873.

5 'The Great Dead of 1873', *Lloyd's Weekly Newspaper*, 4 January 1874.

6 The 'Invisible Prince' idea presumably began with the claim in his obituary in the *Freeman's Journal* that his 'handsome, even distinguished face was wholly missed from society' in the seven years before his death. But Mr and Miss Le Fanu (presumably the eldest, Eleanor, or Ellie) attended a reception at the chief secretary's lodge in January 1866; he returned from

a trip to Britain via Holyhead on September 1866; Mr and Miss Le Fanu were at a dinner given by the lord lieutenant and the marchioness of Abercorn in February 1868 (*Belfast News-Letter*, 14 February 1868); Miss Le Fanu appeared in various amateur theatricals in these years, though it is possible she had a chaperone other than her father; and Mr and Miss Le Fanu were at the Guards' Ball in February 1870. We can also assume that he attended his daughter Eleanor's marriage (21 December 1871) to Lieutenant Patrick Francis Robertson of the 92nd Gordon Highlanders at St Stephen's Church.

7 In the same paragraph in which McCormack claims he was called the 'Invisible Prince', he notes a considerable amount of social activity including 'Club dinners' up until 1869 (p. 197). As late as April 1871, when his health was in decline, McCormack notes that Le Fanu attended a dinner and musical evening (p. 269).

8 Victor Sage, *Le Fanu's Gothic: The rhetoric of darkness* (Houndmills: Palgrave Macmillan, 2004), p. 3.

9 Heather Ingman, *A History of the Irish Short Story* (Cambridge: Cambridge University Press, 2009), p. 41.

10 Those who like coincidences might note that in the same year that the trick-window locked-room mystery of *Uncle Silas* appears, Le Fanu's countryman Dion Boucicault was packing them in with *Arrah-na-Pogue*, in which the great sensation scene reveals Shaun escaping through a faulty prison window, and then, as the set swivels and sinks, shows him from the outside of the same prison, as he climbs the ivy-covered walls.

11 The character of Dr Martin Hesselius is introduced in the framing narrative to the 1869 version of 'Green Tea'. Presumably Le Fanu then saw the possibility of using Hesselius as a narrator to link the stories, old and new, that comprise *In a Glass Darkly*.

12 As the two texts are almost identical, the page references given here are from 'The Familiar', *In a Glass Darkly*, Robert Tracy (ed.) (Oxford: Oxford University Press, 2008), pp. 41–82.

13 Tracy, 'Introduction', *In a Glass Darkly*, pp. viii–xxviii (p. xvi).

14 See, for example, Tom Ferris, *Irish Railways: A new history* (Dublin: Gill & Macmillan, 2008), and Fergus Mulligan, *One Hundred and Fifty Years of Irish Railways* (Belfast: Appletree Press, 1983).

15 Ralph Roth and Marie Noëlle Polino, *The City and the Railway in Europe* (Aldershot: Ashgate, 2003), pp. 192–200.

16 Editorial, *Irish Times and Daily Advertiser*, 5 April 1864.

17 *Dublin Destroyed!, or, The Witches Cauldron of Railway Horror: A mysterious Shakespeareana, in one act* (Dublin: John Wiseheart, 1862). 'William Scribble' (William Smyth, 1813–78) was a comic actor, writer, and painter. I am grateful to Stephanie Rains for bringing his work to my attention.

18 See W.R. Le Fanu, *Seventy Years of Irish Life, Being Anecdotes and Reminiscences* (London: Edward Arnold, 1894), especially pp. 190–203 and pp. 277–8.

19 McCormack, *Sheridan Le Fanu and Victorian Ireland*, p. 121.

20 Editorial (no title), *Freeman's Journal*, 5 June 1868.

21 Page references are to the version of these stories in E.F. Bleiler (ed.), *Best Ghost Stories of J.S. Le Fanu* (New York: Dover, 1964), pp. 361–79 and pp. 419–30.

22 *Apartment Stories: City and home in nineteenth-century Paris and London* (Berkeley: University of California Press, 1999).

23 *Asmodeus; or, The Devil on Two Sticks*, Joseph Thomas (trans.) (London: Joseph Thomas, 1841), p. 20.

24 On the currency of the Asmodeus figures in urban sketches, see Tanya Agathocleous, *Urban Realism and the Cosmopolitan Imagination in the Nineteenth Century* (Cambridge: Cambridge University Press, 2011), p. 82.

25 Cited in Mulligan, *One Hundred and Fifty Years of Irish Railways*, p. 14.
26 'A Run on the Eastern Counties Railway', *Morning Chronicle*, Saturday, 5 October 1850.
27 References are to 'Green Tea', Tracy (ed.), *In a Glass Darkly*, pp. 5–40.
28 An early English-language reference describes a bet made by the duchess of Berri (*sic*) that she could travel from the Tuileries to the Bastille in an omnibus without being recognised. 'Mirror of Fashion', *Morning Chronicle*, 13 December 1828.
29 'On Saturday', *Morning Chronicle*, 6 July 1829.
30 According to Michael Corcoran there had been attempts to create a Dublin service as early as 1834, but these were quashed by legal intervention by the car-men. Corcoran suggests that this impasse continued until 1848, but the newspapers indicate that quite a few routes were operating successfully before then. See Corcoran, *Through Streets Broad and Narrow* (Leicester: Midland, 2000), p. 8. For an example of a clash between the various providers of horse-drawn transport, see, for example, 'Carriage Court – Yesterday', *Freeman's Journal*, 5 November 1846.
31 Frank Hall, *The Properest Thing to Do* (London: L'Enfant & Hodgkins, 1863).
32 Wilkie Collins, *Basil* (Oxford: Oxford University Press, 2005 [1852]), p. 29.
33 On the omnibus in Victorian art, see Christopher Wood, *Victorian Panorama: Paintings of Victorian life* (London: Faber & Faber, 1976), pp. 216–19.
34 'Omnibus Reform', *Punch*, 6 October 1860, p. 139.
35 McCormack, *Sheridan Le Fanu and Victorian Ireland*, p. 125.
36 Bram Stoker draws on this aspect of the story for his own tale of a haunted scholar, 'The Judge's House', which also leans heavily on Le Fanu's 'An Account of Some Strange Disturbances in Aungier Street'.
37 *The Railway Journey: The industrialization of time and space in the nineteenth century* (Berkeley: University of California Press, 1986 [1977]).
38 In *First Class* a young man and woman eye each other as her father sleeps in the corner of the railway carriage. A later version of *First Class*, dated 1855, and painted in response to criticisms of the vulgarity of the theme of the first, renders the original painting more innocent: the father is awake, and talking to the young man.
39 *Uncle Silas* (Oxford: Oxford University Press, 1989 [1864]), p. 390.
40 'The Room in the Dragon Volant', in Tracy (ed.), *In a Glass Darkly*, p. 151.
41 This same device is borrowed by M.E. Braddon for her story 'John Granger', *Belgravia Annual*, 1870, pp. 1–14 and, more recently, by Iain Banks for *The Crow Road* (London: Scribners, 1992).

CHAPTER 4. 'Very little to have been so long about': Pastoralism and William Morris in Yeats' *Poems, 1899–1905* and related writings

1 On the ill-fated *Edition de Luxe*, see: Richard J. Finneran, *Editing Yeats' Poems: A reconsideration* (Basingstoke: Macmillan, 1990), Chapter 1; and 'The Definitive Edition: A history of the final arrangements of Yeats's work', Appendix 6, in A. Norman Jeffares (ed.), *Yeats's Poems* (London: Macmillan, 1989), pp. 706–49.
2 *The Collected Letters of W.B. Yeats, IV, 1905–1907*, John Kelly and Ronald Schuchard (eds) (Oxford: Oxford University Press, 2005), pp. 115–16; see also p. 103.
3 See ibid., p. 65.
4 Ibid., p. 106. *Poems, 1899–1905* (London: A.H. Bullen, 1906) was priced 6*s*.; for Yeats' wish that the volume be affordable, see *The Collected Letters, IV*, pp. 207–8. *Poems: Second series* (London: A.H. Bullen, 1909) alters the arrangement of *Poems, 1899–1905* in positioning *In the Seven Woods*' two narrative poems, 'The Old Age of Queen Maeve' and 'Baile and Aillinn', before its lyric poems, the latter now solely identified as constituting the 1903 collection.

Among other differences between the two volumes, *Poems: Second series* concludes with the 1906 version of *The Shadowy Waters*, the text with which *Poems, 1899–1905* begins.

5 See David Holdeman, *Much Labouring: The texts and authors of Yeats's first modernist books* (Ann Arbor: University of Michigan Press, 1997), pp. 139–40.

6 On Gyles' cover design for *The Secret Rose*, see *The Secret Rose: Stories by W.B. Yeats. A Variorum Edition*, Warwick Gould, Phillip. L. Marcus, and Michael J. Sidnell (eds), 2nd edn (London: Macmillan, 1992), pp. 272–8, and references. The editors of the variorum *Secret Rose* draw attention to a passage Yeats added to 'Rosa Alchemica' – after its initial publication in *The Savoy* (1896), but which, on reflection, he chose to delete from the proofs of the 1897 collection – describing the bound manuscript of the history, doctrine, and symbolism of the Order of the Alchemical Rose: 'In the box was a book bound in vellum, and having *a rose-tree growing from an armed anatomy, and enclosing the faces of two lovers painted on the one side, to symbolize certainly the coming of beauty out of corruption, and probably much else*; and upon the other, the alchemical rose with many spears thrusting against it, but in vain, as was shown by the shattered points of those nearest' (*The Secret Rose*, p. 274). The correspondence between Gyles' design and the deleted words (italicised) and surrounding text has the effect of making *The Secret Rose* analogous to the occult work described therein: the stories, it is implied, are also to be read as secret doctrine. The 'spear' on the spine can also be identified with additions to the story made at proof stage: see *The Secret Rose*, p. 276. Gyles' artistic career, incidentally, had effectively ended in personal trauma with the turn of the century; see *The Collected Letters of W.B. Yeats, II: 1896–1900*, Warwick Gould, John Kelly, and Deirdre Toomey (eds) (Oxford: Oxford University Press, 1997), p. 682.

7 Yeats, *Poems, 1899–1905*, p. xi, p. xii; *The Variorum Edition of the Poems of W.B. Yeats*, Peter Allt and Russell K. Alspach (eds), 3rd imprint (London: Macmillan, 1966), p. 849 (hereafter cited as *VP*).

8 Yeats, *Poems, 1899–1905*, p. xiii, p. 277; *VP*, p. 850.

9 Harold Bloom, *Yeats* (New York: Oxford University Press, 1970), p. 162, p. 161, p. 163, p. 140.

10 Michael J. Sidnell, George P. Mayhew, and David R. Clark, *Druid Craft: The writing of 'The Shadowy Waters'* (Dublin: Dolmen, 1972 [1971]), p. 305.

11 As Richard Cave observes, the 1907 'Acting Version' of the poem is equally 'root[ed] ... firmly in the symbolist tradition as it was manifest in nineteenth-century theatre'. W.B. Yeats, *Selected Plays*, Richard Cave (ed.) (Harmondsworth: Penguin, 1997), p. 274.

12 Yeats, *Poems, 1899–1905*, p. 141; *VP*, p. 198; the Dun Emer version is identical with the later printing.

13 See the letter to *The Times* objecting to the excavations signed by Yeats, Douglas Hyde and George Moore: *The Collected Letters of W.B. Yeats, III: 1901–1904*, John Kelly and Ronald Schuchard (eds) (Oxford: Oxford University Press, 1994), pp. 208–9.

14 Terence Brown, *The Life of W.B. Yeats* (Dublin: Gill & Macmillan, 1999), p. 145.

15 Helen Vendler, *Our Secret Discipline: Yeats and lyric form* (Oxford: Oxford University Press, 2007), p. 158.

16 *The Works of Virgil. Literally Translated into English Prose, with Notes, by Davidson*, new revised edition, by Theodore Alois Buckley (London: George Bell & Sons, 1875), p. 3; cf. *Ecl.* 1.53–8. See Edward O'Shea, *A Descriptive Catalog of W.B. Yeats's Library* (New York: Garland, 1985), no. 2203. On Yeats' knowledge of Virgil (and classical literature and culture in general), see Brian Arkins, *Builders of my Soul: Greek and Roman themes in Yeats* (Gerrards Cross: Colin Smythe, 1990). Arkins (p. 19) observes that, of Virgil's works, the *Eclogues* most influenced Yeats, especially the fourth.

17 Warwick Gould, 'Lips and Ships, Peers and Tears: *Lacrimae Rerum* and tragic joy', in Warwick Gould (ed.), *The Living Stream: Yeats Annual, 18. A Special Issue: Essays in memory*

of A. Norman Jeffares (London: Open Book, 2013), p. 17. See *The Collected Letters, III*, p. 148. 'Edmund Spenser' was collected in *The Cutting of an Agate* (New York: Macmillan Co., 1912), pp. 213–55.

18 W.B. Yeats, *Early Essays*, Richard J. Finneran and George Bornstein (eds) (New York: Scribner, 2007), p. 268.

19 Vendler, *Our Secret Discipline*, p. 159.

20 Jonathan Allison, 'Galway: Coole and Ballylee', in David Holdeman and Ben Levitas (eds), *W.B. Yeats in Context* (Cambridge: Cambridge University Press, 2010), pp. 99–100.

21 Holdeman, *Much Labouring*, p. 62. See, for example, W.B. Yeats, *Autobiographies*, William H. O'Donnell and Douglas N. Archibald (eds) (New York: Scribner, 1999), pp. 280–2 and 484 ff. n. For a detailed account of 'The Vision of the Archer', see the editors' commentary in *The Collected Letters, II*, pp. 658–63. This account, however, draws no explicit connection between the 'vision' and the 'Great Archer' of the 1902 poem: 'WBY used Archer material in some drafts of *The Shadowy Waters*, but did not call upon it again in his poetry until "Parnell's Funeral"' (*The Collected Letters, II*, p. 662).

22 *The Works of Virgil ... by Davidson*, p. 31; cf. *Ecl.* 10.58–60.

23 *The Works of Virgil ... by Davidson* p. 30; cf. *Ecl.* 10.23.

24 The acceptance of which by the *Fortnightly Review* he mentions to Lady Gregory in a letter of 14 December 1901. *The Collected Letters, III*, p. 136. The essay was eventually published in March 1903 and collected in *Ideas of Good and Evil* (London: A.H. Bullen, 1903), pp. 70–89.

25 Yeats, *Early Essays*, p. 42.

26 Ibid., pp. 43–4.

27 *The Collected Works of William Morris*, with introductions by May Morris. Vol. XXI: *The Sundering Flood; Unfinished Romances* (London, 1914; facsimile edn, Cambridge: Cambridge University Press, 2012), pp. 26–7.

28 Yeats, *Poems, 1899–1905*, p. 163; *VP*, p. 199; the Dun Emer version differs only in incidentals. 'The Arrow' was probably written at around the same time as 'In the Seven Woods'.

29 The rhyming couplets of 'The Arrow', moreover, are thrown into relief owing to the unusual 'trueness' of the rhyming words. In Vendler's formulation, 'In the phenomenally extensive charts of language in Yeats's brain, words differing from each other by only one letter (or two) held adjacent places on some great linguistic wheel.' (Vendler, *Our Secret Discipline*, p. 109.)

30 *The Poetical Works of William B. Yeats. I: Lyrical Poems* (New York: Macmillan Co., 1906), p. 280; *VP*, pp. 199–200.

31 See *Autobiographies*, pp. 130–3 and W.B. Yeats, *Memoirs: Autobiography – first draft, journal*, Denis Donoghue (ed.) (London: Macmillan, 1972), p. 20.

32 Holdeman, *Much Labouring*, p. 34. On Dun Emer, see, besides Holdeman, *Much Labouring*, Chapter 1, Liam Miller, *The Dun Emer Press, Later the Cuala Press* (Dublin: Dolmen, 1973), *passim*; and William M. Murphy, *Family Secrets: William Butler Yeats and his relatives* (Dublin: Gill & Macmillan, 1995), Chapter 3.

33 Holdeman, *Much Labouring*, p. 43. Holdeman argues that the narrative and lyric section of the 1903 edition of *In the Seven Woods* possesses a 'comic movement', 'forcing the aristocratic, individualistic, superhuman perfection that it initially describes to stand in tension with a vision of popular, collective, human experience'. Holdeman, *Much Labouring*, p. 30; and cf. pp. 110–11.

34 W.B. Yeats, *In the Seven Woods: Being poems chiefly of the Irish heroic age* (Dundrum: Dun Emer, 1903), p. 23, pp. 24–5, under the title 'The Rider from the North / From the play The Country of the Young'; in *Poems, 1899–1905*, the poem reverts to the title 'The Happy Townland', under which it was first published in the *Weekly Critical Review* (4 June 1903); *VP*, pp. 213–16.

35 Morris, *The Sundering Flood*, pp. 171, 167.
36 *The Collected Letters, III*, p. 346.
37 Yeats, *Poems, 1899–1905*, p. 171; *VP*, p. 205.
38 'Baile and Aillinn' was written in July 1901 and published in July 1902 in the *Monthly Review*: see *The Collected Letters, III*, p. 87; pp. 90–1. *Early Essays*, p. 274.
39 Florence S. Boos, general introduction, *The Earthly Paradise, William Morris Archive*, http://morrisedition.lib.uiowa.edu/general-introduction-to-the-earthly-paradise.
40 Yeats, *Poems, 1899–1905*, p. 156; *VP*, p. 192.
41 Yeats, *Poems, 1899–1905*, pp. 146–8; *VP*, pp. 184–6.
42 See Anna MacBride and A. Norman Jeffares (eds), *The Gonne–Yeats Letters, 1893–1938: Always your friend* (London: Hutchinson, 1992), p. 488; and Mairéad Carew, *Tara and the Ark of the Covenant: A search for the Ark of the Covenant by British Israelites on the Hill of Tara (1899–1902)* (Dublin: Royal Irish Academy, 2003), p. 79.
43 Yeats, *Poems, 1899–1905*, p. 149; *VP*, p. 186.
44 'The Old Age of Queen Maeve' was written in August 1902 and published in *Fortnightly Review*, April 1903: see *The Collected Letters, III*, p. 222.
45 *The Collected Letters, III*, p. 313. See *Autobiographies*, p. 136, for Yeats' account of his growing dissatisfaction with Morris' socialism. On Morris and Nietzsche in Yeats' thought at this period, see Frances Nesbitt Oppel, *Mask and Tragedy: Yeats and Nietzsche, 1902–1910* (Charlottesville: University Press of Virginia, 1987), pp. 115–16.
46 See Tom Villis, *Reaction and the Avant-garde: The revolt against liberal democracy in early twentieth-century Britain* (London: I.B. Tauris, 2006), p. 128.
47 Yeats, *Poems, 1899–1905*, p. 181; *VP*, p. 216.
48 Yeats, *Early Essays*, pp. 43–4; emphasis added.
49 'Between its formation in 1845 and its effective end as a dividend-paying proposition in 1872, Devon Great Consols yielded a net income of £317,927 for the Morris family as a whole. Of this, William Morris Snr, his wife, and children, received £270,624. William Morris earned £8,803. By the standards of the day, these were fabulous sums. When the source of this wealth began to run dry, Morris, together with other members of his family, received a severe financial jolt': Charles Harvey and Jon Press, 'The City and Mining Enterprise: The making of the Morris family fortune', *Journal of William Morris Studies*, vol. 9, no. 1, 1990, p. 12. As Harvey and Press note (p. 3), the source of Morris' income is not accorded detailed treatment in J.W. Mackail's biography, *The Life of William Morris* (London: Longmans, Green, 1899) (and neither, incidentally, is Morris' socialism).
50 *Poems, 1899–1905*, p. 170; *VP*, p. 204.
51 Yeats, *Early Essays*, p. 48.
52 See A. Norman Jeffares and A.S. Knowland, *A Commentary on The Collected Plays of W.B. Yeats* (London: Macmillan, 1975), p. 48.
53 Yeats, *Poems, 1899–1905*, p. 203.

CHAPTER 5. *Fianaise Lom* / Bare Witness: Surrealism and life writing in the work of Celia de Fréine

1 Drago Jančar, 'To Write in the Language of a Small Nation', Tamara M. Sobon (trans.), *Poetry Ireland Review*, vol. 79, 2004, pp. 39–43 (p. 41).
2 English translations created by the author of this essay of titles of, or excerpts from, Irish-language poems by Celia de Fréine, are presented within square brackets throughout. Otherwise, all English-language titles and excerpts are de Fréine's own and are presented in a manner designed to reflect her dual-language poetic practice.

3 Celia de Fréine, *Faoi Chabáistí is Ríonacha* (Indreabhán: Cló Iar-Chonnacht, 2001); Lewis Carroll, 'The Walrus and the Carpenter' (*Through the Looking-Glass*), in *Alice in Wonderland*, 2nd edn, Donald J. Gray (ed.) (New York: W.W. Norton, 1992 [1871]), pp. 140–4 (p. 142).
4 Celia de Fréine, *Scarecrows at Newtownards* (Dublin: Scotus Press, 2005).
5 *Fiacha Fola* (Indreabhán: Cló Iar-Chonnacht, 2004) and *Blood Debts* (Dublin: Scotus Press, 2014).
6 *imram / odyssey* (Galway: Arlen House, 2010) and *Aibítir Aoise / Alphabet of an Age* (Galway: Arlen House, 2011).
7 See: Patricia Coughlan, 'An Léiriú ar Shaol na mBan i dTéacsanna Dírbheathaisnéise Pheig Sayers', in Máire Ní Chéilleachair (eag.), *Peig Sayers, Scéalaí, 1873–1958 (Ceiliúradh an Bhlascaoid 3)* (Baile Átha Cliath: Coiscéim, 1999), pp. 20–57; 'Rereading Peig Sayers: Women's autobiography, social history, and narrative art', in Patricia Boyle Haberstroh and Christine St Peter (eds), *Opening the Field: Irish women, texts, and contexts* (Cork: Cork University Press, 2007), pp. 58–73; '"For nothing can be sole or whole / That has not been rent": Torn motherhood in Máire Mhac an tSaoi's "Love has pitched his mansion ..."', in Louis de Paor (eag.), *Míorúilt an Pharóiste: Aistí ar fhilíocht Mháire Mhac an tSaoi* (Indreabhán: Cló Iar-Chonnacht, 2014), pp. 41–63; '"An t-éitheach; is an fíor?" A note on two late poems by Máire Mhac an tSaoi', in John Carey, Kevin Murray, and Caitríona Ó Dochartaigh (eds), *Sacred Histories: A festschrift for Máire Herbert* (Dublin: Four Courts Press, 2015), pp. 103–14; 'The Poetry of Máire Mhac an tSaoi and the Indivisibility of Love', in Ailbhe Darcy and David Wheatley (eds), *A History of Irish Women's Poetry* (Cambridge: Cambridge University Press, 2021), pp. 255–69.
8 Luz Mar González-Arias, 'Impossible Returns: The trope of the soldier in Celia de Fréine's poetry', *Irish University Review*, vol. 48, no. 2, 2018, pp. 188–201 (p. 189).
9 Nuala Ní Dhomhnaill, *Pharaoh's Daughter* (Loughcrew, Oldcastle: Gallery Press, 2007), p. 155.
10 Nuala Ní Dhomhnaill, *Feis* (Maigh Nuad: An Sagart, 1991), p. 128.
11 Susan Sontag, *Illness as Metaphor and AIDS and Its Metaphors* (New York: Picador, 2001).
12 Elaine Scarry, *The Body in Pain: The making and unmaking of the world* (Oxford: Oxford University Press, 1985).
13 Ibid., p. 6.
14 Ibid.
15 Marina Tsvetayeva, *Selected Poems of Marina Tsvetayeva*, Elaine Feinstein (ed.) (London: Hutchinson, 1986), p. 2, and Nuala Ní Dhomhnaill, *Féar Suaithinseach* (Maigh Nuad: An Sagart, 1984), pp. 17–18.
16 Máire Mhac an tSaoi, 'Réamhrá', in Celia de Fréine, *Fiacha Fola*, pp. 9–12 (p. 12). Máire Mhac an tSaoi, 'Foreword', in Celia de Fréine, *Blood Debts*, pp. 11–17 (p. 15).
17 Luz Mar González-Arias, 'Afterword: Blood that seeps deep into the earth', in Celia de Fréine, *Blood Debts*, pp. 101–7 (p. 106).
18 Lia Mills, 'In Full Voice: Celia de Fréine in conversation with Lia Mills', *Irish University Review*, vol. 48, no. 2, 2018, pp. 169–82 (p. 169).
19 Ibid., p. 170
20 Ibid., p. 171.
21 Ibid., p. 172.

CHAPTER 6. Siblings: Juliet Mitchell and Malory's *Morte Darthur*

1 Sir Thomas Malory, *Le Morte Darthur*, P.J.C. Field (ed.), 2 vols (Cambridge: D.S. Brewer, 2013), 50.2–3. Subsequent references to Malory will be to volume 1 of this edition.
2 Juliet Mitchell, *Siblings: Sex and violence* (Cambridge: Polity Press, 2003). Except where otherwise specified, all subsequent references to Mitchell will be to this volume.

3 Carolyne Larrington, *Brothers and Sisters in Medieval European Literature* (Woodbridge: York Medieval Press, 2015).

4 Kate McClune, '"The Vengeance of My Brethirne": Blood ties in Malory's *Morte Darthur*', in David Clark and Kate McClune (eds), *Arthurian Literature 28: Blood, Sex, Malory: Essays on the 'Morte Darthur'* (Cambridge: D.S. Brewer, 2011), p. 94. See also Catherine La Farge, 'Blood and Love in Malory's *Morte Darthur*', in Peter Brown (ed.), *A Companion to Medieval English Literature and Culture, c.1350–c.1550* (Oxford: Blackwell, 2007), pp. 634–47.

5 Carolyne Larrington, 'Sibling Relations in Malory's *Morte Darthur*', in Clark and McClune, *Arthurian Literature*, pp. 57–74 (p. 57 and p. 61). See also her *King Arthur's Enchantresses: Morgan and her sisters in Arthurian tradition* (London: I.B. Tauris, 2006).

6 Mitchell, *Siblings*, p. 38.

7 As Malory omits the mention in his source, at this stage, of the reconciliation of the eleven kings with Arthur, the action of Lot's wife reads as a continuation of their rebel stance. See *The Works of Sir Thomas Malory*, Eugéne Vinaver (ed.), 3 vols, 3rd edn, revised P.J.C. Field (Oxford: Oxford University Press, 1990), vol. 3, p. 1297, n. 41.12–13.

8 In the French *Merlin*, Arthur's brothers-in-law are enemies of his before they marry his sisters; see Larrington, *King Arthur's Enchantresses*, p. 32.

9 Mitchell, *Siblings*, p. 62 and p. 193.

10 See Vinaver, *The Works of Sir Thomas Malory*, p. 1297, n. 41.12–13

11 See Catherine La Farge, 'Conversation in Malory's *Morte Darthur*', *Medium Ævum*, vol. 56, no. 2, 1987, pp. 225–37.

12 Mitchell, *Siblings*, p. 193, p. 81, pp. 78–9.

13 See Elizabeth Archibald, *Incest and the Medieval Imagination* (Oxford: Clarendon Press, 2001), pp. 50–2, p. 76, n. 65; Mitchell, *Siblings*, p. 41 and p. 92.

14 See Archibald, *Incest and the Medieval Imagination*, pp. 199–220 and her 'Mordred's Lost Childhood', *Arthuriana*, vol. 29, no. 1, 2019, pp. 77–87.

15 See McClune, '"The Vengeance of My Brethirne"', p. 96.

16 Larrington, 'Sibling Relations in Malory's *Morte Darthur*', p. 61. For sibling replication, see Mitchell, *Siblings*, p. xvi.

17 Malory tries to impose order upon doubles Mellyagaunt and Launcelot in a similar way; see Catherine La Farge, 'Blood and Love in Malory's *Morte Darthur*', pp. 638–9 and Mitchell, *Siblings*, p. 215.

18 See Raluca Radulescu, *The Gentry Context for Malory's 'Morte Darthur'*, *Arthurian Studies*, vol. 55 (Cambridge: D.S. Brewer, 2003), pp. 88–9.

19 Enid Balint, 'On Being Empty of Oneself', in Juliet Mitchell and M. Parsons (eds), *Before I was I: Psychoanalysis and the imagination* (London: Free Association Books, 1993 [1963]), pp. 37–55 (p. 40). See also Mitchell, p. 13 and p. 132.

20 Mitchell, *Siblings*, p. 77. Larrington, *Brothers and Sisters in Medieval European Literature*, reads this relationship positively: 'the presence of his sibling-peer, mirroring and completing him, allows Balin at last to function successfully as a unitary self', p. 70.

21 See La Farge, 'Blood and Love in Malory's *Morte Darthur*', p. 641; McClune, '"The Vengeance of My Brethirne"', p. 91.

22 Mitchell, *Siblings*, p. 145.

23 Ibid., p. 211.

24 Ibid., p. 132.

25 See Radulescu, *The Gentry Context for Malory's 'Morte Darthur'*, p. 22.

26 Jill Mann, 'Taking the Adventure: Malory and the *Suite du Merlin*', in Toshiyuki Takamiya and Derek Brewer (eds), *Aspects of Malory* (Arthurian Studies series), vol. 1 (Cambridge: D.S. Brewer, 1981), pp. 71–91 (p. 78).

27 This symmetry somewhat compromises the effect of Malory's avoidance of words such as 'brotherhood' or 'fraternity' for Arthur's fellowship. See Elizabeth Archibald, 'Malory's Ideal of Fellowship', *Review of English Studies*, vol. 43, 1992, pp. 311–28 (p. 315, n. 15) and McClune, '"The Vengeance of My Brethirne"', p. 91.

28 Mitchell, *Siblings*, p. 196. See *La Mort le roi Artu: roman du XIIIe siècle*, J. Frappier (ed.), 3rd edn (Geneva: Droz, 1996), line 125; *Lancelot-Grail: The Old French Arthurian vulgate and post-vulgate in translation*, 5 vols, N.J. Lacey (trans. and ed.) (New York: Garland Publishing, 1995), vol. 4, line 123; the *Stanzaic Morte Arthur*, in *King Arthur's Death: The Middle English stanzaic Morte Arthur and alliterative Morte Arthur*, Larry D. Benson (ed.), revised Edward E. Foster (Kalamazoo: Medieval Institute Publications, 1994), line 1978. For further discussion, see McClune, '"The Vengeance of My Brethirne"', pp. 102–4.

29 See McClune, '"The Vengeance of My Brethirne"', pp. 94–5.

30 Field rejects the Winchester MS's flatter 'I wente ye wolde have smyttyn me', preferring Caxton's wording. Either way, intention is flagged.

31 Mitchell, *Siblings*, p. 37.

32 See La Farge, 'Blood and Love in Malory's *Morte Darthur*', pp. 643–4.

33 Mitchell, *Siblings*, p. 192.

34 See *Le Chevalier au Lion (Yvain)*, M. Roques (ed.) (Paris: Champion, 1971); for the English translation, see *Yvain, or, The Knight with the Lion*, in *Arthurian Romances*, D.D.R. Owen (trans.) (London: J.M. Dent, 1987), pp. 281–373.

35 See *Prudentius*, 2 vols, H.J. Thomson (trans. and ed.) (Cambridge: Loeb Classical Library, 2000 [1949]), vol. 1, pp. 274–343; *Le Roman de la Rose*, Daniel Poirion (ed.) (Paris: Flammarion, 1974); *The Romance of the Rose*, Frans Horgan (trans.) (Oxford: Oxford University Press, 1994).

36 An example from Chrétien's *Yvain* is, for one about men, fairly long; see lines 6024–59.

37 See Michel Foucault, *The History of Sexuality. Volume I: The Will to Knowledge*, Robert Hurley (trans.) (London: Penguin, 1998 [1977]).

38 *La Vita Nuova*, in *Opere di Dante Alighieri*, Fredi Chiappelli and Ugo Mursia (eds) (Milan: Mursia, 1978), ch. 19, canz. 1; the translation is from *La Vita Nuova*, Mark Musa (trans.) (Oxford: Oxford University Press, 1992).

39 See Jill Mann on 'feminized masculinity' in her *Feminizing Chaucer* (Cambridge: D.S. Brewer, 2002), pp. 129–44.

40 See, for instance, Karen Cherewatuk, *Marriage, Adultery, and Inheritance in Malory's 'Morte Darthur'*, *Arthurian Studies 67* (Cambridge: D.S. Brewer, 2006), pp. 60–6; James Noble, 'Gilding the Lily (Maid): Elaine of Astolat', in Bonnie Wheeler and Fiona Tolhurst (eds), *On Arthurian Women: Essays in memory of Maureen Fries* (Dallas: Scriptorium, 2001), pp. 45–57; K.S. Whetter, 'Love and Death in Arthurian Romance', in Karen Cherewatuk and K.S. Whetter (eds), *The Arthurian Way of Death: The English tradition* (Cambridge: D.S. Brewer, 2009), pp. 94–114 (pp. 110–12); Michael Wenthe, 'The Legible Corpses of *Le Morte Darthur*', in Cherewatuk and Whetter (eds), *The Arthurian Way of Death*, pp. 124–35.

41 Juliet Mitchell, *Mad Men and Medusas: Reclaiming Hysteria* (London: Penguin, 2000).

42 Ibid., p. 133.

43 Ibid., p. 5.

44 See Philippe Ariès, *The Hour of Our Death*, Helen Weaver (trans.) (New York: Alfred A. Knopf, 1981) and Mitchell, *Mad Men and Medusas*, pp. 49–50 and pp. 173–4.

45 For another view, see Cherewatuk, *Marriage, Adultery, and Inheritance*, p. 66.

46 Sigmund Freud, '"A Child Is Being Beaten": A contribution to the study of the origins of sexual perversions', in *The Standard Edition of the Complete Psychological Works of Sigmund Freud*, 24 vols, James Strachey (ed. and trans.) (London: Hogarth Press, 1953–74), vol. 12 (1919), pp. 175–204. See Catherine Batt, *Malory's 'Morte Darthur': Remaking Arthurian*

tradition (New York: Palgrave Macmillan, 2002), pp. 153–8 and Earl R. Anderson, '"Ein Kind wird geschlagen": The meaning of Malory's "Tale of the Healing of Sir Urry"', *Literature and Psychology*, vol. 49, no. 3, 2003, pp. 45–74.

47 Mitchell, *Mad Men and Medusas*, p. 84.

48 Ibid., p. 104.

49 Elisabeth Young-Bruel, *Anna Freud: A biography*, 2nd edn (London: Macmillan, 2008), pp. 105–6; *The Writings of Anna Freud*, 8 vols (New York: International University Press, 1966–80), vol. 1 (1922–35), pp. 149–51.

50 Mitchell, *Mad Men and Medusas*, p. 88.

51 Ibid., p. 105.

52 See Mark Lambert, *Malory: Style and vision in 'Le Morte Darthur'* (New Haven: Yale University Press, 1975).

53 Margery Kempe is the most striking fifteenth-century English vernacular example of specular weeping; see *The Book of Margery Kempe*, Lynn Staley (ed.) (Kalamazoo: Medieval Institute Publications, 1996).

54 A perfunctory sublimation inheres in Urry soon becoming Launcelot's junior colleague, habitually twinned henceforth with the similarly assimilated Lavayne.

55 Mitchell, *Mad Men and Medusas*, p. 104.

56 Ibid., p. 104.

57 Freud, '"A Child Is Being Beaten"', p. 197; Mitchell, *Siblings*, p. 95 and p. 104.

58 Mitchell, *Mad Men and Medusas*, p. 99.

59 Terence Cave, *Recognitions: A study in poetics* (Oxford: Clarendon Press, 1988), p. 489.

60 Ibid., p. 213. See Peter Brooks, *The Melodramatic Imagination: Balzac, Henry James, melodrama, and the mode of excess* (New Haven: Yale University Press, 1976), pp. 210–12.

61 Mitchell, *Mad Men and Medusas*, p. 77.

62 See Felicity Riddy, *Sir Thomas Malory* (Leiden: E.J. Brill, 1987), especially pp. 1–30; Felicity Riddy, 'Contextualizing *Le Morte Darthur:* Empire and civil war', in Elizabeth Archibald and A.S.G. Edwards (eds), *A Companion to Malory* (Cambridge: D.S. Brewer, 1996), pp. 55–73; Felicity Riddy, 'John Hardyng's Chronicle and the Wars of the Roses', in Felicity Riddy and James P. Curley (eds), *Arthurian Literature 12* (Cambridge: D.S. Brewer, 1993), pp. 91–108.

CHAPTER 7. Fathers and Sons, Mothers and Daughters: The family romance in Katherine Cecil Thurston's *The Fly on the Wheel*

1 Katherine Cecil Thurston, *The Fly on the Wheel* (London: Virago, 1987 [1908]), p. 2. Subsequent references are to this edition and are given parenthetically in the text.

2 Rosalind Minsky, *Psychoanalysis and Gender* (London: Routledge, 1996), p. 26.

3 Gerardine Meaney, 'Decadence, Degeneration, and Revolting Aesthetics: The fiction of Emily Lawless and Katherine Cecil Thurston', *Colby Quarterly*, vol. 36, 2000, pp. 157–75 (p. 170).

4 Tina O'Toole, '"Nomadic Subjects" in Katherine Cecil Thurston's *Max*', in Patricia Coughlan and Tina O'Toole (eds), *Irish Literature: Feminist perspectives* (Dublin: Carysfort Press, 2008), pp. 79–98 (p. 80, p. 81). For a further discussion of *Max*, see also Tina O'Toole, *The Irish New Woman* (London: Palgrave Macmillan, 2013), pp. 118–28.

5 Meaney, 'Decadence', p. 170.

6 Whitney Standlee, *'Power to Observe': Irish women novelists in Britain, 1890–1916* (Frankfurt: Peter Lang, 2015), p. 133.

7 Declan Kiberd has discussed the tendency apparent in literature of the Irish revival to create symbolic fathers, in the seeming absence of adequate or effective fathers. See *Inventing Ireland* (London: Jonathan Cape, 1995), pp. 380–94. Although this is followed by a chapter entitled

'Mothers and Daughters', Moynagh Sullivan points out that it in fact offers no discussion of intergenerational structures among women, thus rendering the mother ineffective as a site of generation. See Sullivan, 'Raising the Veil: Mystery, myth, and melancholia in Irish studies', in Coughlan and O'Toole (eds), *Irish Literature*, pp. 245–77 (pp. 256–8).

8 Marianne Hirsch, *The Mother/Daughter Plot: Narrative, psychoanalysis, feminism* (Bloomington: Indiana University Press, 1989), p. 10.

9 Sigmund Freud, 'Family Romances', in *The Freud Reader*, Peter Gay (ed.) (London: Vintage, 1995), pp. 297–300.

10 Ibid., p. 299.

11 Marthe Robert, *Origins of the Novel* (Brighton: Harvester Press, 1980), p. 37.

12 The significance of Isabel's education in a French convent is noted by Ciarán O'Neill and Mai Yatani, 'Women, Ambition, and the City, 1890–1910', in Anna Pilz and Whitney Standlee (eds), *Irish Women's Writing, 1878–1922: Advancing the cause of liberty* (Manchester: Manchester University Press, 2016), pp. 100–20 (p. 115). See also Pilz and Standlee, 'Introduction', pp. 1–16 (pp. 11–12).

13 Joseph Valente, *The Myth of Manliness in Irish Culture, 1880–1922* (Urbana: University of Illinois Press, 2011), p. 3. Original emphasis.

14 With the obvious exception of Immanuel Kant (1724–1804), the author of several foundational Enlightenment texts, all the writers to whom Stephen refers are linked by a shared interest in Darwinism. Herbert Spencer (1820–1903) developed what is referred to as social Darwinism; Thomas Henry Huxley (1825–95) was a prominent supporter of Darwin who became known as 'Darwin's bulldog'; Ernst Haeckel (1834–1919) was a German biologist who popularised Darwin's theories in Germany. Fr Cunningham's objection to these writers presumably lies in their challenging of conventional religious belief at the time (Huxley, for example, coined the term 'agnostic'), but is also notable that their ideas would now be seen as contributing to a decidedly right-wing social and political agenda, in which Darwin's theory of evolution became allied with notions of superiority and inferiority among classes and races. Haeckel was a proponent of scientific racism while Spencer's social Darwinism precluded state intervention to alleviate poverty or promote education.

15 Minsky, *Psychoanalysis and Gender*, p. 50 (original emphasis).

16 Hirsch, *The Mother/Daughter Plot*, p. 10. In his discussion of women's role in the Irish revival, Declan Kiberd states in a very similar vein that 'even the more radical thinkers of the modern age defined the revolt of women in terms of the attempt by wives and daughters to break free of the constricting images of the female devised by men' (*Inventing Ireland*, p. 395). It follows then that in this case the daughter's narrative, as Hirsch argues, is dependent on the silencing of the mother.

17 Minsky, *Psychoanalysis and Gender*, p. 142.

18 Ibid., p. 159.

19 Bruce Fink, *The Lacanian Subject: Between language and jouissance* (Princeton: Princeton University Press, 1995), p. 25.

20 See for instance Jean Kimball, 'Family Romance and Hero Myth: A psychoanalytic context for the paternity theme in *Ulysses*', *James Joyce Quarterly*, vol. 20, 1983, pp. 162–73; Cynthia Lewiecki-Wilson, *Writing against the Family: Gender in Lawrence and Joyce* (Carbondale: Southern Illinois University Press, 1994); Christine Van Boheemen, *The Novel as Family Romance: Language, gender, and authority from Fielding to Joyce* (Ithaca: Cornell University Press, 1987); Stephen Sicari, *Joyce's Modernist Allegory: 'Ulysses' and the history of the novel* (Columbia: University of South Carolina Press, 2001), pp. 142–64; Emer Nolan, *James Joyce and Nationalism* (London: Routledge, 1995), pp. 36–54.

21 Kimball, 'Family Romance', p. 169, p. 170.

22 Lewiecki-Wilson, *Writing against the Family*, p. 135.

23 Ibid., pp. 135–6, p. 129.
24 James Joyce, *A Portrait of the Artist as a Young Man*, Jeri Johnson (ed.) (Oxford: Oxford University Press, 2000), p. 171.
25 Ibid.
26 Minsky, *Psychoanalysis and Gender*, p. 159.
27 Standlee likewise reads this scene as signalling Isabel's 'triumph over the confines of her existence'. '*Power to Observe*', p. 140.
28 Sullivan, 'Raising the Veil', p. 266, p. 254.

CHAPTER 8. 'Now in the city there are two worlds': Maeve Brennan's Dublin sequences

1 Anne Enright, 'Introduction', *The Springs of Affection* (Dublin: The Stinging Fly Press, 2016), p. xi. References to Brennan's work in this essay are, unless otherwise stated, to these editions: *The Springs of Affection: Stories of Dublin* (*The Springs of Affection*), Introduction William Maxwell, selected & arranged Christopher Carduff (Berkeley: Counterpoint, 1997); *The Long-Winded Lady: Notes from the 'New Yorker'* (*The Long-Winded Lady*), Christopher Carduff (ed.) (Berkeley: Counterpoint, 1998); *The Rose Garden: Short stories* (*The Rose Garden*), Christopher Carduff (ed.) (Washington, DC: Counterpoint, 2000); *The Visitor*, Christopher Carduff (ed.) (Washington, DC: Counterpoint, 2000).
2 Unless otherwise stated, all information about Brennan and her family comes from Angela Bourke's pioneering biography, *Maeve Brennan, Style, Wit and Tragedy: An Irish writer in New York* (London: Pimlico, 2005 [2004]).
3 See Ellen McWilliams, '"A sort of Rathmines version of a Dior design": Maeve Brennan, Self-fashioning, and the uses of style', *Women: A cultural review*, vol. 27, no. 1, 2016, pp. 42–61, especially pp. 51–2.
4 Bourke, *Maeve Brennan*, p. 143.
5 Ibid., p. 143.
6 Anne McClintock, 'Family Feuds: Gender, nationalism, and the family', *Feminist Review*, Special Issue: Nationalisms and National Identities, no. 44, 1993, pp. 61–80 (pp. 63–4). See also Clair Wills, 'Women, Domesticity, and the Family: Recent feminist work in Irish cultural studies, *Cultural Studies*, vol. 15, no. 1, 2001, pp. 33–57.
7 For further connections to Joyce, see Bourke, *Maeve Brennan*, *passim*; Ellen McWilliams, 'Maeve Brennan and James Joyce', *Irish Studies Review*, vol. 26, no. 1, 2018, pp. 111–23.
8 James Joyce, *A Portrait of the Artist as a Young Man*, Jeri Johnston (ed.) (Oxford: Oxford World's Classics, 2000), p. 55, p. 141.
9 Bourke, *Maeve Brennan*, p. 275.
10 See Maxwell's Introduction, *The Springs of Affection*, p. 2, for Brennan's admiration for Turgenev. Brennan's infrequent but artful naming of books in the *Long-Winded Lady* pieces includes a reference to Benedict Kiely's *Poor Scholar*. See *The Long-Winded Lady*, p. 39.
11 Ellen McWilliams, 'Maeve Brennan, Celebrity, and *Harper's Bazaar* in the 1940s', *Breac*, 17 July 2017, https://breac.nd.edu/articles/maeve-brennan-celebrity-and-harpers-bazaar-in-the-1940s/
12 Bourke, *Maeve Brennan*, p. 69.
13 Ibid., p. 74.
14 See Caitriona Beaumont, 'Women, Citizenship, and Catholicism in the Irish Free State, 1922–1948', *Women's History Review*, vol. 6, no. 4, 1997, pp. 563–85, for examples of legislation attenuating women's citizenship prior to the 1937 constitution. See also Bourke, *Maeve Brennan*, pp. 129–30; Maryann Gialanella Valiulis, 'The Politics of Gender in the Irish Free State, 1922–1937', *Women's History Review*, vol. 20, no. 4, 2011, pp. 569–78.

15 10 December 1937, quoted in Bourke, *Maeve Brennan*, p. 131.
16 Dorothy Macardle, *The Uninvited* (Dublin: Tramp Press, 2015 [1942]).
17 Richard Sennett, *The Fall of Public Man* (London: Faber, 1993), p. 39.
18 *Bunreacht na hÉireann / Constitution of Ireland* (Dublin: Stationery Office, 1945), Article 41.1.1 & 2.
19 Mary F. Corey, *World Through a Monocle: 'The New Yorker' at midcentury* (Harvard: Harvard University Press, 1999), pp. 151–2.
20 Bourke, *Maeve Brennan*, pp. 142–5 and *passim*.
21 Heather Ingman, *A History of the Irish Short Story* (Cambridge: Cambridge University Press, 2009), pp. 206–7. See also Heather Ingman, *Women's Fiction Between the Wars: Mothers, daughters, and writing* (Edinburgh: Edinburgh University Press, 1998), especially pp. 1–21.

CHAPTER 9. The Law of the Mother and the Sibling World: Leeanne Quinn's queer ecologies
1 Leeanne Quinn, 'Acoma', in *Before You* (Dublin: Dedalus Press, 2012), p. 46. All further references will be noted in parentheses.
2 See Nicholas Allen, *Ireland, Literature, and the Coast: Seatangled* (Oxford: Oxford University Press, 2021); *Coastal Works: Cultures of the Atlantic edge*, Nicholas Allen, Nick Groom, and Jos Smith (eds) (Oxford: Oxford University Press, 2017); Borbálo Faragó and Kathryn Kirkpatrick (eds), *Animals in Irish Literature and Culture* (Basingstoke: Palgrave, 2018); Christine Cusick, *Out of the Earth: Ecocritical readings of Irish texts* (Cork: Cork University Press, 2010); Derek Gladwin and Christine Cusick (eds), *Unfolding Irish Landscapes: Tim Robinson, culture and environment* (Manchester: Manchester University Press, 2016); Anne Fogarty, 'Foreword', in Robert Brazeau and Derek Gladwin (eds), *Eco-Joyce: The environmental imagination of James Joyce* (Cork: Cork University Press, 2014), pp. xv–xvii; Oona Frawley, *Irish Pastoral: Nostalgia and twentieth-century Irish literature* (Dublin: Irish Academic Press, 2005); Derek Gladwin, *Contentious Terrains: Boglands, Ireland, postcolonial gothic* (Cork: Cork University Press, 2016); Robert Brazeau (ed.), *Ecological Exile: Spatial injustice & environmental humanities* (Abingdon: Routledge, 2018); Nessa Cronin, 'Achillhenge: Liquid modernity and an archaeology of the Irish anthropocene', *Éire-Ireland*, vol. 55, nos 3 & 4, 2020, pp. 19–43; Centre for Landscape Studies, *Landscape Values: Place and praxis* (Galway: National University of Ireland Galway, 2016); Nessa Cronin, 'Lived and Learned Landscapes: Literary geographies and the Irish topographical tradition', in Marie Mianowski (ed.), *Irish Contemporary Landscapes in Literature and the Arts* (Basingstoke: Palgrave Macmillan, 2012), pp. 106–18; Nessa Cronin, '"The fineness of things": The deep mapping projects of Tim Robinson's art and writings, 1969–72', in Gladwin and Cusick (eds), *Unfolding Irish Landscapes*, pp. 53–72; Nessa Cronin, 'Environmentalities: Speculative imaginaries of the anthropocene', in Renée Fox, Mike Cronin, and Brian Ó Conchubhair (eds), *The Routledge International Handbook of Irish Studies* (Abingdon: Routledge, 2021), pp. 349–61; Maureen O'Connor, *The Female and the Species: The animal in Irish women's writing* (Oxford: Peter Lang, 2010); Maureen O'Connor, 'Mrkgnao!: Signifying animals in the fiction of James Joyce's fiction', in Albert Wachtel (ed.), *Critical Insights: James Joyce* (Pasadena, CA: Salem Press, 2013), pp. 10–19; Maureen O'Connor, '"Extremely nervous on this earth": Fairy tale violence in Edna O'Brien's *In the Forest*', in Tina-Karen Puisse and Heike Schwarz (eds), *Madness in the Woods: Ecopsychopathologies in literature, film, and gaming* (New York: Lexington Books, 2018), pp. 75–89; Maureen O'Connor, 'Irish Animal Studies at the Turn of the Twenty-first Century', in Fox, Cronin, and Ó Conchubhair (eds), *The Routledge International Handbook of Irish Studies*, pp. 362–69; Malcolm Sen, 'An Ordinary Crisis: Covid-19 and Irish studies', in Fox, Cronin, and Ó Conchubhair (eds), *The*

Routledge International Handbook of Irish Studies, pp. 47–84; John Wilson Foster, *Nature in Ireland: A scientific and cultural history* (Dublin: Lilliput Press, 1998); Eamonn Wall, *Writing the Irish West: Ecologies and traditions* (Notre Dame: University of Notre Dame Press, 2011).

3 See Joseph Valente and Margot Gayle Backus, *The Child Sex Scandal and Modern Irish Literature: Writing the unspeakable* (Bloomington: Indiana University Press, 2020). For work on neuroscience and attachment theory see Stephen Porges, *The Polyvagal Theory: Neurophysiological foundations of emotions, attachment, communication, and self-regulation* (New York: Norton, 2011); Marian Dunlea, *Bodydreaming in the Treatment of Developmental Trauma: An embodied therapeutic approach* (Abingdon: Routledge, 2019); Daniela F. Sieff, *Understanding and Healing Emotional Trauma: Conversations with pioneering clinicians and researchers* (Abingdon: Routledge, 2014); Nick Midgley et al., *Mentalization-Based Treatment for Children: A time-limited approach* (New York: American Psychological Association, 2017).

4 Susan Cahill, *Irish Literature in the Celtic Tiger Years 1990 to 2008: Gender, bodies, memory* (London: Bloomsbury Continuum Books, 2011); Claire Bracken, *Irish Feminist Futures* (Abingdon: Routledge, 2016); Margaret O'Neill and Michaela Schrage-Frueh, 'Surplus to Requirements?: The ageing body in contemporary Irish writing', in Fox, Cronin, and Ó Conchubhair (eds), *The Routledge International Handbook of Irish Studies*, pp. 435–47.

5 Tina O'Toole, *The Irish New Woman* (London: Palgrave Macmillan, 2013); see also Tina O'Toole, 'George Egerton's Translocational Subjects', *Modernism-Modernity*, vol. 21, no. 3, 2014, pp. 827–42; Tina O'Toole, 'Cé Leis Tú?: Queering Irish migrant literature', *Irish University Review*, vol. 43, no. 1, 2013, pp. 131–45.

6 See Jason W. Moore, 'The Capitalocene, Part I: On the Nature and Origins of Our Ecological Crisis', *The Journal of Peasant Studies*, vol. 44, no. 3, 2017, pp. 594–630; also Jason W. Moore (ed.), *Anthropocene or Capitalocene? Nature, history, and the crisis of capitalism* (Oakland: Kairos, 2016); and Donna J. Haraway, 'Staying with the Trouble: Anthropocene, capitalocene, chthulucene', in Moore (ed.), *Anthropocene or Capitalocene?*, pp. 34–77.

7 See Patricia Coughlan, 'Hard Times and Sibling Songs: Sibling relations in contemporary Irish literature', in Luz Mar González Arias (ed.), *National Identities and Imperfections in Contemporary Irish Literature* (London: Palgrave Macmillan, 2017); Gerardine Meaney, 'Sex and Nation: Women in Irish culture and politics', in Ailbhe Smyth (ed.), *Irish Women's Studies: A reader* (Dublin: Attic Press, 1993), pp. 230–44; Gerardine Meaney, 'Waking the Dead: Antigone, Ismene, and Anne Enright's narrators in mourning', in Claire Bracken and Susan Cahill (eds), *Irish Writers in Their Time: Anne Enright* (Dublin: Irish Academic Press, 2011), pp. 145–64; Gerardine Meaney, *Gender, Ireland, and Cultural Change: Race sex and nation* (Abingdon: Routledge, 2011).

8 Lucy Collins, Review of *Before You*, *The Stinging Fly*, vol. 21, no. 2, 2012, pp. 119–22.

9 Leeanne Quinn, *Some Lives* (Dublin: Dedalus Press, 2020).

10 Niall McMonagle, cover, Quinn, *Some Lives*.

11 Ibid.

12 Olga Tokarczuk, Nobel lecture, https://www.nobelprize.org/prizes/literature/2018/tokarczuk/lecture; Moynagh Sullivan, 'Interview with Leanne Quinn', July 2020, unpublished.

13 Sullivan, 'Interview'.

14 Ibid.

15 Ibid.

16 Ibid.

17 Ibid.

18 Ibid.

19 Ibid.

20 Juliet Mitchell, *Mad Men and Medusas: Reclaiming hysteria and the effects of sibling relations on the human condition* (London: Penguin, 2000), and *Siblings: Sex and violence* (Cambridge: Polity, 2003).

21 Mitchell, *Mad Men and Medusas*, p. xi; on the law of the mother see Juliet Mitchell, *Psychoanalysis and Feminism* (London: Penguin, 1974) and *Mad Men and Medusas*.

22 For a powerful and comprehensive recent critique of feminist, queer, and gender scholarship in Irish studies, see Bracken, *Irish Feminist Futures*, and Bracken, 'Gender and Irish Studies', in Fox, Cronin, and Ó Conchubhair (eds), *The Routledge International Handbook of Irish Studies*, pp. 230–44

23 Mitchell, *Siblings*, p. 52.

24 Coughlan, 'Hard Times and Sibling Songs', pp. 67–82.

25 Meaney, 'Waking the Dead'.

26 Ibid., p. 146.

27 Seamus Heaney, *Death of a Naturalist* (London: Faber, 1966).

28 Heaney, 'Feeling into Words', in *Preoccupations: Selected prose, 1968–1978* (London: Faber & Faber, 1981), pp. 41–60.

29 Patricia Coughlan, '"Bog Queens": Representations of femininity in the poetry of John Montague and Seamus Heaney', in Toni O'Brien Johnson and David Cairns (eds), *Gender in Irish Writing* (Oxford: Oxford University Press, 1991), pp. 89–111.

30 Ibid.

31 Gerard Dawe (ed.), *The Cambridge Companion to Irish Poets* (Cambridge: Cambridge University Press, 2017).

32 Mitchell, *Siblings*, p. 53.

33 Ibid., pp. 53–4.

34 Ibid.

35 Ibid., p. 53.

36 Tim Robinson, 'A Connemara Fractal', in Timothy Collins, *Decoding the Landscape: Contributions towards a synthesis of thinking in Irish studies on the landscape* (Galway: Centre for Landscape Studies, 2003), pp. 12–30 (p. 16).

37 See Benoît Mandelbrot, 'How Long is the Coast of Britain? Statistical self-similarity and fractional dimension', *Science Magazine*, vol. 156, no. 3,775, May 1967, pp. 636–8.

38 See Porges, *The Polyvagal Theory*, p. 201.

39 Sullivan, 'Interview'.

40 Margaret Whitford, *Luce Irigaray: Philosophy in the feminine* (London: Routledge, 1991), p. 7.

41 Ibid.

42 See The Care Collective: Andreas Chatzidakis, Jamie Hakim, Jo Littler, Catherine Rottenberg, and Lynne Segal, *The Care Manifesto: The politics of interdependence* (London: Verso, 2021).

43 Whitford, *Luce Irigaray*, p. 7

44 See Nicholas Midgley, *Minding the Child: Mentalization-based interventions with children, young people and families* (Abingdon: Routledge, 2012); Nick Midgley, Jacqueline Hayes, and Mick Cooper, *Essential Research Findings in Child and Adolescent Therapy* (London: Sage, 2017); and Philip Graham and Nick Midgley, *So Young, So Sad, So Listen: A parents' guide to depression in children and young people* (Cambridge: Cambridge University Press, 2020).

45 The identification of the family (rather than, for example, the individual) as the basic building block of society is more than pious rhetoric in the Irish Constitution. In post-colonial southern Ireland a particular construction of sexual and familial roles became the very substance of what it meant to be Irish. See Lindsey Earner-Byrne, *Mother and Child:*

Maternity and child welfare in Dublin, 1922–60 (Manchester: Manchester University Press, 2013).

46 The referenda of 2015 and 2108 have gone some considerable way to destabilising the heteronormative family unit as the basis of Irish society, as well as securing a woman's right to make choices about her own body. The Citizens' Assembly on Gender Equality, Saturday, 24 April 2021, recommended a number of inclusive actions in relation to the constitution; leadership and politics; childcare and care; domestic, sexual, and gender-based violence; pay and social protection; and technology and the media. Key to this are recommendations to amend Article 41.2 that hetero-patriarchally identifies women with the house and home:

- Insert a new clause into Article 40 to refer explicitly to gender equality and non-discrimination.
- Delete and replace the text of Article 41.2 (woman in the home) with language that is not gender specific and obliges the state to take reasonable measures to support care within the home and wider community.
- Amend Article 41 so that it would protect private and family life, with the protection afforded to the family not limited to the marital family.

https://www.citizensassembly.ie/en/previous-assemblies/2020-2021-citizens-assembly-on-gender-equality/

47 See Anne Mulhall, '"The well-known, old, but still unbeaten track": Women poets and Irish periodical culture in the mid-twentieth century', *Irish University Review*, vol. 42, no. 1, 2012, pp. 32–52 (p. 33).

48 Sullivan, 'Interview'.

49 Ibid.

50 Amniotic fluid has about 2 per cent salinity. Oceans are 3.0 to 3.5 per cent dissolved salts, https://womenslegacyproject.com/be/oceans-amniotic-fluid/

51 Sullivan, 'Interview'.

52 Eavan Boland, *An Origin Like Water: Collected poems 1957–1987* (Manchester: Carcanet, 1997).

53 Collins, Review of *Before You*.

CHAPTER 10. Female Personal Names in Old English

1 The term 'Anglo-Saxon' is used throughout this essay to refer only to the peoples of early medieval England, to their culture, and to those who work on this period. It is a great pleasure to offer this essay to Patricia Coughlan, in recognition of the many years during which Pat and I have been colleagues and friends.

2 See Fran Colman, *The Grammar of Names in Anglo-Saxon England: The linguistics and culture of the Old English onomasticon* (Oxford: Oxford University Press, 2014).

3 Elisabeth Okasha, *Women's Names in Old English* (Farnham: Ashgate, 2011).

4 Carole Hough, 'Women in English Place-Names', in Carole Hough and Kathryn A. Lowe (eds), *'Lastworda Betst': Essays in memory of Christine E. Fell* (Donnington: Shaun Tyas, 2002), pp. 46–7.

5 Elisabeth Okasha, 'A Second Supplement to *Hand-List of Anglo-Saxon Non-Runic Inscriptions*', *Anglo-Saxon England*, vol. 21, no. 204, 1992, pp. 53–4 and fig. VIc.

6 See Gale R. Owen-Crocker, *Dress in Anglo-Saxon England* (Manchester: Manchester University Press, 1986).

7 Elisabeth Okasha, 'Anglo-Saxon Inscribed Rings', *Leeds Studies in English*, new series, vol. 35, 2003, p. 40.

8 Peter H. Sawyer, *Anglo-Saxon Charters: An annotated list and bibliography* (London: Royal Historical Society, 1968), no. 448.

9 Elisabeth Okasha, *Hand-List of Anglo-Saxon Non-Runic Inscriptions* (Cambridge: Cambridge University Press, 1971), p. 136, no. 155.
10 Ibid.
11 Robin Daniels, *Anglo-Saxon Hartlepool and the Foundations of English Christianity*, Tees Archaeology Monograph Series No. 3 (Hartlepool: Tees Archaeology, 2007), pp. 133–7 and figs.
12 Ibid., p. 133.
13 See Sawyer, *Anglo-Saxon Charters*, no. 445, and Florence E. Harmer (ed.), *Select English Historical Documents of the Ninth and Tenth Centuries* (Cambridge: Cambridge University Press, 1914), p. 12, no. 8.
14 See Daniels, *Anglo-Saxon Hartlepool*, pp. 74–93.
15 See http://www.bl.uk/manuscripts/Viewer.aspx?ref=cotton_ms_domitian_a_vii_f043r
16 David W. Rollason and Lynda Rollason (eds), *The Durham Liber Vitae. London, British Library, MS Cotton Domitian A.VII*, 3 vols (London: British Library, 2007), vol. 1, p. 248.
17 Julius Zupitza (ed.), *Aelfrics Grammatik und Glossar: Text und varianten* (Berlin: Weidmannsche Verlagsbuchhandlung, 1966 [1880]).

CHAPTER 11. Writing Irish Women in South America
1 Margaret Mac Curtain, *Ariadne's Thread: Writing women into Irish history* (Dublin: Arlen House, 2008), p. 60.
2 Ibid.
3 Patricia Coughlan and Tina O'Toole (eds), *Irish Literature: Feminist perspectives* (Dublin: Carysfort Press, 2008), p. 1.
4 Patrick O'Sullivan (ed.), *The Irish World Wide: Irish women and Irish migration* (Leicester: Leicester University Press, 1995), p. 5.
5 Edmundo Murray, *Devenir Irlandés* (Buenos Aires: Eudeba, 2004); *Becoming Irlandés* (Buenos Aires: LOLA, 2006), and Maria Elena Walsh, *La abuela Agnes (1872–1899)* (Buenos Aires: Seix Barral, 1990).
6 Marion Mulhall, *Between the Amazon and Andes or Ten Years of a Lady's Travels in the Pampas, Gran Chaco, Paraguay, and Matto Grosso* (London: E. Stanford, 1881); Barbara Peart, *Tia Barbarita: Memories of Barbara Peart* (London: Faber & Faber, 1932); Kathleen Nevin, *You'll Never Go Back* (Boston: Bruce Humphries, 1946).
7 Sylvia Molloy, *Acto de presencia. La escritura autobiográfica en Hispanoamérica*, José Esteban Calderón (trans.) (México: Fondo de Cultura económica, 1996 [1991]).
8 O'Sullivan (ed.), *The Irish World Wide*, quoting Eiléan Ní Chuilleanáin, p. 7.
9 Thomas Murray, *The Story of the Irish in Argentina* (Cork: Cork University Press, 2011 [1919]).
10 Ibid., p. 32.
11 Ibid., p. 113.
12 Ibid., p. 94; p. 103.
13 Juan Carlos Korol and Hilda Sábato, *Cómo Fue la Immigración Irlandesa en Argentina* (Buenos Aires: Editorial Plus Ultra, 1981), p. 127.
14 Murray, *The Story of the Irish in Argentina*, pp. 113–14.
15 Maria Luddy, 'Women and Politics in Ireland, 1860–1918', in Angela Bourke et al. (eds), *The Field Day Anthology of Irish Writing*, vol. V (Cork: Cork University Press, 2002), pp. 69–70.
16 Borbála Faragó, '"I am the place in which things happen": Invisible immigrant women poets of Ireland', in Coughlan and O'Toole (eds), *Irish Literature*, p. 149.
17 Timothy Bewes, *The Event of Postcolonial Shame* (Princeton: Princeton University Press, 2011), p. 3.

18 Ibid., p. 14.
19 Ibid., p. 24.
20 Ibid., p. 3.
21 Ibid.
22 Maria Luddy and Dympna McLoughlin, 'Women and Emigration from Ireland from the Seventeenth Century', in Bourke et al. (eds), *The Field Day Anthology of Irish Writing*, p. 569, and Maureen Murphy, *Your Fondest Annie* (Dublin: UCD Press, 2005), p. 1.
23 Luddy and McLoughlin, 'Women and Emigration', p. 569.
24 Black people became 'invisible' in rural and urban places in Argentina due to the policies adopted by the government of Domingo Faustino Sarmiento (1868–74) to 'europeanise' the population. Though he modernised and developed the railway, postal and education systems, Sarmiento adopted repressive actions against the black population, forcing them to emigrate to Uruguay and Brazil, to fight in the war of the Triple Alliance, or segregating them in unhealthy neighbourhoods where yellow fever was deadly.
25 The day before Agnes embarked on *The Boyne* in Southampton for Argentina, she wrote to her father on 8 March 1872 from the South Western Hotel saying that the emperor of Brazil was to travel on the same ship, and that she would write again when she arrived in Lisbon.
26 José Ingenieros, *The Treaty of Love*, in Beatriz Sarlo, *El imperio de los sentimientos (The Empire of Feelings)* (Buenos Aires: Siglo XXI Editores, 2011), p. 85.
27 Sarlo, *El imperio de los sentimientos*, p. 85.
28 Ibid., p. 86.
29 Ibid.
30 Ibid., p. 87.
31 See Camila O'Gorman, *Grandes protagonistas de la historia argentina* (Buenos Aires: Editorial Planeta, 1999) and the 1984 Argentine drama film *Camila*, directed by María Luisa Bemberg, based on the story of the nineteenth-century Argentine socialite Camila O'Gorman.
32 'Destinos (1929)', in Juan José Delaney, *Tréboles del Sur* (Buenos Aires: Grupo Editor Latinoamericano, 1994).
33 O'Sullivan (ed.), *The Irish World Wide*, p. xx.
34 Marc Augé, *Non-Places: An introduction to supermodernity*, John Howe (trans.) (London: Verso, 2008 [1992]), p. 63.
35 Ibid.
36 The Irish Eliza Lynch, the mistress of President Francisco Solano Lopes, also plays an important role in Paraguayan history and war.
37 Íde O'Carroll, *Models for Movers: Irish women's emigration to America* (Dublin: Attic Press, 1990), p. 18.
38 Sarah O'Brien, *Linguistic Diasporas, Narrative and Performance: The Irish in Argentina* (Cham: Palgrave Macmillan, 2017). The author interviewed representatives of the Irish-Argentine community and analysed their narratives from the intersecting perspective of migration studies, oral history, and social linguistics. Another recent study is Patrick Speight's *Irish-Argentine Identity in an Age of Political Challenge and Change, 1875–1983* (Bern: Peter Lang, 2019).

CHAPTER 12. 'All I am is feeling': Samuel Beckett, aesthetics, and the matter of mother

1 James Knowlson, *Damned to Fame: The life of Samuel Beckett* (London: Bloomsbury, 1996), p. 352.
2 Russell Smith, '"Uproar, bulk, rage, suffocation, effort unceasing, frenzied, and vain": Beckett's transports of rage', in Elizabeth Barry, Ulrika Maude, and Laura Salisbury (eds), 'Beckett, Medicine, and the Brain', *Journal of the Medical Humanities*, vol. 37, 2016, pp. 137–47.

3 Marx Nixon, *Samuel Beckett's German Diaries, 1936–1937* (London: Continuum, 2011), p. 35. For Beckett's autography, see Hal Porter Abbott, *Beckett Writing Beckett: The author in the autograph* (Cornell: Cornell University Press, 1996).
4 David Lloyd, *Under Representation: The racial regime of aesthetics* (New York: Fordham University Press, 2019), p. 45.
5 G.F.W. Hegel, *Aesthetics: Lectures on fine art*, vol. 1 (Oxford: Oxford University Press, 1975), p. 151, p. 108.
6 Wilhelm Windelband, *A History of Philosophy. Volume II: Renaissance, Enlightenment, Modern* (New York: Harper Torchbook, 1958), p. 457.
7 John Locke, An *Essay Concerning Human Understanding* (Harmondsworth: Penguin, 1997), pp. 229–30.
8 Sigmund Freud, *Beyond the Pleasure Principle and Other Writings* (Harmondsworth: Penguin, 2003), p. 47.
9 Arthur Schopenhauer, 'On Aesthetics', in R.J. Hollingdale (ed.), *Essays and Aphorisms* (London: Penguin, 1970), pp. 155–65 (p. 155).
10 Ibid., p. 157.
11 Ibid., p. 160.
12 Ibid., p. 155.
13 Michel Foucault, *Lectures on the Will to Know: Lectures at the Collège de France, 1970–1971*, Daniel Defert (ed.) (New York: Palgrave Macmillan, 2013), pp. 1–21.
14 Wendy Brown, *Manhood and Politics: A feminist reading in political theory* (New Jersey: Rowman & Littlefield, 1998), pp. 32–52.
15 Ibid., p. 37.
16 Ibid., p. 45.
17 André Gorz, *Critique of Economic Reason* (London: Verso, 1989), p. 14.
18 Brown, *Manhood and Politics*, p. 43.
19 Hélène Cixous, 'Sorties', in Elaine Marks and Isabelle de Courtivron (eds), *New French Feminisms: An anthology* (New York: Schocken Books, 1981), pp. 90–8 (p. 90).
20 Hegel, *Aesthetics*, p. 152, p. 256.
21 Ibid., p. 111.
22 Sigmund Freud, 'Three Essays on Sexual Theory', in Adam Phillips (ed.), *The Psychology of Love* (London: Penguin, 2006), pp. 111–220 (p. 200).
23 Sigmund Freud, 'The Splitting of the Ego in the Defence Processes', in Adam Phillips (ed.), *The Unconscious* (Harmondsworth: Penguin, 2005), pp. 101–6 (p. 105).
24 Ibid., p. 106.
25 Karen Horney, *Feminine Psychology* (New York: W.W. Norton & Company, 1967), p. 134.
26 Luce Irigaray, 'Women-Mothers, the Silent Substratum of the Social Order', in Margaret Whitford (ed.), *The Irigaray Reader* (Oxford: Basil Blackwell, 1991), pp. 47–52 (p. 49).
27 Ibid., p. 47.
28 Nancy Fraser, 'Contradictions of Capital and Care', *New Left Review*, vol. 100, 2016, pp. 99–117 (p. 102).
29 Irigaray, 'The Bodily Encounter with the Mother', in Whitford (ed.), *The Irigaray Reader*, pp. 34–46 (p. 35).
30 Patricia Yaeger, 'Introduction: Dreaming of infrastructure', *PMLA*, vol. 122, no. 1, 2007, pp. 9–26 (p. 16); Irigaray, 'Women-Mothers', p. 47.
31 Luce Irigaray, 'Women-Mothers', p. 49.
32 Samuel Beckett, 'First Love', in S.E. Gontarski (ed.), *The Complete Short Prose, 1929–1988* (New York: Grove Press, 1995), pp. 25–45 (p. 39).
33 Immanuel Kant, *Critique of Practical Reason*, Mary Gregor (ed.) (Cambridge: Cambridge University Press, 2015), p. 129.

34 See Susan Brienza, 'Clods, Whores, and Bitches: Misogyny in Beckett's early fiction', in Linda Ben-Zvi (ed.), *Women in Beckett: Performance and critical perspectives* (Urbana: University of Illinois Press, 1990), pp. 91–105; Rubin Rabinovitz, 'Stereoscopic or Stereotypic: Characterization in Beckett's fiction', in Ben-Zvi (ed.), *Women in Beckett*, pp. 106–16; Mary Bryden, *Women in Samuel Beckett's Prose and Drama: Her own other* (Lanham: Barnes & Noble, 1993), p. 1; Knowlson, *Damned to Fame*, p. 152.

35 Brienza, 'Clods', p. 94; Samuel Beckett, *More Pricks than Kicks* (London: Faber & Faber, 2010), p. 55.

36 Brienza, 'Clods', p. 92.

37 Ibid.

38 Quoted in Jessica Benjamin, 'A Desire of One's Own: Psychoanalytic feminism and intersubjective space', in Teresa de Lauretis (ed.), *Feminist Studies / Critical Studies* (Bloomington: Indiana University Press, 1986), p. 81.

39 Brienza, 'Clods', p. 91.

40 Patricia Coughlan, '"The Poetry is Another Pair of Sleeves": Beckett, Ireland and modernist lyric poetry', in Patricia Coughlan and Alex Davis (eds), *Modernism and Ireland: The poetry of the 1930s* (Cork: Cork University Press, 1995), pp. 173–208 (p. 191).

41 Beckett, *More Pricks than Kicks*, p. 32.

42 Coughlan, '"The Poetry"', p. 191.

43 Beckett, 'First Love', p. 31.

44 *The Letters of Samuel Beckett I, 1929–40*, Martha Dow Fehsenfeld, Lois More Overbeck, Dan Gunn, and George Craig (eds) (Cambridge: Cambridge University Press, 2009), p. 258.

45 Samuel Beckett, *Not I*, in *The Complete Dramatic Works* (London: Faber & Faber, 1990), pp. 376–83 (p. 376).

46 Jean Laplanche, 'Starting from the Fundamental Anthropological Situation', in John Fletcher (ed.), *Freud and the Sexual: Essays 2000–2006* (New York: International Psychoanalytic Books, 2011), pp. 99–114.

47 Beckett, *Psychology Notes*, Trinity College Dublin: TCDMS10971/8, pp. 15–16; Sigmund Freud, *New Introductory Lectures on Psychoanalysis* (London: Pelican, 1975), p. 126.

48 Phil Baker, *Beckett and the Mythology of Psychoanalysis* (London: Macmillan, 1997), p. 6.

49 Samuel Beckett, 'From an Abandoned Work', in Stanley Gontarski (ed.), *The Complete Short Prose, 1929–1988*, pp. 155–64 (p. 155).

50 Charles Rycroft, *A Critical Dictionary of Psychoanalysis* (London: Penguin, 1995), p. 6.

51 Arthur Schopenhauer, 'On Ethics', in Hollingdale (ed.), *Essays and Aphorisms*, pp. 133–47 (p. 144).

52 Arthur Schopenhauer, *The Two Fundamental Problems of Ethics* (Oxford: Oxford University Press, 2010), p. 79.

53 Beckett, *The Psychology Notes*, TCDMS 10971/8, p. 4.

54 Ernest Jones, 'Anal Erotic Character Traits', *Papers on Psycho-Analysis* (Boston: Beacon Press, 1961), pp. 413–38 (p. 423).

55 Beckett, 'First Love', p. 30.

56 Jones, 'Anal Erotic Character Traits', p. 415.

57 Beckett, 'First Love', p. 28.

58 Ibid., p. 34.

59 Sigmund Freud, 'Family Romances', in *On Sexuality* (Harmondsworth: Penguin, 1977), pp. 221–5 (p. 221).

60 Adam Phillips, 'Just Rage', in *The Beast in the Nursery* (New York: Vintage, 1998), pp. 121–40 (p. 130).

61 Samuel Beckett, *Murphy* (London: Calder, 1993), p. 44.

62 Ibid., p. 43.
63 Sigmund Freud, 'Creative Writers and Daydreaming', in *Art and Literature* (Harmondsworth: Penguin, 1985), pp. 129–43 (p. 134); Beckett, *Murphy*, p. 65.
64 Phillips, 'Just Rage', p. 122.
65 Brienza, 'Clods', p. 93.
66 Dirk Van Hulle and Mark Nixon, *Samuel Beckett's Library* (Cambridge: Cambridge University Press, 2013), p. 145; Schopenhauer, 'On Women', in Hollingdale (ed.), *Essays and Aphorisms*, pp. 80–8 (p. 88).
67 Beckett, 'First Love', p. 39.
68 Ibid., pp. 42–3.
69 Beckett, *Murphy*, p. 6.
70 Ibid., p. 17.
71 Ibid., p. 66; Schopenhauer, 'On Aesthetics', p. 155.
72 Locke, *Essay Concerning Human Understanding*, p. 230.
73 Beckett, *Murphy*, p. 102.
74 Ibid., p. 112.
75 Lloyd, *Under Representation*, p. 51.
76 Ibid., p. 45.
77 Schopenhauer, 'On Women', pp. 84–5.
78 Schopenhauer, 'On Aesthetics', p. 155.
79 Schopenhauer, 'On Women', p. 84.
80 Beckett, 'First Love', p. 38.
81 Windelband, *A History of Philosophy II*, p. 449.
82 Kant, *Critique of Practical Reason*, p. 129.
83 Freud, *New Introductory Lectures*, p. 93.
84 Beckett, *Psychology Notes*, TCDMS10971/7, p. 6.
85 Theodor Adorno, *Problems of Moral Philosophy* (Stanford: Polity, 2000), p. 82.
86 Beckett, 'First Love', p.36.
87 Ibid., p. 36, p. 45.
88 Freud, *New Introductory Lectures*, p. 199; Beckett, 'First Love', p. 29.
89 Beckett, *Murphy*, p. 34.
90 Beckett, *Letters I*, p. 552.
91 Smith, '"Uproar"', p. 138.
92 Samuel Beckett, *Molloy* (London: Faber & Faber, 2009), p. 14.
93 Seán Kennedy, 'Mothering Molloy, or Beckett and Cutlery', in Mark Nixon (ed.) '"never neglect the little things in life": Beckett and the everyday', *Journal of Beckett Studies*, vol. 18, no. 1, 2019, pp. 35–51 (p. 37).
94 Beckett, *Molloy*, p. 32.
95 Gabriel d'Aubarède, 'Interview', in Lawrence Graver and Raymond Federman (eds), *Samuel Beckett: The critical heritage* (London: Routledge & Kegan Paul, 1979), pp. 215–17 (p. 217).
96 Beckett, *Molloy*, p. 24.
97 Ibid., p. 13.
98 Ibid., p. 15.

CHAPTER 13. 'Mind Our Men': Fragile masculinity in post-crash Irish men's writing

1 This essay was developed from two keynotes that I gave in 2016: 'Post-Crash Irish Literature and Culture: Its emergence and influence' at the Chinese University of Hong Kong in May 2016; and 'Precarious Subjects' at Trinity College Dublin in June 2016. Thanks to the many

people whose discussion and feedback enabled me to develop my ideas, especially Gavin Doyle and Michael O'Sullivan.

2 See Michael Kimmel, *Manhood in America: A cultural history*, 3rd edn (Oxford: Oxford University Press, 2011); Michael Kimmel, *Angry White Men: American masculinity at the end of an era* (New York: Nation Books, 2015); Suzanne Leonard, 'Escaping the Recession?: The new vitality of the woman worker', in Diane Negra and Yvonne Tasker (eds), *Gendering the Recession* (Durham: Duke University Press, 2014), pp. 31–58.

3 On 'white male injury', see Hamilton Carroll, *Affirmative Reaction: New formations of white masculinity* (Durham: Duke University Press, 2011), p. 2; Leonard, 'Escaping the Recession?', p. 33.

4 Leonard, 'Escaping the Recession?', p. 36. The focus on a causal relation between neoliberal restructuring, the decline of manufacturing industries, and the masculinity crisis predates the most recent recession, of course – see, for example, Susan Faludi, *Stiffed: The betrayal of the American man* (London: Chatto & Windus, 1999).

5 Patricia Coughlan, '"Bog Queens": The representation of femininity in the poetry of John Montague and Seamus Heaney', in Toni O'Brien Johnson and David Cairns (ed.), *Gender in Irish Writing* (Milton Keynes: Open University Press, 1991), pp. 88–111 (p. 88).

6 See Ursula Barry and Pauline Conroy, 'Ireland in Crisis 2008–2012: Women, austerity, and inequality', in Maria Karamessini and Jill Rubery (eds), *Women and Austerity: The economic crisis and the future for gender equality* (London: Routledge, 2013), pp. 186–206; Ursula Barry, *Austerity, Gender, and Inequality: Post-recession Ireland?* (Berlin: Rosa Luxemburg Stiftung, 2020); Alison Spillane, 'The Impact of the Crisis on Irish Women', in Colin Coulter and Angela Nagle (eds), *Ireland Under Austerity* (Manchester: Manchester University Press, 2015), pp. 151–70; and *Central Statistics Office (CSO) Quarterly, National Household Survey*, 2nd Quarter, 2017.

7 Daniel McConnell, Craig Hughes, and John Drennan, 'Burton Vows to End Dole Lifestyle Choice', *Irish Independent*, 17 July 2011, https://www.independent.ie/irish-news/burton-vows-to-end-dole-lifestyle-choice-26752421.html

8 Fionnán Sheahan, 'Kenny Declares War on Welfare Culture', *Irish Independent*, 21 October 2013, https://www.independent.ie/irish-news/kenny-declares-war-on-welfare-culture-29676166.html; Michael Brennan, 'Gilmore: Young People Should Not Be Permanently in Front of Flatscreen TVs', *Irish Independent*, 17 October 2013, https://www.independent.ie/business/budget/gilmore-young-people-should-not-be-permanently-in-front-of-flatscreen-tvs-29668457.html

9 See Ursula Barry, 'Gendered Austerity Policies: Inequality on the rise in the European Union including Ireland', in Beth English, Mary E. Frederickson, and Olga Sanmiguel-Valderrama (eds), *Global Women's Work: Perspectives on gender and work in the global economy* (London: Routledge, 2018), pp. 336–52.

10 Michael Cronin, 'Ireland's Disappeared: Suicide, violence, and austerity', in Colin Coulter and Angela Nagele (eds), *Ireland Under Austerity* (Manchester: Manchester University Press, 2015), pp. 133–50; Paul Corcoran et al., 'Impact of the Economic Recession and Subsequent Austerity on Suicide and Self-harm in Ireland: An interrupted time series analysis', *International Journal of Epidemiology*, vol. 44, no. 3, 2015, pp. 1–9.

11 See for instance Kate Holmquist, 'Men Overboard', *Irish Times*, 5 October 2013, https://www.irishtimes.com/life-and-style/men-overboard-1.1550548; Kate Holmquist, 'Few are Untouched by the "Mancession"', *Irish Times*, 7 October 2013, https://www.irishtimes.com/life-and-style/few-are-untouched-by-the-mancession-1.1550686

12 Donal Ryan, *The Spinning Heart* (Dublin: Doubleday Ireland, 2012), p. 22.

13 Diane Negra, 'Adjusting Men and Abiding Mammies: Gendering the recession in Ireland', *Gender, Sexuality & Feminism*, vol. 1, no. 2, 2014, pp. 23–34 (p. 28, p. 27). Debbie Ging very

usefully develops this point in relation to the 'new gangster genre' in Irish popular culture in 'Memes, Masculinity, and Mancession: *Love/Hate*'s online metatexts', *Irish Studies Review*, vol. 25, no. 2, 2017, pp. 170–92.

14 Lisa McInerney, 'Seize the Means of Publication (Hard Lessons Learned as a Working-Class Writer)', in Declan Meade (ed.), *Beyond the Centre: Writers in their own words* (Dublin: New Island Books, 2017), pp. 207–16 (p. 213).

15 Ging, 'Memes, Masculinity and Mancession', p. 173.

16 Colin Barrett, 'The Moon', in *Young Skins* (London: Vintage, 2015), pp. 33–44 (p. 33).

17 'Calm With Horses', in *Young Skins*, pp. 69–142.

18 Jack Halberstam, *The Queer Art of Failure* (Durham: Duke University Press, 2011), p. 92.

19 Ibid., p. 92.

20 'The Clancy Kid', in *Young Skins*, pp. 3–18 (p. 6).

21 'Kindly Forget My Existence', *Young Skins*, pp. 159–76 (p. 162).

22 Leonard, 'Escaping the Recession?', p. 42. See Kay Hymowitz, *Manning Up: How the rise of women has turned men into boys* (London: Basic Books, 2011).

23 Leonard, 'Escaping the Recession?', p. 42.

24 Kevin Barry, *City of Bohane* (London: Vintage, 2011), p. 3.

25 Ryan, *Spinning Heart*, p. 92; Barrett, 'Bait', in *Young Skins*, p. 22; Barrett, 'The Moon', in *Young Skins*, p. 37.

26 Luke Brown, 'Emasculated: The problem of men writing about sex', *Times Literary Supplement*, 3 July 2020, https://www.the-tls.co.uk/articles/emasculated-the-problem-of-men-writing-about-sex-essay-luke-brown/

CHAPTER 14. 'a permeable membrane gives at the slightest touch': The ecopoetics of houses in the poetry of Vona Groarke and Sinéad Morrissey

1 Vona Groarke, *Other People's Houses* (Loughcrew: Gallery, 1999) and Sinéad Morrissey, *Through the Square Window* (Manchester: Carcanet, 2009). All subsequent references to these volumes will be noted in parentheses.

2 Vona Groarke, *Juniper Street* (Loughcrew: Gallery, 2006), p. 47.

3 Sinéad Morrissey, *Between Here and There* (Manchester: Carcanet, 2002), p. 29.

4 Ibid., p. 31.

5 In his essay 'The Language Habitat: An ecopoetry manifesto', *Octopus*, vol. 9, 2007, James Engelhardt mentions play as one of the connections that to him define the genre: 'the ecopoem must connect to the human capacity to play. More so even than our animal cousins, we are creatures who play. Ecopoems must allow our full range of joy and experimentation as we try to connect to our world and the other creatures here with us. Play allows for interdependent coevolution that explores the contingent within connection, that lets the mind roam without limit. Play reveals deep connections.'

6 James Joyce, *A Portrait of the Artist as a Young Man*, Jeri Johnston (ed.) (Oxford: Oxford University Press, 2000), p. 180.

7 Derrida's book *The Animal That Therefore I Am*, Marie-Louise Mellet (ed.), David Wills (trans.) (New York: Fordham University Press, 2008) is a posthumous collection of various writings on philosophical conceptions of animals. Giorgio Agamben, *The Open: Man and animal*, Kevin Attell (trans.) (Stanford: Stanford University Press, 2004), presents a genealogy of distinctions between human and animal in western thought, as well as the troubling conceptual and practical implications of these distinctions in the posthistorical age.

8 Derrida, *The Animal That Therefore I Am*, p. 148.

9 Ibid., p. 155.

10 Agamben, *The Open*, p. 71.

11 This essay has obvious affinities with the body of interdisciplinary work that has been described as 'the spatial turn' in the humanities and social sciences. As Adam Hanna notes, the geographer Stephen Daniels wrote that 'across the disciplines, the study of space has undergone a profound and sustained transformation. Space, place, mapping, and geographical imaginations have become commonplace topics in a variety of analytical fields in part because globalization has accentuated the significance of location': 'Place and the Geographical Imagination', *Geography*, vol. 77, 1992, pp. 310–22 (p. 310), quoted in Hanna, *Northern Irish Poetry and Domestic Space* (Basingstoke: Palgrave Macmillan, 2015) p. 137, n. 18. Other texts that have been influential for my thinking include Gaston Bachelard, *The Poetics of Space*, Maria Jolas (trans.) (Boston: Beacon Press, 1994 [1964]); Yi-Fu Tuan, *Space and Place: The perspective of experience* (Minneapolis: University of Minnesota Press, 1977); Henri Lefebvre, *The Production of Space*, Donald Nicholson-Smith (trans.) (Oxford: Blackwell, 1991); and Kathleen Stewart, *A Space on the Side of the Road: Cultural poetics in an 'other' America* (Princeton: Princeton University Press, 1996).

12 Johnston uses the term *baroque* to explain this tendency; see his essay '"Hundred-Pocketed Time": Ní Chuilleanáin's baroque spaces', *Irish University Review*, vol. 37, 2007, Special Issue: Eiléan Ní Chuilleanáin, Anne Fogarty (ed.), pp. 53–67.

13 Patricia Coughlan, '"No Lasting Fruit At All": Containing, recognition, and relinquishing in *The Girl Who Married the Reindeer*', *Irish University Review*, vol. 37, 2007 , pp. 157–77 (p. 159).

14 Eiléan Ní Chuilleanáin, *The Sun-Fish* (Loughcrew: Gallery, 2009), p. 26.

15 Medbh McGuckian, *On Ballycastle Beach* (Winston-Salem: Wake Forest University Press, 1988), p. 43.

16 Medbh McGuckian, *Marconi's Cottage* (Loughcrew: Gallery, 1991). Notable studies of voice in early McGuckian include Clair Wills, *Improprieties: Politics and sexuality in Northern Irish poetry* (Oxford: Clarendon Press, 1993); and Leontia Flynn, *Reading Medbh McGuckian* (Sallins: Irish Academic Press, 2014). See also the phenomenological analysis of McGuckian's voice as 'internal other' in Elin Holmsten, 'The Hermeneutics of Otherness in Medbh McGuckian's Poetry', unpublished PhD thesis, Uppsala Universitet, 2006.

17 The scholar most noted for locating and analysing McGuckian's source material is Shane Alcobia-Murphy. See his *Medbh McGuckian: The poetics of exemplarity* (University of Aberdeen: AHRC Centre for Irish and Scottish Studies, 2012). McGuckian's comparison of her methods of composition with birds' nests is discussed in Shane Alcobia-Murphy, *Sympathetic Ink: Intertextual relations in Northern Irish poetry* (Liverpool: Liverpool University Press, 2006), p. 47; and Hanna, *Northern Irish Poetry and Domestic Space*, p. 130.

18 Moynagh Sullivan analyses the concept of a poem as inert container in terms of the maternal body in McGuckian's work; see 'The In-formal Poetics of Medbh McGuckian', *Nordic Irish Studies*, vol. 3, 2004, pp. 75–92. See also Danielle Sered for a perceptive distinction between erasure of authority and a clearing away that 'makes possible its refigured return' (p. 284) in McGuckian's practice: '"By Escaping and [Leaving] a Mark": Authority and the writing subject of the poetry of Medbh McGuckian', *Irish University Review*, vol. 32, 2002, pp. 273–85.

19 Analyses of space, in particular of domestic space, in the work of women writers, are common in second-wave feminist criticism. The trope has also been usefully challenged by, among other efforts, Black and majority-world feminist criticism in the wake of the Combahee River Collective; see Trudier Harris, *Depictions of Home in African American Literature* (Lanham: Lexington Books, 2021). See also Kyla Schuller, *The Biopolitics of Feeling: Race, sex, and science in the nineteenth century* (Durham: Duke University Press, 2017), which argues that the scientific discourse of sexual division arose as a subset of racial theory. According

to Schuller, this genealogy underpins contemporary biopolitics no less than the historical cultures where 'angels of the house' co-existed with a wide range of female people who were not allowed to stay home, or indeed to have homes to inhabit.

20 Vona Groarke, *Flight and Earlier Poems* (Winston-Salem: Wake Forest University Press, 2004), p. 19.

21 Martin Doyle, 'Brought to Book: Vona Groarke on the unbearable lightness of reviews', interview with Vona Groarke, *Irish Times*, 30 May 2014, https://www.irishtimes.com/culture/books/brought-to-book-vona-groarke-on-the-unbearable-lightness-of-reviews-1.1806730

22 Augé's distinction between what he terms spaces and non-spaces in the globalised world raises a number of aesthetic as well as social issues; see *Anthropology for Contemporaneous Worlds*, Amy Jacobs (trans.) (Stanford: Stanford University Press, 1999 [1994]) and *Non-Places: An introduction to supermodernity*, John Howe (trans.) (London: Verso, 2008 [1992]).

23 Vona Groarke, *Spindrift* (Loughcrew: Gallery, 2009).

24 Vona Groarke, *Four Sides Full* (Loughcrew: Gallery, 2016).

25 Ibid., p. 53.

26 Louis MacNeice, 'Snow', in *Collected Poems*, Peter McDonald (ed.) (London: Faber & Faber, 2007), p. 24.

27 Slavka Sverakova, 'Review of *A Seed of Zero*, Golden Thread Gallery, Belfast, December 2006 – January 2007', *Circa Art Magazine*, 2007. See https://circaartmagazine.net/a-seed-of-zero-golden-thread-gallery-belfast-december-2006-january-2007/

28 Vona Groarke, *Lament for Art O'Leary. From the Irish of Eibhlín Dubh Ní Chonaill* (Loughcrew: Gallery, 2008).

CHAPTER 15. Alienated Subjects: Post-feminist control and contemporary Irish femininity

1 Patricia Coughlan, 'Irish Literature and Feminism in Postmodernity', *Hungarian Journal of English and American Studies*, vol. 10, nos 1–2, 2004, pp. 175–202 (p. 178).

2 See Wanda Balzano and Moynagh Sullivan, 'Editorial: The contemporary ballroom of romance', Special Issue: Irish Feminisms, *Irish Review*, vol. 35, 2007, pp. 1–6; Claire Bracken, 'Post-Feminism and the Celtic Tiger: Deirdre O'Kane's television roles', in Claire Bracken and Emma Radley (eds), *Viewpoints: Theoretical perspectives on Irish visual texts* (Cork: Cork University Press, 2013), pp. 169–83; Debbie Ging, 'All-Consuming Images: New gender formations in post-Celtic-Tiger Ireland', in Debbie Ging, Michael Cronin, and Peadar Kirby (eds), *Transforming Ireland: Challenges, critiques, and resources* (Manchester: Manchester University Press, 2009), pp. 52–70.

3 Susan Cahill, 'A Girl Is a Half-Formed Thing?: Girlhood, trauma, and resistance in post-Tiger Irish women's fiction', *Literature Interpretation Theory*, vol. 28, no. 2, 2017, p. 155. On representations of Irish girlhood, see Susan Cahill, 'Where Are the Irish Girls? Girlhood, Irishness, and L.T. Meade', in Claudia Mitchell and Carrie Rentschler (eds), *Girlhood Studies and the Politics of Place: Contemporary paradigms for research* (New York: Berghahn Books, 2016), pp. 212–27; Susan Cahill, 'Making Space for the Irish Girl: Rosa Mulholland and Irish girls in fiction at the turn of the century', in Kristine Moruzi and Michelle J. Smith (eds), *Colonial Girlhood in Literature, Culture and History, 1840–1950* (Basingstoke: Palgrave, 2014), pp. 167–79; Jane Elizabeth Dougherty, 'Nuala O'Faolain and the Unwritten Irish Girlhood', *New Hibernia Review*, vol. 11, no, 2, 2007, pp. 50–65.

4 Cahill, 'Making Space', p. 153.

5 Coughlan, 'Irish Literature', p. 177.

6 See the introductory chapter of Stéphanie Genz and Benjamin A. Brabon, *Postfeminism: Cultural texts and theories* (Edinburgh: Edinburgh University Press, 2009), pp. 1–50.

7 Ibid., p. 6.

8 Diane Negra, *What a Girl Wants? Fantasizing the reclamation of the self in postfeminism* (London; Routledge, 2009); Yvonne Tasker and Diane Negra, 'Introduction: Feminist politics and postfeminist culture', in Yvonne Tasker and Diane Negra (eds), *Interrogating Postfeminism: Gender and the politics of popular culture* (Durham: Duke University Press, 2007), pp. 1–25.

9 Angela McRobbie, *The Aftermath of Feminism: Gender, culture, and social change* (London: Sage, 2009), p. 2.

10 Ibid., p. 57

11 Ibid.

12 Negra, *What a Girl Wants?*, p. 5.

13 Gilles Deleuze, *Negotiations: 1972–1990*, Martin Joughin (trans.) (New York: Columbia University Press, 1995), p. 178.

14 Ibid., p. 179.

15 Ibid.

16 Ibid.

17 As Luce Irigaray argues, female rivalry is based on the Oedipal configuration of the 'one' place for woman, the mother: 'In this way, a woman becoming a mother will be *the Mother*, totally identified with maternity through a kind of murder of *her own mother*.' Luce Irigaray, *Speculum of the Other Woman*, Gillian C. Gill (trans.) (Ithaca: Cornell University Press, 1985), p. 76.

18 Deleuze, *Negotiations*, p. 179.

19 McRobbie makes a similar point in the specific context of consumerism, noting that 'by generating bodily dissatisfaction, the beauty and fashion industries respond directly to the fraught state of non-identity which we all inhabit and which is predicated on unfathomable loss'. McRobbie, *The Aftermath of Feminism*, p. 62.

20 Anne Enright, 'Natalie', in *Taking Pictures* (London: Jonathan Cape, 2008), pp. 41–51 (p. 41). All further references will be noted in parentheses.

21 Elke D'hoker, 'Distorting Mirrors and Unsettling Snapshots: Anne Enright's short fiction', in Claire Bracken and Susan Cahill (eds), *Anne Enright* (Dublin: Irish Academic Press, 2011), pp. 33–50 (p. 43).

22 Somewhat like the US prom, the Debs [debutantes' dance] is a formal dinner dance (generally black tie) held after graduating from secondary school in Ireland.

23 Hedwig Schwall, in her reading of *The Portable Virgin*, argues that subjects in Enright's fiction are 'dividual', rather than 'individual', reading the dividual differently, as a symbol of interaction, between self and other, subject and world. See Schwall, '*The Portable Virgin*: Anne Enright's translations of philosophy into literature', in Laura Izarra and Beatriz Kopschitz X. Bastos (eds), *A New Ireland in Brazil: Festschrift in honour of Munira Hamud Mutran* (São Paulo: Humanitas, 2008), pp. 339–50 (p. 350).

24 Anne Enright, 'An Interview with Anne Enright, August 2009', in Bracken and Cahill (eds), *Anne Enright*, pp. 13–32 (p. 25).

25 See Coughlan 'Irish Literature', pp. 182–6, for an incisive analysis of embodied inter-subjective relations in Enright's first novel *The Wig My Father Wore*. With respect to *The Pleasure of Eliza Lynch*, Coughlan notes that 'A third term, largely unattended to in the *world* which the book constructs, though not in *the book itself*, which brings it forcefully before the reader's mind, is compassionate inter-subjectivity, which is daily betrayed in people's consumption of one another, in war, in the abuse of power, and the struggle between the wealthy and the wretched'. '"Without a blink of her lovely eye": *The Pleasure of Eliza Lynch* and visionary skepticism', *Irish University Review*, vol. 35, no. 2, 2005, pp. 349–73 (p. 357).

26 Susan Cahill specifically reads Grace's swimming body at the end of *The Wig My Father Wore* as 'a powerful image of intersubjectivity between the generations'. Susan Cahill, *Irish*

Literature in the Celtic Tiger Years 1990–2008: Gender, bodies, memory (London: Continuum, 2011), p. 112.

27 Leanne O'Sullivan, *Waiting for My Clothes* (Tarset: Bloodaxe Books, 2004). Further allusions to this text will be noted in parentheses.

28 See Leanne O'Sullivan, *Cailleach: The Hag of Beara* (Tarset: Bloodaxe Books, 2009); *The Mining Road* (Tarset: Bloodaxe Books, 2013); *A Quarter of an Hour* (Tarset: Bloodaxe Books, 2018).

29 Luz Mar González-Arias, '"The Famine of the 90s": Female starvation and religious thought in Leanne O'Sullivan's *Waiting for My Clothes*', *Estudios Irlandeses*, vol. 0, 2005, pp. 50–7 (p. 53). See also Eavan Boland, *In Her Own Image* (Dublin: Arlen House, 1980).

30 González-Arias, '"The Famine of the 90s"', p. 51.

31 Ging, 'All-Consuming Images', p. 63.

32 The collection also stages a critique of Ireland's patriarchal past, with González-Arias identifying the recurrence of religious imagery in *Waiting for My Clothes*, persuasively connecting it to a Catholic legacy of denial and denigration of the female body and sexuality, something evident in 'Famine', a third-person poem concerning a girl that 'sits at the dinner table' refusing food (p. 14). The poem's title recalls a traumatic period of Ireland's past, while resolutely locating this in the present, 'the famine of the 90s', and the pressures of the beauty myth: 'She is beautiful'. The title's reference to Ireland's past is important in placing the poem, and the collection as a whole, as performing a critique of both present and past.

33 Coughlan, 'Irish Literature', p. 186.

34 Belinda McKeon, 'About a Girl', *Irish Times*, 6 November 2004.

35 Bonnie Moradi, Danielle Dirks, and Alicia V. Matteson, 'Roles of Sexual Objectification Experiences and Internalization of Standards of Beauty in Eating Disorder Symptomatology: A test and extension of objectification theory', *Journal of Counseling Psychology*, vol. 52, no. 3, 2005, pp. 420–8.

36 Negra, *What A Girl Wants?*, p. 121.

37 For other examples of the doubled self in the collection see: 'When We Were Good'; 'My Father Asks Me Why'; 'Hunger'; 'Hangover of Years'; 'What Doesn't Kill Us'.

38 Coughlan, 'Irish Literature', p. 185.

39 See also 'My Father Asks Me Why' for an association of foetal curling and the death of self.

40 This is evident, for example, in the poem 'Crescendo' and also 'My Father's Fleece'.

41 Ivana Bacik, 'From Virgins and Mothers to Popstars and Presidents: Changing roles of women in Ireland', Special Issue: Irish Feminisms, *Irish Review*, vol. 35, 2007, pp. 100–7 (p. 105).

42 For example, see Rebecca Pelan, *Two Irelands: Literary feminisms North and South* (Syracuse: Syracuse University Press, 2005), pp. 3–7.

43 See Jennifer De Wan, 'The Practice of Politics: Feminism, activism, and social change in Ireland', in John Hogan, Paul F. Donnelly, and Brendan K. Rourke (eds), *Irish Business and Society: Governing, participating, and transforming in the 21st century* (Dublin: Gill Books, 2010), pp. 520–36. Ailbhe Smyth, 'Momentary Views: A personal history', *The Irish Review*, vol. 35, 2007, pp. 7–24. In 2001, at the height of the Tiger boom, the African Women's Network (AkiDWa) was established, an organisation whose mission is 'to promote equality and justice for migrant women living in Ireland', http://www.akidwa.ie. For excellent accounts of feminist activism in the second wave in Ireland, see Linda Connolly, *The Irish Women's Movement: From revolution to devolution* (Dublin: Lilliput Press, 2003) and Linda Connolly and Tina O'Toole, *Documenting Irish Feminisms: The second wave* (Dublin: Woodfield Press, 2005).

44 Coughlan, 'Irish Literature', p. 179.

Patricia Coughlan Publications

EDITED COLLECTIONS:

Coughlan, Patricia, *Spenser and Ireland: An interdisciplinary perspective* (Cork: Cork University Press, 1990)

Coughlan, Patricia and Alex Davis (eds), *Modernism and Ireland: The poetry of the 1930s* (Cork: Cork University Press, 1995)

Coughlan, Patricia and Tina O'Toole (eds), *Irish Literature: Feminist perspectives* (Dublin: Carysfort Press, 2008)

CHAPTERS IN BOOKS:

'The Recycling of Melmoth: "A Very German Story"', in Wolfgang Zach and Heinz Kosok (eds), *Literary Interrelations: Ireland, England, and the world*, vol. II (Tübingen: Günter Narr, 1987), pp. 181–92

'"Fold over fold, inveterately convolv'd": Some aspects of Mangan's intertextuality', in Birgit Bramsback and Martin Croghan (eds), *Anglo-Irish and Irish Literature, vol. II (Acta Universitatis Upsaliensis)* (Uppsala: University of Uppsala, 1988), pp. 191–200

'Doubles, Shadows, Sedan Chairs, and the Past: The ghost stories of J.S. Le Fanu', in Michael Allen and Angela Wilcox (eds), *Critical Approaches to Anglo-Irish Literature* (Gerrards Cross: Colin Smythe, 1989), pp. 17–39

'"Some secret scourge which by her shall come unto England": Ireland and alterity in Spenser', in Patricia Coughlan (ed.), *Spenser and Ireland: An interdisciplinary perspective* (Cork: Cork University Press, 1990), pp. 46–74

'"Cheap and common animals": The English anatomy of Ireland in the seventeenth century', in Thomas Healy and Jonathan Sawday (eds), *Literature and the English Civil War* (Cambridge: Cambridge University Press, 1990), pp. 205–23

'"Bog Queens": The representation of femininity in the poetry of Seamus Heaney and John Montague', in Toni O'Brien Johnson and David Cairns (eds), *Gender in Irish Writing* (Milton Keynes: Open University Press, 1991), pp. 88–111

'Kate O'Brien: Feminine beauty, feminist writing, and sexual role', in Eibhear Walshe (ed.), *Ordinary People Dancing: Essays on Kate O'Brien* (Cork: Cork University Press, 1993), pp. 59–84

'Natural History and Historical Nature: The project for a natural history of Ireland', in Mark Greengrass, Michael Leslie, and Timothy Ryder (eds), *Samuel Hartlib and Universal Reformation: Studies in intellectual communication* (Cambridge: Cambridge University Press, 1994), pp. 298–318

'"The poetry is another pair of sleeves": Beckett, Ireland, and modernist lyric poetry', in Patricia Coughlan and Alex Davis (eds), *Modernism and Ireland: The poetry of the 1930s* (Cork: Cork University Press, 1995), pp. 173–208

'*Entre le galet et la mer*: Reading a Beckett poem between two languages', in Stephen F. Boyd and John C. Barnes (eds), *Cross-Currents in European Literature* (Dublin: UCD Dept. of Italian, 1996), pp. 69–79

'"Bog Queens": The representation of women in the poetry of John Montague and Seamus Heaney', in Michael Allen (ed.), *Seamus Heaney* (New Casebooks) (London: Palgrave, 1997), pp. 185–205

'Women and Desire in the Work of Elizabeth Bowen', in Eibhear Walshe (ed.), *Sex, Nation, and Dissent* (Cork: Cork University Press, 1997), pp. 103–34

'An Léiriú ar Shaol na mBan i dTéacsanna Dírbheathaisnéise Pheig Sayers' ('The Representation of Women's Lives in the Autobiographical Texts of Peig Sayers'), in Máire Ní Chéilleachair (eag.), *Peig Sayers, Scéalaí, 1873–1958 (Ceiliúradh an Bhlascaoid 3)* (Baile Átha Cliath: Coiscéim, 1999), pp. 20–57

'Cross-Currents in Colonial Discourse: The political thought of Vincent and Daniel Gookin', in Jane H. Ohlmeyer (ed.), *Political Thought in Seventeenth-Century Ireland* (Cambridge: Cambridge University Press, 2000), pp. 56–82

'"The poetry is another pair of sleeves": Beckett, Ireland and modernist lyric poetry', in Jennifer Birkett and Kate Ince (eds), *Samuel Beckett (Longman Critical Readers)* (London: Longman, 2000), pp. 65–82

'"The modell of its sad afflictions": Henry Burkhead's *Tragedy of Cola's Furie or Lirenda's Miserie*', in Mícheál Ó Siochrú, *Kingdoms in Crisis: Ireland in the 1640s* (Dublin: Four Courts Press, 2001), pp. 192–211

'"Bog Queens": The representation of women in the poetry of John Montague and Seamus Heaney', in Claire Connolly (ed.), *Theorizing Ireland* (London: Palgrave Macmillan, 2003), pp. 41–60

'Introduction' [co-authored, Tina O'Toole], in Tina O'Toole (ed.), *A Dictionary of Munster Women Writers, 1800–2000* (Cork: Cork University Press. 2005), pp. xv–xxxvi

'Killing the Bats: O'Brien, abjection, and the question of agency', in Kathryn Laing, Sinéad Mooney, and Maureen O'Connor (eds), *Edna O'Brien: New critical perspectives* (Cork: Cork University Press, 2006), pp. 171–95

'Rereading Peig Sayers: Women's autobiography, social history, and narrative art', in Patricia Boyle Haberstroh and Christine St Peter (eds), *Opening the Field: Irish women, texts and contexts* (Cork: Cork University Press, 2007), pp. 58–73

'"The whole strange growth": Heaney, Orpheus, and women', *Irish Review*, vol. 35, 2007, pp. 25–45

'Introduction', in Patricia Coughlan and Tina O'Toole (eds), *Irish Literature: Feminist perspectives* (Dublin: Carysfort Press, 2008), pp. 1–15

'"Not like a person at all": Bowen, the 1920s, and "The Dancing-Mistress"', in Eibhear Walshe (ed.), *Elizabeth Bowen* (Dublin: Irish Academic Press, 2008), pp. 40–65

'"Chipped and Tilted Marys': Two Irish poets in their contemporary contexts', in Britta Olinder and Werner Huber (eds), *Place and Memory in the New Ireland (Irish Studies in Europe, Volume 2)* (Trier: WVT Wissenschaftlicher Verlag Trier, 2009), pp. 71–100

'Introduction', in *'A Tragedie of Cola's Furie, Or Lirenda's Miserie' by Henry Burkhead* (Dublin: Four Courts Press, 2009), pp. 9–32

'Doubles, Shadows, Sedan-Chairs, and the Past: The ghost stories of J.S. Le Fanu', in Gary William Crawford, Jim Rockhill, and Brian J. Summers (eds), *Reflections in a Glass Darkly: Essays on J. Sheridan Le Fanu* (New York: Hippocampus Press, 2011), pp. 137–60

'"Without a blink of her lovely eye": *The Pleasure of Eliza Lynch* and visionary scepticism', in Claire Bracken and Susan Cahill (eds), *Anne Enright* (Dublin: Irish Academic Press, 2011), pp. 107–26

'"An t-éitheach; is an fíor? ...": A note on two late poems by Máire Mhac an tSaoi', in John Carey, Kevin Murray, and Caitríona Ó Dochartaigh (eds), *Sacred Histories: A festschrift for Máire Herbert* (Dublin: Four Courts Press, 2015), pp. 103–14

'"For nothing can be sole or whole / That has not been rent": Torn motherhood in Máire Mhac an tSaoi's "Love has pitched his mansion ..."', in Louis de Paor (eag.), *Míorúilt an Pharóiste: Aistí ar fhilíocht Mháire Mhac an tSaoi* (Indreabhán: Cló Iar-Chonnacht, 2015), pp. 41–62

'Hard Times and Sibling Songs: Sibling relations in contemporary Irish literature', in Luz Mar González-Arias (ed.), *National Identities and Imperfections in Contemporary Irish Literature* (London: Palgrave Macmillan, 2017), pp. 67–82

'Elizabeth Bowen', in Heather Ingman and Clíona Ó Gallchoir (eds), *A History of Modern Irish Women's Literature* (Cambridge: Cambridge University Press, 2018), pp. 204–26

'The Poetry of Máire Mhac an tSaoi and the Indivisibility of Love', in Ailbhe Darcy and David Wheatley (eds), *A History of Irish Women's Poetry* (Cambridge: Cambridge University Press, 2021), pp. 255–69

ESSAYS IN JOURNALS:

'"A noise of wet kisses and washing in a tub": Samuel Beckett and the idea of fiction', *Maynooth Review*, vol. 6, no. 1, 1980, pp. 35–48

'"Enter Revenge": Henry Burkhead and *Cola's Furie*', *Theatre Research International*, vol. 15, 1989, pp. 1–17

'The Local Context of Mutabilitie's Plea', *Irish University Review*, vol. 26, no. 2, 1996, pp. 320–41

'"Does a man die at your feet …": Gender, history, and representation in *The Catastrophist*', *Irish University Review*, vol. 33, no. 2, 2003, pp. 371–91

'Irish Literature and Feminism in Post-Modernity', *Hungarian Journal of English and American Studies*, vol. 10, no. 2, 2004, pp. 175–202

'"Without a blink of her lovely eye": Anne Enright's *The Pleasure of Eliza Lynch* and visionary scepticism', *Irish University Review*, vol. 35, no. 1, 2005, pp. 349–73

'Banville, the Feminine, and the Scenes of Eros', *Irish University Review*, vol. 36, no. 1, 2006, pp. 81–101

'"No lasting fruit at all": Containing, recognition, and relinquishing in *The Girl Who Married the Reindeer*', *Irish University Review*, vol. 37, no. 1, 2007, pp. 157–77

'"The whole strange growth": Heaney, Orpheus, and women', *Irish Review*, vol. 35, 2007, pp. 25–45

'"High Tide: Amagansett", Thomas Kinsella', *Irish University Review*, vol. 39, no. 2, 2009, pp. 367–84

'Paper Ghosts: Reading the uncanny in Alice McDermott', *Éire-Ireland*, vol. 47, nos 1 & 2, 2012, pp. 123–46

'"So am I detached / From the fabric which claims me": Women, fabric, and poetry', *Review of Irish Studies in Europe*, vol. 2, no. 1, 2018, pp. 241–61

'"We get all sealed up": An essay in five deaths', *Irish University Review*, special issue on Elizabeth Bowen, Tina O'Toole (ed.), vol. 51, no. 1, 2021, pp. 9–23

Bibliography

Abbott, Hal Porter, *Beckett Writing Beckett: The author in the autograph* (Cornell: Cornell University Press, 1996)

Adorno, Theodor, *Problems of Moral Philosophy* (Stanford: Polity, 2000)

Agamben, Giorgio, *The Open: Man and animal*, Kevin Attell (trans.) (Stanford: Stanford University Press, 2004)

Agathocleous, Tanya, *Urban Realism and the Cosmopolitan Imagination in the Nineteenth Century* (Cambridge: Cambridge University Press, 2011)

Alcobia-Murphy, Shane, *Sympathetic Ink: Intertextual relations in Northern Irish poetry* (Liverpool: Liverpool University Press, 2006)

—, *Medbh McGuckian: The poetics of exemplarity* (University of Aberdeen: AHRC Centre for Irish and Scottish Studies, 2012)

Allen, Nicholas, *Ireland, Literature, and the Coast: Seatangled* (Oxford: Oxford University Press, 2021)

Allen, Nicholas, Nick Groom, and Jos Smith (eds), *Coastal Works: Cultures of the Atlantic edge* (Oxford: Oxford University Press, 2017)

Allison, Jonathan, 'Galway, Coole, and Ballylee', in David Holdeman and Ben Levitas (eds), *W.B. Yeats in Context* (Cambridge: Cambridge University Press, 2010), pp. 98–108

Anderson, R., '"*Ein Kind wird geschlagen*": The Meaning of Malory's "Tale of the Healing of Sir Urry"', *Literature and Psychology*, vol. 49, no. 3, 2003, pp. 45–74

Archibald, Elizabeth, 'Malory's Ideal of Fellowship', *Review of English Studies*, vol. 43, 1992, pp. 311–28

—, *Incest and the Medieval Imagination* (Oxford: Clarendon Press, 2001)

—, 'Mordred's Lost Childhood', *Arthuriana*, vol. 29, no. 1, 2019, pp. 77–87

Ariès, Philippe, *The Hour of Our Death*, Helen Weaver (trans.) (New York: Alfred A. Knopf, 1981)

Arkins, Brian, *Builders of My Soul: Greek and Roman themes in Yeats* (Gerrards Cross: Colin Smythe, 1990)

Augé, Marc, *Anthropology for Contemporaneous Worlds*, Amy Jacobs (trans.) (Stanford: Stanford University Press, 1999 [1994])

—, *Non-Places: An introduction to supermodernity*, John Howe (trans.) (London: Verso, 2008 [1992])

Bachelard, Gaston, *The Poetics of Space*, Maria Jolas (trans.) (Boston: Beacon Press, 1994 [1964])

Bacik, Ivana, 'From Virgins and Mothers to Popstars and Presidents: Changing roles of women in Ireland', Special Issue: Irish Feminisms, *Irish Review*, vol. 35, 2007, pp. 100–7

Baker, Phil, *Beckett and the Mythology of Psychoanalysis* (London: Macmillan, 1997)

Balint, Enid, 'On Being Empty of Oneself', in Juliet Mitchell and M. Parsons (eds), *Before I Was I: Psychoanalysis and the imagination* (London: Free Association Books, 1993 [1963]), pp. 37–55

Balzano, Wanda and Moynagh Sullivan, 'Editorial: The contemporary ballroom of romance', Special Issue: Irish Feminisms, *Irish Review*, vol. 35, 2007, pp. 1–6

Banks, Iain, *The Crow Road* (London: Scribners, 1992)

Barrett, Colin, *Young Skins* (London: Vintage, 2013)

Barry, Kevin, *City of Bohane* (London: Vintage, 2011)

Barry, Ursula, *Austerity, Gender, and Inequality: Post-recession Ireland?* (Berlin: Rosa Luxemburg Stiftung, 2020)

Barry, Ursula and Pauline Conroy, 'Ireland in Crisis 2008–2012: Women, austerity, and inequality', in Maria Karamessini and Jill Rubery (eds), *Women and Austerity: The economic crisis and the future for gender equality* (London: Routledge, 2013), pp. 186–206

Barton, Ruth, *Irish National Cinema* (London: Routledge, 2004)

Batt, Catharine, *Malory's 'Morte Darthur': Remaking Arthurian tradition* (New York: Palgrave Macmillan, 2002)

Beaumont, Caitriona, 'Women, Citizenship, and Catholicism in the Irish Free State, 1922–1948', *Women's History Review*, vol. 6, no. 4, 1997, pp. 563–85

Beckett, Samuel, *Not I*, in *The Complete Dramatic Works* (London: Faber & Faber, 1990), pp. 376–83

—, *Murphy* (London: Calder, 1993)

—, 'First Love', in S.E. Gontarski (ed.), *The Complete Short Prose, 1929–1988* (New York: Grove Press, 1995), pp. 25–45

—, 'From an Abandoned Work', in S.E. Gontarski (ed.), *The Complete Short Prose, 1929–1988* (New York: Grove Press, 1995), pp. 155–64

—, *The Letters of Samuel Beckett I, 1929–40*, Martha Dow Fehsenfeld, Lois More Overbeck, Dan Gunn, and George Craig (eds) (Cambridge: Cambridge University Press, 2009)

—, *More Pricks than Kicks* (London: Faber & Faber, 2010)

—, *Psychology Notes*, Trinity College Dublin: TCDMS10971/8

Benjamin, Jessica, 'A Desire of One's Own: Psychoanalytic feminism and intersubjective space', in Teresa de Lauretis (ed.), *Feminist Studies/Critical Studies* (Bloomington: Indiana University Press, 1986), pp. 78–101

Ben-Zvi, Linda (ed.), *Women in Beckett: Performance and critical perspectives* (Urbana: University of Illinois Press, 1990)

Bergin, Osborn, *Irish Bardic Poetry*, compiled and edited by David Greene Fergus Kelly (Dublin: Dublin Institute for Advanced Studies, 1984)

Bewes, Timothy, *The Event of Postcolonial Shame* (Princeton: Princeton University Press, 2011)

Bloom, Harold, *Yeats* (New York: Oxford University Press, 1970)

Boland, Eavan, *In Her Own Image* (Dublin: Arlen House, 1980)

—, *An Origin Like Water: Collected Poems 1957–1987* (Manchester: Carcanet, 1997)

Boos, Florence S., 'General Introduction', *The Earthly Paradise, William Morris Archive*, http://morrisedition.lib.uiowa.edu/Poetry/EarthlyParadise/epintro.html

Bourke, Angela et al. (eds), *The Field Day Anthology of Irish Writing, vol. V* (Cork: Cork University Press, 2002)

Bourke, Angela, *Maeve Brennan: Style, wit, and tragedy. An Irish writer in New York* (London: Pimlico, 2005)

Bracken, Claire, 'Post-Feminism and the Celtic Tiger: Deirdre O'Kane's television roles', in Claire Bracken and Emma Radley (eds), *Viewpoints: Theoretical perspectives on Irish visual texts* (Cork: Cork University Press, 2012), pp. 157–71

—, *Irish Feminist Futures* (Abingdon: Routledge, 2016)

—, 'Gender and Irish Studies: 2008 to the present', in Renée Fox, Mike Cronin, and Brian Ó Conchubhair (eds), *The Routledge International Handbook of Irish Studies* (Abingdon: Routledge, 2021), pp. 230–44

Bracken, Claire and Susan Cahill (eds), *Anne Enright* (Dublin: Irish Academic Press, 2011)

Braddon, M.E., 'John Granger: A ghost story', *Belgravia Annual*, 1870, pp. 1–14

Brah, Avtar, *Cartographies of Diaspora: Contesting identities* (London: Routledge, 1996)

Brazeau, Robert (ed.), *Ecological Exile: Spatial injustice & environmental humanities* (Abingdon: Routledge, 2018)

Breatnach, Pádraig A., 'Metamorphosis 1603: Dán le hEochaidh Ó hEódhasa', *Éigse*, vol. 17, 1977–8, pp. 169–80

Brennan, Maeve, *The Springs of Affection: Stories of Dublin*, Introduction by William Maxwell; selected and arranged by Christopher Carduff (Berkeley: Counterpoint, 1997)

—, *The Long-Winded Lady: Notes from the New Yorker*, Christopher Carduff (ed.) (Berkeley: Counterpoint, 1998)

—, *The Rose Garden: Short stories*, Christopher Carduff (ed.) (Washington, DC: Counterpoint, 2000)

—, *The Visitor*, Christopher Carduff (ed.) (Washington, DC: Counterpoint 2000)

—, *The Springs of Affection*, Introduction by Anne Enright (Dublin: The Stinging Fly Press, 2016)

Brennan, Michael, 'Gilmore: Young People Should Not Be Permanently in Front of Flatscreen TVs', *Irish Independent*, 17 October 2013, https://www.

independent.ie/business/budget/gilmore-young-people-should-not-be-permanently-in-front-of-flatscreen-tvs-29668457.html

Brienza, Susan, 'Clods, Whores, and Bitches: Misogyny in Beckett's early fiction', in Ben-Zvi (ed.), *Women in Beckett*, pp. 91–105

Briggs, Julia, *Night Visitors: The rise and fall of the English ghost story* (London: Faber, 1977)

Brooks, Peter, *The Melodramatic Imagination: Balzac, Henry James, melodrama, and the mode of excess* (New Haven: Yale University Press, 1976)

Brown, Luke, 'Emasculated: The problem of men writing about sex', *Times Literary Supplement*, 3 July 2020, https://www.the-tls.co.uk/articles/emasculated-the-problem-of-men-writing-about-sex-essay-luke-brown/

Brown, Terence, *The Life of W.B. Yeats* (Dublin: Gill & Macmillan, 1999)

Brown, Wendy, *Manhood and Politics: A feminist reading in political theory* (New Jersey: Rowman & Littlefield, 1998)

Bryden, Mary, *Women in Samuel Beckett's Prose and Drama: Her own other* (Lanham: Barnes & Noble, 1993)

Bulfin Papers, National Library of Ireland (Manuscripts)

Bunreacht na hÉireann / Constitution of Ireland (Dublin: Stationery Office, 1945)

Burrow, Colin, 'Re-embodying Ovid: Renaissance afterlives', in Philip Hardie (ed.), *The Cambridge Companion to Ovid* (Cambridge: Cambridge University Press, 2002), pp. 301–19

Caball, Marc, *Poets and Politics: Reaction and continuity in Irish poetry, 1558–1625* (Cork: Cork University Press / Field Day, 1998)

—, 'Ó hEódhusa (O'Hussey), Eochaidh', *Dictionary of Irish Biography* (Cambridge: Cambridge University Press, 2010)

Cahill, Susan, *Irish Literature in the Celtic Tiger Years 1990–2008: Gender, bodies, memory* (London: Continuum, 2011)

—, 'Making Space for the Irish Girl: Rosa Mulholland and Irish girls in fiction at the turn of the century', in Kristine Moruzi and Michelle J. Smith (eds), *Colonial Girlhood in Literature, Culture and History, 1840–1950* (Basingstoke: Palgrave, 2014), pp. 167–79

—, 'Where Are the Irish Girls?: Girlhood, Irishness, and L.T. Meade', in Claudia Mitchell and Carrie Rentschler (eds), *Girlhood Studies and the Politics of Place: Contemporary paradigms for research* (New York: Berghahn Books, 2016), pp. 212–27

—, 'A Girl Is a Half-Formed Thing?: Girlhood, trauma and resistance in post-Tiger Irish women's fiction', *Literature Interpretation Theory*, vol. 28, no. 2, 2017, pp. 153–71

Canny, Nicholas, *Making Ireland British, 1580–1650* (Oxford: Oxford University Press, 2001)

Cantrell, Carol Helmstetter, 'Cartesian Man and the Woman Reader: A feminist approach to Beckett's *Molloy*', in Ben-Zvi (ed.), *Women in Beckett*, pp. 117–33

The Care Collective: Andreas Chatzidakis, Jamie Hakim, Jo Littler, Catherine Rottenberg, and Lynne Segal, *The Care Manifesto: The politics of interdependence* (London: Verso, 2021)

Carew, Mairéad, *Tara and the Ark of the Covenant: A search for the Ark of the Covenant by British Israelites on the Hill of Tara (1899–1902)* (Dublin: Royal Irish Academy, 2003)

'Carriage Court-Yesterday', *Freeman's Journal*, 5 November 1846

Carroll, Clare, *Circe's Cup: Cultural transformations in early modern writing about Ireland* (Notre Dame: University of Notre Dame Press / Field Day, 2001)

Carroll, Hamilton, *Affirmative Reaction: New formations of white masculinity* (Durham: Duke University Press, 2011)

Carroll, Lewis, *Alice in Wonderland*, 2nd edn, Donald J. Gray (ed.) (New York: W.W. Norton, 1992 [1871])

Cave, Terence, *Recognitions: A study in poetics* (Oxford: Clarendon Press, 1988)

Central Statistics Office [CSO], *Quarterly National Household Survey*, 2nd Quarter 2017

Centre for Landscape Studies, *Landscape Values: Place and praxis* (Galway: National University of Ireland Galway, 2016)

Cherewatuk, Karen, *Marriage, Adultery, and Inheritance in Malory's 'Morte Darthur'*, *Arthurian Studies 67* (Cambridge: D.S. Brewer, 2006)

Cherewatuk, Karen and K.S. Whetter (eds), *The Arthurian Way of Death: The English tradition* (Cambridge: D.S. Brewer, 2009)

Citizens' Assembly on Gender Equality, 24 April 2021, https://www.citizensassembly.ie/en/previous-assemblies/2020-2021-citizens-assembly-on-gender-equality/

Cixous, Hélène, 'Sorties', in Elaine Marks and Isabelle de Courtivron (eds), *New French Feminisms: An anthology* (New York: Schocken Books, 1981), pp. 90–8

Collins, Lucy, 'Review of *Before You*', *The Stinging Fly*, vol. 21, no. 2, 2012, pp. 119–22

—, *Contemporary Irish Women Poets* (Liverpool: Liverpool University Press, 2015)

Collins, Wilkie, *Basil* (Oxford: Oxford University Press, 2005 [1852])

Colman, Fran, *The Grammar of Names in Anglo-Saxon England: The linguistics and culture of the Old English onomasticon* (Oxford: Oxford University Press, 2014)

Connelly, Ailish, 'The Celtic Kittens Are in Control', *Irish Times*, 11 December 2006

Connolly, Claire, *A Cultural History of the Irish Novel, 1790–1829* (Cambridge: Cambridge University Press, 2012)

Connolly, Linda, *The Irish Women's Movement: From revolution to devolution* (Dublin: Lilliput Press, 2003)

Connolly, Linda and Tina O'Toole, *Documenting Irish Feminisms: The second wave* (Dublin: Woodfield Press, 2005)

Corcoran, Michael, *Through Streets Broad and Narrow* (Leicester: Midland, 2000)

Corey, Mary F., *World Through a Monocle: The New Yorker at midcentury* (Harvard: Harvard University Press, 1999)

Coughlan, Patricia, '"Some secret scourge which by her shall come unto England": Ireland and alterity in Spenser', in Patricia Coughlan (ed.), *Spenser and Ireland: An interdisciplinary perspective* (Cork: Cork University Press, 1990), pp. 46–74

—, 'Doubles, Shadows, Sedan-Chairs, and the Past: The ghost stories of J.S. Le Fanu', in M. Allen and A. Wilcox (eds), *Critical Approaches to Anglo-Irish Literature* (Gerrards Cross: Colin Smythe, 1989), pp. 17–39

—, '"Cheap and common animals": The English anatomy of Ireland in the seventeenth century', in Thomas F. Healy and Jonathan Sawday (eds), *Literature and the English Civil War* (Cambridge: Cambridge University Press, 1990), pp. 205–26

—, '"Bog Queens": Representations of femininity in the poetry of John Montague and Seamus Heaney', in Toni O'Brien Johnson and David Cairns (eds), *Gender in Irish Writing* (Milton Keynes: Open University Press, 1991), pp. 88–111

—, '"The poetry is another pair of sleeves": Beckett, Ireland and modernist lyric poetry', in Patricia Coughlan and Alex Davis (eds), *Modernism and Ireland: The poetry of the 1930s* (Cork: Cork University Press, 1995), pp. 173–208

—, 'An Léiriú ar Shaol na mBan i dTéacsanna Dírbheathaisnéise Pheig Sayers', in Máire Ní Chéilleachair (eag.), *Peig Sayers, Scéalaí, 1873–1958 (Ceiliúradh an Bhlascaoid 3)* (Baile Átha Cliath: Coiscéim, 1999), pp. 20–57

—, 'Irish Literature and Feminism in Postmodernity', *Hungarian Journal of English and American Studies*, vol. 10, nos 1–2, 2004, pp. 175–202

—, '"Without a blink of her lovely eye": *The Pleasure of Eliza Lynch* and visionary skepticism', *Irish University Review*, vol. 35, no. 2, 2005, pp. 349–73

—, 'Rereading Peig Sayers: Women's autobiography, social history, and narrative art', in Patricia Boyle Haberstroh and Christine St Peter (eds), *Opening the Field: Irish women, texts, and contexts* (Cork: Cork University Press, 2007), pp. 58–73

—, '"No lasting fruit at all": Containing, recognition, and relinquishing in *The Girl Who Married the Reindeer*', *Irish University Review*, Special Issue: Eiléan Ní Chuilleanáin, Anne Fogarty (ed.), no. 37, 2007, pp. 53–67

—, '"For nothing can be sole or whole / That has not been rent": Torn motherhood in Máire Mhac an tSaoi's "Love has pitched his mansion ..."', in Louis de Paor (eag.), *Míorúilt an Pharóiste: Aistí ar fhilíocht Mháire Mhac an tSaoi* (Indreabhán: Cló Iar-Chonnacht, 2015), pp. 41–62

—, '"An t-éitheach; is an fíor?" A note on two late poems by Máire Mhac an tSaoi', in John Carey, Kevin Murray, and Caitríona Ó Dochartaigh (eds), *Sacred Histories: A festschrift for Máire Herbert* (Dublin: Four Courts Press, 2015), pp. 103–14

—, 'Hard Times and Sibling Songs: Sibling relations in contemporary Irish literature', in Luz Mar González-Arias (ed.), *National Identities and Imperfections in Contemporary Irish Literature* (London: Palgrave Macmillan, 2017), pp. 67–82

Coughlan, Patricia and Tina O'Toole (eds), *Irish Literature: Feminist perspectives* (Dublin: Carysfort Press, 2008)

Cronin, Michael 'Ireland's Disappeared: Suicide, violence, and austerity', in Colin Coulter and Angela Nagle (eds), *Ireland Under Austerity* (Manchester: Manchester University Press, 2015), pp. 133–50

Cronin, Nessa, 'Lived and Learned Landscapes: Literary geographies and the Irish topographical tradition', in Marie Mianowski (ed.), *Irish Contemporary Landscapes in Literature and the Arts* (Basingstoke: Palgrave Macmillan, 2012), pp. 106–18

—, '"The fineness of things": The deep mapping projects of Tim Robinson's art and writings, 1969–72', in Gladwin and Cusick (eds), *Unfolding Irish Landscapes*, pp. 53–72

—, 'Achillhenge: Liquid modernity and an archaeology of the Irish anthropocene', *Éire-Ireland*, vol. 55, nos 3 & 4, 2020, pp. 19–43

—, 'Environmentalities: Speculative imaginaries of the anthropocene', in Fox, Cronin, and Ó Conchubhair (eds), pp. 349–61

Crowe, Catriona, 'The Commission and the Survivors', *The Dublin Review*, vol. 83, Summer 2021, pp. 60–83

Cusick, Christine, *Out of the Earth: Ecocritical readings of Irish texts* (Cork: Cork University Press, 2010)

d'Aubarède, Gabriel, 'Interview', in Lawrence Graver and Raymond Federman (eds), *Samuel Beckett: The critical heritage* (London: Routledge & Kegan Paul, 1979), pp. 215–17

Daniels, Robin, *Anglo-Saxon Hartlepool and the Foundations of English Christianity*, Tees Archaeology Monograph Series No. 3 (Hartlepool: Tees Archaeology, 2007)

Daniels, Stephen, 'Place and the Geographical Imagination', *Geography*, vol. 77, 1992, pp. 310–22

Darcy, Ailbhe and David Wheatley (eds), *A History of Irish Women's Poetry* (Cambridge: Cambridge University Press, 2021)

D'Arcy, Kathy, 'Why Uncomplicated Recovery Isn't Enough: Rhoda Coghill, her letters, and the Fired! movement', *The Honest Ulsterman*, June 2020, n.p., https://humag.co/features/why-uncomplicated-recovery-isn-t-enough

Dawe, Gerald (ed.), *The Cambridge Companion to Irish Poets* (Cambridge: Cambridge University Press, 2017)

'Death of Mr Lefanu', *Freeman's Journal*, 10 February 1873

de Fréine, Celia, *Faoi Chabáistí is Ríonacha* (Indreabhán: Cló Iar-Chonnacht, 2001)

—, *Fiacha Fola* (Indreabhán: Cló Iar-Chonnacht, 2004)

—, *Scarecrows at Newtownards* (Dublin: Scotus Press, 2005)

—, *imram / odyssey* (Galway: Arlen House, 2010)

—, *Aibítir Aoise / Alphabet of an Age* (Galway: Arlen House, 2011)

—, *Blood Debts* (Dublin: Scotus Press, 2014)

Delaney, Juan José, *Tréboles del Sur* (Buenos Aires: Grupo Editor Latinoamericano, 1994)

Deleuze, Gilles, *Negotiations: 1972–1990*, Martin Joughin (trans.) (Ithaca: Columbia University Press, 1995)

De Troyes, Chrétien, *Le Chevalier au Lion (Yvain)*, M. Roques (ed.) (Paris: Champion, 1971)

—, 'Yvain, or, The Knight with the Lion', *Arthurian Romances*, D.D.R. Owen (trans.) (London: J.M. Dent, 1987), pp. 281–373

Derricke, John, *Image of Irelande with a Discoverie of Woodkarne* (Edinburgh: A&C Black, 1883 [1581])

Derrida, Jacques, *The Ear of the Other: Otobiography, transference, translation*, Avita Ronell and Peggy Kamuf (trans.) (Lincoln: University of Nebraska Press, 1985)

—, *Specters of Marx: The state of the debt, the work of mourning, and the New International* (London: Routledge, 1994)

—, *The Animal That Therefore I Am*, Marie-Louise Mellet (ed.), David Wills (trans.) (New York: Fordham University Press, 2008)

De Wan, Jennifer, 'The Practice of Politics: Feminism, activism, and social change in Ireland', in John Hogan, Paul F. Donnelly, and Brendan K. Rourke (eds), *Irish Business and Society: Governing, participating and transforming in the 21st century* (Dublin: Gill & Macmillan, 2010), pp. 520–36

D'hoker, Elke, 'Distorting Mirrors and Unsettling Snapshots: Anne Enright's short fiction', in Bracken and Cahill (eds), *Anne Enright*, pp. 33–66

Dictionary of the Irish Language (Dublin: Royal Irish Academy, 1983)

Dougherty, Jane Elizabeth, 'Nuala O'Faolain and the Unwritten Irish Girlhood', *New Hibernia Review*, vol. 11, no, 2, 2007, pp. 50–65

Doyle, Martin, 'Brought to Book: Vona Groarke on the unbearable lightness of reviews', interview with Vona Groarke, *Irish Times*, 30 May 2014, https://www.irishtimes.com/culture/books/brought-to-book-vona-groarke-on-the-unbearable-lightness-of-reviews-1.1806730

Dunlea, Marian, *Bodydreaming in the Treatment of Developmental Trauma: An embodied therapeutic approach* (Abingdon: Routledge, 2019)

Earner-Byrne, Lindsey, *Mother and Child: Maternity and child welfare in Dublin, 1922–60* (Manchester: Manchester University Press, 2013)

Editorial, *Freeman's Journal*, 5 June 1868

Editorial, *Irish Times and Daily Advertiser*, 5 April 1864

Edwards, David, 'Beyond Reform: Martial law and the Tudor reconquest of Ireland', *History Ireland*, vol. 5, no. 2, 1997, pp. 16–22

—, 'The Escalation of Violence in Sixteenth-Century Ireland', in David Edwards, Pádraig Lenihan, and Clodagh Tait (eds), *Age of Atrocity: Violence and political conflict in early modern Ireland* (Dublin: Four Courts Press, 2007), pp. 34–78

—, 'Tudor Ireland: Anglicisation, mass killing and security', in Cathie Carmichael and Richard C. Maguire (eds), *The Routledge History of Genocide* (London: Routledge, 2015), pp. 23–37

Engelhardt, James, 'The Language Habitat: An ecopoetry manifesto', *Octopus*, vol. 9, 2007, http://derece.blogspot.com/2008/06/language-habitat-ecopoetry-manifesto.html

Enright, Anne, *Taking Pictures* (London: Jonathan Cape, 2008)

—, 'Call Yourself George: Gender representation in the Irish literary landscape', in *No Authority: Writings from the laureateship* (Dublin: UCD Press, 2019), pp. 69–88

Enright, Anne, Claire Bracken, and Susan Cahill, 'An Interview with Anne Enright, August 2009', in Bracken and Cahill (eds), *Anne Enright*, pp. 13–32

Faludi, Susan, *Stiffed: The betrayal of the American man* (New York: Harper Collins, 1999)

Faragó, Borbála, '"I am the place in which things happen": Invisible immigrant women poets of Ireland', in Coughlan and O'Toole (eds), *Irish Literature*, pp. 145–66

Faragó, Borbála and Kathryn Kirkpatrick (eds), *Animals in Irish Literature and Culture* (Basingstoke: Palgrave, 2018)

Felski, Rita, *Hooked: Art and attachment* (Chicago: University of Chicago Press, 2020)

Ferris, Tom, *Irish Railways: A new history* (Dublin: Gill & Macmillan, 2008)

Fink, Bruce, *The Lacanian Subject: Between language and jouissance* (Princeton: Princeton University Press, 1995)

Finneran, Richard J., 'The Definitive Edition: A history of the final arrangements of Yeats's work', in A. Norman Jeffares (ed.), *Yeats' Poems* (London: Macmillan, 1989), pp. 706–49

—, *Editing Yeats' Poems: A reconsideration* (Basingstoke: Macmillan, 1990)

Flynn, Leontia, *Reading Medbh McGuckian* (Sallins: Irish Academic Press, 2014)

Fogarty, Anne, 'Foreword', in Robert Brazeau and Derek Gladwin (eds), *Eco-Joyce: The environmental imagination of James Joyce* (Cork: Cork University Press, 2014), pp. xv–xviii

Foster, John Wilson, *Nature in Ireland: A scientific and cultural history* (Dublin: Lilliput Press, 1998)

Foucault, Michel, *The History of Sexuality. Volume I: The Will to Knowledge*, Robert Hurley (trans.) (London: Penguin, 1998 [1977])

—, *Lectures on the Will to Know: Lectures at the Collège de France, 1970–1971*, Daniel Defert (ed.) (New York: Palgrave Macmillan, 2013)

Fox, Renée, Mike Cronin, and Brian Ó Conchubhair (eds), *The Routledge International Handbook of Irish Studies* (Abingdon: Routledge, 2021)

Fraser, Nancy, 'Contradictions of Capital and Care', *New Left Review*, vol. 100, 2016, pp. 99–117

Frawley, Oona, *Irish Pastoral: Nostalgia and twentieth-century Irish literature* (Dublin: Irish Academic Press, 2005)

Freud, Anna, *The Writings of Anna Freud*, 8 vols (New York: International University Press, 1966–80)

Freud, Sigmund, '"A Child Is Being Beaten": A contribution to the study of the origins of sexual perversions' (1919) , in *The Standard Edition of the Complete Psychological Works of Sigmund Freud*, 24 vols, James Strachey (ed. and trans.) (London: Hogarth Press, 1953–74), vol. 12 (1919), pp. 175–20

—, *New Introductory Lectures on Psychoanalysis* (London: Pelican, 1975)

—, 'Family Romances', in *On Sexuality* (Harmondsworth: Penguin, 1977), pp. 221–5

—, 'Creative Writers and Daydreaming', in *Art and Literature* (Harmondsworth: Penguin, 1985), pp. 129–43

—, 'Family Romances', in Peter Gay (ed.), *The Freud Reader* (London: Vintage, 1995), pp. 297–300

—, *Beyond the Pleasure Principle and Other Writings* (Harmondsworth: Penguin, 2003)

—, 'The Splitting of the Ego in the Defence Processes', in Adam Phillips (ed.), *The Unconscious* (Harmondsworth: Penguin, 2005), pp. 101–6

—, 'Three Essays on Sexual Theory', in Adam Phillips (ed.), *The Psychology of Love* (London: Penguin, 2006), pp. 111–220

Gamble, Sarah, 'Postfeminism', in Sarah Gamble (ed.), *The Routledge Companion to Feminism and Postfeminism* (London: Routledge, 2006), pp. 36–45

Genz, Stéphanie and Benjamin A. Brabon, *Postfeminism: Cultural texts and theories* (Edinburgh: Edinburgh University Press, 2009)

Gibbons, Luke, 'Projecting the Nation: Cinema and culture', in Joe Cleary and Claire Connolly (eds), *The Cambridge Companion to Modern Irish Culture* (Cambridge: Cambridge University Press, 2005), pp. 206–24

Gillespie, Michael, *The Myth of an Irish Cinema: Approaching Irish-themed films* (Syracuse: Syracuse University Press, 2008)

Ging, Debbie, 'All-Consuming Images: New gender formations in post-Celtic-Tiger Ireland', in Debbie Ging, Michael Cronin, and Peadar Kirby (eds), *Transforming Ireland: Challenges, critiques, and resources* (Manchester: Manchester University Press, 2009), pp. 52–70

—, 'Memes, Masculinity, and Mancession: *Love/Hate*'s online metatexts', *Irish Studies Review*, vol. 25, no. 2, 2017, pp. 170–92

Ging, Debbie, Michael Cronin, and Peadar Kirby (eds), *Transforming Ireland: Challenges, critiques, and resources* (Manchester: Manchester University Press, 2009)

Gladwin, Derek, *Contentious Terrains: Boglands, Ireland, postcolonial gothic* (Cork: Cork University Press, 2016)

Gladwin, Derek and Christine Cusick (eds), *Unfolding Irish Landscapes: Tim Robinson, culture, and environment* (Manchester: Manchester University Press, 2016)

Gontarski, S.E. (ed.), *Samuel Beckett: The complete short prose, 1929–1988* (New York: Grove Press, 1995)

González-Arias, Luz Mar, '"The Famine of the 90s": Female starvation and religious thought in Leanne O'Sullivan's *Waiting for My Clothes*', *Estudios Irlandeses*, vol. 0, 2005, pp. 50–7

—, 'Impossible Returns: The trope of the soldier in Celia de Fréine's poetry', *Irish University Review*, vol. 48, no. 2, 2018, pp. 188–201

Gorz, André, *Critique of Economic Reason* (London: Verso, 1989)

Gould, Warwick, 'Lips and Ships, Peers and Tears: *Lacrimae rerum* and tragic joy', in Warwick Gould (ed.), *Yeats Annual, 18. A Special Edition: Essays in Memory of A. Norman Jeffares* (London: Open Book, 2013), pp. 15–55

Graham, Philip and Nick Midgley, *So Young, So Sad, So Listen: A parents' guide to depression in children and young people* (Cambridge: Cambridge University Press, 2020)

Groarke, Vona, *Other People's Houses* (Loughcrew: Gallery, 1999)

—, *Flight and Earlier Poems* (Winston-Salem: Wake Forest University Press, 2004)

—, *Juniper Street* (Loughcrew: Gallery, 2006)

—, *Lament for Art O'Leary. From the Irish of Eibhlín Dubh Ní Chonaill* (Loughcrew: Gallery, 2008)

—, *Spindrift* (Loughcrew: Gallery, 2009)

—, *Four Sides Full* (Loughcrew: Gallery, 2016)

Halberstam, Jack, *The Queer Art of Failure* (Durham and London: Duke University Press, 2011)

Hall, Frank, *The Properest Thing to Do* (London: L'Enfant & Hodgkins, 1863)

Hanna, Adam, *Northern Irish Poetry and Domestic Space* (Basingstoke: Palgrave Macmillan, 2015)

Haraway, Donna J., 'Staying with the Trouble: Anthropocene, capitalocene, chthulucene', in Moore (ed.), *Anthropocene or Capitalocene?*, pp. 34–77

Hardie, Philip, 'Ovid and Early Imperial Literature', in *The Cambridge Companion to Ovid*, Philip Hardie (ed.) (Cambridge: Cambridge University Press, 2002), pp. 34–45

Harmer, Florence H. (ed.), *Select English Historical Documents of the Ninth and Tenth Centuries* (Cambridge: Cambridge University Press, 1914)

Harris, Trudier, *Depictions of Home in African American Literature* (Lanham: Lexington Books, 2021)

Harvey, Charles and Jon Press, 'The City and Mining Enterprise: The making of the Morris family fortune', *Journal of William Morris Studies*, vol. 9, no. 1, 1990, pp. 3–14

Heaney, Seamus, *Death of a Naturalist* (London: Faber, 1966)
—, 'Feeling into Words', *Preoccupations: Selected Prose, 1968–1978* (London: Faber & Faber, 1981), pp. 41–60
Hegel, G.F.W., *Aesthetics: Lectures on fine art*, vol. 1 (Oxford: Oxford University Press, 1975)
Hirsch, Marianne, *The Mother/Daughter Plot: Narrative, psychoanalysis, feminism* (Bloomington: Indiana University Press, 1989)
Hogan, Caelainn, *Republic of Shame* (London: Penguin, 2019)
Holdeman, David, *Much Labouring: The texts and authors of Yeats' first modernist books* (Ann Arbor: University of Michigan Press, 1997)
Holmquist, Kate, 'Men Overboard', *Irish Times*, 5 October 2013, https://www.irishtimes.com/life-and-style/men-overboard-1.1550548
—, 'Few Are Untouched by the "Mancession"', *Irish Times*, 7 October 2013, https://www.irishtimes.com/life-and-style/few-are-untouched-by-the-mancession-1.1550686
Holmsten, Elin, 'The Hermeneutics of Otherness in Medbh McGuckian's Poetry', unpublished PhD thesis, Uppsala Universitet, 2006
Horney, Karen, *Feminine Psychology* (New York: W.W. Norton & Company, 1967)
Hough, Carol, 'Women in English Place-Names', in Carol Hough and Kathryn A. Lowe (eds), *'Lastworda Betst': Essays in memory of Christine E. Fell* (Donnington: Shaun Tyas, 2002), pp. 41–106
Hymowitz, Kay, *Manning Up: How the rise of women has turned men into boys* (London: Basic Books, 2011)
'Impact of the Economic Recession and Subsequent Austerity on Suicide and Self-harm in Ireland: An interrupted time series analysis', *International Journal of Epidemiology*, 2015, pp. 1–9
Ingenieros, José, *The Treaty of Love*, in Beatriz Sarlo, *El imperio de los sentimientos. The Empire of Feelings* (Buenos Aires: Siglo XXI Editores, 2011)
Ingman, Heather, *Women's Fiction Between the Wars: Mothers, daughters, and writing* (Edinburgh: Edinburgh University Press, 1998)
—, *A History of the Irish Short Story* (Cambridge: Cambridge University Press, 2009)
Irigaray, Luce, *Speculum of the Other Woman*, Gillian C. Gill (trans.) (Ithaca: Cornell University Press, 1985 [1974])
—, *This Sex Which Is Not One*, Catherine Porter and Carolyn Burke (trans.) (Ithaca: Cornell University Press, 1985 [1977])
—, 'Women-mothers: The silent substratum of the social order', in Whitford (ed.), *The Irigaray Reader*, pp. 47–53
—, 'The Bodily Encounter with the Mother', in Whitford (ed.), *The Irigaray Reader*, pp. 34–46
James, Heather, 'Ovid and the Question of Politics in Early Modern England', in Yvonne Bruce (ed.), *Images of Matter: Essays on British literature of the middle ages and Renaissance. Proceedings of the Eighth Citadel Conference on*

Literature, Charleston, South Carolina, 2002 (Newark: University of Delaware Press, 2005), pp. 92–122

Jančar, Drago, 'To Write in the Language of a Small Nation', Tamara M. Sobon (trans.), *Poetry Ireland Review*, vol. 79, 2004, pp. 39–43

Jaski, Bart, *Early Irish Kingship and Succession* (Dublin: Four Courts Press, 2000)

Jeffares, A. Norman and A.S. Knowland, *A Commentary on The Collected Plays of W.B. Yeats* (London: Macmillan, 1975)

Johnston, Dillon, '"Hundred-Pocketed Time": Ní Chuilleanáin's baroque spaces', *Irish University Review*, Special Issue: Eiléan Ní Chuilleanáin, Anne Fogarty (ed.), no. 37, 2007, pp. 53–67

Johnston, Maria and Conor Linnie (eds), *Irish Women Poets Rediscovered: Readings in poetry from the eighteenth to the twentieth century* (Cork: Cork University Press, 2021)

Jones, Ernest, 'Anal Erotic Character Traits', in *Papers on Psycho-Analysis* (Boston: Beacon Press, 1961), pp. 413–38

Joyce, James, *A Portrait of the Artist as a Young Man*, Jeri Johnson (ed.) (Oxford: Oxford Classics, 2000)

Kant, Immanuel, *Critique of Practical Reason*, Mary Gregor (ed.) (Cambridge: Cambridge University Press, 2015)

Kelleher, Margaret, *The Feminization of Famine: Expressions of the inexpressible?* (Cork: Cork University Press, 1997)

Kennedy, Seán, 'Mothering Molloy, or Beckett and Cutlery', in Mark Nixon (ed.) '"never neglect the little things in life": Beckett and the everyday', *Journal of Beckett Studies*, vol. 18, no. 1, 2019, pp. 35–51

Kempe, Margery, *The Book of Margery Kempe*, Lynn Staley (ed.) (Kalamazoo: Medieval Institute Publications, 1996)

Kiberd, Declan, *Inventing Ireland* (London: Jonathan Cape, 1995)

Kim, Rina, *Women and Ireland as Beckett's Lost Others: Beyond mourning and melancholia* (Houndmills: Palgrave Macmillan, 2010)

—, *King Arthur's Death: The Middle English stanzaic Morte Arthur and alliterative Morte Arthur*, Larry D. Benson (ed.), revised Edward E. Foster (Kalamazoo: Medieval Institute Publications, 1994)

Kimball, Jean, 'Family Romance and Hero Myth: A psychoanalytic context for the paternity theme in *Ulysses*', *James Joyce Quarterly*, vol. 20, 1983, pp. 162–73

Kimmell, Michael, *Manhood in America: A cultural history*, 3rd edn (Oxford and New York: Oxford University Press, 2011)

—, *Angry White Men: American masculinity at the end of an era* (New York: Nation Books, 2015)

Knott, Eleanor, *The Bardic Poems of Tadhg Dall Ó Huiginn (1550–1591)*, 2 vols (London: Irish Texts Society, 1922–6)

—, *An Introduction to Irish Syllabic Poetry of the Period 1200–1600*, 2nd edn (Dublin: Dublin Institute for Advanced Studies, 1957)

Knowlson, James, *Damned to Fame: The life of Samuel Beckett* (Bloomsbury: London, 1996)

Korol, Juan Carlos and Hilda Sábato, *Cómo fue la immigración irlandesa en Argentina* (Buenos Aires: Editorial Plus Ultra, 1981)

—, *La Mort le roi Artu: roman du XIIIe siècle*, J. Frappier (ed.), 3rd edn (Geneva: Droz, 1996)

La Farge, Catherine, 'Conversation in Malory's *Morte Darthur*', *Medium Ævum*, vol. 56, no. 2, 1987, pp. 225–37

—, 'Blood and Love in Malory's *Morte Darthur*', in Peter Brown (ed.), *A Companion to Medieval English Literature and Culture, c.1350–c.1550* (Oxford: Blackwell, 2007), pp. 634–47

Lambert, Mark, *Malory: Style and vision in 'Le Morte Darthur'* (New Haven: Yale University Press, 1975)

Lancelot-Grail: The Old French Arthurian Vulgate and Post-Vulgate in Translation, 5 vols, N.J. Lacey (trans. and ed.) (New York: Garland Publishing, 1995)

Landowski, Eric, *Presenças do Outro* (São Paulo: Editora Perspectiva, 2002)

Laplanche, Jean, 'Starting from the Fundamental Anthropological Situation', in John Fletcher (ed.), *Freud and the Sexual: Essays 2000–2006* (New York: International Psychoanalytic Books, 2011), pp. 99–114

Larrington, Carolyne, *King Arthur's Enchantresses: Morgan and her sisters in Arthurian tradition* (London: I.B. Tauris, 2006)

—, 'Sibling Relations in Malory's *Morte Darthur*', in David Clark and Kate McClune (eds), *Arthurian Literature, 28: Blood, Sex, Malory. Essays on the 'Morte Darthur'* (Cambridge: D.S. Brewer, 2011), pp. 57–74

—, *Brothers and Sisters in Medieval European Literature* (Woodbridge: York Medieval Press, 2015)

Le Fanu, J. Sheridan, *Best Ghost Stories of J.S. Le Fanu*, E.F. Bleiler (ed.) (New York: Dover, 1964)

—, *Uncle Silas* (Oxford: Oxford University Press, 1989 [1864])

—, *In a Glass Darkly*, Robert Tracy (ed.) (Oxford: Oxford University Press, 2008)

Le Fanu, W.R., *Seventy Years of Irish Life, Being Anecdotes and Reminiscences* (London: Edward Arnold, 1894)

Lefebvre, Henri, *The Production of Space*, Donald Nicholson-Smith (trans.) (Oxford: Blackwell, 1991)

Leonard, Sue, 'Escaping the Recession? The new vitality of the woman worker', in Diane Negra and Yvonne Tasker (eds), *Gendering the Recession* (Durham: Duke University Press, 2014)

Lesage, Alain René, *Le diable boiteux (1707). Asmodeus; or, The Devil on Two Sticks*, Joseph Thomas (trans.) (London: Joseph Thomas, 1841)

Lewiecki-Wilson, Cynthia, *Writing against the Family: Gender in Lawrence and Joyce* (Carbondale: Southern Illinois University Press, 1994)

Lloyd, David, *Under Representation: The racial regime of aesthetics* (New York: Fordham University Press, 2019)

Locke, John, *An Essay Concerning Human Understanding* (Harmondsworth: Penguin, 1997)

Luddy, Maria, 'Women and Politics in Ireland, 1860–1918', in Angela Bourke et al. (eds), *The Field Day Anthology of Irish Writing*, pp. 69–74

Luddy, Maria and Dympna McLoughlin, 'Women and Emigration from Ireland from the Seventeenth Century', in Bourke et al. (eds), *The Field Day Anthology of Irish Writing*, pp. 567–9

Lutz, Deborah, 'Gothic Fictions in the Nineteenth Century', in John Kucich and Jenny Bourne Taylor (eds), *The Oxford History of the Novel in English. Volume 3: The Nineteenth-Century Novel, 1820–1880* (Oxford: Oxford University Press, 2011), pp. 76–89

Macardle, Dorothy, *The Uninvited* (Dublin: Tramp Press, 2015 [1942])

MacBride, Anna and A. Norman Jeffares (eds), *The Gonne–Yeats Letters, 1893–1938: Always your friend* (London: Hutchinson, 1992)

Mac Craith, Mícheál, 'Gaelic Ireland and the Renaissance', in Glanmor Williams and Robert Owen Jones (eds), *The Celts and the Renaissance: Tradition and innovation. Proceedings of the Eighth International Congress of Celtic Studies 1987* (Cardiff: University of Wales Press, 1990), pp. 57–88

—, 'Fun and Games Among the Jet Set: A glimpse of seventeenth-century Gaelic Ireland', in Joseph Falaky Nagy (ed.), *Memory and the Modern in Celtic Literatures, CSANA Yearbook* 5 (Dublin: Four Courts Press, 2006), pp. 15–36

—, 'The Political and Religious Thought of Florence Conry and Hugh McCaughwell', in Alan Ford and John McCafferty (eds), *The Origins of Sectarianism in Early Modern Ireland* (Cambridge: Cambridge University Press, 2006), pp. 183–202

Mac Curtain, Margaret, *Ariadne's Thread: Writing women into Irish history* (Dublin: Arlen House, 2008)

Mack, Peter, *Elizabethan Rhetoric: Theory and practice* (Cambridge: Cambridge University Press, 2004)

Mackail, J.W., *Life of William Morris* (London: Chiswick Press, 1899)

MacNeice, Louis, *Collected Poems*, Peter McDonald (ed.) (London: Faber & Faber, 2007)

Malory, Thomas, *The Works of Thomas Malory*, Eugène Vinaver (ed.), 3 vols, 3rd edn, revised by P.J.C. Field (Oxford: Oxford University Press, 1990)

—, *The Works of Sir Thomas Malory*, P.J.C. Field (ed.), 2 vols (Cambridge: D.S. Brewer, 1990)

Mandelbrot, Benoît , 'How Long Is the Coast of Britain? Statistical self-similarity and fractional dimension', *Science Magazine*, vol. 156, no. 3,775, May 1967, pp. 636–8

Mann, Jill, 'Taking the Adventure: Malory and the *Suite du Merlin*', in Toshiyuki Takamiya and Derek Brewer (eds), *Aspects of Malory* (Arthurian Studies series), vol. 1 (Cambridge: D.S. Brewer, 1981), pp. 71–91

—, *Feminizing Chaucer* (Cambridge: D.S. Brewer, 2002)

Marcus, Sharon, *Apartment Stories: City and home in nineteenth-century Paris and London* (Berkeley: University of California Press, 1999)

McClintock, Anne, 'Family Feuds: Gender, nationalism, and the family', Special Issue: Nationalisms and National Identities, *Feminist Review*, vol. 44, 1993, pp. 61–80

McClune, Kate, '"The Vengeance of My Brethirne": Blood ties in Malory's *Morte Darthur*', in David Clark and Kate McClune (eds), *Arthurian Literature, 28: Blood, Sex, Malory. Essays on the 'Morte Darthur'* (Cambridge: D.S. Brewer, 2011), pp. 89–106

McConnell, Daniel, Craig Hughes, and John Drennan, 'Burton Vows to End 'Dole Lifestyle Choice', *Irish Independent*, 17 July 2011, https://www.independent.ie/irish-news/burton-vows-to-end-dole-lifestyle-choice-26752421.html

McCormack, W.J., *Sheridan Le Fanu and Victorian Ireland* (Oxford: Clarendon Press, 1980)

McGuckian, Medbh, *On Ballycastle Beach* (Winston-Salem: Wake Forest University Press, 1988)

—, *Marconi's Cottage* (Loughcrew: Gallery, 1991)

McInerney, Lisa, 'Seize the Means of Publication (Hard Lessons Learned as a Working-Class Writer)', in Declan Meade (ed.), *Beyond the Centre: Writers in their own words* (Dublin: New Island Books, 2017), pp. 207–16

McKenna, Lambert (ed. and trans.), *Aithdioghluim Dána*, 2 vols (Dublin: Irish Texts Society, 1939–40)

McKeon, Belinda, 'About a Girl', *Irish Times*, 6 November, 2004

McKibben, Sarah E., *Endangered Masculinities in Irish Poetry, 1540–1780* (Dublin: UCD Press, 2010)

—, 'In their "owne countre": Deriding and defending the early modern Irish nation after Gerald of Wales', *Eolas: The Journal of the American Society of Irish Medieval Studies*, vol. 8, 2015, pp. 39–70

McManus, Damian and Eoghan Ó Raghallaigh, *A Bardic Miscellany: Five hundred bardic poems from manuscripts in Irish and British libraries* (Dublin: Department of Irish, Trinity College Dublin, 2010)

McQuillan, Peter, *Native and Natural: Aspects of the concepts of 'right' and 'freedom' in Irish* (Cork: Cork University Press / Field Day, 2004)

—, 'Courtesy and Civility in Early Modern Irish Literature', XIV International Congress of Celtic Studies, Maynooth, 4 August 2011 (conference presentation)

—, 'A Bardic Critique of Queen and Court: "Ionmholta malarit bhisigh", Eochaidh Ó hEodhasa, 1603', in Brendan Kane and Valerie McGowan-Doyle (eds),

Elizabeth I and Ireland (Cambridge: Cambridge University Press, 2014), pp. 60–85

McRobbie, Angela, *The Aftermath of Feminism: Gender, culture, and social change* (London: Sage, 2009)

McWilliams, Ellen, '"A Sort of Rathmines Version of a Dior Design": Maeve Brennan, self-fashioning, and the uses of style', *Women: A cultural review*, vol. 27, no. 1, 2016, pp. 42–61

—, 'Maeve Brennan, Celebrity, and *Harper's Bazaar* in the 1940s', *Breac*, July 2017, https://breac.nd.edu/articles/maeve-brennan-celebrity-and-harpers-bazaar-in-the-1940s/

—, 'Maeve Brennan and James Joyce', *Irish Studies Review*, vol. 26, no. 1, 2018, pp. 111–23

Meaney, Gerardine, 'Sex and Nation: Women in Irish culture and politics', in Ailbhe Smyth (ed.), *Irish Women's Studies: A reader* (Dublin: Attic Press, 1993), pp. 230–44

—, 'Landscapes of Desire: Women and Ireland on film', *Women: A cultural review*, vol. 9, no. 3, 1998, pp. 237–51

—, 'Decadence, Degeneration, and Revolting Aesthetics: The fiction of Emily Lawless and Katherine Cecil Thurston', *Colby Quarterly*, vol. 36, 2000, pp. 157–75

—, 'Waking the Dead: Antigone, Ismene, and Anne Enright's narrators in mourning', in Bracken and Cahill (eds), *Anne Enright*, pp. 145–64

—, *Gender, Ireland, and Cultural Change: Race, sex, and nation* (New York: Routledge, 2011)

Mhac an tSaoi, Máire, 'Réamhrá', in Celia de Fréine, *Fiacha Fola*, pp. 9–12

—, 'Foreword', in Celia de Fréine, *Blood Debts*, pp. 11–17

Midgley, Nicholas, *Mentalization-Based Treatment for Children: A time-limited approach* (Abingdon: Routledge, 2012)

Midgley, Nick, Jacqueline Hayes, and Mick Cooper (eds), *Essential Research Findings in Child and Adolescent Therapy* (London: Sage, 2017)

Miller, Liam, *The Dun Emer Press, Later the Cuala Press* (Dublin: Dolmen, 1973)

Mills, Lia, 'In Full Voice: Celia de Fréine in conversation with Lia Mills', *Irish University Review*, vol. 48, no. 2, 2018, pp. 169–82

Minahane, John, 'Hiding Ireland' (review of Jane Ohlmeyer, *Making Ireland English: The Irish aristocracy in the seventeenth century*), *The Dublin Review*, vol. 31, 25 March 2013, https://www.drb.ie/essays/hiding-ireland

Minsky, Rosalind, *Psychoanalysis and Gender* (London: Routledge, 1996)

'Mirror of Fashion', *Morning Chronicle*, 13 December 1828

Mitchell, Juliet, *Psychoanalysis and Feminism* (London: Penguin, 1974)

—, *Mad Men and Medusas: Reclaiming hysteria* (London: Penguin, 2000)

—, *Siblings: Sex and violence* (Cambridge: Polity Press, 2003)

Molloy, Sylvia, *Acto de presencia. La escritura autobiográfica en Hispanoamérica*, José Esteban Calderón (trans.) (México: Fondo de Cultura económica, 1996 [1991])

Moore, Jason W. (ed.), *Anthropocene or Capitalocene? Nature, history, and the crisis of capitalism* (Oakland: Kairos, 2016)

—, 'The Capitalocene, Part I: On the Nature and Origins of our Ecological Crisis', *The Journal of Peasant Studies*, vol. 44, no. 3, 2017, pp. 594–630

Moradi, Bonnie, Danielle Dirks, and Alicia V. Matteson, 'Roles of Sexual Objectification Experiences and Internalization of Standards of Beauty in Eating Disorder Symptomatology: A test and extension of objectification theory', *Journal of Counseling Psychology*, vol. 52, no. 3, 2005, pp. 420–8

Morgan, Hiram, 'Giraldus Cambrensis and the Tudor Conquest of Ireland', in Hiram Morgan (ed.), *Political Ideology in Ireland, 1541–1641* (Dublin: Four Courts Press, 1999), pp. 22–44

Morin, Christina, *The Gothic Novel in Ireland, c.1760–1829* (Manchester: Manchester University Press, 2018)

Morris, William, *The Collected Works of William Morris*, with introductions by May Morris. Vol. XXI: *The Sundering Flood; Unfinished Romances* (London, 1914; facsimile edn, Cambridge: Cambridge University Press, 2012)

Morrissey, Sinéad, *Between Here and There* (Manchester: Carcanet, 2002)

—, *Through the Square Window* (Manchester: Carcanet, 2009)

—, *Parallax and Selected Poems* (New York: Farrar, Straus & Giroux, 2015)

Mulhall, Anne, '"The well-known, old, but still unbeaten track": Women poets and Irish periodical culture in the mid-twentieth century', Special Issue: Irish Poetry Cultures 1930–1970, Lucy Collins (ed.), *Irish University Review*, vol. 42, no. 1, 2012, pp. 32–52

Mulhall, Marion, *Between the Amazon and Andes or Ten Years of a Lady's Travels in the Pampas, Gran Chaco, Paraguay, and Matto Grosso* (London: E. Stanford, 1881)

Mulligan, Fergus, *One Hundred and Fifty Years of Irish Railways* (Belfast: Appletree Press, 1983)

Murphy, Maureen, *Your Fondest Annie* (Dublin: UCD Press, 2005)

Murphy, William M., *Family Secrets: William Butler Yeats and his relatives* (Dublin: Gill & Macmillan, 1995)

Murray, Edmundo, *Devenir Irlandés* (Buenos Aires: Eudeba, 2004); *Becoming Irlandés* (Buenos Aires: LOLA, 2006)

Murray, Thomas, *The Story of the Irish in Argentina* (Cork: Cork University Press, 2011 [1919])

Negra, Diane, *What a Girl Wants? Fantasizing the reclamation of the self in postfeminism* (London: Routledge, 2009)

—, 'Adjusting Men and Abiding Mammies: Gendering the recession in Ireland', *Gender, Sexuality & Feminism*, vol. 1, no. 2, 2014, pp. 23–34

Nevin, Kathleen, *You'll Never Go Back* (Boston: Bruce Humphries, 1946)

Ní Chuilleanáin, Eiléan, *The Sun-Fish* (Loughcrew: Gallery, 2009)

Ní Dhomhnaill, Nuala, *Féar Suaithinseach* (Maigh Nuad: An Sagart, 1984)

—, *Feis* (Maigh Nuad: An Sagart, 1991)

Ní Dhuibhne, Éilís, 'Introduction', in Éilís Ní Dhuibhne (ed.), *Look! It's A Woman Writer: Irish literary feminisms, 1970–2020* (Dublin: Arlen House, 2021), pp. 13–33

Nixon, Mark, *Samuel Beckett's German Diaries, 1936–1937* (London: Continuum, 2011)

Noble, James, 'Gilding the Lily (Maid): Elaine of Astolat', in Bonnie Wheeler and Fiona Tolhurst (eds), *On Arthurian Women: Essays in memory of Maureen Fries* (Dallas: Scriptorium, 2001), pp. 45–57

Nolan, Emer, *James Joyce and Nationalism* (London: Routledge, 1995)

O'Brien, Sarah, *Linguistic Diasporas, Narrative, and Performance: The Irish in Argentina* (London: Palgrave Macmillan, 2017)

Ó Buachalla, Breandán, 'Poetry and Politics in Early Modern Ireland', *Eighteenth-Century Ireland*, vol. 7, 1992, pp. 149–75

—, 'James Our True King: The ideology of Irish royalism in the seventeenth century', in D. George Boyce, Robert Eccleshall, and Vincent Geoghegan (eds), *Political Thought in Ireland Since the Seventeenth Century* (London: Routledge, 1993), pp. 7–35

O'Carroll, Íde, *Models for Movers: Irish women's emigration to America* (Dublin: Attic Press, 1990)

O'Connor, Maureen, *The Female and the Species: The animal in Irish women's writing* (Oxford: Peter Lang, 2010)

—, '"Mrkgnao!": Signifying animals in the fiction of James Joyce', in Albert Wachtel (ed.), *Critical Insights: James Joyce* (Pasadena: Salem Press, 2013) pp. 101–19

—, '"Extremely nervous on this earth": Fairy tale violence in Edna O'Brien's *In the Forest*', in Tina-Karen Puisse and Heike Schwarz (eds), *Madness in the Woods: Ecopsychopathologies in literature, film and gaming* (New York: Lexington Books, Rowman & Littlefield, 2018), pp. 75–89

—, 'Irish Animal Studies at the Turn of the Twenty-first Century', in Fox, Cronin, and Ó Conchubhair (eds), *The Routledge International Handbook of Irish Studies*, pp. 362–9

Ó Corráin, Ailbhe, *The Dark Cave and the Divine Light: Verses on the human condition by Giolla Brighde Ó hEódhasa* (Oslo: Institute for Comparative Research in Human Culture, Novus Press, 2016)

Ó Dúshláine, Tadhg, 'Dál na mBeach a Bharamhail: An dúlra mar dhlúth faoi inneach shaothar an fhile, Eochaidh Ó hEoghusa', *Léachtaí Cholm Cille* vol. 11, 1980, pp. 97–119

O'Gorman, Camila, *Grandes protagonistas de la historia Argentina* (Buenos Aires: Editorial Planeta, 1999)

Okasha, Elisabeth, *Hand-list of Anglo-Saxon Non-Runic Inscriptions* (Cambridge: Cambridge University Press, 1971)

—, 'A Second Supplement to *Hand-List of Anglo-Saxon Non-Runic Inscriptions*', *Anglo-Saxon England*, vol. 21, 1992, pp. 53–4

—, 'Anglo-Saxon Inscribed Rings', *Leeds Studies in English*, New Series, vol. 35, 2003, pp. 29–43

—, *Women's Names in Old English* (Farnham: Ashgate, 2011)

O'Leary, Philip, 'Foreseeing Driver of an Old Chariot: Regal moderation in early Irish literature', *Cambridge Medieval Celtic Studies*, vol. 11, 1986, pp. 1–16

Olwig, Kenneth, *Landscape, Nature, and the Body Politic: From Britain's Renaissance to America's New World* (Madison: University of Wisconsin Press, 2002)

'Omnibus Reform', *Punch*, 6 October 1860, p. 139

O'Neill, Ciarán and Mai Yatani, 'Women, Ambition, and the City, 1890–1910', in Anna Pilz and Whitney Standlee (eds), *Irish Women's Writing, 1878–1922: Advancing the cause of liberty* (Manchester: Manchester University Press, 2016), pp. 100–20

O'Neill, Margaret and Michaela Schrage-Frueh, 'Surplus to Requirements? The ageing body in contemporary Irish writing', in Fox, Cronin, and Ó Conchubhair (eds), *The Routledge International Handbook of Irish Studies*, pp. 435–47

'On Saturday', *Morning Chronicle*, 6 July 1829

Oppel, Frances Nesbitt, *Mask and Tragedy: Yeats and Nietzsche, 1902–1910* (Charlottesville: University of Virginia Press, 1987)

O'Shea, Edward, *A Descriptive Catalog of W.B. Yeats' Library* (New York: Garland, 1985)

O'Sullivan, Leanne, *Waiting for My Clothes* (Tarset: Bloodaxe Books, 2004)

—, *Cailleach: The Hag of Beara* (Tarset: Bloodaxe Books, 2009)

—, *The Mining Road* (Tarset: Bloodaxe Books, 2013)

—, *A Quarter of an Hour* (Tarset: Bloodaxe Books, 2018)

O'Sullivan, Patrick (ed.), *The Irish World Wide: Irish women and migration*, vol. 1 (Leicester: Leicester University Press, 1995)

O'Toole, Emer, 'Waking the Feminists: Re-imagining the space of the national theatre in the era of the Celtic phoenix', *Literature, Interpretation, Theory*, vol. 28, no. 2, 2017, pp. 134–52

O'Toole, Tina, '"Nomadic Subjects" in Katherine Cecil Thurston's *Max*', in Coughlan and O'Toole (eds), *Irish Literature*, pp. 79–98

—, *The Irish New Woman* (London: Palgrave Macmillan, 2013)

—, 'Cé Leis Tú? Queering Irish migrant literature', *Irish University Review*, vol. 43, no. 1, 2013, pp. 131–45

—, 'George Egerton's Translocational Subjects', *Modernism-Modernity*, vol. 21, no. 3, 2014, pp. 827–42

—, 'The New Woman Flaneuse or Streetwalker?: George Egerton's urban aestheticism', in Bénédicte Coste, Catherine Delyfer, and Christine Reynier (eds), *Reconnecting Aestheticism and Modernism* (Abingdon: Routledge, 2017), pp. 19–31

Owen-Crocker, Gale R., *Dress in Anglo-Saxon England* (Manchester: Manchester University Press, 1986)

Palmer, Patricia, *Language and Conquest in Early Modern Ireland: English Renaissance literature and Elizabethan imperial expansion* (Cambridge: Cambridge University Press, 2001)

—, 'Missing Bodies, Absent Bards: Spenser, Shakespeare, and a crisis in criticism', *English Literary Renaissance*, vol. 36, no. 3, Autumn 2006, pp. 376–95

Peart, Barbara, *Tia Barbarita: Memories of Barbara Peart* (London: Faber & Faber, 1932)

Pelan, Rebecca, *Two Irelands: Literary feminisms north and south* (Syracuse: Syracuse University Press, 2005)

Perry, Curtis, *The Making of Jacobean Culture: James I and the renegotiation of Elizabethan literary practice* (Cambridge: Cambridge University Press, 1997)

Phillips, Adam, 'Just Rage', in *The Beast in the Nursery* (New York: Vintage, 1998), pp. 121–40

Pilz, Anna and Whitney Standlee, 'Introduction', in Anna Pilz and Whitney Standlee (eds), *Irish Women's Writing, 1878–1922: Advancing the cause of liberty* (Manchester: Manchester University Press, 2016), pp. 1–16

Porges, Stephen, *The Polyvagal Theory: Neurophysiological foundations of emotions, attachment, communication, and self-regulation* (New York: Norton, 2011)

Prudentius, 2 vols, H.J. Thomson (trans. and ed.) (Cambridge, MA: Loeb Classical Library, 2000 [1949])

Quinn, Leeanne, *Before You* (Dublin: Dedalus Press, 2012)

—, *Some Lives* (Dublin: Dedalus Press, 2020)

Rabinovitz, Rubin, 'Stereoscopic or Stereotypic: Characterization in Beckett's fiction', in Ben-Zvi (ed.), *Women in Beckett*, pp. 106–16

Radulescu, Raluca, *The Gentry Context for Malory's 'Morte Darthur'*, *Arthurian Studies*, vol. 55 (Cambridge: D.S. Brewer, 2003)

Renan, Ernest, 'What is a nation?', Martin Thom (trans.), in Homi K. Bhabha (ed.), *Nation and Narration* (London: Routledge, 1990), pp. 8–22

Rhodes, Neil, Jennifer Richards and Joseph Marshall (eds), *King James VI and I: Selected writings* (Aldershot: Ashgate, 2003)

Riddy, Felicity, *Sir Thomas Malory* (Leiden: E.J. Brill, 1987)

—, 'John Hardyng's Chronicle and the Wars of the Roses', in Felicity Riddy and James P. Curley (eds), *Arthurian Literature*, vol. 12 (Cambridge: D.S. Brewer, 1993), pp. 91–108

—, 'Contextualizing *Le Morte Darthur:* Empire and civil war', in Elizabeth Archibald and A.S.G. Edwards (eds), *A Companion to Malory* (Cambridge: D.S. Brewer, 1996), pp. 55–73

Robert, Marthe, *Origins of the Novel* (Brighton: Harvester Press, 1980)

Robinson, Tim, 'A Connemara Fractal', in Timothy Collins (ed.), *Decoding the Landscape* (Galway: Centre for Landscape Studies, 2003), pp. 12–30

Rollason, David W. and Lynda Rollason (eds), *The Durham Liber Vitae. London, British Library, MS Cotton Domitian A.VII*, 3 vols (London: British Library, 2007)

Le Roman de la Rose, Daniel Poirion (ed.) (Paris: Flammarion, 1974)

The Romance of the Rose, Frances Horgan (trans.) (Oxford: Oxford University Press, 1994)

Roth, Ralph and Marie Noëlle Polino, *The City and the Railway in Europe* (Aldershot: Ashgate, 2003)

'A Run on the Eastern Counties Railway', *Morning Chronicle*, Saturday, 5 October 1850

Ryan, Donal, *The Spinning Heart* (Dublin: Doubleday Ireland, 2012)

Rycroft, Charles, *A Critical Dictionary of Psychoanalysis* (London: Penguin, 1995)

Sage, Victor, *Le Fanu's Gothic: The rhetoric of darkness* (Houndmills: Palgrave Macmillan, 2004)

Sarlo, Beatriz, *El imperio de los sentimientos (The Empire of Feelings)* (Buenos Aires: Siglo XXI Editores, 2011)

Sawyer, Peter H., *Anglo-Saxon Charters: An annotated list and bibliography* (London: Royal Historical Society, 1968)

Scarry, Elaine, *The Body in Pain: The making and unmaking of the world* (Oxford: Oxford University Press, 1985)

Schivelbusch, Wolfgang, *The Railway Journey: The industrialization of time and space in the nineteenth century* (Berkeley: University of California Press, 1986 [1977])

Schopenhauer, Arthur, *Essays and Aphorisms*, R.J. Hollingdale (ed.) (London: Penguin, 1970)

—, 'On Aesthetics', in R.J. Hollingdale (ed.), *Essays and Aphorisms* (London: Penguin, 1970)

—, *The Two Fundamental Problems of Ethics* (Oxford: Oxford University Press, 2010)

Schuller, Kyla, *The Biopolitics of Feeling: Race, sex, and science in the nineteenth century* (Durham: Duke University Press, 2017)

Schwall, Hedwig, '*The Portable Virgin*: Anne Enright's translations of philosophy into literature', in Laura Izarra and Beatriz Kopschitz X. Bastos (eds), *A New Ireland in Brazil: Festschrift in honour of Munira Hamud Mutran* (São Paulo: Humanitas, 2008), pp. 339–50

Scribble, William, *Dublin Destroyed!, or, The Witches Cauldron of Railway Horror: A Mysterious Shakespeareana, in One Act* (Dublin: John Wiseheart, 1862)

Sen, Malcolm, 'An Ordinary Crisis: Covid-19 and Irish studies', in Fox, Cronin, and Ó Conchubhair (eds), *The Routledge International Handbook of Irish Studies*, pp. 471–84

Sennett, Richard, *The Fall of Public Man* (London: Faber, 1993)

Sered, Danielle, 'By Escaping and [Leaving] a Mark': Authority and the writing subject of the poetry of Medbh McGuckian', *Irish University Review*, vol. 32, 2002, pp. 273–85

Sheahan, Fionnán, 'Kenny Declares War on Welfare Culture', *Irish Independent*, 21 October 2013, https://www.independent.ie/irish-news/kenny-declares-war-on-welfare-culture-29676166.html

Sicari, Stephen, *Joyce's Modernist Allegory: 'Ulysses' and the history of the novel* (Columbia: University of South Carolina Press, 2001)

Sidnell, Michael J., George P. Mayhew and David R. Clark, *Druid Craft: The writing of 'The Shadowy Waters'* (Dublin: Dolmen, 1972 [1971])

Sieff, Daniela F., *Understanding and Healing Emotional Trauma: Conversations with pioneering clinicians and researchers* (Abingdon: Routledge, 2014)

Sieghardt, Mary Ann, *The Authority Gap: Why women are still taken less seriously than men* (London: Doubleday, 2021)

Smith, Andrew, *The Ghost Story, 1840–1920* (Manchester: Manchester University Press, 2010)

Smith, Russell, '"Uproar, bulk, rage, suffocation, effort unceasing, frenzied, and vain": Beckett's transports of rage', in Elizabeth Barry, Ulrika Maude, and Laura Salisbury (eds), 'Beckett, Medicine and the Brain', *Journal of the Medical Humanities*, vol. 37, 2016, pp. 137–47

Smyth, Ailbhe, 'Momentary Views: A personal history', *The Irish Review*, vol. 35, 2007, pp. 7–24

—, 'The Obvious Explanations of How Power Is Held and Exercised Over Women Are Very Basic', in Una Mullally (ed.), *Repeal the 8th* (London: Unbound, 2018), pp. 129–42

Snyder, R. Clarke, 'What Is Third-Wave Feminism?: A new direction essay', *Signs*, vol. 34, no. 1, 2008, pp. 175–96

Sontag, Susan, *Illness as Metaphor and AIDS and Its Metaphors* (New York: Picador, 2001)

The Southern Cross, Buenos Aires, 16 January 1875–present

Speight, Patrick, *Irish-Argentine Identity in an Age of Political Challenge and Change, 1875–1983* (Oxford: Peter Lang, 2019)

Spillane, Alison, 'The Impact of the Crisis on Irish Women', in Coulter and Nagle (eds), *Ireland Under Austerity*, pp. 151–70

Standlee, Whitney, *'Power to Observe': Irish women novelists in Britain, 1890–1916* (Frankfurt: Peter Lang, 2015)

Stewart, James, 'How the Eagle Cools It: An apologue and its analogues', *Éigse*, vol. 25, 1991, pp. 165–72

Stewart, Kathleen, *A Space on the Side of the Road: Cultural poetics in an 'other' America* (Princeton: Princeton University Press, 1996)

Sullivan, Jack, *Elegant Nightmares: The English ghost story from Le Fanu to Blackwood* (Athens: Ohio University Press, 1978)
Sullivan, Moynagh, 'The In-formal Poetics of Medbh McGuckian', *Nordic Irish Studies*, vol. 3, 2004, 75–92
—, 'Treachery of Wetness: Seamus Heaney, Irish studies, and the politics of parturition', *Irish Studies Review*, vol. 13, no. 4, 2005, pp. 451–68
—, 'Raising the Veil: Mystery, myth, and melancholia in Irish studies', in Coughlan and O'Toole (eds), *Irish Literature*, pp. 245–77
—, 'Interview with Leeanne Quinn', July 2020, unpublished
Sverakova, Slavka, 'Review of *A Seed of Zero*, Golden Thread Gallery, Belfast, December 2006–January 2007', *Circa Art Magazine*, 2007, https://circaartmagazine.net/a-seed-of-zero-golden-thread-gallery-belfast-december-2006-january-2007/
Tasker, Yvonne and Diane Negra, 'Introduction: Feminist politics and postfeminist culture', in Yvonne Tasker and Diane Negra (eds), *Interrogating Postfeminism: Gender and the politics of popular culture* (Durham: Duke University Press, 2007), pp. 1–25
'The Great Dead of 1873', *Lloyd's Weekly Newspaper*, 4 January 1874
Thurston, Katherine Cecil, *The Fly on the Wheel* (London: Virago, 1987 [1908])
Tokarczurk, Olga, Nobel lecture 2018, https://www.nobelprize.org/prizes/literature/2018/tokarczuk/lecture/
Tsvetayeva, Marina, *Selected Poems of Marina Tsvetayeva*, Elaine Feinstein (ed.) (London: Hutchinson, 1986)
Tuan, Yi-Fu, *Space and Place: The perspective of experience* (Minneapolis: University of Minnesota Press, 1977)
Valente, Joseph, *The Myth of Manliness in Irish Culture, 1880–1922* (Urbana: University of Illinois Press, 2011)
Valente, Joseph and Margot Gayle Backus, *The Child Sex Scandal and Modern Irish Literature: Writing the unspeakable* (Bloomington: Indiana University Press, 2020)
Valiulis, Maryann Gialanella, 'The Politics of Gender in the Irish Free State, 1922–1937', *Women's History Review*, vol. 20, no. 4, 2011, pp. 569–78
Van Boheemen, Christine, *The Novel as Family Romance: Language, gender and authority from Fielding to Joyce* (Ithaca: Cornell University Press, 1987)
Van Hulle, Dirk and Mark Nixon, *Samuel Beckett's Library* (Cambridge: Cambridge University Press, 2013)
Vendler, Helen, *Our Secret Discipline: Yeats and lyric form* (Oxford: Oxford University Press, 2007)
Villis, Tom, *Reaction and the Avant-Garde: The revolt against liberal democracy in early twentieth-century Britain* (London: I.B. Tauris, 2006)
The Works of Virgil: Literally translated into English prose, with notes, by Davidson, new revised edn by Theodore Alois Buckley (London: George Bell & Sons, 1875)

La Vita Nuova, Fredi Chiappelli and Ugo Mursia (eds), *Opere di Dante Alighieri* (Milan: Mursia, 1978)

La Vita Nuova, Mark Musa (trans.) (Oxford: Oxford University Press, 1992)

Wall, Eamonn, *Writing the Irish West: Ecologies and traditions* (Notre Dame: University of Notre Dame Press, 2011)

Walsh, Maria Elena, *Novios de Antaño (1930–1940) & La abuela Agnes (1872–1899)* (Buenos Aires: Seix Barral, 1990)

Wenthe, Michael, 'The Legible Corpses of *Le Morte Darthur*', in Cherewatuk and Whetter (eds), *The Arthurian Way of Death*, pp. 124–35

Whetter, K.S., 'Love and Death in Arthurian Romance', in Cherewatuk and Whetter (eds), *The Arthurian Way of Death*, pp. 94–114

Whitford, Margaret (ed.), *The Irigaray Reader* (Oxford: Blackwell Publishers, 1991)

Wills, Clair, *Improprieties: Politics and sexuality in Northern Irish poetry* (Oxford: Clarendon Press, 1993)

—, 'Women, Domesticity, and the Family: Recent feminist work in Irish cultural studies, *Cultural Studies*, vol. 15, no. 1, 2001, pp. 33–57

Windelband, Wilhelm, *A History of Philosophy. Volume II: Renaissance, Enlightenment, Modern* (New York: Harper Torchbook, 1958)

Wood, Christopher, *Victorian Panorama: Paintings of Victorian life* (London: Faber & Faber, 1976)

Wormald, Jenny, 'James VI and I (1566–1625)', *Oxford Dictionary of National Biography* (Oxford: Oxford University Press, 2004), http://www.oxforddnb.com/view/article/14592

Yaeger, Patricia, 'Dreaming of Infrastructure', *PMLA*, vol. 122, no. 1, 2007, pp. 9–26

Yeats, William Butler, *In the Seven Woods: Being poems chiefly of the heroic age* (Dundrum: Dun Emer, 1903)

—, *Ideas of Good and Evil* (London: A.H. Bullen, 1903)

—, *Poems 1899–1905* (London: A.H. Bullen, 1906)

—, *The Poetical Works of William B. Yeats. I: Lyrical poems* (New York: Macmillan Co., 1906)

—, *Poems: Second series* (London: A.H. Bullen, 1909)

—, *The Cutting of an Agate* (London: Macmillan, 1912)

—, *The Variorum Edition of the Poems of W.B. Yeats*, Peter Allt and Russell K. Alspach (eds), 3rd imprint (London: Macmillan, 1966)

—, *Memoirs: Autobiography – first draft, journal*, Denis Donoghue (ed.) (London: Macmillan, 1972)

—, *Yeats' Poems*, A. Norman Jeffares (ed.) (London: Macmillan, 1989)

—, *The Secret Rose: Stories by W.B. Yeats: A variorum edition*, Warwick Gould, Philip. L. Marcus and Michael J. Sidnell (eds), 2nd edn (London: Macmillan, 1992)

—, *The Collected Letters of W.B. Yeats, III: 1901–1904*, John Kelly and Ronald Schuchard (eds) (Oxford: Oxford University Press, 1994)

—, *The Collected Letters of W.B. Yeats, II: 1896–1900*, John Kelly, Warwick Gould, and Deirdre Toomey (eds) (Oxford: Oxford University Press, 1997)

—, *W.B. Yeats: Selected plays*, Richard Cave (ed.) (Harmondsworth: Penguin, 1997)

—, *Autobiographies*, William H. O'Donnell and Douglas N. Archibald (eds) (New York: Scribner, 1999)

—, *The Collected Letters of W.B. Yeats, IV: 1905–1907*, John Kelly and Ronald Schuchard (eds) (Oxford: Oxford University Press, 2005)

—, *Early Essays*, Richard J. Finneran and George Bornstein (eds) (New York: Scribner, 2007)

Young-Bruel, Elisabeth, *Anna Freud: A biography*, 2nd edn (London: Macmillan, 2008)

Zupitza, Julis (ed.), *Aelfrics Grammatik und Glossar: Text und varianten* (Berlin: Weidmannsche Verlagsbuhhandlung, 1966 [1880])

Index

NOTE: Literary titles are indicated in italics. Compound titles separated by a hyphen indicate that the work was in both Irish and English; or subsequently published under a different name.

3 Women, 120

Abbey Theatre, the, 2
abortion referendum (2018), the, 2
Act of Oblivion (1603), the, 46
Adams, Walton, 68
Adorno, Theodor, 218
affective turn, the, 11, 207, 219
Agamben, Giorgio, 243–244
Ahmed, Sara, 22
Akhmatova, Anna, 160
All the Year Round, 51
Allison, Jonathan, 69
Altman, Robert, 120
Ammons, A.R., 160
Amsterdam Company, the, 31
Anchieta, Jose de, 23
Anglo-Irish, the, 52
Anglo-Saxon (Old English) names and grammatical gender, 9, 185–191
Argentinian civil wars, the, 205
Aristotle, 209
Ark of the Covenant, the, 68
Arredondo rebellion (1874), the, 204
Asmodeus, 59–60
Auden, W.H., 248
Augé, Marc, 203, 252
Author's Club award, the, 236

Bacik, Ivana, 272–273
Backus, Margot, 158
Bagot stories of Maeve Brennan, the, 8, 144, 145, 146, 148, 151, 154–157
Baker, Francis
  Tremulous Private Body, The, 22
Banville, John, xxv
  Sea, The, xxii
Barrett, Colin, 10, 221, 222, 223
  'Bait', 240
  'Calm With Horses', 231–234, 235
  'Clancy Kid, The', 235
  'Kindly Forget My Existence', 235
  'Moon, The', 230–231, 240
  Young Skins, 10, 222, 229–236, 239, 240
Barry, Frederick, 55
Barry, Kevin, 10, 221, 223, 229
  City of Bohane, The, 10, 222, 229, 236–240
Barry, Ursula, 223
Barton, James, 55
Bauman, Zygmunt, 260
Beckett, Samuel, xx, xxv, 9, 207, 208, 210–214, 215–220
  'Anal Erotic Character Traits', 213–214
  'Ding-Dong', 212

Beckett, Samuel *(continued)*
'First Love', 10, 212, 213–214, 216, 217–219, 220
'I', 219
Krapp's Last Tape, 207
Molloy, 219–220
More Pricks than Kicks, 211, 212
Murphy, 217–218, 219
'Wet Night, A', 211
Belfast News-Letter, 52
Belgravia, 51
Bell, Lian, 3
Bellarmine, Robert (Roberto Bellarmino), 44
Benjamin, Jessica, 211
Benjamin, Walter
'Paris, Capital of the Nineteenth Century', 53
Bennett, Ronan, xxii
Bewes, Timothy, 196
bias against female contributions in the arts, 2–3
Bion, Wilfred, 212
Bishop, Elizabeth, 159, 160, 162
blood relations and sexual prejudice in surrealist Irish-language poetry, 96
blood sacrifice in surreal Irish language poetry and the Hepatitis C scandal, 92–95
Bloom, Harold, 66–67
boat as an image of hope, the, 87
Boland, Eavan, 175, 247, 269
'Anorexic', 269
book-making and design, 66, 74
Boos, Florence S., 75–76
Bourke, Angela, 151, 153
Bowen, Elizabeth, xxi, xxii, xxiv
Brabon, Benjamin A., 262
Bracken, Claire, 11, 158, 162
Bradley, Marion Zimmer, 120
Bradshaw, Brendan, 38
Bramsback, Birgit, xx
Brazilian-Angolan slave trade, the, 34
Brennan, Maeve, xxiv, 8, 144–157
'Attack of Hunger, An', 151
'Barrel of Rumours, The', 149
'Beginning of a Long Story, The', 145
'Bride, The', 144
'Carpet with the Big Pink Roses on It, The', 145
'Christmas Eve', 145, 155
'Clever One, The', 149
'Day We Got Our Own Back, The', 146, 149
'Devil in Us, The', 149
'Drowned Man, The', 146
'Eldest Child, The', 145
'Free Choice, A', 146
'Holy Terror, The', 150
'Joker, The', 148
'Lie, The', 149
Long-Winded Lady, The, 144, 145, 150, 157
'Morning after the Big Fire, The', 148
'Old Man of the Sea, The', 148
'Poor Men and Women, The', 150
Rose Garden, The, 144, 145, 148, 156
'Sofa, The', 154
'Spinning Wheel, The', 149–150
'Springs of Affection, The', 156
Springs of Affection, The, 144, 145, 146, 148–150, 151–155
'Stories of Africa', 145, 155
'Twelfth Wedding Anniversary, The', 145
Visitor, The, 147–148, 150, 157
'Young Girl Can Spoil Her Chances, A', 145, 146, 151
Brienza, Susan, 211
Brooks, Peter, 126
Brown, Luke
'Emasculated', 240
Brown, Terence, 68

Brown, Wendy
Manhood and Politics, 209
Bulfin, William
Southern Cross, The, 194, 203
Bullen, A.H., 65, 66
Burke, Edmund, 208
Burkhead, Henry
Tragedy of Cola's Furies or Lirenda's Miserie, A, xix
Burton, Joan, 223

Caball, Marc, 38, 39
Cahill, Susan, 158, 261
Cannon, Moya, xxii, xxiii
Carleton, William
Traits and Stories of the Irish Peasantry, 148
Carroll, Clare, 38, 39, 42, 49
Carroll, Lewis
Alice in Wonderland, 80, 254, 255–256
Through the Looking-Glass, 80
case study of inscribed finger-rings and gender determination of their owner, 187–188
case study of inscribed name-stones and gender determination, 188–189
case study of names in the Durham *Liber Vitae* manuscript, 189–190
Catholic middle class in provincial Ireland, the, 128, 130
(*see also Fly on the Wheel, The*)
Cave, Terence, 126
Celtic Tiger period, the
and the building of family homes, 173, 249
and feminism, 272–273
and representations of girlhood, 270–272, 274, 275
Cervantes, Miguel
Don Quixote, 28
character as a product of childhood, 214
Chichester proclamation (1605), the, 43
child narratives of family romance, 130–131, 140
Christian morality and unconditional love, 201
cities as public and private spaces, 147
Citizens' Assembly Report on Gender Equality (2021), the, 174
Cixous, Hélène, 209
cognitive perceptions of threat, 169–170
Collins, Lucy, 159, 176
Collins, Wilkie
Basil, 61–62
Colman, Fran, 185
colonial relations and narrative shame, 195–196
Connolly, Linda, 3
conscience and the Creator, 218
conservatism of bardic poetry, the, 38
constructions of beauty, 270
conversions to Catholicism of the Guarani of South America, 25–26
Corey, Mary, 153
Corless, Catherine, 2
Coughlan, Patricia, xviii–xxvi, 11, 26, 29, 30, 37, 40, 51, 52, 81, 105, 159, 162, 192, 211, 244–245, 262, 268, 270, 271, 274
'An Léiriú ar Shaol na mBan i dTéacsanna Dírbheathaisnéise Pheig Sayers', xx–xxi
'Bog Queens', xxi, 163, 222, 259
'Gente Blanca', 22
History of Irish Women's Poetry, A, xxiv, 3
History of Modern Irish Women's Literature, xxiv

Coughlan, Patricia (*continued*)
Irish Literature: Feminist perspectives, xxii
'Irish Literature and Feminism in Postmodernity', 260
Modernism and Ireland: The poetry of the 1930s, xx
Spenser and Ireland: An interdisciplinary perspective, xviii–xix
'Waking the Dead: Antigone, Ismene, and Anne Enright's narrators in mourning', 163
'We get all sealed up', xxiv
Creagh, Janet, 23
Croker, B.M., 51
Cronin, Michael, 224
Cronin, Nessa, 158
Cruikshank, George
Omnibus, 61
Cuña Atenare, the, 30
Cuna Muchu, 30–31, 35
Cusick, Christine, 158

Daly, Nicholas, 5, 6
Dante (Dante Gabriel Rossetti), 70, 121
Darcy, Ailbhe, 3
Dargan, William, 55
Dark Blue, The, 51
Davis, Alex, xx, 6
Dawe, Gerald
Cambridge Companion to Irish Poets, The, 2, 164
de Burca, Benjamin
The Journey's End, 254–255
Things Will Always Be the Same, Again, 255
Trouble with Context, The, 255
de-coupling of house and home and the family, the, 173–174
de Fréine, Celia, 6–7, 80, 81–105
'A Dheirfiúracha Dílse' / 'Sisters', 101–102
'A Ghasúir' / 'Dear Children', 99
'A Iníon' / 'Daughter', 101
'Achainí' / 'Petition', 95
'ag bualadh craicinn le Beethoven a Naoi' / 'having sex to Beethoven's Ninth', 83
'Ag Gluaiseacht leis an gCeol' / 'Moving to the Music', 83
Aibítir Aoise / Alphabet of an Age, 81, 87, 90–92
'Aibítir Aoise' / 'Alphabet of an Age', 90
'Ailp na Seirce' / 'Love Bite', 96
'Áit a mBíonn Toit' / 'Where There's Smoke', 99
'Áit Álainn' / 'Beauty Spot', 90
'An Leabhar Fianaise' / 'The Book of Evidence', 101
'An Seic' / 'The Cheque', 101
'An Tromluí is Troime' / 'The Worst Nightmare', 99
'Ar a Téad Rite Arís' / 'On Her High Wire Again', 95
'Ar Mhuin an Albatrais' / 'On the Back of the Albatross', 83
'Bhí Cogadh ar Siúl' / 'There Was a War On', 82
'Bíobla Lae'/ 'Daily Bible', 88
'Boladh an Mhismín Fhiáin' / 'The Scent of Wild Mint', 90
'Cailís Mo Chuid Fola' / 'Chalice of My Blood', 93
'Cluichí Oilimpeacha Los Angeles' / 'Los Angeles Olympics', 96
'Coinnigh Ort' / 'Pray Continue', 95
'Cóisir Bhainise' / 'Wedding Feast', 83
'Comfort', 96
'Crainn' / 'Trees', 88

de Fréine, Celia (*continued*)
'Cuireadh' / 'Invitation', 89
'Cúraimí' / 'Responsibilities', 93–94
'De Cheal an Chogaidh' / 'In the Absence of War', 89
'Do na Mná' / 'For the Women', 97
'Dóchas' / 'Hope', 87
'Escaping the Circus', 86
'Faigh Réidh Leo' / 'Nip It in the Bud', 97
Faoi Chabáistí is Ríonacha, 80–81, 82, 83, 85, 86
'Fáthmheas' / 'Diagnosis', 101
'Fear sa Teach' / 'A Man about the House', 82
'Féileacán ar Foluain' / 'A Butterfly Aflutter', 91
Fiacha Fola / *Blood Debts*, 6, 81, 92–105
'Fianaise / 'Witness', 91–92
'Gadaí' / 'Thief', 88
'Gan Pána a Bhriseadh' / 'Without Breaking a Pane', 99
'Giosta' / 'Yeast', 88
'Grace', 99–101
'Gráinneog / 'Hedgehog', 88
'Hearsay', 99
'Hotel Koper', 89–90
'Huth ná Hath' / 'Here nor There', 92
'I gCoibhneas a Chéile' / 'In Relation to Each Other', 92
'I Wanna Sleep Forever', 95
imram/odyssey, 81, 87–90
'In Uisce Té' / 'In Hot Water', 96
'Íobairt' / 'Blood Sacrifice', *101*
'Lámhachta?' / 'Taken Out and Shot?', 103–104
A Leannáin' / 'Lover', 99
'Lionn Buí na gCaolán' / 'Yellow Humour,' 93
'Mála' / 'Bag', 88
'Meán Fómhair – Mí na mBreithlaethanta' / 'September – Month of Birthdays', 93–94
'Mochthráth an Mhic Tíre' / 'The Hour of the Wolf', 97–99
'Morning Ireland', 99
'Not of Woman Born', 96
'Nuacht / 'News', 84–85
'Ocras' / 'Hunger', 82
'Picnic i Reilig sa Bhílearúis' / 'Picnic in a Cemetery in Belarus', 85
'Piontaí / 'Pints', 99
'Samhain in the City', 86
'Scarecrows at Newtownards', 86–87
Scarecrows at Newtownards, 81, 82, 83, 85, 86–87
'Scáth' / 'Shade', 88
'Scéal Eile ó Shahrazad' / 'Another Tale from Shahrazad', 101
'Sea' / 'Yes', 99
'Stórtha Arda' / 'Tall Storeys', 83
'Táimid Damanta, a Dheirféaracha / 'We are Damned, my Sisters', 101–103
'Talamh Eadrána' / 'No Man's Land', 88
'Teanga' / 'Tongue', 89
'Tenders of His Affection', 83
'Theastaigh Grianghraf Bainise Uaithi' / 'She Wanted a Wedding Photograph', 83
'There Was a Soldier', 82
'Trap an tSorcais' / 'Circus Trap', 85–86
'Tréadaí' / 'Pastor', 95
de Paor, Louis, xxiii, 38
del Techo, Nicolas
Historia de la Provincia del Paraguay de la Compañía de Jesús, 23
Delaney, Juan José, 202
Deleuze, Gilles, 261, 263–264

Derdon stories of Maeve Brennan, the, 8, 144, 146, 148, 150–154, 155, 156
Derrida, Jacques, 243–244
Descartes, René, 22
'Desolation, Haunting, Power: Changing the city imaginary', xxv
D'hoker, Elke, 265
di-thematic names, 185, 186
diaspora of Irish women in South America, the, 9, 29–32, 35–36, 192–206
Dickens, Charles, 53
  Bleak House, xxv
  Christmas Carol, A, 60
  Dombey and Son, 59
  'Signalman, The', 63
Dillon, Fr Patrick, 203
Dillon, Gerald, 161, 162
Donoghue, Emma
  Pull of the Stars, The, 241
Doré, Gustav, 60
Dublin Corporation, 55
Dublin in the 1790s and 1840s, 54–56, 57–58
Dublin in the short stories of Maeve Brennan, 8, 144, 147, 151–152, 157
Dublin Penny Journal, 59, 60
Dublin University Magazine, 51, 53
Dun Emer Press, 66, 67, 72, 73, 74, 75, 76
Dunne, Tom, xxv

economic crash and impact on masculinity, the, 221, 223–224
  (*see also* masculinity in post-economic crash fiction)
ecopoetry and ecocritical discourse on the environment, 242–243
  (*see also* Groarke, Vona; Morrisey, Sinéad)
Edward VII, King, 68, 69, 75
Egley, William Maw
  Omnibus Life in London, 62
Éire-Ireland, xxiii
English pirate attack on Jesuit missionaries, 23–24, 32–33, 34, 35
Enright, Anne, 4, 30, 144, 260, 273
  Gathering, The, xxiv
  'Natalie', 11, 261, 262, 265–269, 271, 272
  Pleasure of Eliza Lynch, The, xxii, 22, 26, 29, 30, 268
  Taking Pictures, 265
  Wig My Father Wore, The, 260, 268, 271
Ephron, Nora, 75
exploration in the sixteenth century, 21
  (*see also* Jesuit missions to Paraguay and South America, the)

Fahy, Fr, 194
family, the
  and the Irish constitution, 153, 173–174
  in Maeve Brennan's stories, 155, 156
fantasy beatings among siblings and Freudian psychoanalysis, 122–124, 125
Feilitzen, Olof von, 186
Felski, Rita
  Hooked, 11
female literary characters and misogyny, 211–217
female sexuality and Freudian psychoanalysis, 137
feminism and Irish women poets, 10–11, 247
  (*see also* Groarke, Vona; Morrisey, Sinéad; O'Sullivan, Leanne)
feminism in Ireland, 2, 3, 151, 173–174, 222, 272
Fihily, William, 23
Fogarty, Anne, xxv

forgetfulness and the creation of a nation, 47
Forward Book of Poetry, The, 168
Forward Prize for Poetry, the, 168
Foster, John, Wilson, 158
Foster, R.F., 22
Foucault, Michel
  Will to Know, The, 209
Foundling and Bastard narratives in the family romance, 130–131
framing conceit in bardic poetry, 42
Fraser, Nancy, 210
freedom and the aesthetic judgement, 208
freedom of conscience, 44
freedom of speech, 43, 48
Freeman's Journal, 52, 57, 75
French, Tana, xxv
Freud, Anna, 123, 124, 125
Freud, Sigmund, 122, 129–131, 132, 137, 140, 208, 213, 218, 219
  'On Family Romances', 130, 215
  Three Essays on the Theory of Sexuality, 209–210

gender and sexuality and the Irish Catholic middle class (*see Fly on the Wheel, The*)
gender imbalances and inequalities, 2–3, 170–171, 174, 223, 224
gendering of Irish literary tradition, the, 162–163
Genz, Stéphanie, 262
Gerald of Wales, 40
gestation imagery, 271–272
ghost story and Irish gothic, the, 51, 60
Gilmore, Eamon, 223
Gilroy, Paul, 34
Ging, Debbie, 230, 270
Gladwin, Derek, 158
Gonne, Maud, 66–67, 70, 73, 77
Gookin, Daniel, xix
Gookin, Vincent, xix
Gould, Warwick, 68
Gregory, Lady Augusta, 65
Griffith, Arthur, 77
Groarke, Vona, xxii, xxiii, 10, 244–245, 257
  Flight and Earlier Poems, 247
  'For the Unkept House', 247–248
  'Four Sides Full', 252–253
  'House Rules', 249–250
  'House Style', 252
  Juniper Street, 242
  'Lighthouse, The', 250–251
  Other People's Houses, 242, 248–252
  Shale, 247
  'Spindrift', 252
  translation: *'Caoineadh Airt Uí Laoghaire'*, 258
  'Why I Am Not A Nature Poet', 242
Groom, Charles, 67–68
Guarani, the, 25–26, 27, 35
Guardian First Book Award, the, 229
Gutiérrez, Fr Uladislao, 201–202
Gyles, Althea, 66

hagiographic subjects as metaphors, 26–27
Haitian earthquake disaster (2010), the, 174
Halberstam, Jack, 234
Harper, Margaret Mills, 10–11
Haussmann, Baron, 55
Haverty, Anne, xxii
  One Day as a Tiger, 260
Hawkshaw, John, 55
Heaney, Seamus, xxi, xxiii, 164, 222, 259
  'Digging', 163
Hegel, G.F.W., 9, 208
Heidegger, Martin, 243–244
Hepatitis C scandal, the, 81, 92, 97, 99–101
Herbert, George, 256

Herbert, Máire, xxiii
Herbert's Retreat stories of Maeve Brennan, the, 144, 150
Hill of Tara excavations (1899), the, 67–68, 69, 76, 77
Hirsch, Marianne, 7, 130, 138
Hobbes, Thomas, 208
Hoddis, Jakob van, 160
Holdeman, David, 66, 69, 74, 75
Horney, Karen, 210
Hough, Carole, 186, 187
house and spatial presentations in poetry, the, 247–250
Hughes, Eamonn, 8
human relationships with animals, 243–244
Hymowitz, Kay
  Manning Up: How the rise of women has turned men into boys, 236
hysteria and sibling trauma, 122

'I' pronoun of the poetic voice, the, 246, 251, 252
identity in postmodern construction, 26
IMPAC Dublin Literary Award, the, 236
incest and siblings, 112
infantile sexuality and Freud, 209–210, 213, 218
Ingenieros, José, 202
  Treaty of Love, The, 200–201
Ingman, Heather, 52, 154
intelligence in the material world, 168–169, 171
interdependent connections and the replacement of the patrimonial, 164, 172–174, 176
Intermission, 230
intertwined workings of power and space, 4, 8, 11
'Invisible Prince' and Sheridan Le Fanu, the, 52, 64
Ireland under King James I and VI, 41–49
Irigaray, Luce, 170–171, 210
Irish barbarousness, 40–41
Irish bardic poetry, 37–38, 39–50
Irish Blood Transfusion Board, the, 92
Irish community in Argentina, the, 193–206
Irish constitution and the family, the, 153, 173, 174
Irish feminist literary criticism, 222 (*see also* Coughlan, Patricia)
'Irish Gothic' literature, xix–xx, 5–6, 51–54, 55, 58–59, 60–64
Irish literary tradition and English colonialism, the, 38–39
Irish male literary voice, the, 148, 150
Irish nationalism in the early twentieth century, 140
Irish Railway Gazette, 55
Irish Research Council, the, xxiv–xxv
Irish Review, xxi, xxiii
Irish Times, The, xx, 4, 55, 224
Irish University Review, xxiv
Irish Women and Irish Migration, 193
Irish Women Poets Rediscovered: Readings in poetry from the eighteenth to the twentieth century, 3
'irreducibility of the body,' the, 26
Izarra, Laura, 9

James VI and I, King, 5, 39, 40, 41, 42, 43, 44, 45–46, 47–49, 50
  Basilikon Doron, 48
Jerrold, Blanchard
  London: A pilgrimage, 60
Jesuit missions to Paraguay and South America, the, 22–28, 32–35
Johnston, Dillon, 245

Johnston, Maria, 3
Jones, Ernest, 213
Jordan, Neil, xxv
Joy, George William
Bayswater Omnibus, 62
Joy, Thomas Musgrave
Charing Cross to Bank Omnibus, The, 62
Joyce, James, xxiv, 244
'Dead, The', 135
Dubliners, 148, 151
Portrait of the Artist as a Young Man, A, xxiv, 135, 140–142, 147, 148, 243

Kant, Immanuel, 9, 207–208, 210, 214, 220
Critique of Judgement, 207, 217
Critique of Practical Reason, 218
Kelmscott Press, 74
Kemble, J.M., 186
Kennedy, Seán, 9–10
Kimball, Jean, 140
Kinsella, Thomas, xxii, xxiii
Korol, Juan Carlos, 194
Kosok, Heinz, xx
Kristeva, Julia, xxii

La Farge, Catherine, 7
'La Pampa Gringa' (1870–1892), 205
Lacanian concept of the Real, the, 139
Land League, the, 140
Landseer, Edwin, 52
Laplanche, Kean, 212
Larrington, Carolyne, 111, 114
law of the mother and sibling relations, the, 165–166, 178
Le Fanu, Joseph Sheridan, xix, 5–6, 55–58
'Account of Some Strange Disturbances in Aungier Street, An', 58
'Authentic Narrative of a Haunted House, An', 58, 60
'Carmilla', 51, 52
'Familiar, The', 53
In a Glass Darkly, 53, 54, 58, 63
'Green Tea', 53, 60–61, 62–63
Old Carlisle Bridge, 56
'Room in the Dragon Volant, The', 64
Uncle Silas, 51, 52, 64
'Watcher / 'The Familiar,' The', 53–54, 55, 58–59, 60
as 'William Scribble': *Dublin Destroyed!, or, The Witches Cauldron of Railway Horror: A Mysterious Shakespeareana, in One Act*, 55–56
Wylder's Hand, 64
Le Fanu, William, 57
Lefebvre, Henri, 4
Lennon, Colm, 22
Leonard, Suzanne, 221, 235–236
Lerner, Gerda, 192
Lesage, Alain René, 60
Le Diable boiteux, 59
Lewiecki-Wilson, Cynthia, 140, 141
Lewis, C.S., 70
LGBT+ sexualities, 3
Linebaugh, Peter, 35
Linnie, Conor, 3
literary awards, 168, 229, 236
Lloyd, David, 217
Under Representation, 207
Lloyd's Weekly Newspaper, 52
Locke, John, 208
locked room in Victorian supernatural fiction, the, 52–53
London General Omnibus Company, the, 62
London Guiana Company, the, 31

Lorimer, Joyce
English and Irish Settlement on the River Amazon, 29
Love/Hate, 230
Lovett, Ann, 261
Low, Sampson, 51
Lowell, Robert, 162
Lozano, Pedro, 24, 26, 27, 32, 33
Historia de la Compañía de Jesús en la Provincia del Paraguay, 23
Luddy, Maria, 194, 196
lyric and the lyric poem, the, 243, 245–246
Lytton, Edward Bulwer
'Asmodeus at Large', 59

Mac an Bhaird, Fearghal Óg, 39, 48
'Trí coróna i gcairt Shéamuis', 39
Mac Craith, Mícheál, 38
Macardle, Dorothy
Uninvited, The, 151
MacBride, John, 70, 73
MacCurtain, Margaret, 192
Mackail, J.W.
Life of William Morris, The, 78
MacNeice, Louis
'Snow', 253
Macready, William, 52
MacSwiney, Terence, 79
Maguire, Hugh, 40, 41
male doctors and the patriarchy, 6–7
Malory, Sir Thomas, 4, 7, 111–115, 126–127
(*see also Le Morte Darthur*)
Malory, Thomas
Le Morte Darthur, 7, 8, 111, 112–119, 120, 121–126
'Man Overboard', 224
'mancession' tropes (*see* masculinity in post-economic crash fiction)
Mandelbrot, Benoît, 167
Mandelstam, Nadezhda, 160
Mandelstam, Osip, 160
Mangan, James Clarence, xix
Mann, Jill, 118
Mar González-Arias, Luz, xxiv, 82, 269
Marcus, Sharon, 58
Marcuse, Herbert, 211
Maric, Mileva, 92
marriage equality, 2
Mary, Queen of Scots, 39
masculinity as a fictional narrative (*see Fly on the Wheel, The*)
masculinity in post-economic crash fiction, 10, 221–222, 224–241
masochism and the pleasure principle, 208
Mathews, Elkin, 65
matter of mother and misogyny, the, 207–208, 211
Maturin, Charles, xix
Maynooth Review, xx
McCabe, Patrick, 239
McCann, William, 194
McCarthy, Thomas
'City Without God', 183
McClintock, Anne, 146–147
McClune, Kate, 111
McCole, Brigid, 92, 99
McCormack, Mike
Solar Bones, 240
McDermott, Alice, xxii, xxiii
McGuckian, Medbh, 10, 160, 245, 246–247, 251
'Harem Trousers', 246
Marconi's Cottage, 246
'Time Before You, The', 246
McInerney, Lisa, 229
McKeon, Belinda, 270
McLoughlin, Dympna, 196
McMonagle, Niall, 159
McQuillan, Peter, 38, 49

McRobbie, Angela
Aftermath of Feminism, The, 262–263
McWilliams, Ellen, 148
Meaney, Gerardine, 129, 159, 162, 163
medical experts and the treatment of diseased women in Irish language poetry, 10, 92, 101
(*see also* Hepatitis C scandal, the)
Meehan, Paula
'Lionhearted, The', 181–182
Merwin, W.S., 160
metamorphosis and *Metamorphoses*, 41
metaphysical constructions of gender, 170–171
Mhac an tSaoi, Máire, xxii, xxiii–xxiv, 81, 104
migrants and rites of passage in literary narratives, 21–22
Minsky, Rosalind, 137
Misión San Vincente, 23
misogyny
in literature, 9–10, 211–217, 238, 240
and the matter of mother, 207–208, 211
Mists of Avalon, The, 120
Mitchell, Juliet, 7, 111, 117, 118, 121–122, 123, 124, 125, 126, 159, 164–165, 166
Mad Men and Medusas, 162
Siblings: Sex and violence, 112, 162
Mitre, Bartolomé, 205
monogamy and prostitution, 216
Montague, John, xxi, 163, 222, 259
Moore, Sally, 193, 198, 199, 202, 203, 204–205
Morning Chronicle, 59–60, 61
Morris, William, 6, 72, 74, 75, 77
'Adam's Curse', 79
Earthly Paradise, The, 70–71, 75–76
Hollow Land, The, 71
News from Nowhere, 78
Sundering Flood, The, 70, 71–72, 75, 78
Water of the Wondrous Isles, The, 70
Morrissey, Sinéad, xxv, 10, 244–245, 247, 258
'Clangers, The', 256, 257
'Device for Monitoring Brain Activity by Shining Light into the Pupil, A', 257
'Hanging Hare, The', 256
Between Here and There, 242
'Invitation, The', 253–254, 255
'Jo Gravis in His Metal Garden', 242
'Lighthouse', 257
'Our Flower Garden', 242
Parallax, 257
Through the Square Window, 242, 253–254, 255–257
Morrissy, Mary, xxii
Pretender, The, 260
mother fixation and psychoanalysis, 212–215, 219–220
Mountjoy, Lord, 46
Muldoon, Paul, 87
Mulhall, Anne, 10
Mulhall, Edward, 203
Mulhall, Marion, 193, 195, 197–198
Mulhall, Michael, 203
Munster Women Writers project, the, xxii
Murphy, Fanny, 193, 199, 202
Murphy, Kate, 193, 197, 198, 199–200, 202
Murphy, Robert, 200
Murphy, Sally, 200
Murphy (née Daly), Mary, 200
Murray, Edmundo, 198, 199, 200, 202, 204, 205
Becoming Irlandés, 193, 197
Murray, Thomas
Story of the Irish in Argentina, The, 193

myth and truth boundaries in sixteenth century literary narratives, 23–24, 30, 32, 33

Nabokov, Vladimir
Lolita, xxv
narratives as rites of passage, 21
natural world and the human body, the, 172, 174–175, 176–177
necessity and masculine autonomy, 209–210, 215, 216–218
Negra, Diane, 229, 263
neo-liberalism and post-feminism, 11, 262–269, 272–274
Nevin, Kathleen
You'll Never Go Back, 193, 194–196, 197, 205
'new gangster genre' in Irish film and television, the, 230, 240
New Monthly Magazine, 59
New Woman writing, 7, 129
New Yorker, the, 148, 153
Ní Chuilleanáin, Eiléan, xxii, xxiv, 10, 245–246, 247, 251
'Flood, The', 245
'Stabat Mater', 19
Sun-Fish, The, 245
Ní Dhomhnaill, Nuala, xxiv, 101, 104, 247
'Ceist na Teangan' / 'The Language Issue', 87
'Cuimhne an Uisce', 15–16
Ní Dhuibhne, Eilís, xxii
Dancers Dancing, The, 260
Ní Ghráda, Máiréad, 104
Ní Ghríofa, Doireann
'While Bleeding', 13–14
Nic Eoin, Máirín, 6, 7
Nietzsche, Friedrich, 77
Nine Years War, the, 41, 42
NYPD Blue, 99
Ó Buachalla, Breandán, 38, 39, 48
Ó Dálaigh, Aonghus
'Dia libh, a laochruidh Gaoidhiol', 46
Ó Dálaigh, Lochlainn
'Cáit ar ghabhadar Gaoidhil?', 45
Ó Gallchoir, Clíona, 7
Ó hEodhasa, Eochaidh, 5, 39, 43–44, 47–48
'Mór theasda dh'obair Óivid', 39–40, 41–50
Ó Maolchonaire, Flaithrí, 44
O'Brien, Don Bernardo del Carpio, 29–32, 35, 36
O'Brien, Edna, xxi–xxii, xxv
O'Brien, Fitzjames, 51
O'Brien, Kate, xxi
O'Brien, Sarah
Linguistic Diasporas, Narrative and Performance: The Irish in Argentina, 206
O'Callaghan, Eve, 253
O'Connor, Maureen, 158
O'Donoghue, Bernard, xxiv, 162–163
'Home Sickness', 109
Oedipal phase and the Oedipus complex, the, 130, 132, 137, 162, 163, 164, 213, 220
O'Fihily, Thomas, 5, 22–23, 24, 25, 26–28, 32, 35, 36
O'Gorman, Camila, 201–202
oikos (realm of the home), the, 209, 210, 217, 220
Okasha, Elisabeth, 9
Oliver, Mary, 160
Omnibus, The, 61
omnibuses in nineteenth-century literature and art, 61–63
O'Neill, Daniel, 86
O'Neill, Hugh, 28, 42
O'Neill, Margaret, 158

Orage, A.R.
New Age, The, 77
Ortega, Fr, 24, 25
O'Sullivan, Leanne, 11
'Famine', 271
'Graduating', 272
'Journey, The', 272
'Mirror', 270–271
'Thing of Beauty, A', 269–270
Waiting for My Clothes, 11, 261–262, 269–273
O'Sullivan, Patrick, 192, 193
Otherness, 7, 112, 244, 256
O'Toole, Tina, xxii, 7, 129, 159
outline of the book, 4–5
Ovid, 39, 41–42
Metamorphoses, 40, 41, 50
Owen-Crocker, Gale, 186

Paley, Grace, 99
Palmer, Patricia, 5
paternal articulations in poetry, 163
patriarchy, the, 6–7, 209, 210
and prejudices against women, 3–4, 164, 215
Peart, Barbara
Tia Barbarita: The memories of Barbara Peart, 193, 202, 205
Pettit, John James, 197, 202–203
Philip IV, King, 31
Phillips, Adam
'Just Rage', 214–215
Pieta House 'Mind Our Men' campaign, 224
Poe, Edgar Allan
'Murders in the Rue Morgue, The', 52–53
polis (political sphere) and manly action, the, 209, 210
politics in surreal Irish language poetry, 88–89, 92, 99–101
polygamy and male desire, 216
Porter, John Grey C.
'Few Observations Upon Our Present Railway System in Ireland, A', 55
post-feminism, 11, 262–269, 272–274
postmodernism and Irish gender politics and feminism, 260–261, 270
prejudice in the medical system, 6–7
prostitution and the literature of Samuel Beckett, 216, 219
psychoanalysis
and fantasy beatings among siblings, 122–124, 125
and female sexuality, 137
and mother fixation, 212–215, 219–220
and social feminism, xxii
psychomachia and sibling sameness among women, 120–121
Punch, 62
Purcell, Rev Francis, 51

queer critiques of heteronormative life, 235–236
'queer failure' and heteronormativity, 234
Quinn, Caroline, 159, 161, 162, 166
Quinn, John, 77
Quinn, Leeanne, 4, 8, 158–178
'Absence of Memory', 170, 178
'Accidents', 160, 168, 169, 171
'After Violence', 172, 177
'Before You', 168, 177
'Berlin', 165, 168
'Chorus', 169, 176
'Cockle Picker (Morecambe Bay)', 171–172, 178
'Gertrude Stein Poses for Man Ray', 160–161, 175

Quinn, Leeanne (*continued*)
'Graffiti on the Plant Store', 171, 172, 178
'House in the Ocean', 175
'Houses', 174
'Impact, The', 158, 168, 172
'Imprints', 159, 163, 164, 165, 166, 170, 171
'In Paint', 161
'Letter to Leonard Woolf', 160, 177
'Mosquitoes', 158, 159, 165–166, 167, 170, 174, 177
'Nano's Dream Castle', 161, 162
'Naples', 159
'New Heart, The', 178
'Ode to Memory', 171
'Peculiar Alphabets', 159, 161, 177, 178
'Permafrost', 168, 170
'Rhapsody Blackout', 178
'Rubble', 174–175, 176
'Siesta', 170
Some Lives?, 159, 160
'Water', 169
'Winter Coat', 176
Before You, 8, 159–160, 161, 163–164, 167, 170, 173–178

railway development in nineteenth century Ireland, 54–57, 58
Rank, Otto, 142
Myth of the Birth of the Hero, The, 140
Ray, Man, 160
Redin, Mats, 186
reduciones, the, 35
Reid, Nano, 161–162
relic of a martyred virgin of St Ursula, the, 32–34
Renan, Ernest, 47
reverse labour migration to Ireland from Argentina, 206
Riddell, Mrs. J.H., 51
Ridgway, Keith, xxv, 237
Robert, Marthe, 131
Robinson, Tim, 167
Roe, Sir Henry, 29, 30
Rollason, David, 190
Rollason, Lynda, 190
Roman de la Rose, 120
Rosas, Juan Manuel de, 202
Ryan, Donal, 10, 221, 223, 236
Spinning Heart, The, 10, 222, 224–229, 240
Rycroft, Charles, 213

Sábato, Hilda, 194
Sage, Victor, 52
salt water as transformative effect, 175
Saltair na Rann, 21
Sarlo, Beatriz
El imperio de los sentimientos, 200–201
Sarmiento, Domingo Faustino, 197
Facundo, 198
Sayers, Peig, 81
Scarry, Elaine
Body in Pain, The, 97
Schivelbusch, Wolfgang
Railway Journey, The, 63
Schopenhauer, Arthur, 208–209, 213, 217
'On Women', 216
Schrage-Frueh, Michaela, 158
second-wave feminism, 3, 247
Sedley, Charles
Asmodeus; or, The Devil in London, 59
self-figurations as narratives of the self by women, 205–206
Shelley, Percy Bysshe, 70
Shelton, Thomas, 28
Shuah, Belacqua, 212, 215

sibling relations, 7, 8, 111–127, 159, 163, 164–167, 178
sibling sameness in medieval romance, 120–121, 122
Sisters of Mercy, the, 193
Smyth, Ailbhe, 3
social norms and moralities of love, 200–201
social status and Irish middle-class Catholics, 128–129
Solomon, Abraham
 'First Class – The Meeting ...' And at first meeting loved", 63
sovereignty motif in Irish bardic poetry, the, 40
spatial presentations in literature, 52–53, 58–59, 245–251, 253, 256
Spenser, Edmund, xviii, xix, 48
 View of the Present State of Ireland, A, 68–69
Spillane, Alison, 223
St Peter, 188
St Ursula, 32–34
Standard, The, 203
Standlee, Whitney, 129
stanza, the, 250
Stein, Gertrude, 160–161
Stoker, Bram, 51
Stuart, James, 39
Suárez, Francisco, 44
suicide and mental health among men and the economic crash, 223–224
Sullivan, Moynagh, 8, 143, 259
surrealism in Irish language poetry, 80–90, 92–105
Sverakova, Slavka, 254–255
Sweet, Henry, 186
Symbolic and being a speaking subject, the, 139
Synge, J.M.
 Playboy of the Western World, The, 226
Tavistock Clinic, London, the, 212
Techo, Nicolás del, 23, 33
Tejedor, Carlos, 205
Temple Bar, 51
textual 'interweaving,' xxi
third-wave feminism, 3
Thurston, Katherine Cecil, 7
 Fly on the Wheel, The, 7–8, 128, 129–130, 131–143
 Max, 129
Times, The, 52
Tohoku earthquake/tsunami disaster (2011), the, 175
Tokarczuk, Olga, 160
Toklas, Alice B., 160
Tolkien, J.R.R., 70
Tracy, Robert, 54
trading in the Amazon, 31, 35, 36
translocation and queer subjections, 159
translocation networks through letters from Irish emigrés, 203–205
transport and commuting in Irish Gothic fiction, 62–63, 64
trauma and psychoanalysis, 213
Triple Alliance War (1864–70), the, 204
Troyes, Chrétien de
 Yvain, 120
Tsvetayeva, Marina, 160
 'We Shall Not Escape Hell,' 101
Turgenev, Ivan
 Sportsman's Sketches, 148
Twitter streams, 273
 #FiredIrishPoets, 3
 #WakeUpIrishPoetry, 3
 #WakingTheFeminists campaign, the, 3, 273

undocumented burial of babies at Bon Secours home, Tuam, the, 2

unemployment after the 2008 economic crash, 222–223
United Irishman, 68, 77

Valente, Joseph, 134, 158
Vendler, Helen, 68, 69
Victoria, Francisco de, Bishop of Tucumán, 34, 35
Virgil
Eclogues, 68, 69–70, 74
visual culture in poetry, 161–162

'Waking the Nation' theatre programme, the, 2
Walker, Emery, 74
Walsh, Agnes, 195, 198–199, 200, 203, 205
Walsh, Catherine, 260
Walsh, Maria Elena
La abuela Agnes, 193
Novios de antaño, 198
Walshe, Eibhear, xxii
war as a theme in surrealist Irish-language poetry, 82, 89
Welsh, Irvine
Trainspotting, 234
Wheatley, David, 3
White, Ali
Me, Moller, 2
whiteness as a category through experience, 22, 36
Windelbrand, Wilhelm
History of Philosophy, 208
women and role in Irish society after military conflicts, 151, 194
women and the workplace, 205
Woolf, Virginia, 160

Yeats, Elizabeth Corbet 'Lolly,' 74
Yeats, W.B., 6, 65–68
'Arrow, The', 72, 73, 74
'Baile and Aillinn', 72, 75
On Baile's Strand, 66, 67
Collected Works in Verse and Prose of William Butler Yeats, The, 65, 72
Edition de Luxe, 65
'Folly of Being Comforted, The', 73, 74
'Happiest of the Poets, The', 70, 74, 78, 79
'In the Seven Woods', 67–69, 72, 73, 74, 76, 77
King's Threshold, The, 67, 79
'Never Give all the Heart', 74
'Old Age of Queen Maeve, The', 72, 75, 76–77
'Old Memory', 74
Plays in Prose and Verse, 79
Poems, 1899–1905, 6, 65, 66, 67, 72, 73, 74, 75, 78–79
Poems: Second series, 65, 66
Poems Lyrical and Narrative, 65, 72, 73
Poems of Spenser, The, 68, 75
Poetical Works of William B. Yeats, The, 65, 72, 73
'Rider from the North, The' / 'The Happy Townland', 77–78
Secret Rose, The, 66
Seven Poems and a Fragment, 79
In the Seven Woods, 66, 67, 68, 72, 74–75
Shadowy Waters, The, 66, 67
Wild Swans at Coole, The, 66
Wind Among the Reeds, The, 65–66, 67
Yorke, Barbara, 186
You've Got Mail, 75

Zach, Wolfgang, xx
Zachary, Pope, 21